THE
ALPINE JOURNAL
2022

George Finch's photograph of Capt Geoffrey Bruce making notes at base camp in 1922. Finch wrote of him: 'tall, of athletic build, strong, endowed with a great fund of mental energy – an invaluable asset on ventures of this kind – and cheerful in any situation.' Bruce would set a world altitude record on his first climb. *(Alpine Club Photo Library)*

THE
ALPINE JOURNAL
2022

The Journal of the Alpine Club

A record of mountain adventure
and scientific observation

Editor: Ed Douglas

Production: Nathan Ryder

Volume 126
Number 370

Supported by the
MOUNT EVEREST FOUNDATION

Published by
THE ALPINE CLUB

© 2022 by the Alpine Club

THE ALPINE JOURNAL 2022
Volume 126. Number 370

www.alpine-club.org.uk

Address all editorial communication to the Hon Editor:
Alpine Club, 55 Charlotte Rd, London EC2A 3QF

Address all sales and distribution communications to:
Cordee, 11 Jacknell Rd, Dodwells Bridge Ind Est, Hinckley LE10 3BS

Back numbers:
Apply to the Alpine Club, 55 Charlotte Rd, London EC2A 3QF or,
for 1969 to date, apply to Cordee, as above.

First published in 2022 by The Alpine Club
Typeset by Ryder Design – www.ryderdesign.studio
Printed and bound by Novoprint SA, Barcelona

A CIP catalogue record for this book is available from The British Library

ISBN 978-1-7399535-1-5

Front cover: Tom Livingstone on the 'interminable' summit ridge of
Tengkangpoche on the first ascent of Massive Attack in late October 2021.
See page p16. *(Matt Glenn)*

Endpapers
Front: An excerpt from the team photo of the 1922 Everest Expedition, featured
in Mick Conefrey's new history, featuring the indigenous high-altitude workers
who enabled the attempt. Conefrey's book is reviewed on p292. *(AC Photo Library)*
Back: An early example of data visualisation: 'Des Principales Montagnes et des
Principaux Fleuves du Monde', published in 1829 by J Andriveau-Goujon, some
of it derived from Alexander Humboldt and appearing in Lachlan Fleetwood's new
history of the scientific exploration of the Himalaya, reviewed on p306.

Foreword

At the end of 1943 Geoffrey Winthrop Young gave his valedictory address as president of the Alpine Club: 'For the first time in our history the term of a presidency has been begun and ended under the shadow of war.' Hitler's war put several dents in the Club. GWY's first act had been to disperse the Alpine Club Library, so the Luftwaffe wouldn't get it. Yet with the books went 'the last chance of consoling ourselves for the loss of active mountaineering'. In the First World War, the proximity of the western front had allowed younger members on active service to return to London. That wasn't so easy now, Winthrop Young explained, with fighting so widely dispersed. What's more, rationing of food and travel, limits on lighting and heating, and the dwindling numbers qualified and able to join a mountaineering club necessarily diminished the Club's prospects.

I thought of this moment in the Club's history after Russia's invasion of Ukraine. As we report, a team of Ukrainians had made what must be regarded as one of the greatest Himalayan ascents in late 2021: the inaccessible and outlandish south-east ridge of Annapurna III. No one had gone higher than Nick Colton and Tim Leach had during a futuristic attempt in 1981, despite the world's best trying. Then the Ukrainians arrived. The style Nikita Balabanov, Mikhail Fomin and Viacheslav Polezhaiko employed to overcome this immense challenge was exemplary. In an era of what the Slovenian alpinist Marko Prezelj calls 'business climbing', here was magic. And yet, within weeks, their homeland was facing an existential threat as Russian troops poured across Ukraine's borders. Now is the time, Fomin said, for Ukrainian climbers to don soldiers' helmets and put aside their passion for the mountains.

I wonder if these courageous men are still thinking about what they achieved on Annapurna III last year and miss the sense of freedom and possibility that time in the mountains can offer. Even though war left the Alpine Club on its uppers, Winthrop Young was determined to keep a small flame burning. The *Alpine Journal*, reduced in size and starved of material, still appeared. Its wartime content was what you might expect from such disruption: nostalgia for happier times, a reappraisal of the past (Winthrop Young's own essay 'Mountain Prophets' is an excellent example), and reports from what members were still able to achieve, either as relief from war or in its service. Wilfrid Noyce, whose life and times Simon Pierse recalls in this edition of the *Alpine Journal*, was teaching mountain skills to air crew in Kashmir. Edward Peck, a diplomat in Turkey, was exploring the Ala Dağ with Robin Hodgkin. Raymond Greene and Fred Pigott wrote on mountain rescue in war and peace. Bill Tilman's 1943 piece 'Zaghouan by Verey Light' is well worth seeking out, bringing the gritty tension of war to the process of climbing a mountain. In another piece he described being in northern Italy 'ostensibly with a view to prosecuting the partisan war there, in reality to see some hills.'

Tilman, you feel, would have rolled his eyes at the media's new buzzword: 'perma-crisis'. Yet one aspect of today's gloomy headlines needs our close attention. While I was stuck at home editing the *Alpine Journal*, I was in frequent contact with Alpine guides who were describing to me how rising temperatures were impacting their summer season. During the Second World War, those fighting knew the mountains would still be there at the end of it. Now the mountains themselves are changing under the impact of climate change; glacial ice melts away, prompting a new intensity of rock fall. In this issue, Stuart Dunning describes an astonishing event last year in the Nanda Devi region when a large chunk of Ronti Peak weighing 49 million tonnes detached itself, landing with the force of 15 Hiroshima atomic bombs. Such events are not only the consequence of our changing climate. The world is rarely so simple. But it's clear our carbon emissions are responsible for the rapid changes we're witnessing in mountain ranges around the world.

How we respond to these changes is complicated. Do we give up? I hope not. But it's time to press pause on the consumerist attitude many climbers developed in the era of cheap travel. Just as the disruption of the Second World War made alpinists reflect on what they held to be most important in life, so climate change will make us stop and think: a difficult task in this age of constant communication. But I don't think we really have a choice, and the lessons learned from a more thoughtful approach to adventure will surely offer benefits in the future. We must learn once again to savour our adventures rather than gobble them up.

I had intended this to be my last edition of the *Alpine Journal*. Indeed, one member of the Club took the trouble to write suggesting this should be the last edition ever. In the internet age, he suggested, isn't the *Alpine Journal* simply out of date? It's an engrossing question but one that largely answers itself. When I started writing about climbing in the 1980s there were lots of mountaineering magazines around the world. The internet killed most of them; this past year, the longstanding American magazine *Climbing* stopped its print publication. Social media is fun but marketing departments at outdoor brands dominate that world. If you want perspective and context from inside our community, then increasingly you're left with club journals. And as the oldest such publication in the world, I think the Alpine Club would do well to keep going with its own journal, just as Winthrop Young did during the war.

The lack of an immediate successor has meant a delay to my departure. Hopefully, this time next year the new editor will be in post. Meanwhile I want to thank Rod Smith for his work on the In Memoriam section, and our Area Notes correspondents. I want to thank once again Chris Russell, who has handed over his column 100 Years Ago to Peter Foster. We would not have a journal at all without the dedication of volunteers and we thank them for their efforts.

Ed Douglas

Contents

continued …

In this centenary of the first full expedition to Everest, this year's frontis-pieces celebrate the art of Everest, particularly the works of members of the Alpine Club who participated in 1922, namely Howard Somervell (1890-1975) and Edward Norton (1884-1954), but also including work by Elsie Dixon (1889-1980), Philip MacLeod Coupe (1944-2013) and Rob Fairley (b1953). The selection was made as usual by Robin Campbell, whose article on his choices appears on p100. See also David Seddon's piece on Howard Somervell on p86.

Climbs & Expeditions

'Everest group from the Singalila Ridge', T Howard Somervell,
oil, 29cm × 36cm, 1943?. *(Courtesy of Tony Astill)*

Climbs & Expeditions

TIM MILLER

The Phantom Line

A First Ascent in Nepal's Jugal Himal

Tim Miller starting on the crux section of steep chimneys on Jugal Spire's
The Phantom Line. Sacks were hauled as the climbing required
getting inside the chimney and squirming. *(Paul Ramsden)*

One thing we knew for certain on our trip to Nepal was that at some point each afternoon there would be snow, usually hail and often thunder and lightning. Every day for a month without fail we encountered an afternoon storm. Frequently it would cloud over from 9am onwards, affording us only a couple hours of sun in the morning. So as we sat in our little tent in base camp after completing our climb as the heavens opened and thunder raged, we couldn't believe we had managed to snatch such a brilliant route from such improbable conditions.

The adventure began two years earlier when Paul Ramsden invited Richard Kendrick and me to a Gritstone Club hut nestled under a cliff in the Lake District. Inside, Paul swore us to secrecy before showing us a few of his highly

3

Below the wall of chimneys, the key to the face. *(Tim Miller)*

confidential new route ideas on his laptop. We discussed them, then picked one and started to make plans for a trip. Not long after, Covid-19 hit and scuppered plans for that autumn – and the following autumn as well. The route we had planned was climbed in the meantime and Richard then had to drop out due to other commitments. By this point Paul and I were frustrated at having our plans fall through so often despite all our efforts at rearranging. We decided on a new objective and planned to go in spring; we didn't want to wait another year.

I first met Paul one winter's day about eight years ago while climbing on Ben Nevis by myself. I was at the CIC hut getting ready to head down at the end of the day. Two other climbers were also packing bags so I asked them if they would be driving past Glasgow and could I get a lift. They were heading all the way to middle England and so they sped me back to Glasgow in double quick time. Paul was one of them and he told me how he had once witnessed a murder while hitchhiking to the Alps when he was younger. One of the lovely things about the world of climbing is how it is so small but welcoming. There are few sports where you can read about your heroes in books, the next day bump into them and a few years later be on a trip together.

We arrived at Kathmandu airport and after the slight panic of not finding our bags (another team had removed them from the conveyor belt) were met by our tour agent with a garland of flowers and driven to our hotel. Paul showed me around the sights of the city while we picked up our permit, gas canisters and other last-minute supplies. We were introduced to our team of porters and then we all jumped on a bus and were off out of the city. The roads got smaller, steeper, became single track and then turned to lumpy dirt tracks.

Paul Ramsden squirming. *(Tim Miller)*

Before long, the bus was bumping and swinging round hairpin bends while clinging miraculously to the edge of steep mountainsides. At the end of the road we arrived in the small mountain village of Bhotang, surrounded by rice terraces and humid jungle.

What's interesting about our objective is that it hadn't seen a previous attempt or any interest at all despite being only a six-hour drive and four-day walk. It's one of the closer 6,000m peaks to Kathmandu. Its obscurity may lie in the fact that its face is hidden and the peak sits in front of the bigger and more famous Dorje Lhakpa so it doesn't stand out on the skyline.

It was obvious on the first day of the approach that there was quite a divide in experience among the porters. Chatting to them in broken English, we discovered a few had never portered before but had previously worked as hotel clerks in Dubai, before Covid-19 had brought an end to the tourism industry there and they had lost their jobs. Now forced to take whatever work they could get, it must have been quite a contrast to their previous lives. They started to lag far behind the fitter porters up front, who hadn't understood where we wanted to stop for the night and carried on to the next stop, forcing us all to continue.

It was now that we were introduced to the regular weather pattern with an afternoon thunderstorm. Tired and bedraggled, the last porters arrived in camp 12 hours after setting off on what should have been a two-day journey. We had gained 2,000m of ascent and were concerned the porters, who were from Kathmandu and not acclimatised, might suffer from the altitude. Luckily for us, next morning everyone woke up well and was able to continue. A much shorter day took us to the famous Panch Pokhari religious shrine, a pretty collection of five mountain lakes at 4,100m a popular pilgrimage site.

Nut hunting on *The Phantom Line*.
(*Paul Ramsden*)

Ramsden's patented homemade
snow-hammock allowing the team to pitch
a tent on a steep slope. (*Tim Miller*)

Up to this point we had been walking on well-constructed paths that allowed
pilgrims and tourists to visit the lakes. These now stopped and we were on
to rough tracks over passes and round mountainsides. A few of the porters
decided at this point to switch from flip-flops to trainers. White rugged
peaks pierced the crisp blue skies, rocky ridges led steeply down to misty
green valleys bellow. And from the top of one pass we got our first view of
the mountain we hoped to climb.

We trekked for two more days, sometimes in the fog and occasionally
getting a brief glimpse of our peak. Just before arriving at base camp, and
not having seen another soul in days, we noticed a solitary figure a few hundred metres behind the group. He must have been following us in the shadows. Despite the snowy passes we had crossed, he arrived with only the
clothes on his back, flip-flops on his feet and no bag. Our sirdar spoke to him
and declared him 'a mad man' who was on some sort of religious journey.
He hadn't eaten for days, so that night we fed him and he was walked back
down with the porters the following day.

Base camp was situated in a valley of lateral moraine that was quite muddy from the frequent rain and not a place we felt inspired to hang around for
too long. So we set off straightaway, with light bags, on a reconnaissance
mission. Our aims were to find a practical route through the maze of the
glacier leading to our peak and try to get a view of the face if we were lucky
enough for it not to cloud over before we arrived.

Travelling across highly crevassed and moraine-covered glaciers is always
an extremely slow and awkward task. Paul pointed out that it was often at
these points that injuries happen and the most important thing for us to do
now was stay fit and healthy. As soon as he said this, I slipped on a wobbly
boulder, fell backwards and put my hand out to catch myself. In doing so I
bent my fingers into an unnatural position and tweaked some of the liga-
ments in one of the fingers. I didn't want it to affect the expedition but for

The route's second 'White Spider' where Ramsden and Miller spent their third night on the wall. The steep headwall pitches loom above. *(Tim Miller)*

days after I struggled to hold a knife and fork and tie laces with that hand. I just hoped I would still be able to hang off an ice axe when the time came.

The rest of that day we continued up the glacier, eventually climbing an embankment of moraine that brought us to a little alpine lake surrounded by grass and large boulders with views of the peak. It was an idyllic spot. But our first view of the face blew us away. Looking at it in profile we realised it was much steeper than we had thought. The one photo we had seen of the face was from a Spanish team that showed it straight on. We also realised our photo had been taken after a storm, making it look very white and leading us to believe there were lots of lower-angled ice fields on the face. Now we realised it was made up primarily of vertical granite with the exception of one long scar of ice across it. We couldn't see yet if this ice linked up all the way but walking back down the glacier we knew we had discovered an incredible face. Yet there were several big question marks as to whether it was climbable. On the plus side we discovered a brilliant path that took us down a grassy moraine valley straight back to base camp. Both tasks for the day were complete.

With fresh motivation, the following day we launched straight into the acclimatisation phase. With huge bags packed with food for seven days and all the kit we would want for the climb later, we set off up the moraine valley. Plodding slowly under the weight of the bags and our unacclimatised lungs, we arrived eventually at the 'hanging garden' of the little alpine lake. We had hoped to lounge around, here stretching and relaxing in sunshine on the grass but the weather had different plans and we found ourselves reading in the tent all afternoon while it snowed around us.

Next day, we stashed under a boulder all the kit that we knew we would

Paul on the breakfast pitch, day four. *(Tim Miller)*

need for the climb but wouldn't want for the acclimatisation. Then we continued up a large flat glacier. Our acclimatisation generally involved slogging for a few hours each morning to gain an extra 400m of elevation and then putting up the tent up and lying there for the next 18 hours mostly reading and sleeping and occasionally eating and getting up to pee. We continued thus to 5,700m and with splitting headaches decided to stop and stay an extra night before descending. What took five days to get up took us a morning to get down.

Back at base camp it was sinking in that months of planning and weeks of in-country preparation was now coming to a climax. We meticulously went through gear, cutting out anything that would add extra grams to our bags and triple-counting our rations. Then it snowed for two days and we were forced to rest in the tent reading books while the thought of the mountain hung over us. With apprehension building it was a funny thing to be tent-bound while so mentally ready to go. Then a nice morning came along and off we went.

Our first stop was at the stash we had left under the boulder. We repacked and with bags now overflowing continued gingerly up the glacier, each of us struggling over boulders while wondering how on earth we were going to climb a face that is 1.5km high. That evening we set up camp not far from our planned descent route, leaving two meals and a handful of bars stashed under a rock for the likely scenario that we would be starving hungry and needing a break when we got to this point after the route.

The following day we continued up the glacier right beneath the face. It towered over us looking monstrously steep and imposing. We dumped our

Steep climbing on day four. *(Paul Ramsden)*

bags and walked up to the bergschrund. All we could see above was a sea of granite, our line of ice totally obscured from below. Paul seemed slightly subdued at this point and I can understand why. At the time I didn't know what to make of such an impressive wall other than that I was in awe of it. I went to sleep looking forward to giving it a go but I sensed Paul had doubts over it being possible, having seen the wall up close. Had all our weeks and months of preparation been for nothing? Had we bitten off more than we could chew?

At 3am next morning our alarms beeped and we were tugged from our dreams to the monumental task at hand. Without a word we packed our bags in the cold morning air and retraced our steps from the previous afternoon across the glacier just as the sun started to light the tops of faraway peaks. Not yet in a rhythm, I struggled under the weight of my pack while I fought my way up steep snow over the bergschrund. I would stop every so often to pant furiously and warm my numb fingers. As soon as I could, I stopped to make a belay to give myself a rest and pass the work over to Paul.

The route started to steepen, the snow turned to ice and we now fell into a rhythm that worked. Climbing in lots of quick 40m pitches allowed each of us a frequent rest and prevented the belayer getting too cold. After 13 pitches of this we had climbed a huge third of the face, admittedly the easiest portion. On one of the last pitches of the day I arrived at a belay ledge and kicked the ice with the side of my crampon to make a small stance. As I did so the metal loop connecting the ankle strap to the crampon base popped off. The crampon was no longer attached to my foot and skidded down the ice a few meters, then stopped precariously in a patch of snow.

Loose mixed climbing at 6,200m. The snow mushroom in front of
Miller fell off a few seconds after this picture was taken. *(Paul Ramsden)*.

As Paul climbed up towards me, he was able to simply pluck it out the snow and hand it back to me without any further drama. We marvelled at the ease with which the situation was solved and grimaced at the thought of the complex retreat that might have followed had it disappeared for good, spelling the end of the trip and months of planning.

Having arrived at a potential bivy site we had spotted earlier through binoculars, to our surprise we discovered an overhanging rock cave with snow beneath that we were able to flatten off and pitch a tent on, albeit with the edges hanging in space. We couldn't have asked for a better place to stay on such a steep face. Still clipped in and with harness on, the rest of the evening passed quickly with snow melting for tea, juice, dinner and finally tea again, all with the familiar routine to prevent spills, promote efficiency and avoid too much steam condensing on the walls of the tent.

The main task for the following day was to tackle the so-called 'crux chimneys'. These were a gap in the line of ice and formed one of the bigger question marks that separated us from success. After packing up camp we rounded the corner and our eyes met a 100m steep wall of rock split by an ugly curving chimney. This was the wall's only line of weakness and we had to get up it. Leaving my rucksack at the belay allowed me to get inside the chimney at points and squirm my way up, feet peddling on small edges and my chest grating against its walls causing several ragged tears to open

Paul seconding with plenty of exposure. *(Tim Miller)*

in my jacket. Loose rocks clattered down as I struggled to hook anything with my axes. I was grateful for my Scottish winter apprenticeship; it had prepared me well for this type of climbing.

After three pitches of this, along with the exhausting job of hauling rucksacks, we re-joined the ice ramp. Hauling was a much harder job for Paul, who not only had to climb the pitch but also simultaneously dislodge the rucksacks with one hand, as they seemed to jam every few metres. Had the face been unlocked? Could we celebrate? Not yet. We knew there were further challenges up ahead but solving the problem of the chimneys was a big step forward.

We completed another few pitches that brought us to a feature we dubbed the 'first white spider', one of two circular snowfields reminiscent of their namesake on the Eiger. The hard labour never stopped and after a quick brew we set to work preparing our accommodation for the night. This involved Paul's very own homemade snow hammock, an invention that when fastened to an anchor at either end can be filled with snow while a ledge is also cut to form a platform big enough to pitch a tent on. That's quite an unexpected luxury on a 60° ice slope. But as we lay in the tent after dinner, content at having finished a day of good progress, Paul, who had his back to the slope, found himself forcefully pushed forward. A large amount of snow had fallen down the gap between the tent and the face. This was not good news.

I jumped from my sleeping bag, threw on my down jacket, boots, gloves and head torch and stepped outside. Unbeknownst to us, it had been snowing while we were in the tent. The face was too steep to be of any avalanche danger but streams of spindrift were cascading down and accumulating behind the tent, threatening to push it off its perch. We had to work constantly,

Tim Miller and Paul Ramsden
celebrate on the summit.

one at either side, to dig out the snow before the next assault came. Wind-whipped snow, reflecting the beam of our torches inches from our faces, and the outline of the other were all we could make out for several hours. After struggling for a while, we real-ised this wasn't sustainable. So we pulled the tent in towards the slope and the spindrift fell on its side, flattening it into the platform. Before long it was buried under a meter of snow but at least this way we wouldn't lose it off the cliff. All we could do now was stand with our backs to the slope while inter-mittent torrents of snow poured down on us deep into the night. We turned our torches off, slipped into a trance state and embraced the grim position we found ourselves in: standing in a snow storm, strapped to the side of a mountain at 6,000m in the middle of the night.

After an immeasurable amount of time the volume of spindrift partially subsided and we became too cold. So we uncovered the tent, removed the poles and sat inside it like a double bivy bag. Whenever a shower of spindrift fell on us, we pressed our backs against the slope to stop it accumulating behind us and using our arms raised the tent fabric in front of us to help the snow slide off the tent. This prevented us being buried but also kept us busy all night.

Eventually, to our huge relief, the sky started to lighten and brought a bit of warmth with it. We packed up our kit and set off climbing for the day. Having had virtually no sleep our progress was noticeably slower. A couple of pitches got us across the 'white spider' and then the ground started to drop away wildly to our left. Below us lay a huge 700m sweep of granite while our ramp continued across the top of it in a brilliantly exposed position. Then the good ice disappeared to be replaced with large amounts of uncon-solidated snow on top of rock slabs. Once again I left my bag at the belay and led a pitch of Scottish-style tenuous mixed climbing up a groove that led to just below the second 'white spider'. More hauling faff followed, made worse by our exhausted state. We had only climbed 150m higher but were in dire need of a rest. Who knew where the next possible bivy spot lay? Once again, the snow hammock saved the day and allowed us to pitch the tent. At one point we were given a scare when a flurry of spindrift came down; we thought we were about to have a repeat of the previous night but thankfully it was a one-off. That evening we were even treated to a glorious sunset but were so knackered we hardly appreciated it. We were asleep in-stantly despite our cold and cramped sleeping quarters.

Three very steep and looming pitches on the headwall lay between the final snow slopes and us. Paul started on these next morning; the ice was good and squeaky and the first two pitches proved to be very enjoyable. On the third, the ice thinned out, then disappeared as the groove system moved left around a protruding bulge of rock. Once again, this required bag-free climbing and all my Scottish winter experience of choss before I finally collapsed onto the bottom of the summit ice slopes. It was only 11am so we decided to press on and aim for a shoulder we had spotted just below the summit where we would be able to pitch the tent easily.

By now the altitude had truly caught up with us. Our pace reduced to a few steps before we were forced to stop for air. The ice required a frustrating amount of force before it took pick placements, sapping further our limited remaining energy. Then the sun burst from behind a cloud and, reflecting off the snow, started to boil us in all our layers. Each pitch was taking longer and longer. Even talking became a big effort so conversation was reduced to short, measured bursts squeezed between bouts of heavy breathing. Then the sun set and our saturated gloves froze immediately around our hands as the temperature plummeted. We went from being cooked alive to being forced to warm our hands and swing our feet every few paces to keep them from frostbite.

The top of the slope was getting close and I led a pitch to the bottom of a small rock band. As I approached this, I realised it was an overhang with a perfect cave formed beneath with a lip of ice protecting it. I rolled into the cave and lay there panting for several minutes, utterly exhausted and ex-tremely relieved we had found a suitable spot for the night. The cave was only a few feet high, and all our bulky jackets made it tricky to move around, but we managed to create a flat sleeping platform. Just as we were having dinner and laying our sleeping bags out, snow began to blow into the cave and circulate around, settling on our kit. This required an urgent reset to keep things as dry as possible. All this had to be done in bitter cold and simple jobs like opening packets and eating required gloves on. During the previous few days Paul had been developing an altitude cough and exacer-bated by the extreme cold and elevation it now became alarmingly constant and rasping. He didn't tell me till later, but at the time he was concerned it might develop into HAPE and we would have to go down immediately, missing the summit.

We then endured an extremely cold night trying to keep our numb digits from freezing. Waking in the morning, we wrapped ourselves in all the lay-ers we had and stumbled out of the cave. Two pitches of easy snow brought us onto the shoulder and then up to the summit. Dazed by the morning sun and the desperate cold, we fumbled to take a few photos and absorb the view. Any emotions were largely suppressed by a stifling sense of exhaus-tion. We had summited an unclimbed and unnamed peak via an exception-al route over five days and 37 pitches.

Retreating back to the shoulder, we put together a plan of descent. We had spotted an obvious couloir on the opposite side of the mountain that

The Phantom Line on Jugal Spire.

ran from a col 500m below the summit straight back to the glacier. All we had to do was abseil on V-threads down the ice slope and into the couloir yet even this was knackering for our tired bodies in the morning sun. We developed a routine making sure no mistakes were made at this late stage in the game. Once we were halfway down the couloir the angle eased enough to allow us to down-climb the rest of the way with a final abseil over the bergschrund and onto the glacier. What had taken five days to climb had taken five hours to descend.

By now the cloud had rolled in for the day and snow was starting to fall. Feeling utterly drained we stumbled across the glacier in the fog. The crampons I was wearing had steel front points and aluminium bases to save weight. On the climb they had been great but now, after days of being worn down, I was forced to front-point backwards down any slightly steep decline. Despite this we made it back to our much-appreciated food stash where we decided to stop for the day since we needed the rest and crossing the moraine-covered glacier with an extra layer of snow on the boulders was too much to handle at that point. Finally able to relax, we felt the relief of being down safe and the satisfaction of our achievement began to wash over us. I wasn't able to get to sleep for a while despite being warm and having a flat bed for the first time in several nights.

We woke to grey skies and with snow still covering the moraine the going was slow and our steps clumsy with fatigue. With a bit of guesswork we crossed the glacier in thick fog to the grassy moraine valley on the side of the glacier. Every so often, while we walked, we would whistle into the mist to tell base camp we were on the way, being a day late by this point. A few hundred metres from base camp our cook crew came out to greet us with an extremely welcome flask of hot juice, a KitKat and some cheese that provided the essential energy to stumble the rest of the way to camp. We threw our bags down and collapsed into our tent feeling weak but happy.

The next few days passed in a blur of eating the many brilliant meals provided by our cook and sleeping. Our thoughts drifted back to the climb and we simmered in satisfaction. The porters arrived a day later and we started the slow march home. On the first day of the walkout a hailstorm blew in that then turned to snow making the going hard work. Since descending the peak, Paul's cough had continued and now with this added fatigue he suddenly collapsed. He picked himself back up and was able to walk to our camp for that night where he took antibiotics for a chest infection and over the following days his condition dramatically improved.

We spoke to several locals to ask if they had a name for the mountain that we had climbed, but none did, only referring to the whole group as Jugal Himal. So we settled on Jugal Spire. We then named the route *The Phantom Line* as we were never sure whether the line would have ice all the way and several big question marks lingered right up to the end. Was it there or was it not? Did it exist as a climbable entity?

There were two essential ingredients that allowed this trip to be a success: the first, discovering such an amazing and improbable route on an immaculate, unclimbed face that leads to an unclimbed summit is extremely rare and very special. Finding these gems takes a lot of cunning and knowhow. The second ingredient was the tactical understanding that allows such big routes to be climbed safely and successfully: where to stop, how to bivy, how much food and kit to bring, when to pitch and so forth. Both these ingredients are Paul's specialty and it is thanks to his experience in these areas that we were able to succeed. I can't thank him enough for inviting me along on another of his brilliant adventures.

TOM LIVINGSTONE
Massive Attack
Hard Climbing and Controversy on Tengkangpoche

The lower portion of the north-east pillar of Tengkangpoche partly shrouded in cloud and a topo (opposite) illustrating where the route goes on the lower portion of the mountain. *(Tom Livingstone)*

October 2021. I'm hanging from a single peg in front of my face, watching it flex under my weight. Anxiously scratching the snow, I search for another placement. The key to Tengkangpoche's upper headwall is contained within this single crack. All our efforts up to this moment have been focussed on one question: could we climb through this feature? How I've wondered, worried and longed to see what was around this corner. Would it go? A gust blew ice against my numb face and stung my eyes, shaking the rope like it was useless string. Straddling the blunt arête, a thousand metres of air dropped away beneath my boots. The valley below was already dark: night was rushing in.

'Move!' I shouted at myself, trying to maintain pace whilst aid climbing. The building drumbeat of Massive Attack's 'Angel' thundered round my head, filled my ears. *You are my angel / Come from way above.* I climbed another metre and looked up, simultaneously registering the setting sun suddenly on my face – bright but without warmth – and the end of the headwall.

I could see easier névé leading to the summit ridge. I leant out above the void and glanced back at Matt Glenn, huddled in all his clothes. Punching the air, I screamed.

'Yeah! It goes! Also, watch me.'

Six weeks earlier. I had been eager to climb in Nepal for many years. Its history and culture is intertwined with mountains and alpinism. I'd heard many stories of the kind Sherpa people, living in the shadows of the world's highest mountains. Since I'd already visited Pakistan three times and India once, the Nepali Himalaya and Khumbu in particular made sense. In September 2021, Matt Glenn and I agreed on a last-minute climbing trip there.

Matt's strength of mind compensated for his relatively green experience in the Greater Ranges. He is also a member of the UK's Young Alpinist Group, the mentoring programme I set up a few years ago. The previous winter we shared a rope on the north faces of La Meije, the Grandes Jorasses and Les Droites, quickly developing a strong partnership and mutual affinity for techno music and hedonistic parties. He speaks with a light Northern Irish accent and his eyes light up when he enthuses about 'the sesh'. I also saw in him a familiar psyche for difficult alpine routes.

Matt and I searched for objectives that fit our requirement for a relatively short trip in October: the mountain couldn't be too high, so as to limit the acclimatisation needed; it mustn't be too far from civilisation, so as to limit the trekking approach; not too expensive; and either something that grabbed our attention, like an aesthetic and already climbed line, or a new route that appeared high quality. I found a couple of mountains but filed them away for another time as being either too high or too remote. Then, scrolling around Google Earth, I saw a mysterious peak. There was the tell-tale sign of a large pointed shadow jutting from its base. The altitude was good, there was a village nearby and the face looked steep. I messaged Dawa at Dream Himalaya Adventures but he replied immediately: 'that's Tsoboje, the Slovenians' objective.'

I'd just spent 10 days in Slovenia with my girlfriend Christelle, seeing all my friends there. We knew of each other's trips to Nepal but I hadn't asked

Tom Livingstone with Sherku Sherpa, the team's trekking guide, and Matt Glenn with Everest, Lhotse and Makalu over his shoulder. *(Tom Livingstone)*

about their ideas. I called Luka Stražar and we laughed. 'You've discovered our plans,' he said, 'and you're welcome to join us.' We joked this could be a rematch between the UK and Slovenia (after teams have unexpectedly and unintentionally met in the same base camp).

'Thanks,' I replied, 'but if you're going to this mountain, Matt and I will look elsewhere.' Whilst I enjoy sociable trips, I prefer isolation.

I re-checked my list of 'amazing unclimbed peaks', noting I'd written 'Tengkangpoche'. I'd already messaged Quentin Roberts in June 2021, congratulating him on his previous attempts to climb this 6,487m mountain in Nepal's Khumbu region. He'd spent six days on the sharp and sheer northeast pillar in 2019 with Juho Knuuttila and tried it again in spring 2021 with Jesse Huey. I asked if he was planning to return and if conditions were much worse in the autumn. Quentin's reply made the peak sound better in the spring – more sun and a more pleasant-looking snow ridge – so I initially ruled it out.

The search continued, Matt and I stressing about our departure date looming in just two weeks. Eventually, I suggested the Thame valley. It fitted our requirements and had a host of mountains nearby: Kwande, Kongde Ri, Tengkangpoche, Tengi Ragu Tau and several things we couldn't name but liked the look of. I figured we'd find something when we arrived and saw the peaks first hand. We'd keep our options open. Or more accurately, as I often do, we just postponed the decision. I messaged Quentin again on 17 September: 'we're going exploring but I feel it's important to be honest – Tengkangpoche is something we're interested in! Reading about your first attempt makes me think it was a really good effort and there doesn't seem to be a feasible way up it … but then if you went back for a second time you think it'll go …?!'

Quentin replied, 'I appreciate the honesty!! It is a beautiful mountain! Yes I hope so but sadly wasn't able to find out. Keep in touch when you're in the Khumbu. I'm excited to hear how things go for you guys. Especially [with regards to] weather and conditions. If you've got any questions hit me up of course. Jesse and I are planning to go back in the spring. Would you be keen? Or going back to Pakistan?'

Over the next two days we exchanged dozens of messages about Tengkangpoche. Quentin kindly offered lots of beta about route choice, gear and logistics. Much of it was stuff I'd already figured out from my own experience in the mountains but I was grateful to Quentin for sharing his first-hand experience. In fact, there was plenty of information from Quentin's two previous attempts on the mountain: articles, reports, photos, a kit list, a podcast interview and videos. This publicity had certainly generated interest within the alpine community, and I wondered if we'd meet other teams in Nepal with more concrete ideas of trying Tengkangpoche.

I asked Dawa for a permit to the Thame valley. My experience in Pakistan and India has been that permits are a pointlessly bureaucratic and occasionally expensive process. On three of my trips the agent has essentially 'fudged' the permit, either ignoring it or combining it with another team. I've also heard of permits being issued after the route has been climbed. Dawa explained the easiest method was to apply for Tengkangpoche. Being under 6,500m meant minimal paperwork. With flights hurriedly booked and only days to go, Matt and I agreed: put Tengkangpoche on the form and we can sort it out later, if and when we climbed anything. The permit was not a binding obligation.

When Matt saw the gear explosion in my garage, he laughed. I kept stuffing gear into duffels.

'You rocket.' He often used this phrase to mean someone or something that was a bit crazy of or wild. Although after 10 trips to the Greater Ranges I'm boring enough to have a spreadsheet to remind me what to bring. I still forget things though.

We threw a going-away party. Amongst the guests were Gabriel and his girlfriend. Gab was also going to Nepal, with the French young alpinist team. We chatted and planned to meet in Kathmandu after our trips. I said goodbye to Christelle at the airport. 'Come back safe,' she replied.

Our teahouse base camp was a mud-lined building dug into into the hillside of the Thengbo valley. Low clouds scudded over juniper bushes slowly browning with autumn. A stream burbled past some excellent bouldering. If it weren't for the yaks grazing nearby and the occasional glimpse of snow-covered summits high above, it could've been the Scottish Highlands. This sense of familiarity, of home, relaxed me only for the distant mountains to emerge from the clouds, reigniting my nerves.

Matt and I stooped through the door and blinked in the darkness. Tsongee Sherpa greeted us with her wide smile. A stove smoked with yak shit. We sipped sweet masala tea. 'This'll do nicely for the next month!' we agreed.

Just before we left Thame village and our last connection to wifi, Quentin messaged me saying he was upset we might try Tengkangpoche. He'd seen a post by our agent with the caption 'Tengkangpoche Expd'. I explained about putting the mountain on our permit because it was easiest (and cheapest) and how it was just one of many options we had in mind, including the

Climbing the lower slabs. *(Tom Livingstone)*

mountain's north face, rather than its pillar. I respected the fact he had put in a lot of effort. I suggested it was better to talk again at the end of our trip.

Once in Thengbo, the quietness allowed us to focus. We switched off our phones and began to feel the rhythm of the mountains. We scoped our surroundings through our budget binoculars. Down valley, Kwande appeared like a fortress: a bulk of rock and ice. Kongde Ri rose in a jumble of walls, like a double Grandes Jorasses. At the head of the cirque, Tengi Ragu Tau stood tall and imposing. And straight in front of us, Tengkangpoche soared. It reminded me of Les Drus in Chamonix, a pointed spire ready to blast off, almost ripping the fabric of the sky.

We stood outside our teahouse in the cool of the morning, coffees in hand. 'Angel' by Massive Attack was pounding darkly through the speaker, a storm of energy.

'Belter,' Matt commented.

Our fingers traced imaginary lines up the mountains but our uncertainty left them hanging in the air to float with our unfinished sentences.

'If you go up that ramp system, maybe you can ...?'

Eventually we drifted back to earth, not yet daring to believe. Instead, shouldering packs, we trudged up the valley to acclimatise. Then, with more red-blood cells, we returned to Thame village for internet and hot showers. A weather window appeared on our forecasts. Tengkangpoche's north-east pillar seemed the most suitable objective. It was in the best condition, with dry rock and little snow; it also looked like the most impressive and obvious. We were slightly intimidated, since Quentin and Juho had found a lot of hard free and aid climbing. We were also somewhat hesitant. Quentin had tried it twice before and invested a lot of effort, but we reasoned we'd just 'have a look.' Matt and I packed our bags with quiet apprehension, minimising gear as much as possible. I was optimistic; we had a good partnership. But I was also apprehensive. Could we climb so many hard pitches, day after day?

Livingstone described the climbing as split equally between hard aid and free climbing and mixed climbing. Although they didn't offer a grade, they agreed with previous assessments of around 5.11, A3 and M7. *(Tom Livingstone)*

At first light the following day we stood at the base of the pillar. Our trekking guide Sherku had kindly carried a bag up the grassy slopes too. Now, with everything inside, our packs weighed about 17kg each. I worried we had too much junk but reasoned that big routes need big bags.

We scrambled up easy slabs until steeper ground called for the rope. It was strangely reminiscent of Idwal Slabs in north Wales. That was a comfort. Matt led, stretched out on smooth ripples of stone, double boots clunking against the granite.

'Shit!' he shouted, skidding and tumbling down the rock. Thankfully his fall was stopped by his last piece of gear. 'Sorry man,' he said as he dusted himself off. He was fine.

'You rocket!' I said.

Moving together along ledge systems and zigzagging up the face, the terrain grew steeper and the walls began to loom. Transitioning to crampons and axes, we raced up snow and ice through a feature we'd nicknamed 'the smiles': two upward arcs of snow we spotted from base camp. Above, impressive rock walls were cut with large snow terraces, like thin layers within a cake. We hoped to find comfortable bivys at these terraces.

Around noon, we reached a snow terrace where previous teams had camped.

'We can't stop here. It's only noon.' Matt and I were agreed. I'm all for taking it slow and stopping early on these Himalayan marathons but sleeping there seemed counter-productive. We shrugged on our giant red backpacks again and weaved back left. Just before the next snow terrace, one long mixed pitch had me hot and pumped, cursing the strangely compact-yet-loose granite. I left my backpack on a piece of gear about 15m from the belay so Matt had to second the pitch whilst dragging it.

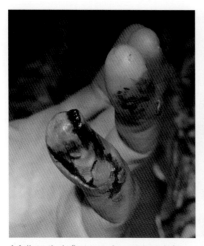

A fall on their first two-day attempt left Livingstone with a damaged little finger that spelled descent and recovery. *(Tom Livingstone)*

Despite injuring his finger, the pair fixed their ropes and returned to their previous night's bivy before jumaring back up, still hopeful they could make progress. With only Glenn able to lead, they decided to retreat. *(Tom Livingstone)*

'You rocket.'

Stomping out our first bivy in the snow, the sun painted the surroundings in gold. Everest, Makalu, Cho Oyu and hundreds of other impressive peaks smouldered.

'I guess that's Everest!' I said, pointing to the highest peak.

'You think?!' Matt teased. 'It looks strangely close … funny to see it in reality, and to think it's made of snow and rock, just like everything else.'

We also saw Quentin's backpack from his attempt in the spring. He and Jesse had put in a good effort but had had bad luck with the weather. We looked inside then left it alone. Diving into the tent, we tried not to think about the 300m headwall looming above.

Next day we aimed to fix our single and tagline ropes up the lower headwall but after an hour of glorious sunshine, we shuddered in fridge-like temperatures again.

'It looks like the Dawn Wall,' I thought. I started aid climbing up sporadic crack systems and patches of ice, my limited aid experience making things slow. On the second pitch, after about 20m, I saw an in-situ copperhead and gingerly weighted it. Using my axe to pull up, I suddenly felt a crunch. The axe had ripped and I slumped onto the copperhead, which immediately ripped. I was caught by a good cam some way down the wall but scraped my little finger on the rock on the way down. Blood dripped out of a deep cut. I found I could wiggle the nail around.

Back at the bivy, we bandaged the wound. 'You rocket,' Matt said. 'Let's keep climbing for now.' We jumared back to my pitiful high point. I couldn't believe I'd fallen off and scraped my little finger – of all things. It was my ego that was most bruised but we were concerned the finger might get infected.

Matt led three more pitches until, late in the afternoon, we had the inevitable conversation.

'What do you think?' Matt asked.

Climbers always start an awkward conversation like this; the words are heavy, loaded with subtext.

'I can only jumar with a giant mitt and my finger hurts but it's okay. I guess it really needs a doctor. Sorry mate. Shit. Maybe we could keep going but you'd have to lead a lot?'

'I think it needs medical attention. You don't want it to get infected and we have about five more days to go.'

We rapped down to our bivy, pulling the ropes. The following day we descended, taking all our gear with us. With heavy legs and quiet thoughts, we walked to Thame in search of a doctor. Of all the reasons to bail, this seemed the most pathetic. The doctor in Thame valley winced when he saw my finger. 'Hmm... that needs cleaning,' he said, squirting iodine into the wound. He slowly dressed it and gave me antibiotics.

Five days later, the clouds cleared. Matt and I could finally see the mountaintops. The peaks had been transformed, now completely plastered with snow. I nursed my bandaged finger and swore. I was pissed off about my injury and the poor weather but glad the forecast showed another opportunity for us to try something. I was grateful Matt was still psyched and not outwardly annoyed at me for blowing our best opportunity. We walked back up to our teahouse in Thengbo, lost in our thoughts. What should we try? Would conditions be good enough? The weather stable? Would my finger be healed enough?

After the bad weather, we decided Tengkangpoche's north-east pillar was again our most logical option. The surrounding peaks of Kongde Ri, Kwande and Tengi Ragu Tau remained buried in powder snow which cleared slowly due to their northerly aspect; they also avalanched often and remained dangerous. Tengkangpoche's pillar was steep and thus mostly devoid of snow; it was also cleaning the quickest and received some sun. The pillar had a low avalanche danger and would be slightly sheltered from the strong westerly winds. Plus, we had gained knowledge of the first section.

We also decided to use some bars, gas and a few items of equipment we'd seen in Quentin's stashed pack. In hindsight, we shouldn't have taken this 'lazy' option; it wasn't the best decision. At the time, we reasoned we would each save a kilo or two on the first day of climbing. It wouldn't make the difference between climbing the mountain or not, since the pack was low on the pillar, but the weight-saving was useful. In my messages with Quentin, he'd said the gear 'might be bad by now already.' Matt and I also agreed that if we bailed from the pillar, we'd replace everything we had used with our excess food and gas, thus leaving the stash in its original condition. We had the necessary food, gas and gear in base camp, but the rapid change of conditions, the failure of our first attempt and the knowledge of what to expect on that first day meant we made the easier choice.

Matt Glenn aid climbing on the second attempt. *(Tom Livingstone)*

We packed our bags, feeling a sense of déjà vu from our first attempt. I threw the same items into the same rucksack, bouncing to electronic music blasting from the speaker.

'Are you going for more acclimatisation?' Sherku asked.

'We're going up there!' I said excitedly, pointing to the pillar.

'Oh!' he exclaimed. 'I'll watch for you.'

Next morning, beneath a thousand soft stars, we launched. Sherku again helped us by carrying some of our gear to the base of the mountain. By dawn, we were climbing. Instead of soloing dry rock, this time we donned crampons and waded slowly through unconsolidated powder, taking turns to dig. Finally reaching steeper ground and the feature we'd dubbed 'the smiles', we moved faster, weaving through the lower section of the pillar. On the harder mixed pitch below the first bivy, I was prepared; I hauled my pack and knew what pieces of gear to place. I'd been dreading this section but it actually went smoothly: it's always better to expect the climbing to be difficult.

We reached the first bivy, satisfied the ascent had gone smoothly so far. Early on the second day, we quested onto the lower headwall. I felt anxious about the upcoming climbing but through experience and many sleepless nights, I've learnt not to think too much about what may – or may not – happen on an alpine route. Time will tell, and the best way to find out was to start.

By sunrise, now only touching our wall for 45 minutes, I was aiding again. I reached the second pitch, dubbed 'the Livingstone lob', and this time climbed without incident. The cracks were more choked with ice than our previous attempt and the temperatures noticeably cooler.

'Not much point in using the rock shoes,' I joked. Matt jugged the single rope wearing his down jacket then took over. He aided another two pitches, steadily inching higher. The long silence was broken with warnings to watch

Glenn tucking in at the alcove bivouac. *(Tom Livingstone)*

him and then: 'Is it legit to aid on your ice axes?' We rappelled back down to our bivy late in the afternoon, fixing our tagline and single rope in order to re-ascend them next morning. This would give us a fast start through the lower headwall and then we could gun for the next snow terrace above.

On day three we again woke early, apprehensive about the 300m of hard aid climbing above. Rubbing our fuzzy eyes, we robotically heated water, racked up and packed the tent. In the soft pastel colours of dawn, we took turns to jug the ropes. I tried to switch off my brain as I slid the jumars methodically up the 6mm tagline, dubiously eyeing the furry orange cord. I was glad to be moving upwards efficiently but disliked both the act and the risk involved. I suppose in this instance jugging made sense.

Matt steadily led several pitches then I took over. We followed the only cracks on this otherwise compact wall, always chasing the arc of the sun as it slipped away, just out of reach. The tempo of aid climbing gave the belayer plenty of time to think, whilst the leader's heart hammered out of their chest as they stared at the bendy half-in peg in front of their face, gingerly stepping higher in the etrier.

'I almost enjoy aid,' I shouted down to Matt during one particularly long pitch. 'It's engaging and hard and while it's not as fun as climbing, you can get into a good rhythm.' Our Nomic ice axes were now battered, the constant placing of pegs and peckers taking its toll. I was impressed at the steepness of the wall. Only occasional foot ledges offered the slightest relief.

At sunset, I started up slabbier ground. We were relieved to have made it through the steepest section of the lower headwall and eager to reach the next snow terrace. With slow dread, we realised it was still far away.

'This is relentless; it just goes on and on.' In the darkness I climbed into a dead-end, eventually went the correct way, tried to excavate a one-seat bivy then finally found a small alcove that must've been occupied by Quentin and Juho in 2019.

Livingstone aids steep terrain on the third day of their second attempt. *(Matt Glenn)*

As Matt's headtorch lit up the ledge something tumbled from his harness and he swore. 'That's my second crampon heel bail.'

'What?' I looked at his crampons hanging from his harness. The heel bails were obviously missing.

'I think I can make some out of cord later,' he replied. 'Let's get some food first.'

We excavated the alcove and slumped into an uncomfortable semi-spooning position. It was 1am by the time we half-pulled our double sleeping bag over us. Doubts drifted through my head. Are we too tired and too slow? Can we climb this thing? We joked darkly that we'd fixed ropes on the lower part of the headwall specifically to avoid this alcove bivy, yet here we were. At least the night was calm.

On the fourth day, I climbed several mixed pitches of névé, enjoying the quicker style of movement. Some sections were only 20cm wide and required delicate, considered swings. I welcomed the good cam placements and supportive crunch of my crampons, enjoying the more familiar feel of free climbing. I finally reached the snow terrace but frowned as the sun immediately left my belay.

Finding a good bivy site and being both tired, we decided to stop early. The 'marathon pace' of Himalayan climbing had finally been beaten into us. We were really psyched to have made it through the lower headwall, which was demanding but we knew it had already been climbed. The real crux lay above. The upper headwall was the biggest 'unknown' of the route and we didn't know if it was even possible. We might find blank slabs too, we mused. However, we'd seen a right-trending ramp system from the valley and now camped below it, were pleased to see cracks split the rock.

I took stock of our food, counting out bars and my favourite peanut butter sachets. 'We'll run out after lunch on day seven,' I said, wishing anyway that this be our last. We'd already begun sharing our meals. Yet we went to sleep optimistic and hopeful, daring to believe we could make it through the wall and onto the snow ridge above.

The glorious, warming, life-giving sunshine hit us as we aided on the fifth day. Our rhythm was now familiar: Matt started leading then I took over.

Livingstone climbing thin ice runnels on day four, which he described as 'a nice change after all the aid climbing on the previous day'. *(Matt Glenn)*

'Take as long as you like,' I joked as he pegged upwards. 'I'm just happy to be warm.' He steadily progressed up the cracks we'd seen from the bivy, laughing in the sun. The gear was often small or fiddly but never too desperate; there weren't lots of 'bodyweight only' placements in a row. Still, Matt took a small fall when a micro cam blew, grunting with surprise then resuming with determination. I took over, desperately hoping for easy ground leading out of the headwall. We could see Quentin and Juho's highpoint just below our ramp system and really felt for them; they had come so close.

Finally I reached the exposed arête with the single crack running through it, battering in pegs and wires as hard as I could. Hammered by the wind, I could still see the final lock was opened. Matt seconded the pitch with wild, wide eyes, but he cracked a grin when he saw we'd made it through the headwall. Another perfect bivy, sheltered by a cliff band, appeared in the flash of my headtorch a few metres away. Happiness spread through me at the prospect of comfort. We put up the tent and collapsed inside. Exchanging messages with friends via our Garmin InReach, they reassured us about the forecast. 'Keep safe!' they said.

There was a final question mark in our minds. Could we find a way through the cliff band that we'd stopped under? On our sixth day, Matt searched for a passage through, both of us hoping for an easy way out. We'd been tried and tested and pushed for days. Now, all we wanted was respite; our slim bodies were like tired engines, burning more energy than they consumed. Instead, we found an overhanging step that looked hard. Tired and buffeted by the bitter wind, I willed Matt to climb fast. He backed off, unsure if he could free it.

'I'm not sure if it's possible,' he said. I swore to myself, not wanting to bail from here.

'Can you switch to aid?' I suggested, grateful he was leading. In his fatigue, he hadn't even considered aid climbing but with renewed energy he tried again.

The purgatory of the summit ridge on day seven. *(Matt Glenn)*

Wearing every item of his clothing, the wind whistling, Matt methodically aided through the cliff band and belayed on its lip.

'This is totally wild!' he shouted. He was right: the belay seemingly hung straight over the valley in an outrageous, adrenaline-pulsing position. Using my axes and crampons, I then tried to mantle onto the névé slope above, picks dragging through the soft snow. Stepping onto the top piece of the belay and trying not to stab Matt, I leant into the slope and delicately pull on my axes, expecting everything to rip and for me to crash onto the anchor. With heart thumping and my breath stolen by the wind, I inched higher, face hovering above the snow until I could swing into solid névé and breathe again.

Matt seconded, his crampons now attached with thin cord. I was impressed he'd fashioned a solution to his missing heel bails. Then we slugged up the snow ridge, the occasional ice screw offering a little safety in the soft sugar. The arête felt 'classically Himalayan', a beautiful white arc rising towards the still-distant summit. Soon, there was basically no gear or belays. We plunged our axes into the unsupportive snow, sinking up to our elbows as we overcame tricky steps in the ridge.

I took stock at sunset. 'We're still miles from the top. I think we're going to have to bivy again. This thing is a monster,' I said, feeling cold. Matt nodded;

words were now expensive and tiring. Flecks of ice pelted our face and we huddled against the wind cutting into the ridge. Then we hunkered inside the tent, occasional gusts punching and shaking the fabric. We both agreed that we had to be finished next day, or we'd be very hungry.

Matt did a brilliant job leading on the final, seventh morning, sticking to the crest and breaking trail. I followed, drained. I was hypnotised by loose snow whipping from the ridge and flying into the distance. Then, having eaten an entire sachet of peanut butter, I took over with new energy.

Eventually, finally, I belly-flopped onto the summit at around noon, screaming down to Matt. 'I can't believe it. I can't believe we've actually done it!' Then I looked around in case there was a higher point. With so many unknown variables and so much difficult climbing, we'd been half-expecting to bail. There were so many times when we wanted an easy pass, a break from the hard or bold pitches, but the route was relentless. We'd wondered, sometimes aloud, about the cruxes: could we find a passage through the upper wall? Would we be able to protect the snow ridge? At each moment, at each test, we were lucky to make it through. And here we were: tired, elated and at the top.

Our descent down the east ridge was thankfully quick and straightforward. From a col, we then rappelled and down-climbed about 1,500m back to the Thame valley. Wasted, covered in white sun cream, but deeply satisfied, we staggered back into our teahouse as night fell on our seventh day. Sherku hugged us tightly, his smile flashing brightly in the light of our headtorches. We texted our friends: 'Back safe.'

Next morning Matt and I lay on a huge boulder outside the teahouse, soaking in the warm sunshine. We both thought the climb was finished, that we'd weathered the storm. However, there was another one gathering on the horizon. 'The yaks have already taken your bags to the village,' Sherku said, so we shouldered our climbing packs again and staggered down the valley, double boots clumping around our shoulders.

'Mmm, food,' I said, stopping to lie in the grass after only a kilometre. We looked back at Tengkangpoche, its snowy spine proudly showing. It felt surreal to think we were on the summit only yesterday, our lives distilled into climbing and survival. The route had been relentless, each day our bodies weaker and thinner.

Connecting to wifi in Thame village, I messaged Quentin Roberts. I felt it was important he learnt of our ascent from us rather than finding out online. I also contacted my parents and girlfriend Christelle, learning the tragic news that Gabriel Miloche, Louis Pachoud and Thomas Arfi had died on the nearby peak Mingbo Eiger. Gab and Louis had been great friends and I'd hoped to meet them in Kathmandu. My mind reeled. Suddenly, our ascent felt empty and meaningless.

Posting on Instagram about our route, I was surprised at the storm I generated. Quentin was upset I hadn't immediately acknowledged using gear from his backpack. I intended to publish a full account at a later date, with due credit, but I underestimated how necessary it would be to immediately

specify publicly each piece of gear
we had borrowed or used. Instead of
Quentin contacting me so I could
fully credit him, an article appeared
on an American climbing blog that
threw a metaphorical Molotov cocktail at Matt and me, sparking an online backlash. We were called 'scum'
and critics promised to contact our
sponsors, which was amusing as far
as Matt was concerned since he
doesn't have any. My sponsors I'm
grateful to say were supportive. At no
stage were we asked to comment
and the errors in the piece weren't
corrected. We could only look on in
horror as controversy raged. The
blog author Andrew Bisharat ap-
pealed for calm but it was too little
too late as far as we were concerned.

Thankfully, I was speaking with
the alpinist Rolo Garibotti throughout this maelstrom: he offered support and good advice. 'If aggressive
behaviour is all they can muster in
response, it does not much matter.
Over the Cerro Torre bolt affair
someone cut my car tires, and I recall being relieved, because it was not
the kind of reasoned analysis that would make me question myself and
lose sleep.'

Traditionally, climbing news was subject to scrutiny by an editor (of a
magazine, for example). Responses were equally examined, and published
if they represented a legitimate or sensible opinion. Nowadays, the role of
the editor has been removed. News and comments can be published by
anyone with an online platform, to anyone. The distance and effortlessness
of typing on a screen desensitises people. It's easier to write something
you would never say to someone's face, and easier to add a comment online
than write a letter or email. And climbers like their echo chambers just as
much as everyone else. Suffice to say I was grateful that Colin Haley wrote
a more measured piece on his Facebook page that changed the views of
many of our critics.

For a while I felt hounded and apologetic. But on reflection, I would
attempt Tengkangpoche's north-east pillar again. I don't believe anyone
owns an alpine route or mountain. I did have some reservations before our
attempts because I know Quentin and that he had invested time, energy
and money in this mountain. However, Tengkangpoche's pillar was the

Topos illustrating the completed line of *Massive Attack*, climbed between 24 and 30 October. *(Tom Livingstone)*

most obvious, attractive and safest choice for us. Also, we weren't at all confident we would climb it.

With hindsight, we wouldn't have used anything from Quentin and Jesse's backpack, which was stashed low on the mountain. We made the wrong decision given what followed. We should have brought all the gear necessary from our base camp, rather than choosing the lazier option by taking gear from their pack. I told Quentin that 'we didn't have loads of food and gas to start with,' but we certainly had all we needed. Matt and I apologised for using Quentin and Jesse's gear without their permission.

Others pointed out that equipment left on a mountain over seasons might be seen as garbage, as Colin Haley wrote: 'I definitely don't think it was unethical of them [Tom and Matt] to do so [take their gear].' Rolo Garibotti made similar comments, saying our actions were the right thing to do and understandable. The gear in the backpack was 'wall garbage' and therefore 'fair game'. Of course, a stash can be a good tactic if you intend to return, but this is never guaranteed. I know of stashes that have been subsequently abandoned in the mountains. Unfortunately, some peaks in Nepal have thousands of metres of fixed ropes littering them, those who fixed them being either too tired or not bothered to clean up.

Yet I have learned lessons. It's important to clearly state the full story, and not to rush into publicising it. Social media is a potentially dangerous place, and not always conducive to constructive, well-thought-out debate. I wouldn't wish my experience of a social-media pile-on on anybody. Overall, though, I found the climbing community to be incredibly supportive. I think 'spraying' about not climbing a route and then getting upset when someone climbs 'your' project is a little sad. Nobody owns projects in the mountains.

Summary
First ascent of *Massive Attack*, the north-east pillar of Tengkangpoche (6487m), Khumbu region, Nepal, 24-30 October 2021.

Acknowledgments
Mountain Equipment, Petzl, La Sportiva, Julbo and Fatmap. Rob Smith for weather forecasts. Dawa and Sherku at Dream Himalaya Adventures. Gyaltsen and family at the Third Pole Summitter Lodge, Thame village. Mrs T at Thengbo Lodge.

MIKE TURNER

Thunderstruck

First Ascents in the Kichatna Spires

The east face of Kichatna Spire. *(Mark Thomas)*

I can't exactly remember how many trips I've made to the Kichatna Spires, that knot of stunningly beautiful granite peaks 110km south-west of Denali in the Alaska Range. It has to be around a dozen or so. I've been most years since the turn of the millennium. There are so many big faces there and loads to do. It's way more impressive than most of Patagonia and I've done a lot in Patagonia. For me, part of the appeal is the remoteness. True, you fly in to the glacier but once you're there you're committed. Rescue is difficult. Denali is a different world in that respect; that's more like being in the Alps.

I've only been in the Kichatna once when there's been another team climbing there: a Polish trio in 2003. That spring Krysztof Belczynski, Marcin Tomaszewski and Dawid Kaszlikowski climbed a new route on the east face of The Citadel, above the Shadows glacier: *Last Cry of the Butterfly* (1,000m, VI 5.10+, A4, 80°). Their line took the prow of the east face, just left of a new route I'd climbed the year before with Stuart McAleese called *Off the Wall Bonkers* (850m, VI, 5.11a, A2), the direct start to the face's original 1976 route. As it happened we were back on The Citadel at the

High above the glacier on the perpendicular crack that splits the upper wall. A cam dropped from high on the face landed near kit left at its base. *(Mark Thomas)*

same time as the Poles, climbing a more alpine route to the left that we dubbed *The Supa Dupa Couloir* (1000m, ED, WI5+). We reached the top two hours after the Poles did.

In the intervening years I've done more new routes in the Kichatna's. In 2004 I was back with Stu, our third trip in three years, and Dai Lampard. There'd been a four-day storm just before we arrived and the faces were plastered with new snow. Crossing from the landing site on the Tatina glacier to the Monolith glacier was dangerous but we managed to estalbish our camp between the west face of Middle Triple Peak and the kilometre-long east face of Mount Nevermore. Our line was on the farthest right of this face, straight up to the summit.

Mark Thomas and Mike Turner, veteran
of the Kichatnas. *(Mark Thomas)*

We spent two days fixing the first 200m, climbing in waterfalls created by the melting snow. Then we started up capsule style, just as the weather turned cold and snowy again. For another five days we climbed through bad weather, generally following a continuous crack up steep walls of excellent rock, clear snow and ice as we went. On the eighth day the weather improved and we made faster progress, free climbing up perfect cracks to a little cave where we were able to pitch our tent and enjoy a comfortable bivy for a change. Next day we made the summit, the first climbers to do so since the existing route on the face hadn't gone to the top. We called our route *The Perfect Storm* (1,000m, ED, E4, A2). The weather crapped out as the day wore on and we abseiled through the night to make it back to the glacier and our flight out of the mountains.

I say that I've only ever met one other team in the Kichatnas, but that's really because of a technicality. In 2012, when Dave Gladwin and I landed on the Tatina glacier, we discovered two climbers already there, a Brit called Stu Inchley and Tasmanian guide Kim Ladiges, who this year made the second ascent of the west wall of Changabang. This was my seventh trip to the Kichatnas and only the second other group I'd seen there. Stu and Kim were looking at the same objective as we were, the right-hand side of Middle Triple Peak, Nevermore's near-neighbour, and given condition were so hazardous, with everything plastered in snow and ice, it made sense to combine forces.

We spent a couple of days stocking an advanced base but the amount of ice and snow was exceptional. It had been a 50-year record snowfall that spring. The climb started with 500m of snow and ice, always with the worry of avalanches, followed with a precarious traverse to the base of the pillar, a big wall of superb granite topped with some outrageous snow ridges. We took a direct line linking perfect cracks and iced-up corners that needed a combination of steep aid and mixed climbing, reaching the top after six days.

We made it back to our mid-way bivy that night but were then stuck in a two-day storm, waiting until we deemed it safe before continuing down. Having survived the climb eating block of butter, we called the route *Hard Arteries* (1,000m, A3, V, Scottish V). Not the hardest route I've done but the conditions were burly and I felt in the conditions it was a major effort.

Thomas' hands after 10 days on the face. *(Mark Thomas)*

It was certainly one of the most beautiful. Kim and Stu got a solid grounding in Alaskan suffering. I've never seen such wet down pits as those lads had.

Middle Triple's neighbour North Triple was my objective in 2016, this time climbing with Tim Blakemore, my tenth trip to the Kichatnas, aiming for the icy north-west couloir and climbing in pure alpine style. The result was *No Country for Old Men* (800m, ED, AI6), climbed in 18 long pitches from the bergschrund to the summit, starting up an ephemeral ice smear to reach the couloir and follow it to the top. The weather was pretty bad on that trip – wind, cloud and rime ice – so we knew we'd have to move fast when a window arrived. The route was done in 24 hours of continuous movement, taking advantage of a break in the weather.

I think it was on that first trip to Kichatna in 2002 that I first looked at this year's line up the east face of Kichatna Spire. We backed off low down faced with 30m or so of steep loose rock that looked unjustifiable. This spring, Paul Roderick of Talkeetna Air Taxi, a keen climber and skier himself, once again flew us into the mountains, as he has for two decades now. Back on the Tatina glacier, I discovered the rotten section that had stopped us 20 years ago had fallen off in the interim leaving something altogether more climbable.

This spring I was climbing with Mark Thomas, who I would rate as among the very toughest alpine climbers in Britain right now. He's on a different level to almost anyone: an absolute monster. We'd arrived in Alaska on the Saturday night, flown in with Paul on the Sunday morning and we started climbing that day having skipped breakfast. For the first couple of days we had to contend with the difficult loose section low down, more or less the third pitch. It took Mark two days to lead this on aid, with lots of hook moves and bird beaks. It sounds ridiculous but he was climbing flat out over those two days: it was an amazing lead. And once we'd got past it we were

The line of *Thunderstruck. (Mark Thomas)*

into an amazing crack that fired straight up the face for 900m. How straight? Near the top of the wall I dropped a cam and it landed next to the bag we'd stashed at the bottom. Eat your heart out Emilio Comici.

After six days we'd fixed all the rope we'd brought, around 540m, but had reached a comfortable ledge and so we pulled everything up and moved in. Being on the east face meant we got a lot of sunshine that this spring was the best season in decades, certainly since I've been going. We had a thunderstorm one morning, when it came in really black and a hailstorm, but that was it: quite the contrast to 2012 when conditions were so gnarly. Temperatures in the sun were pleasant and we climbed in fleeces but when it went away it got cold quickly. Mostly we climbed in double boots for the aid and easy free climbing but we put on rock boots for harder free sections.

Mike 'Twid' Turner on the bivy ledge halfway up *Thunderstruck* on the Kichatna Spire, surrounded by reusable shopping bags. *(Mark Thomas)*

After another five days or so climbing and fixing the upper part of the wall we reached the top and the demanding alpine ridge beyond. Leaving our ledge at 4am, we'd jugged back up the wall to the top of the ropes and then pitched along the ridge with climbing up to VS and HVS on a section that turned a roof. There were bits of loose rock and a lot of snow and ice above to the summit, which we reach on our twelfth day. It was an incredible moment and an amazing summit, the kind you only climb a few times over the years. Then we started down, calling Paul to come and get us on the way. He was busy that afternoon we reached the glacier – he might have had a party on – but he was back next morning. Thanks to our flight schedule we were straight back to Anchorage. We didn't even have time for a beer in the Fairview Inn. I'd lost three and a half kilos in a fortnight, which shows how much effort we put in.

Summary
First ascent of *Thunderstruck* (1,200m, VI, A3+/A4, 6c, 33 pitches), Kichatna Spire, Alaska range, Mike 'Twid' Turner and Mark Thomas.

VICTOR SAUNDERS
The Murkhun Valley

Pregar on the right, situated in the Murkhun valley in the Karun Koh region of the
Karakoram. The peak on the left is c6,000m. *(Victor Saunders)*

A team of three comprising Frenchman Bruno Dupety, Italian Giovanni
Rossi and myself left Chamonix to visit the Hunza valley in July 2021.
The target was the Murkhun valley, west of Karun Koh. This region was
chosen for several reasons. In Pakistan permits and liaison officers are not
required below 6,500m if not too close to the frontier. None of the team had
been to this valley, so it would be new territory for all and there seemed to be
a number of unclimbed 6,000m peaks in the region. There were also reports
of previous expeditions to the area from 1984 to 2016, so there was good
background information to support the exploration. Logistically it appeared
to be fairly simple with easy access to the road head on the Karakoram
Highway followed by a two-day trek to a base camp at 4,000m, which was
important given that we had a relatively short window of three weeks; it was
necessary to have sufficient time to acclimatise and select an objective and
explore approaches to it.

It was notably simple to travel from France to Pakistan. We booked flights
with Etihad through Abu Dhabi and the team flew from Paris to Islamabad.

On the two-day approach to base camp from the village of Murkhun. *(Victor Saunders)*

Covid-19 inevitably made things difficult. We needed to take PCR tests 72 hours before passing through security at the airport. We also required double vaccinations. Masks were mandatory on the flight and on arrival in Islamabad we had swab tests. The local population in Hunza were very Covid aware and masks were worn in all public spaces. Our two base-camp staff members were vaccinated. The porters on the trek kept their distance from us. Our sojourn in base saw very few visitors and Covid was not an issue during the climbing period. The level level of Covid compliance in rural Pakistan was broadly impressive.

In Islamabad, our excellent agent Ishaq Ali of North Pakistan Adventure met us. Having missed the next flight to Gilgit we took the Karakoram Highway to Gilgit in 13 hours, continuing on to Karimabad the next day in three hours. If I can offer advice for future expeditions to Hunza: it is preferable to spend a night in Islamabad and fly to Gilgit. The government seem to be losing the battle to stop the road reverting to mountainside. We spent a delightful day in Karimabad collecting supplies, including two chickens, for base camp, then made a two-hour jeep drive to Murkhun where we collected our cook and local porters for the trek to base camp. From Murkhun there is a spectacular gorge leading to Boibar, less a settlement than a remote group of shielings. The gorge continues to the herder hamlet of Prariar. There's a beautiful turf camp 300m higher at 4,000m with a spring-fed stream at the entrance to a side valley leading to the north side of Zartgarbin (5850m). This was our chosen base. There are further campsites a day's trek up the Karun Koh valley between 4,500m and 4,600m but they are not as well appointed as the Zartgarbin site.

The site of base camp at 4,000m on the north side of Zartgarbin. *(Victor Saunders)*

Base camp was established on 5 July and dismantled on 20 July, giving a 15-day period at or above base. Three of the possible objectives, Jurjur Kona Sar, Zartgarbin and Pregar II (marked as Pt 6200m on the Jerzy Wala 1992 map) were discounted for different reasons. The obvious and highly attractive route on Pregar II turned out to be an avalanche trap in the conditions we had in early July.

After several exploratory sorties it was decided to attempt Pregar (c6185m) from the west. Advance base was established at 4,900m under Pregar on the right bank of the Murkhun glacier. We left ABC at 4am on 17 July to attempt the climb. This involved five rope lengths in an atmospheric canyon-sided couloir to reach a long glacial shelf, a serac barrier (turned on the orographic left bank on the south side) and finally 10 rope lengths up an ice field to the summit block. The final pitches sported insecure snow undercut by cornices and were poorly protected with horizontal snow stakes buried deeply. It is not easy to give an alpine grade to the climb, given the length of the route and conditions we found but AD would seem about right.

The top of the mountain had a double summit, the slightly higher one, in good mountaineering fashion, being hidden till the last moment. The summit was reached at approximately 1.30pm. Doug Scott used to say it was respectful of the sacred nature of mountains to stop just below the top at a point where the climber can see over the highest point. That is what our team did. The descent was prolonged by quickly deteriorating snow conditions. After 10 rappels, the formerly crisp surfaces of the glacial shelf and serac barrier had become thigh deep porridge in the late afternoon, producing conditions that were in places simultaneously tiring and hazardous.

Giovanni Rossi at the summit.
(Victor Saunders)

Dupety and Rossi high on the route. The
flat-topped peak on the right is Pregar II,
currently unclimbed. Across the glacier on
the left are peaks of the Tupopdan group.
(Victor Saunders)

The access couloir was rappelled in deteriorating conditions down small streams of water where in the early morning there had been ice. The descent took as long as the ascent with the team back at their tents by 11pm.

Our return home was somewhat complicated by the UAE banning travel from Pakistan and Etihad cancelling our flights not once but twice, forcing us to purchase new flights with Qatar. Again PCR tests (administered in Islamabad) were required to board the flight and double vaccination for avoiding quarantine in France.

Our route was possibly a first ascent of the mountain and a new route. In 1984, an Austrian expedition made the first ascent of Karun Koh (c6977m), shortly after an attempt by Chris Bonington and Alan Rouse. They reported making an ascent of a peak west of Karun Koh. Peter Thompson, who came close to the summit of Pregar in 2016, speculated the Austrians may have climbed Pregar, which was not a name used on maps in the 1980s. However, the *American Alpine Journal* reports that the Austrian leader, Harry Grün, confirmed they climbed two peaks of more than 6,000m, but that these were small, snowy tops on the long ridge connecting Pregar and Karun Koh, easily accessible from the upper Murkhun glacier and likely marked 6,040m and c6,000m on the Jerzy Wala map.

Two views of the route up Pregar's south face. *(Victor Saunders)*

TOM BELL

Of Ice and Tanks

Climbing in Russia on the Eve of War

Tom and Steve at the hotel in Dargavs. *(Andrey)*

My downtime at work used to be whiled away flicking through online articles. No more. This is the first time in my life I've not been able to face the news. I have grown up with war. For all my life there has been a war somewhere, with all the destruction and pointless waste of life it brings. Nor is this the first time I've seen white faces in war zones, nor even the first war in Europe, and it wouldn't matter if it were. Logically this war shouldn't feel different to those other times, but war isn't logical. So even though I know I shouldn't be affected more by this particular conflict, I find that I am. We seem to be stumbling ever deeper into global calamity with no clear idea of why and how or any plan to get out of it. The world does not feel a nice place to be right now.

It wasn't like that early in February when our plane touched down in Mineralnye Vody. We had been planning this trip to the Russian ice-climbing venue of Midagrabin for three years; the ice had thawed and refrozen

Driving the Midagrabin gorge on the way to the icefalls. *(Andrey)*

Steve on the first pitch of *Duck Stories*. *(Tom Bell)*

twice in the time it had taken to get here. Covid-19 had derailed everyone's lives but finally my passport had arrived back with a visa in place and the border permit accepted. I had had to copy my application into Cyrillic with the help of our agent Andrey but it had worked, and with everything back on, and international travel finally allowed, I was on a plane bound for the other side of the tattered iron curtain on an ice-climbing trip to Russia.

Steve and I formed the entirety of the Alpine Club contingent on this trip. We landed in the early hours and negotiated a taxi ride to the hostel we had been recommended and grabbed a few hours sleep. Then we stood on a dusty main road contemplating which mystery breakfast meat product was most likely to set us up for the long ride ahead while looking towards North Ossetia and our final destination: the snow-capped mountains we could see rising towards the Caucasus where Russia ends and Georgia begins.

As we sat in the back of a 4WD Lada, our luggage piled high beside us, a column of tanks and troop vehicles passed in the other direction, headed for the Ukrainian border. At the time we assumed it was all just posturing, the alpha displaying his plumage. At random points along the road the police had set checkpoints and we were pulled over and trundled through the Russian bureaucratic system by smiling guards curious to know what bought us to this out-of-the-way corner of Russia. From long experience I have found

Tom Bell on the third pitch of *Duck Stories. (Andrey)*

explaining icefall climbing to friends who know me and speak my language to be fraught with confusion and likely to end in bemused expressions. So our total lack of Russian and the police's minimal English did not make for a fruitful international dialogue. Music is the great leveller however, and once we had clarified I had a shameful ignorance of Russian rap stars we settled on the Beatles, more of an international language than Esperanto ever was. After some badly sung bars we were cheerfully waved through, our axes welcome to hit whatever ice we were lucky enough to find, no further explanation required.

We picked up Andrey, swapped the Lada (much to Steve's delight) for a Land Rover that would be more suited to the roads ahead, and drove on towards the hotel that was to be our base for the coming week. As a climber I am not used to holidays with any level of appreciable luxury. Quite often the only running water is direct from the glacier. So being presented with a menu was a pleasant change. I've always been flexible with my vegetarian proclivities when in mountain huts, and recognise that sometimes it is not a fight worth having. So this time when I was informed a vegetarian diet would be challenging (in the end it turned out to be no problem at all). So I ordered the fresh trout. It arrived with a subtle, lemon vinaigrette and perfectly cooked, a reminder of all I am choosing to miss out on. That first night we were sharing the hotel with the last evening of a couples' yoga retreat. It wasn't long before Steve was roped in, to an exercise charting the week's mediative journey through the medium of glitter and face paint. As he himself had not been on the journey and was functioning in a foreign language with a total stranger his efforts were only to be commended. This set the tone for a warm and welcoming week in our accommodation.

The ice itself is very reliable. Midagrabin gorge, the mountain valley we climbed in, had been -20°C during the day for the week prior but a more hospitable -5°C for us. The ice is always formed and the only question is how fat it is. Conditions for us were comparatively lean but still excellent. Access to the climbing is via a gradually disintegrating dirt road; you are limited by vehicle and driver. We had the Land Rover and Steve, the perfect blend: design and indestructibility combined with skill and an infectious joy behind the wheel. Our walk-ins therefore were very short.

We had all had several years away from water-ice climbing and were taking it easy on the first day. Rediscovering a rhythm and flow and gaining confidence in your placements meant the whole week was a pleasingly steep learning curve and we were all climbing much harder and more fluidly by the end. The Midagrabin gorge is one of Russia's top ice venues but it still doesn't see the volume of traffic that the big European venues do. There was very little drafting of placements: you had to earn your rope lengths.

We climbed every day, with a day of via ferrata as our only rest day. Much of the climbing is multi-pitch and you would have to be good and moving quickly to reach the top of the longer routes in daylight. On a memorable final day, as the midday sun finally crested the steep valley sides, we found ourselves hanging exposed, a couple of pitches up, below huge ice daggers as the sun hit them and the face we were climbing. Small shivers of ice started to rain down on us and there was, for the first time, a respite from the creaking frozen silence as water started trickling down the face beneath the ice. With one pitch left we debated if we had time to make a dash for the top. But as it turned out physics made the decision for us: the sun disappeared behind the mountains surrounding us, the dripping stopped, silence returned and we were free to carry on. The final pitch was one of the best of the week, as the sun had warmed the ice to one-swing toffee placements and the pitch was transformed from steep and intimidating to a joyous celebration of what had been a wonderful trip.

Andrey specialises in introducing Brits and other Europeans to climbing and skiing in some of the incredible mountain areas of Russia, helping navigate government bureaucracy and the challenges of a language that few Europeans speak or write. Experiences that would have been nigh on impossible without his support were instead an enjoyable, stress-free week's holiday. I spoke to Andrey soon after the war started, wondering how he was affected by events in Ukraine. His hard work in developing trips like ours may well have been in vain. He is worried for his young family and how best to protect them. He loves his country in many ways, but is horrified at what is happening. It goes without saying that Russians face draconian punishment for any sort of protest. It is unsafe for anyone to speak out. A good, gentle and inspiring man has, in the space of a few weeks, had his world turned inside out. There will be many ordinary Russians experiencing the same thing.

Art & Literature

'Everest from Pang La', Edward Norton, watercolour and gouache, 18cm × 25cm, 26 May 1924. *(Courtesy of Norton Family Archives)*

SIMON PIERSE

Letters from the Fish's Tail

The Life and Climbs of Wilfrid Noyce

Wilfrid Noyce (1917-62), photographed on Everest in 1953.

In its obituary, the *Himalayan Journal* described Wilfrid Noyce as 'almost certainly the greatest British mountaineer of his time'.[1] This year, 2022, marks the 60th anniversary of his death and the 65th anniversary of the expedition that included Noyce to climb Machapuchare, in Nepali 'Fishtail' or the 'Fish's Tail'.[2] Noyce died in tragic circumstances in 1962 during an Anglo-Soviet expedition to the Pamirs. Roped together with Robin Smith, in the briefest of unsecured manoeuvres, they slipped and fell to their deaths. The bodies were recovered and buried in a crevasse.

Noyce was just 44 years old but had already achieved a great deal, not only as a mountaineer but also as a scholar, author, poet and teacher. He was a loving husband and supportive father, which sometimes caused him

1. T Braham, 'C W F Noyce, Obituary', *Himalayan Journal*, vol 23, section 19.
2. Sometimes spelt Machhapuchhare. See W Noyce, *Climbing the Fish's Tail*, Heinemann, London, 1958, p146.

All in the family. Wilfrid Noyce with Rosemary, Jeremy and Tenzing Norgay, Godalming, 1957.

interrogate his motives for climbing and to question whether it was fair and reasonable for a family man with two young sons to do so. In 1937, he had fallen on Scafell and owed his life to Menlove Edwards who roped down and managed to stop the bleeding. The 19-year-old Noyce underwent plastic surgery to rebuild his face. Noyce had another accident in 1946 when a violent gust of wind blew him from his holds on Great Gable and he fell 30ft, sustaining a broken leg. This accident, the third in nine years, 'acted very nearly as an obituary to his climbing' and caused him to question the path he had chosen.[3] It 'was designed clearly to teach me,' he wrote, 'and perhaps that my lines have been all wrong, at any rate that I've got to give them up for a while …'[4] When Noyce accepted the offer of a teaching job at Malvern College later the same year he found a situation where he could combine scholarship and modern languages with the opportunity to teach climbing and develop his career as an author and poet. He married Rosemary Davies in August 1950.

In a script for a radio broadcast recorded in February 1957, a few months before joining an expedition led by Lt Col J O M Roberts to climb Machapuchare, Noyce spoke of the impossibility of explaining 'difficulty' and 'danger' to his wife who had never climbed, however bravely she might face the idea of separation.[5]

I am leaving her for some months with our two boys, one aged four, the other two. It will be harder for her on her own to look after house and children; there will be more responsibility. Suppose they get ill? Or have an accident? Suppose there is a fire? And all because I am nailing myself to a bit of snow thousands of miles away.

This thought makes me ask myself most seriously why I climb. Am I just being selfish, or do I get something out of it which makes even this separation worthwhile?[6]

3. T Braham, op cit.
4. S Hawkins, Far, Far the Distant Peak: *The Life of Wilfrid Noyce, Mountaineer, Scholar, Poet*, Curbans Books, Cambridge, 2014, p130.
5. W Noyce, 'Why I Climb', BBC German Service, rec 24 February 1957.
6. Ibid.

The letters Noyce wrote during the Machapuchare expedition reveal both love and a sense of responsibility to Rosemary and their young family. The correspondence also shows how he was never quite free of the concerns of his literary career. Book reviews to consider, an article for the *Daily Herald* to write, and poetry to be composed – even in the shadow of the mountain that he was struggling to climb.

Action and reflection, far from being a conflict between two sides of Noyce's personality, were in fact, complementary and part of the same impulse. In the preface to a book of poems published by Noyce in 1960, Frances Cornford wrote of the 'fundamental impulse common to mountaineer and poet, this surprising feat is not the result of possessing a dual nature, but a harmonious one; though it is everlastingly true, as these poems bear witness, that nobody can be a whole human being who has not, at some time or other in life, suffered deeply and been lost.'[7]

Noyce's poetry is sometimes experimental, as in 'Breathless', written at 21,000ft on Everest, where every two-syllable line evokes a gasp for breath, at the same time forming a long trail of words downwards across the page like footprints in the snow. More often Noyce's poetry is lyrical; sometimes using details of nature observed on expeditions as the sounding board for inner feelings. In 'The Chough', seen at 28,000ft on Everest, the bird flies effortlessly to heights that man struggles to reach, mocking and encouraging in turn. In 'Before the Last Climb (written under Machapuchare, May 1957)', birds and flowers induce a quiet reverie:

Mosses and primula soothe, where I am sitting.
Swallow and redstart flit on the tumbling stream.
All these call me to calm in the Abiding,
In sacred thought, not in ambitious dream.

A striving to understand the poetic and adventurer instincts within his own personality is traceable in much of what Noyce published, whether it is in the eclectic research of *Scholar Mountaineers* (1950) or the more accessible *The Springs of Adventure* (1958). In *Why I Climb* (1957), Noyce identified collaboration as one of four key motivations. 'Climbing with one or two others you are no longer a single person, you are a "party", or, in bigger ranges, an "expedition". You move as one, fall as one; sometimes your very life depends upon your thinking as one.'[8]

I have felt this same pleasure on the bigger climbs of the Himalaya … and particularly in 1953 on Mount Everest. We felt that we were a team, and that the important thing was not "who" got to the top but that "we" got to the top.[9]

7. F Cornford, Foreword to *Poems* by Wilfrid Noyce, Heinemann, London, 1960, p12.
8. W Noyce, 'Why I Climb'.
9. Ibid.

Machapuchare, 1957. Standing, left to right: David Cox, Jimmy Roberts, Dikshya Man (liaison officer). Sitting, left to right: Dhanbahadur, Charles Wylie, Roger Chorley, Ang Nyima, Ang Tsering, Tashi.

Noyce recalled how he felt 'no twinge of jealousy, only a great joy' as his Sherpa pointed towards the distant figures of Hillary and Tenzing on the lower, south summit.[10] Expedition leader John Hunt was in no doubt that Noyce could have reached the summit: 'I know, from a quiet uncomplaining word to me at Base Camp on May 8th ... that he felt this, too. It was some comfort to us both that we were to have made a third attempt together, if such had been needed.'[11]

South Col, the book Noyce wrote of his time on Everest, is one of the best Himalayan expedition books ever written. Noyce wrote of 'being irresistibly tempted to try what may be impossible, and what a leader's expedition book does not from its very nature do ... there may remain a further interest in what the members of the party, their untidy everyday individual selves, were seeing and feeling and thinking through all those months; in the closer expression of their fears and doubts and delights.'[12] The success of *South Col* gave Noyce the confidence he needed to further his writing career and give up teaching which he did in 1961. It makes his untimely death the following year all the more poignant.

10. Ibid.
11. J Hunt, 'In Memoriam', *Alpine Journal*, vol 67, pp389-91.
12. W Noyce, *South Col: One Man's Adventure on the Ascent of Everest*, 1953 Heinemann, London, 1954, xvii.

On 22 May 1957, Noyce was at base camp beneath Machapuchare, having just returned from a strenuous stint above camp IV driving in pitons and fixing ropes. There was a stack of mail waiting for him from friends and family. He wrote to his wife, 'Romie', explaining that he had returned to get more rope, stakes and food, adding that:

> *Another reason for 'reculer pour mieux sauter' has been the weather which was* **bloody** *(there's no other word) almost the whole time. Nearly always it was fine in the early morning. Then about 10.00am clouds were creeping up, and by 12.00 or 1.00pm it was snowing or hailing fine pea-sized hailstones with no cohesion whatever, which had to be bailed off the tents with anything that came to hand, till 7.00 or 8.00pm in the evening.*[13]

Wilfrid described how pleasant it was to be resting a day or two on a bank amongst primulas, 're-reading all your letters and looking at the splendid photos Mum sent.' Sucking penicillin lozenges to alleviate the symptoms of a gumboil which flared up about once a year, he wrote: 'It certainly is a difficult mountain, but a very safe one.'[14]

> *Much of the work has been fixing ropes, there are now 1,300 feet strung out, 100 between I & II, 700 between II & III, 500 between III & IV. I have taken a certain fierce pride in having led every bit of the route and cut all the steps and stuck in all the pitons. You remember the problem was to get onto the ridge. We managed that by going straight up the face above II, up a snow gully and then a steep snow … where the fixed rope is, then left at the level top of a huge ice bulge which overhangs in the lower part, but [the] top makes a nice level III, before Chas lost his sleeping bag – it was blown off and went nearly right down to II.*[15]

Roger Chorley had contracted polio on his way out to join the expedition and Jimmy Roberts had to take him down the mountain on an improvised sedan chair with carriers. It 'must have been a tough job,' Wilfrid wrote, 'and he is now having to do a month's quarantine at Pokhara mission. … [Jimmy] really is a splendid person, and has never murmured at having to miss half the expedition taking Roger down. Unassuming, modest, humorous. Knows the Indians and Nepalis backwards.'[16]

Affairs of home were never far from Noyce's mind. In his letters, he commented on news about the start of the spring term (Cricket Quarter) at Charterhouse. He had missed the candidates meeting to award places and lamented that the academic standard that year hadn't been better. Heinemann had shortened the preface to one of his publications and reviews of *Snowdon Biography* had appeared in the British press. *The Times* wrote of the

---

13. W Noyce to R Noyce, 22 May 1957.
14. Ibid.
15. Ibid.
16. Ibid.

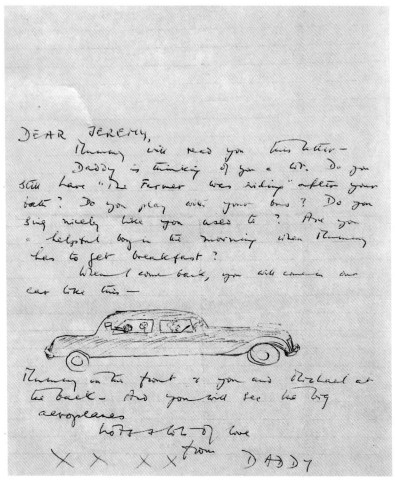

Letters home, to Jeremy, above, and Michael, opposite.

book's significance and how it was likely to replace 'the classic but outdated *Mountains of Snowdonia*'. The reviewer paid tribute to Noyce's contribution: 'a chapter on the literature [that] rescues much attractive writing from the limbo of climbing-club journals.'[17] 'I have had *The Times* review in Thomas's letter,' Wilf wrote to Romie, 'and Jo Briggs, in a letter to David says it has had very good reviews. I hope so.'[18]

On the flight to India, Noyce had spent the time writing the first chapter to *The Springs of Adventure*, which would be published by John Murray the following year.[19] There was also a poetry prize that Rosemary had written

17. 'Climbing High', review of Snowdon Biography by G Winthrop Young, G Sutton and W Noyce, The Times, 25 April 1957, p11.
18. W Noyce to R Noyce, 22 May 1957.
19. W Noyce to R Noyce, postmarked 6 April 1957.

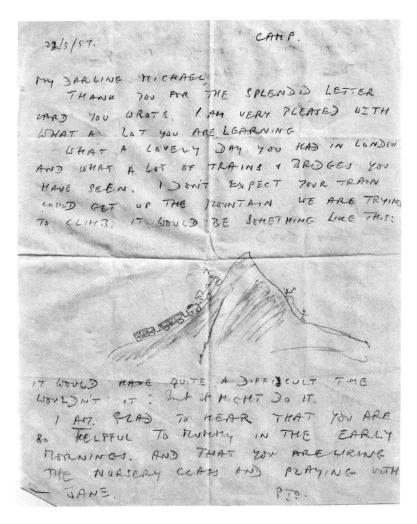

about in one of her letters. The deadline was 6 July. 'If I am inspired here I will send', Wilf wrote. 'I don't think there's a chance in a million, but if not here, I will seek out when I get home – I don't think you could find anything in my study – there is a folder – but you are at liberty to try and choose.'[20]

Rosemary had encouraged the boys to write to their father and Wilf enclosed notes addressed to each of them in turn. To his younger son, Jeremy, aged just two, he promised birthday presents on his return from Nepal and was hoping to see him at the airport.[21] To Michael (aged four) he wrote of how impressed he was by the 'splendid letter card' Michael had written and thanking him for helping his mother in the early mornings.

20. W Noyce to R Noyce, 22 May 1957.
21. *Climbing the Fish's Tail* is dedicated to Jeremy.

The summit of Machapuchare (6993m), photographed during the 1957 expedition.

What a lovely day you had in London and what a lot of trains and bridges you have seen. I don't expect your train could get up the mountain we are trying to climb – it would be something like this: [drawing]. It would have quite a difficult time, wouldn't it? But it might do it. ... Keep on crossing off the days and helping Mummy – then we'll have a lovely birthday! P.S. keep on writing I do think your letter is very good. Keep on writing![22]

Noyce had cabled to Dehli to secure the return flight to London and was hoping to be at the airport in time to celebrate his son Michael's birthday. 'I could ramble on indefinitely among the primulas,' he concluded. 'It may be a fortnight or so before another [letter] gets off. I do hope the Indians lay off these stamps: I'll ask the parents in a letter card to let you know they have heard and am writing a note to Mum too.'[23]

Charles Wylie wrote to Rosemary Noyce from base camp on 24 May 1957, praising Wilfrid's achievements on the mountain:

22. W Noyce to M Noyce, 22 May 1957.
23. W Noyce to R Noyce, 22 May 1957.

Without exaggeration, he is the tower of strength of the expedition on the mountain. I have been astounded with his prowess as a mountaineer and his quite indestructible stamina. He has done literally all the work on the mountain so far – led every inch of the way, and most of it several times over, fixed all the ropes, cut all the steps ... If we get to the top it will be Wilf's climb entirely.[24]

Before the final attempt on the mountain, Noyce wrote a poem, addressing the mountain directly: 'I have long fought you and now, stayed at your feet, ask how I came here, why so prayed to bestride you, your cold hard body. Where was the use of it? ... I only know that tomorrow I shall be stepping up the patterned ridge, towards the rockhead crown; as if it were all, for one hour to be standing on a crested wave of the world. And then come down.'

Noyce's 'ambitious dream' was not to be realised. On the morning of 2 June, it was snowing hard. Just before 11am, they saw 'four or five columns of blue ice, like the claws of some great dragon ... it was the summit itself, perhaps a little under 150 feet above our heads.'[25] Climbing with David Cox, Noyce had almost reached the summit but was forced to turn back due to the bad weather.

Back at base camp on 8 June, it was with a sense of irritation rather than disappointment that Noyce considered whether or not they could be said to have climbed Machapuchare. *Climbing the Fish's Tail*, the title of the book he wrote about the expedition is intentionally ambiguous. To this day, Machapuchare has never officially been climbed to its summit.[26]

The five years that followed the Machapuchare expedition were a time of fulfilment for Wilfrid Noyce. In 1960, he was invited to lead an Anglo-American expedition to the Karakoram where, with Jack Sadler, he made the first ascent of Trivor (7577m). The same year Heinemann published a volume of Noyce's poetry [27]. And again in 1960, *Samson*, a book on the life and writings of Menlove Edwards[28], co-authored with Geoffrey Sutton, was published privately.

Wilfrid Noyce died on 24 July 1962, together with his climbing companion Robin Smith, after ascending Mount Garmo (6595m) in the Pamirs. They were members of Sir John Hunt's 18-man Anglo-Soviet expedition. In 2009, the climber's younger son Jeremy visited the site of Noyce's burial in Tajikistan where Russian mountaineers of the Sports Society Spartak had erected a memorial to Noyce and Smith overlooking the glacier where they were buried.

In Noyce's obituary, Trevor Braham paid tribute to the 'sensitive temperament of his character ... richly blended with courage, gentleness, modesty and integrity ... Nobody had more friends, or enjoyed friendships more,

24. C Wylie to R Noyce, 24 May 1957.
25. S Hawkins, op cit, p231.
26. To respect local opinion, the Nepali government does not grant permits to climb this especially sacred peak. New Zealander Bill Denz (1951-83) is believed to have made an illegal ascent in the early 1980s.
27. W Noyce, Poems, Heinemann, London, 1960.
28. G Sutton & W Noyce, Samson: The Life and Writings of Menlove Edwards, The Cloister Press, Stockport, 1960.

Memorial to Wilfrid Noyce and Robin Smith, Garmo valley, Tajikistan, September 2009.

although his quiet, almost hesitant, manner made him a difficult person to know well.'[29] In the *Alpine Journal*, Sir John Hunt wrote movingly of his long friendship with Noyce. They had met in an army camp in Thetford in 1940 and were initially brought together by the mutual experience of surviving serious climbing accidents. Together they taught soldiers the basics of climbing in Snowdonia. Hunt's description of Wilf as a 'diffident, seemingly dreamy young officer, who was wont quietly to drift off on his own after a long day's training, … content to commune with himself and with nature' is key to understanding Noyce's character.[30]

Acknowledgements

I am grateful to Jeremy and Michael Noyce for giving me permission to quote from family correspondence and to reproduce photographs from their father's archive.

29. T Braham, op cit.
30. J Hunt, op cit.

ABBIE GARRINGTON

The Rock in Rock and Roll

A Short History

Climbers now look like athletes. They used to look like rock stars. The famous photo of Billy Westbay, Jim Bridwell and John Long after the first one-day ascent of the Nose in 1975 and an archive shot of Alex MacIntyre and John Porter on St George's Field, part of the Leeds University campus, in 1973.
(John Long/Bernard Newman)

Vasquez Rocks, the Sierra Pelona Mountains, California. A lone guitarist stalks up the sandstone and plugs the jack of his guitar lead into a socket in the rock. He plays an angular, skittering riff while silhouetted against the skyline, and the video for Greta Van Fleet's 'When the Curtain Falls' (2018) is underway. This is Jake Kiszka, student of the history of rock and roll and its rhythm and blues origins, and member of a group intent upon picking up those traditions and seeing where they might be taken today. His plugging in to the stone is not only an arresting visual choice within a video already committed to the fantastical (featuring hooded figures, strange eclipses and faces in the mountainside), but also underscores just such a musical heritage, its sedimentary layers accreting over the decades. Further, it emphasises the significance of geological rock itself, of mountain formations, in the history of rock and roll (including psychedelic, hard, folk and blues rock). When Kiszka chooses stone-as-amplifier, he makes these histories sound once again.

Street fightin' men: Mick Jagger and editor and publisher Ken Wilson. Jagger was a rock climber in his youth, thanks to father Joe's interest. Joe Jagger was hired as a consultant on an ATV sports documentary 'Seeing Sport' and Mick appeared on it, interviewed by the runner John Disley. It was produced, improbably, by Ned Sherrin.

The long-term entanglement between rock music and climbing cultures comes to a particular pitch in the 1960s and 1970s in UK and US contexts, when mountains influence a huge range of rock and rollers including The Grateful Dead, Led Zeppelin and The Rolling Stones, cropping up in lyrics and album cover art, as well as inspiring sonic innovations (how do you make your guitar sound like a wall of rock, an avalanche, or a descending body?). Musicians might also join the pan-Asian 'hippy trail' of the era and explore mountainous regions themselves, in search of sounds and experiences that can be converted into song ('We were just the same as the other hippies really,' Robert Plant of Zeppelin told *Mojo* in 2010, recalling a Moroccan road trip of the early 1970s). Meanwhile, mountaineers and climbers in these decades bring rock and roll with them 'on the hill', sound-tracking important attempts, as memoirs and expedition accounts record. British mountaineer Alex MacIntyre's sound-system transported folk rockers Fleetwood Mac to the Hindu Kush of Afghanistan for 1977's Koh-i-Bandaka expedition.

'Alex was never without music,' team member John Porter later wrote, noting it 'fuelled' the work at high altitude. This two-way traffic, with the mountains moving into rock and roll, and rock and roll moving into the mountains, sheds light on the importance of high places to the counterculture at this time. As Maria Coffey has written, by the mid-1970s the climbing world 'seemed to draw certain characters whose spirits were capable of freeing themselves from convention.' Mountains are therefore, like rock and roll concerts, spaces of potential rebellion and communion, where an attempt can be made to think differently in musical, sexual and socio-political terms.

Another possible route to escape is provided by drugs, particularly hallucinogens, of interest to both mountaineers and rock and rollers in these decades. The weirdness of an LSD trip or a mescaline dream might replicate the sensory confusion of high-altitude mountaineering and vice versa, while mountain landscapes could be conjured up during a trip. (Lucy was, after all, in the sky with her diamonds.) Coffey, writing of her boyfriend Joe Tasker, a significant figure alongside MacIntyre in the 'fast and light' generation of Himalayan climbers, who died on Everest in 1982, recalls him confiding that he had taken LSD during his student days and 'It was the same [as] coming down off Dunagiri – I saw people who weren't there. But somehow I made it down.' In his renowned climbing memoir *Savage Arena* (1982), Tasker directly compares climbing and drug-taking, calling the former 'an addiction' requiring 'ever stronger doses.' He was said to be a fan of The Doors, and their 'The End' (1967) deploys just the kind of phantasmagoric landscapes that the heights or the highs might bring about: 'In a desperate land / Lost in a Roman wilderness of pain / And all the children are insane.' English musician Julian Cope credits The Doors with taking 'shamanism into arenas', indicating lead singer Jim Morrison's manner of performance, which seems to invite spirits into the body. Shamanism, in turn, has a long association with mountain pilgrimage, and attributes spirits and powers to high places. Nevertheless, the use of 'The End' on the soundtrack for Francis Ford Coppola's

Vietnam War-set film *Apocalypse Now* (1979), which Tasker watched shortly before departure on his final expedition, emphasises that it's conflict rather than shamanic summoning that might well create such a 'desperate land' and that the wars of the era, too, had the quality of hallucination.

Yet love as well as battle might need a landscape to express it, as Fleetwood Mac's 'Landslide' (1975) shows: 'I took my love, I took it down / I climbed a mountain and I turned around / And I saw my reflection in the snow-covered hills / 'Til the landslide brought me down.' Songwriter Stevie Nicks later recalled writing in Aspen, staring at the Rocky Mountains, and telling then band-mate and boyfriend Lindsey Buckingham 'We're going to the top!' – affirming their continuing in the music business after disappointing album sales (of 1973's *Buckingham Nicks*) which had brought avalanches to mind. The Colorado snows offer 'my reflection', or a chance for contemplation and self-analysis while lifted out of ordinary existence. Eric Clapton's 'High' (1975; originally recorded with Derek and the Dominos) aims at something similar: 'High upon a mountain top / Where the eagle builds his nest / I shall go wandering, / Trying to put my mind at rest.' Fleetwood Mac were a favourite of Tasker's climbing partner Pete Boardman, who favoured the album *Bare Trees* (1972) and took it with him to Everest on cassette. The track 'The Ghost' might appeal to an ambitious mountaineer: 'Blue hills are lookin' good to me / I go there when I'm fast asleep.' The lines seem apt for Boardman in particular, since the year of the track's release saw him climb the north face of Koh-i-Mondi in the Hindu Kush, a trip written up by fellow climber Martin Wragg as 'Realisation of a Dream'.

John Denver's 'Rocky Mountain High' (1972), released the year before Nicks wrote 'Landslide,' addresses the same region as the later track, and can function as a cautionary tale for both the climber and the drug-taker. First, 'He climbed cathedral mountains, he saw silver clouds below / He saw everything as far as you can see' indicates not only the vast purview of the summit or the mind-expansion of hallucinogens or opiates but, via 'cathedral', a move towards the heavens. (See also Linda Ronstadt's recording of the hymn 'Life is Like a Mountain Railway' (1970): 'And the angels there to join us / In God's grace forever more.') But next, Denver's lines 'And they say that he got crazy once and he tried to touch the sun / And he lost a friend but kept the memory' bring us towards Icarus of Greek myth, whose ambitious attempt to fly close to the sun leads to his fall. Soon after, the Stones' 'Loving Cup' (1972) opens with an oblique reference to Pieter Bruegel the Elder's painting 'Landscape with the Fall of Icarus' (c1555): 'I'm the man on the mountain, come on up / I'm the plowman in the valley with a face full of mud.' The summit might permit a clear-eyed look at your circumstances, but get above yourself, or get 'crazy,' and a landslide or an avalanche can fling you down to grubby earth.

Nevertheless, the possibility of *not* 'mak[ing] it down' from on high does not only indicate lost love or failed ambitions. It also links climbers and drug-takers, with 'the fallen' of these years, lost to drug experiments or to mountain disasters, coming to haunt mountain spaces real and imagined.

UK and US musicians passing away through substance abuse and related illness or accident (Morrison; Jimi Hendrix; Brian Jones of the Stones; John Bonham of Zeppelin; Janis Joplin; Phil Lynott of Thin Lizzy; Carl Radle of Derek and the Dominos) here line up next to those who meet their end on the hill (Robert Broughton and George Bogel; Ian Clough; John Harlin; Alison Chadwick-Onyszkiewicz and Vera Watson; Nick Estcourt; Boardman and Tasker; MacIntyre, and many more). Icarus might be seen to represent them all. The subsequent elegiac function of mountains, permitting a reunion with the dead, is clearest in Fairport Convention's 'Meet on the Ledge' (1968) which, while it in fact draws on lyricist Richard Thompson's tree-climbing childhood, has become an anthem for mountaineers as well as Fairport fans: 'Too many friends who tried / Were blown off this mountain with the wind [...] We're gonna meet on the ledge / When my time is up I'm gonna see all my friends.' Whether your experiments are chemical or climb-related, then, it turns out to be hard, as Zeppelin's 'Stairway to Heaven' (1971) has it, 'to be a rock and not to roll.'

That Zeppelin track, perhaps inevitably, gives its name to several rock climbs in the US, an honour it shares with Jefferson Airplane's 'White Rabbit' (1967). Though primarily influenced by Lewis Carroll's novel *Alice's Adventures in Wonderland* of 1865, the latter track also takes up some of the disorientation of high-altitude mountaineering – playing with scale, including the line 'And you know you're going to fall,' and depicting the moment 'When logic and proportion / Have fallen sloppy dead.' The book's original title was *Alice's Adventures Under Ground*, but The Airplane take us to the skies. Cecil Day-Lewis's book-length poem *The Magnetic Mountain* (1933) offers some of the same inversions and weird experiences: 'Near that magnetic mountain / Compass and clock must fail, / For space stands on its head there / And time chases its tail.' Carroll's White Rabbit, who 'chases [his] tail' in the sense of forever being late, carries a pocket watch that does not seem to help him. Canadian folk musician Gordon Lightfoot's 'Brave Mountaineers' (1972), while it refers to climbing bridges rather than mountains, picks up on this move outside of regulated time that links childhood and the climber (just as Thompson sought to do): 'we would climb / Like brave mountaineers / We were never much bothered by time.' In this way, rock and roll of the 1960s and 1970s draws on a long history of writing about mountain strangeness and the baffling of the senses, in turn intersecting with landscapes of hallucination, memory and dream – 'First there is a mountain, then there is no mountain, then there is,' as Donovan's 'There is a Mountain,' another hit of 1967, puts it.

To 'drop out' in these decades might therefore be to pursue the hippy trail, become a mountaineer, join a band, or ingest the drugs that take you down the rabbit hole, through the looking glass, or to the summit – all providing a new perspective, presuming you don't 'drop' in another sense and join 'the fallen.' Day-Lewis and his fellow poets of the W H Auden generation of the 1930s used imagined journeys to fictional landscapes to eschew overt social commentary, while tackling the deepest political questions of the era with

Cosmic dancers: Alex MacIntyre and Marc Bolan of T Rex.

fresh eyes (and several of them wrote about Icarus too). In a similar way, the mountains of rock and roll offer a space to look again at personal, social and chemical experiences. 'White Rabbit' found its way onto the soundtrack of Peter Mortimer and Nick Rosen's *Valley Uprising* documentary of 2014, tracing the 'dirtbag' climbers' counterculture of Yosemite through the years. Dropping out or falling down are not the only moves of interest once mountains are in the mix: rising up or rebelling are important too.

The late 1960s to mid-1970s saw a notably intense phase of mountain influence in rock and roll music, with high places becoming a convention of the genre, across lyrics, cover art (most notably in the case of the *band* Mountain, active 1969-74) and soundscapes. This is also a period when Himalayan and high-altitude mountaineering in particular experienced a shift from the military-style expeditions of earlier decades towards a fast-and-light alpine approach – 'a guerrilla attack and not a siege,' as Tasker wrote of his 1979 Kangchenjunga expedition (to a soundtrack of '[British radio DJ] John Peel and Punk Rock,' his notes record); or 'upstaging the older generation [and] what we perceived as their outmoded methods,' in fellow climber Nick Colton's words. With all of the 8,000m peaks scaled by 1964, new routes and approaches remained as the available challenges in the Greater Ranges. As Porter has written, the new 'alpine-style purity' was driven by considerations of 'cost as well as ethics and aesthetics.' You no longer had to be a well-funded member of the establishment to afford participation in a globally significant expedition although other privileges of time, physical capacity and social contacts remained in play.

Mountaineers were also finding new possibilities in regions encompassed by the hippy trail, including Morocco and Afghanistan, while climbers involved in the Californian counterculture found themselves in a location of great significance to the music scene. Boardman, writing of Europeans' ambitious new climbs in the Hindu Kush in the early 1970s, claimed that mountaineers here 'established traditions away from the ache of commercialism' which were 'anarchic gestures of freedom' and 'romantic dashes of colour in a world of determined cause and effect.' With a greater mix of participants involved, such mountain trips became more explicitly tied to an outsider identity, and needed a soundscape of rebellion to accompany attempts: 'always loud music wherever we went,' as Porter wrote in MacIntyre's obituary in the present journal. On the Kangchenjunga north ridge expedition of 1979, Tasker reported that the expedition party took to scaring one another with past accounts of the difficulty of the climb, and that as a result base camp became a space in which to be 'cushioned from our surroundings by immersion in books to a background of Rock Music on a cassette player.' Rebels who had escaped to the mountains might need to retreat even further, via tape and tinny speaker, into musical ranges too.

While mountaineers were pitting themselves against the harsh realities of Himalayan conditions, accompanied en route and at camp by a rock-and-roll soundtrack, and while Nicks and Denver worked with specific Colorado snows, imagined or fabled mountains remained of interest to

Living on a thin line: the British 1967-8 Cerro Torre expedition and The Kinks.

other musicians of the era. The Grateful Dead's 'Mountains of the Moon' of 1969 takes its title from legends across the ancient world about an east African mountain range at the source of the Nile. Tales of the river's origin had been stirred up again by the previous year's joint Ethiopian-British expedition led by John Blashford-Snell to find the source of the Blue Nile, with a team including mountaineer Sir Chris Bonington and pilot Maj Alan Calder RE, great uncle of the present author. (The Blue Nile, known in the 1960s as 'the Everest of rivers' as 'Blashers' recalled, also gives us the name of the significant Glasgow rock band, founded in 1981. They drew the name from Alan Moorehead's 1962 historical study of the river.) The Grateful Dead's lyricist Robert Hunter opens 'Mountains of the Moon' with a reference to 'Cold Mountain', aka Chinese poet and highland hermit of the seventh century Hanshan, whose work had been translated into English by Gary Snyder in 1958. The rest of the song accrues further residents of the heights, often with associations in myth and fable: a 'carrion crow' (from a traditional nursery rhyme), a 'laurel' (worn as a symbol of victory, but with a variant that grows on high land), and a 'fairy Sybil [sic] flying.' J R R Tolkien's 'On Fairy-Stories' of 1947 reminds us of the 'uncharted world of time' of the fairylands, completely at odds with the clock time of human realms (hence the White Rabbit's woes). Hunter's reference to the 'marsh king's daughter' makes a further link to imaginary worlds, via Hans Christian Andersen's 1858 fairy-tale of the same name. Donovan's disappearing and reappearing mountain recurs here, as Hunter has high places flicker between the real and surreal, while stacking the centuries in geological layers through which the song moves with ease.

Hunter and The Grateful Dead return to the mountains in 1970's 'New Speedway Boogie,' where the skewed temporality of high realms gets an oblique mention in the lines: 'I spent a little time on the mountain / I spent a little time on the hill / Things went down we don't understand / But I think *in time* we will.' The anticipation of retrospection ('I think in time we will.') emphasises the common notion that a mountain summit supplies a view, weather permitting, not only across vast tracts of land, but also through time – the mountain's geological endurance, and its status as haunted space, seems to ensure this. Yet we are in the realms of commemoration and elegy here in a further important sense, since the song was written in response to journalist Ralph J Gleason's account of the Altamont Speedway disaster of 6 December 1969, when a rock-and-roll concert in the hills near Livermore, California turned into a brawl which saw the death by stabbing of 18-year-old Meredith Hunter (no relation). Three further deaths were recorded, including one caused by drowning while under the influence of LSD. The Grateful Dead were booked to play, but were deterred by the increasing violence, although fellow rock and rollers Jefferson Airplane and the Stones took part. The event, originally planned as a West Coast Woodstock, drifted a long way from the alleged peace-and-love spirit of the era, and once again time 'on the hill' is mooted as a way to process loss and to gain eventual perspective.

Of all the rock and rollers of the period, those with one of the most sustained engagements with mountain landscapes, with moving (as their song title of 1973 has it) 'Over the Hills and Far Away,' was Led Zeppelin. Not only can high places be seen to influence their lyrics and experiments in sound, but particular mountain landscapes have also proved an intrinsic part of the writing process for the band at important junctures in their career. *Led Zeppelin III* (1970) was in part written at Bron-Yr-Aur, an eighteenth-century cottage near Machynlleth in Wales's Dyfi valley ('Bron-Yr-Aur Stomp' is one of the resulting tracks; the instrumental 'Bron-Yr-Aur' appeared on 1975's *Physical Graffiti*). Guitarist Jimmy Page attributed some of the creative energy of that time to the 'panoramic views' of the location, later telling Cameron Crowe that it instigated Zeppelin's use of travel to inspire new music. (Page's interest in buildings with a distinctive atmosphere can also be seen in his 1970 purchase of Boleskine House in the Scottish Highlands, previously home to mountaineer and notorious occultist Aleister Crowley.) Zeppelin's 'Rock and Roll' (1971) might therefore be expected to be a mountain manifesto, but instead focuses on sexual longing and desire: 'It's been a long time since I rock and rolled / […] It's been a long time since the book of love.' But the rock-and-roll tradition is in fact poised between this specifically sexual rocking and rolling, and the same moves being made in response to godly inspiration, since the genre's development in the early days drew on Pentecostal worship traditions. By the time Zeppelin are writing, rock and roll's interest in salvation and the holy could be said to have abated but, via mountain spaces, the band continued to link high places to ecstasy and transcendence, just as drug-taking and mountaineering cultures of the period were wont to do.

Lead singer Plant, born in West Bromwich in the industrial West Midlands of England, had since boyhood been in the habit of retreating with his family to the relative peace of the 'Misty Mountains' of Snowdonia, north Wales. While Plant was interested in the Celtic history of the area (and explored this in the band's film *The Song Remains the Same*, released 1976), the Misty Mountains are also a fictional range, situated between Eriador and Wilderland, in Tolkien's *The Hobbit* and the three-volume *The Lord of the Rings* (the latter taken by Bonington on the Everest south-west face attempt of 1972). 'Misty Mountain Hop' (1971) can therefore be seen to draw on the mountains of both Wales and Middle Earth. It returns us to the temporal skew of both highs and high places via the line 'Hey Boy do you want to score?' followed by 'I really don't know what time it was oh, oh.' It also invokes the tradition of contrasting mountain and valley, summit and street, in asserting that 'Folk down there really don't care' and ending with a statement of mountaineer's intent: 'So I'm packing my bags for the Misty Mountains / Where the spirits go now / Over the hills where the spirits fly,' turning back toward the shamanic, the fairylands or the realms of 'the fallen'. Yet music journalist Nigel Williamson has suggested that the song is primarily a response to the events of a rally for the legalisation of marijuana in London's Hyde Park on 7 July 1968, which was heavily policed and led to arrests.

In common with 'New Speedway Boogie,' mountain spaces are used here to process difficult events, to memorialise, and to imagine a different world. And once again, 'getting high,' whether by lighting up or by climbing, is an important act of rebellion.

In addition to these more conspicuous references to mountains real and imagined, Zeppelin were keen to explore sonic equivalents to mountain experience, and to draw on travel in mountainous regions beyond the UK to assist in such experiments. 'Black Mountain Side' (1969), an instrumental included on the band's first album, drew the attention of the Beat Generation author William S Burroughs, who in 1975 was sent on assignment by then-prominent music magazine *Crawdaddy* to review a Zeppelin concert, and afterwards to interview Page. The resulting article, 'Jimmy Page, Led Zeppelin and Rock Magic' was published in the June edition, in which Burroughs claimed that the atmosphere of the gig meant that 'leaving the concert hall was like getting off a jet plane,' or descending from the heights. He discussed with Page the dangers of 'handling the fissionable material of the mass unconscious,' recorded debates about riots at large events with the mysterious line 'Sounds like falling mountains of the risks involved' (though the Altamont Speedway fails to get a mention), and explained that he heard in Zeppelin's musical textures 'a lot, really, in common with Moroccan trance music.' Yet again, mountains loom when ecstatic states are indicated, with climbing expeditions, hallucinogens and the trance-inducing sound of drums and guitars all lifting participants out of quotidian experience.

Page, recalling this interview in *Guitar World* in 1993 (the year of a Zeppelin reunion tour in Morocco, collaborating with local Gnaoua musicians), stated that Burroughs had first heard an 'Arabic' influence in 'Black Mountain Side,' and had advised him to go to Morocco – a trip he eventually took. Plant, however, had already been on a Moroccan road journey in 1973, which resulted in the writing of the lyrics for 'Kashmir', a staple of Zeppelin live performance (the geographical distance of the region from Morocco did not deter the author). Those lyrics reanimate some psychedelic tropes of wasted landscapes and relentless desert sun, and also state: 'Like Shangri-La beneath the summer moon / I will return again,' referencing the fictional location within the Kunlun described in James Hilton's novel *Lost Horizon* of 1933. Both 'Black Mountain Side' and 'Kashmir' are played in 'DADGAD' tuning, typically associated with British folk guitarist Davey Graham, and drawing on both Celtic and Moroccan traditions; Page refers to it as 'my CIA tuning', acknowledging Celtic, Indian and Arabic influence. 'Kashmir' has become one of the most familiar songs in the rock-and-roll repertoire, and its two riffs, one rising step-wise, the other declining increasingly rapidly, even echo mountain ascent and fall. As in so many areas, Zeppelin led the way when it came to interpolating mountain landscapes, cultures, sounds and literary references into their musical experiments, merging Wales, Morocco, Kashmir, Shangri-La and Middle Earth as they did so.

A new day yesterday: the first ascent team on the Cyrn Las classic Lubyanka and prog rockers Jethro Tull. *(Rob Matheson/Alamy)*

As outlined thus far, the narrative of mountain-influenced rock music looks markedly white and predominantly male. Yet, as Zeppelin's efforts indicate, cultures beyond the white West had a foundational role to play in the formulation of these mountain routes for the development of rock and roll. 'Far too many white performers thrive and survive on personas and performances that are studies in ventriloquism and minstrelsy, careless footnotes to a badly read blues text,' as Margo Jefferson wrote in *Harper's Magazine* in 1973. Just as the 'hidden histories of exploration' (to use historian Felix Driver's term) must be uncovered to offer a counterbalance to the white-centred narratives of expeditionary achievement, so a more nuanced reading of the rocks in rock and roll reveals that the deepest geological layers are of Black musical tradition and expertise. In conspicuously blues-influenced guitarist Joe Bonamassa's 2016 track 'Mountain Climbing', he sings 'Lost in the struggle, there's a mountain in my way' but also observes 'Whoa, it's blues at the bottom,' neatly indicating both the upward journey out of strife that makes apt a mountain metaphor, and the fundamental place of the blues in any rock-and-roll mountain lineage. In the late 1950s and early 1960s, the UK experienced what has become known as the 'R&B boom', in which British musicians influenced by Black US artists such as Howlin' Wolf, Muddy Waters and Chuck Berry (the latter with a Pentecostal background) drew blues principles into club bands which had until then been working in jazz and folk genres. The counter-move was the mid-1960s' 'British invasion' of rock and rollers from the UK into the US, exporting blues-invigorated music, albeit in bands often led by white men.

Music historian Patrick Burke has identified a tendency in 1960s rock and roll toward 'white musicians casting themselves as political revolutionaries by enacting a romanticised vision of African American identity.' Mountains are caught up in these debates, not least because they are attached to just such notions of 'uprising' and the countercultural. Dr Martin Luther King's 'I have a dream' speech asserting African-American civil rights had been delivered in August 1963, and contains seven references to mountains, five to hills. Indeed, one iteration of the famous line begins: 'I have a dream that one day every valley shall be exalted, every hill and mountain shall be made low.' Meanwhile, his final speech, delivered the day before his assassination in 1968, is known by its resonant phrase 'I've been to the mountaintop.' Dr King knew the power of landscape to convey a sense of radical upheaval, a fundamental shift in the social order. The rhetorical power here has an explicitly Biblical tenor (drawing on Isaiah 40:4 in particular) and mountains' path from the Bible, to African-American spirituals and gospel music, to the blues should not be overlooked, supplementing Pentecostalism's so-called 'holy rollers'. While artists including Zeppelin and the Stones were consistent in their praise for and collaboration with Black blues musicians, the whiteness of the line-up of rock and roll 'torch bearers' in the era might well give you the 'Black Mountain Blues' (a 1930 track by Black artist Bessie Smith made famous by white Janis Joplin's 1975 cover version). 'Nothing in American vernacular music holds still,' Greil Marcus wrote of Bob Dylan's

'Like a Rolling Stone' (1965), citing that track's roots in the work of blues greats Waters and Son House; the stones keep rolling on down the mountain.

Notable exceptions to the whiteness of rock and roll's frontmen include the aforementioned Hendrix, and Lynott of Thin Lizzy. The latter drew on his Irish heritage (he was born, like Plant, in West Bromwich, but his mother hailed from Dublin, his father from then British Guiana, now Guyana) to write 'Emerald' (1976), which deploys several of the mountain tropes outlined above to stage a combination of imaginary quest and English colonial violence: 'Down from the glen came the marching men'; 'They had come to claim the Emerald.' Lynott also refers to 'the fallen,' although the scene of battle moves between the 'glen' and the sounds of the band's duelling guitars. Without that Irish heritage, and referring to a 'peaceful army' rather than marauding colonialists, Greta Van Fleet's 'Heat Above' (2021) uses the same landscape of battle ('Fire still burning on the ground') to, ultimately, state the value of 'Ascending to the stars as one'; bringing us back to mountain communion. But the band have a longer history of engagement with high places, with 'Mountain of the Sun' (2018) seeming to urge a modern Icarus to 'Climb the mountain even higher / To kiss the sun,' and the otherwise Aldous Huxley-influenced 'Brave New World' (2018) speaking of 'drifters of the high rift plains.' Greta's use of mountain landscapes, in videos and album cover art as well as lyrics (and in a 2017 cover of 'Meet on the Ledge'), both relies on the heritage sketched in this article including that of Black precursors, and shifts the use of those imagined spaces toward the contemplation of environmental catastrophe. Denver, whom the band have claimed as an influence, was in early with this narrative of mountain desecration, since 'Rocky Mountain High' contains the lines: 'he cannot comprehend / Why they try to tear the mountains down to bring in a couple more / More people, more scars upon the land.' In continuing this conversation, Greta demonstrate the enduring importance of the rocks in rock and roll, and highlight the ability of the endlessly resonant symbol of a mountain to reflect the concerns of its time. Tracing rock geologies – following the mountains in the music – is therefore one powerful way to trace rock genealogies, leading from R&B, to the classic era of the 1960s and 1970s, to those taking up the traditions today. Rock and roll might be ever changing, but the mountains at least endure. Or, as Donovan's 'The Mountain' (1976) expresses it: 'First there is a mountain, then it seems the mountain's gone, / But then, if you take a look, why, it's been there all along.'

Indicative Bibliography

P Boardman, 'Hindu Kush: Alpine Style', *Alpine Journal*, vol 79, pp110-14, 1974.

P Burke, 'Tear Down the Walls: Jefferson Airplane, Race, and Revolutionary Rhetoric in 1960s Rock', *Popular Music* 29.1 pp61-79, January 2010.

W Burroughs, 'Jimmy Page, Led Zeppelin and Rock Magic', *Crawdaddy*, June 1975.

M Coffey, *Fragile Edge*, Chatto & Windus, London, 1989.

C Day Lewis, *The Magnetic Mountain*, Hogarth Press, London, 1933.

F Driver, *Hidden Histories of Exploration*, Royal Geographical Society, London, 2009.

M Jefferson, 'Ripping Off Black Music', *Harper's Magazine*, pp40-5, January 1973.

C Carson & K Shepard (eds), '"I Have a Dream": Address Delivered at the March on Washington for Jobs and Freedom', *A Call to Conscience: The Landmark Speeches of Dr Martin Luther King* Warner Books, New York, pp75-88, 2001.

J Porter, 'In Memoriam: Alexander MacIntyre,' *Alpine Journal* vol 88, pp276-279, 1983.

J Porter, *One Day as a Tiger: Alex MacIntyre and the Birth of Light and Fast Alpinism*, Vertebrate, Sheffield, 2015.

J Tasker, 'Kangchenjunga North Ridge 1979', *Alpine Journal*, vol 85, pp49-58, 1980.

J Tasker, 'Notes on Kangchenjunga North Ridge 1979', Joe Tasker Collections, Mountain Heritage Trust, TAS/05/02.

J Tasker, *Savage Arena*, Methuen, London, 1982.

J Tolkien, 'On Fairy-Stories', *Essays Presented to Charles Williams*, Books for Libraries Press, New York, pp38-90, 1947.

N Williamson, *The Rough Guide to Led Zeppelin*, Rough Guides, London, 2013.

M Wragg, 'Realisation of a Dream', *Nottingham University Mountaineering Club Journal* 10, pp5-8, 1973.

The Alpine Journal and its Editors

Part IV: 1954-82[a]

Francis Keenlyside with HM The Queen at the Club's centenary
celebrations in 1957. *(AC Photo Library)*.

F H Keenlyside (1954-61)

The sacking of T Graham Brown from the editorship of the *Alpine Journal*
in 1954[b] was largely the result of his having antagonised Geoffrey Winthrop
Young but there had been other, more cogent grounds: the *Journal* was in a
rut, backward looking and out of touch, criticisms that had also been aimed
at the Club itself and which had led to the formation of the Alpine Climbing
Group. As W H Murray observed:

> *I and several other members of the club who joined the recently formed Alpine
> Climbing Group were impelled to do so because it had become no longer possi-
> ble within the AC to keep ourselves adequately informed about Alpine climbing
> developments … The AJ has become the last place one looks to get news of
> routes and reconnaissances.[1]*

a. Parts I-III, written by T S Blakeney, appeared in AJs vols 79, 80 and 81.
b. P Foster & G Jones, 'Sacking the Editor', Alpine Journal, vol 119, pp262-77, 2015.

Reform was required and Francis Keenlyside was chosen to deliver it, although at first sight he was not obviously the person best qualified to do so. He had been elected to the Club six years earlier on the strength of a walking holiday in the Alps (and an ascent of the Great Pyramid) in 1938, a few minor climbs with guides in 1939 and two seasons immediately after the Second World War; his sentiments were pre-war, inclining more to those of Winthrop Young than Strutt's. For Keenlyside, mountaineering was a route to an 'aesthetic experience'; and he had his own doubts about his suitability. In a letter to Graham Brown, he wrote:

> I had no wish to be editor, certainly no wish to succeed you but was persuaded in all the circumstances I should do so ... I am fully aware that my qualifications fall very far short of yours: the rather unflattering interest of the Committee seemed to be to secure an 'efficiency' expert available in London. And I am not even that.[2]

But the AC Committee, having identified its quarry, seemingly had no qualms about poaching him from the Climbers' Club whose journal he edited at the time.

Keenlyside set out his stall in an editorial note:

> When the Alpine Club was founded mountaineering was the activity of a handful of unusual men in very few countries. Now it is the recreation of large numbers of men and women throughout the world. The task of maintaining contact with mountaineering development and achievement has consequently become vastly more difficult, if not impossible. Nevertheless we feel that this task, so far as it lies in our powers, is imposed on the Alpine Journal.[3]

The period of his editorship coincided with an international explosion in Himalayan climbing and a resurgence of the British in the Alps. These developments are captured in his journals. There were reports from the leaders of the expeditions that made the first ascents of Nanga Parbat (Austro-Germans), K2 (Italians), Cho Oyu (Austrian), Kangchenjunga (British), Makalu (French), Lhotse and the second ascent of Everest (Swiss).

In the Alps, the second ascent of the west face of the Dru by Joe Brown and Don Whillans was reported in an article by Ron Moseley, a fellow member of the Rock and Ice; Hamish MacInnes described his ascent of the Bonatti Pillar, during which he suffered a fractured skull along with the second British ascent of the Walker Spur, following the trail of empty tubes of Smarties discarded by Robin Smith and Gunn Clark who were one bivouac ahead; and Chris Bonington contributed technical accounts of three climbs on the north faces of the Tre Cime di Lavaredo including the *Brandler-Hasse* on the Cima Grande, which on the first ascent had required fifteen bolts and about 200 pitons. Strutt would surely have been spinning in his grave while his ghost still haunted the Club.

A few years earlier Keenlyside had commissioned and published an article on the techniques of artificial climbing which prompted Tom Peacocke to write the following:

> *I would humbly suggest that the article … is somewhat out of place in the Alpine Journal and would better grace the pages of an engineering journal. The methods … are alien to the traditions of the Alpine Club and to British mountaineering generally.*[4]

To keep abreast of mountaineering worldwide, Keenlyside established a network of foreign correspondents whose regular reviews and updates appeared as Area Notes, which remain a feature of the *Journal* to this day. He also secured articles by leading Continental climbers, such as Kurt Diemberger, Gaston Rébuffat and André Roch, their contributions usually appearing in translation although several were published in their original French, including Monsieur Seylaz's[c] six-page review of *The First Ascent of Mont Blanc* by Graham Brown and de Beer, published to mark the Club's centenary. (Was there no native English-speaker in the Club willing to write a review and risk a feud with TGB?)

The Club celebrated its centenary in 1957 and the *Journal's* content for that year was overwhelmingly retrospective, charting the history of mountaineering and the Club in contributions from, amongst others, Geoffrey Young, Arnold Lunn, Jack Longland and Tom Longstaff. In his article, 'Fifty Years Ago', Longstaff provided delicious vignettes of some of the senior members who had occupied the front row in the lecture hall at the turn of the century: Sir Edward Davidson, 'scarcely approachable in his majestic self-confidence'; Douglas Freshfield, 'very dangerous to cross swords with and never popular'; James Bryce, 'a more urbane, friendly and accomplished personality I am never likely to meet'; and Clinton Dent, whose 'malice was delicious without a trace of anger … the most intriguing character I have ever known.'

Accounts of the centenary celebrations spilled over into the next number, filling half its pages. The reception held in the great hall of Lincoln's Inn and attended by the Queen and Prince Philip had been a glittering occasion. In a description perhaps more suited to *Vogue* than the *AJ*, readers were informed that the Queen wore 'a lovely, full-skirted dress of cream and gold brocade, diamond tiara, necklace and earrings of diamonds, and the star and blue sash of the Order of the Garter' and 'made a radiant picture, vivid, smiling and relaxed, clasping a charming bouquet of edelweiss, deep-blue trumpet gentians and other alpine flowers.'[5] The dinner at the Dorchester Hotel commenced with turtle soup, 'allaying any fears of what was to come', and was accompanied by 'well-chosen' wines, inducing in the reporter 'a feeling of how appropriate it had all been to the occasion, and how well in keeping with the Club's own character: sufficient formality but without stiffness, and above all, a pleasantly relaxed atmosphere of ease, friendship

---

c. Editor of the Swiss Alpine Journal, *Les Alpes*.

and good fellowship.'[6] Understandably, this was the *Journal* at its most parochial but by the time Keenlyside relinquished the editorship he had made considerable strides towards countering Bill Murray's criticism, delivering a *Journal* in which the reader could confidently expect to find information about new climbs and exploration in mountain ranges throughout the world.

A D M Cox (1962-7)

Medieval historian and Oxford don David Cox had started rock climbing as a schoolboy in the late 1920s on the tors of Dartmoor. Ten years later, he was operating at the highest level, repeating routes such as *Longland's* and *Kirkus' Great Slab* on Cloggy, and adding his own new route, *Sunset Crack*, on its East Buttress. His Alpine career had started slowly and was interrupted by the Second World War, during which he was engaged in mountain-warfare training in Britain and Lebanon but in the 1950s he enjoyed a series of successful seasons, often in the company of Sir John Hunt. In 1957 he had visited the Himalaya and with Wilfrid

David Cox, the Oxford don whose 'impulse was always towards a younger, more enterprising style.'
(AC Photo Library)

Noyce just failed to reach the summit of Machapuchare. The following year he contracted polio, which left him with permanently weakened arms and chest, terminating his climbing career.

Like Keenlyside, Cox's formative years had been spent in the shadow of Young and Strutt, the former, recalled Cox's contemporary and great friend Robin Hodgkin, held in 'profound but slightly satirical affection' and the latter considered 'absurdly chauvinist.' But Cox had sensed that a new era was in the offing – he had even placed a piton for a belay on his first ascent in 1935 of the *Climbers' Club Ordinary* on the Dewerstone – and 'the compromises between the old and the threatening new were veiled in jokes.'[7] As editor he would display a natural sympathy for the young and the novel.

On assuming the editorship, Cox continued the task of keeping a finger on the pulse of mountaineering around the world. Set-piece, national expeditions to 8,000m peaks were giving way to smaller, cheaper expeditions, and interest in the mountains of South America as an alternative to the

Himalaya grew. In a neat coincidence of generations, the veteran Eric Shipton described his travels in Patagonia and Tierra del Fuego in the same volume of the *Journal* as the thrusting Bonington provided an account of the first ascent of the Central Tower of Paine. Significant developments in alpinism were covered in articles from Bonington on the first ascent of the Central Pillar of Frêney, John Harlin on the first ascent of the direct route up the west face of the Dru and Peter Gillman on the epic winter ascent of the Eiger's *Harlin Route*.

The siege tactics employed and the danger tolerated during the latter were castigated in a letter to the *Journal*, raising once again the ghost of Strutt: it was a commercial stunt; the route was artificial, fixed ropes providing a 'handrail' down which climbers 'were able to descend at any time to the "almost hysterical atmosphere" of a well appointed hotel, which provided good meals, the comfort of a well heated room and a warm bed, a good wine-list, a dance band and the pleasures of female company;'[8] and following Harlin's death continuing the climb was unjustifiable. By contrast, Cox wrote in his review of *Eiger Direct*, by Gillman and Dougal Haston:

> one can only admire the planning of the climb and the skill and endurance by which it was achieved ... To a reviewer not of that generation, it seems that climbing is done for enjoyment; that there are many ways of enjoying it; that extreme climbing, if one is competent to do it, is one of them; and that very few people should mind if unorthodox means were used on a new route on the north face of the Eiger.[9]

Cox's 'impulse was always towards a younger, more enterprising style.'[10] He welcomed articles from young alpinists and allowed a more flippant tone. Here, for example, is Tony Smythe on expedition planning:

> Barrie Biven and I decided to go to Alaska one Sunday afternoon in January, 1962, when we were eating fish and chips in a café in Bristol. We had met for the first time only twenty minutes before, and twenty minutes later we parted, having arranged a rendezvous in Canada for the following April. Somewhere I read that if an expedition can't be organised on the back of an old envelope, it isn't going to be any fun; at that meeting, Barrie and I didn't seem to have even a pencil between us![11]

And Mick Burke, recalling his precarious situation high up on the north face of the Matterhorn during a winter ascent with Haston:

> The problem was a 60-70ft. cliff composed of dry stone walling, but it was all leaning towards me. It looked dangerous to stand underneath let alone climb on it. Still who is afraid of these slight problems? (Anyone who is please get in contact – I'm forming a club). For a short while the cold weather disappeared and was followed by a hot spell. I was really sweating ... I was so frightened I can't remember that passage very well.[12]

Like his predecessor, Cox enjoyed the support of two assistant editors: Tom Blakeney and Fred Dangar. Amongst Blakeney's papers stored in the British Library[13] is correspondence with Cox illustrating some of the trials of an editor. Contributors required careful handling: 'what a pity it is that Odell, who is a nice chap in many ways, gets prickly so easily'; Longland 'writes well – though he is a tiresome chap to pin down'; and he tussled with Charles Evans over the obituary notice of his friend, Graham Brown: 'I have given a good deal of thought to the tiresome Graham Brown problem, the crucial question ... has all along been what weight should be attached to GB's wishes?'

There were other controversies to be tactfully resolved. In 1937 F Spencer Chapman had made an audacious first ascent of Chomolhari, situated on the border between Tibet and Bhutan, reaching the summit with an inexperienced Sherpa and enduring a lengthy and harrowing descent. At the time there had been whisperings of doubt as to whether Chapman had actually reached the summit, for amongst his contemporaries he had gained the reputation for a tendency to exaggerate his feats;[d] 29 years later this doubt was expressed in two separate articles published in *Mountain World* and *Les Alpes*, provoking indignation on the part of Blakeney and Dangar who authored a refutation of this perceived calumny against a war-hero.[e] Cox's emollient opinion was that it was 'a storm in a teacup'.

News of the first ascent of Everest from the north by the Chinese in 1960 had been greeted with scepticism and the expedition's photographic evidence was scrutinised in the pages of the *Journal*. In the absence of a view from the summit – the Chinese had arrived in darkness – much effort and ingenuity were applied to establishing the height and position from which the expedition's highest picture had been taken: probably at about 8,700m from a point on the north-east ridge a little above the Second Step. Yet in some minds there lingered the possibility that the photograph could have been taken from an aeroplane.

Then there was the perennial challenge of controlling the ever-rising cost of production of the *Journal*. By the end of 1966 Cox had decided to resign the editorship and the search for a successor began. 'If the Committee plumped for a young man on the Youth Must be Served principle,' opined Blakeney a trifle sniffily, 'then Blackshaw suggests himself.'

Alan Blackshaw (1968-70)

Blackshaw, then aged 35, was a product of the vibrant Oxford University Mountaineering Club of the early 1950s and a member of the ACG. A career civil servant possessing considerable energy and intellect, he was in the fast lane for promotion and had already risen to the rank of principal private secretary.

---

d. Jack Longland, who had been at Cambridge with him, contributed Chapman's entry in the *Dictionary of National Biography*, and in it wrote of his exploits: 'Remarkable as these were, they lost nothing in the telling.'

e. During the Second World War Chapman had spent three years operating behind enemy lines in Malaya and at one stage had been presumed dead. For his services he received the DSO and bar; the Supreme Allied Commander South East Asia Command, Lord Mountbatten, declared that he should have been awarded the Victoria Cross.

Alan Blackshaw, president of the Alpine Club 2002-04 and a formidable campaigner. *(AC Photo Library)*

Alan Blackshaw leading an artificial pitch on the east ridge of the Dent du Crocodile, photographed by Roger Chorley on 20 July 1953. *(AC Photo Library)*

He was a natural campaigner – 'causes and disputes were a speciality' – and he would make important contributions in matters of land access, conservation and mountaineering administration, serving as president of the British Mountaineering Council, the UIAA and the Alpine Club. His tenure of the editorship was brief but in 1969 he introduced a major change to the *Journal*, making it a single-issue annual volume, an innovation first mooted during Graham Brown's editorship and pressed for by Keenlyside. The long-standing practice of producing two issues per year had necessarily involved duplication of effort and cost, posing practical problems for the editor and financial pressure on the Club, and had become unsustainable. The new format with wider coverage was well received and sales of the *Journal* almost trebled, half of them abroad, requiring a reprint.[f]

E C Pyatt (1971-82)

Ted Pyatt's Alpine experience was modest, comprising two seasons in the Bernese Oberland immediately after the war, but he was immensely knowledgeable about mountains and mountaineering and he brought 'boundless, almost relentless energy' to the role.[14] He was persuasive, too. Chris Russell recalls being induced to write his column, *100 Years Ago*, still a regular feature 50 years later, during a good meal accompanied by fine wine, and he assembled an expanded team of assistants, delegating masterfully. Pyatt's editorial notes make clear the challenges he faced: 'an annual publication of the present quality and proportions is a publishing proposition comparable

---

f. To stimulate sales the cover price had been reduced from 42s to 35s but rising costs of production necessitated a return to the original price in the following year.

Ted Pyatt, editor in the 1970s, was forced to deal with spiralling costs but managed to maintain the *Journal's* breadth of coverage.

with or even larger than, the average book,' making it impractical to compete for topical information with the burgeoning bimonthly magazines, especially Ken Wilson's *Mountain*, then in its heyday, and necessitated 'a change of basic style.'[15]

The 1970s were a period of extraordinary advances in mountaineering. The decade began with the ascent of the south face of Annapurna followed a few years later by the first ascent of the south-west face of Everest, both achieved by Bonington's large and hugely expensive expeditions which used traditional siege tactics but attained a new level of difficulty in high-altitude climbing. These climbs were duly reported in the *Journal*. But a new generation that embraced a different style – 'the struggle'– was emerging.

We did not want to overcome a mountain with ease, we needed to struggle, needed to be at the edge of what was possible for us, needed an outcome that was uncertain.[16]

That was the view of Joe Tasker, who with Peter Boardman, Alan Rouse, Alex MacIntyre and others led the way. They sought out difficulty, choosing audacious lines and attempting them often in adverse conditions without logistical support, and accepted greater risk, with the result that, as John Porter has observed, the generation 'nearly climbed itself into extinction.' Their exploits rarely reached the pages of the *AJ*, the zeitgeist of this generation finding expression in articles for *Mountain* magazine.

In 1975 the Ladies' Alpine Club merged with the AC bringing 150 new members to the Club. The *Journal's* subtitle was amended to recognise the incorporation of the journal of the LAC and in the following three numbers Pyatt published a series of articles by Cicely Williams, entitled 'The Feminine Share of Mountain Adventure'. Yet over the next few years the ladies contributed fewer than a handful of articles. Barbara Swindin's piece, 'Perpetual Second', offers a clue to their reticence:

Perhaps nowadays with the so-called liberation of women we should all be forcing ourselves forward to the sharp end of the rope, with its undoubted excitements and rewards, but this might mean forgoing many of the pleasures gained from pushing oneself slightly beyond one's limits in the security of climbing with a far more competent companion.'[17,g]

Pyatt, whose professional life was spent at the National Physical Laboratory undertaking and supervising research (his expertise was in electronics), accorded greater prominence to science in the *Journal* to reflect its rubric: 'a record of mountain adventure and scientific observation', more than doubling the number of scientific articles published by his three predecessors combined, and introducing a specific section, Scientific Notes, which regularly ran to three pages. Diverse subjects were covered: glaciology, geology, meteorology and medicine; graphs, formulae and equations became almost commonplace. Pyatt was also concerned about the future of the mountain environment and pleaded for relevant contributions, 'otherwise it will look as though the AC has nothing to say concerning matters of the moment;'[18] the only response was Ronald Clark's 1978 essay on the pollution of the Alps, illustrated ominously with pictures of traffic jams on the St Gotthard, a massive concrete dam in Valgrisanche, cranes and scaffolding in Breuil and ski lifts in Alpe d'Huez.

Pyatt's 12-year tenure of the editorship was second only to George Yeld's, which lasted 30 (1896-1926). They had not been easy years. The 1970s were a disastrous decade for the nation's prosperity: economic stagnation combined with rising inflation and rising unemployment, culminating in the notorious winter of discontent. Escalating costs of production of the *Journal* forced Pyatt to retrench: he cut the number of pages by about one fifth but by reducing the font size for large sections and insisting on brevity from his contributors he maintained the breadth of coverage, and he experimented with cheaper printing methods resulting in some decrease in quality. There were additional difficulties which he stated bluntly:

I acknowledge with deep gratitude the dwindling numbers of contributors, whose efforts are reproduced herewith and the very considerable efforts they have made towards this production ... I acknowledge with quite different feelings all those who refused for not very obvious reasons to contribute, those who hurriedly put forward an utterly useless alternative to themselves and those who engaged to contribute and then disappeared beyond the range of all enquiry and entreaty; they make the Editor's task considerably more arduous than it needs to be.'[19]

Nevertheless, Pyatt's efforts had sustained the *Journal* during a period when there had been moments of serious doubt about its viability.

---

g. Swindin would go on to reach all but one of the 4,000m summits in the Alps.

References
1. AC archives B59 (1)
2. National Library of Scotland Acc 4338/13
3. AJ **59**: 492
4. AJ **61**: 234
5. AJ **63**: 82
6. AJ **63**: 65
7. Oxford Mountaineering 1973 p.6
8. AJ **72**: 193
9. AJ **72**: 166
10. *High* magazine, pp59-63, January 1995.
11. AJ **68**: 262
12. AJ **73**: 44
13. British Library Add Ms 63123
14. AJ **91**: 287
15. AJ **78**: 269
16. J Tasker, *Savage Arena*, London, p20, 1982.
17. AJ **85**: 102
18. AJ **80**: 287
19. AJ **79**: 275

DAVID SEDDON

Everest from Rongbuk, 1922

A Tale of Two Pictures

'Everest from Shilling', 1922 watercolour. *(Alpine Club Collection)*

T H Somervell (1890-1975) noted in his autobiography *After Everest* that in the first week or so of May 1922, he painted a series of six oil pictures and over 10 watercolours of Everest from Rongbuk.[1] He had already sketched distant views of Everest from Kampa Dzong[2], Shilling and the Pang La. Of the view of Everest from Rongbuk, Somervell would write:

[Everest's] outline is stately rather than fantastic, and its dignity is the solid dignity of Egyptian buildings ... Everest is, on its northern aspect, rather a cubist mountain, and ... it offered constant satisfaction as a subject for numerous sketches.

1. T H Somervell, *After Everest*, Hodder & Stoughton, London, 1936.
2. D J Seddon, 'The Unseen Somervell', *Alpine Journal*, vol 124, pp97-104, 2020

Everest from Pang La, 45 miles away.

'Everest from the Pang La', undated watercolour. *(Alpine Club Collection)*

The fate of two of the Everest from Rongbuk pictures intrigued me. One of these, dated 1922, was reproduced as the frontispiece of *After Everest* with the title 'Everest from the Base Camp'. The other illustrated *The Fight for Everest: 1924* by E F Norton.[3] This picture, also dated 1922, bears the caption, 'Mount Everest from Basecamp'. However, by March 2020 and with no evidence that either picture had survived, I considered them both 'lost'.[4] However, by October 2021, both pictures would be identified.

In 1935-6, Somervell took 15 months leave from his work as a surgeon in south India and returned to Britain. This coincided with the publication of *After Everest* in 1936. To illustrate this volume, he selected one of his pictures of Everest from Rongbuk. It is impossible to know whether this was also the one picture of Everest from Rongbuk he selected for exhibition at the Alpine Club (11-30 December 1922 and 21 January-6 February 1923) and the Fitzwilliam Museum, Cambridge (24 February-12 March 1923).

What is certain is that following Somervell's death in 1975, his widow Margaret exhibited 43 pictures from her husband's personal collection at Abbot Hall Gallery (7 February-7 March 1976). Included in these was an oil picture given the title 'Everest Base Camp, North Face' (cat no 37). She exhibited this picture again in 1979, also at Abbot Hall Gallery, and there is a photograph in the *Westmorland Gazette* of a very spry Noel Odell inspecting

3. E F Norton, *The Fight for Everest*, Edwin Arnold & Co, London, 1925.
4. D J Seddon, op cit.

'Everest from Rongbuk', 1922 oil, 49.8cm x 61.3cm. *(Private collection)*

a picture of Everest from Rongbuk.[5] But was this the picture reproduced in *After Everest*?

In October 2021, an oil picture of Everest from Rongbuk was one of several pictures by Somervell that appeared for auction in Stroud. Although damaged, this picture was the one reproduced, albeit cropped at the sides in *After Everest*. This picture is 49.8cm × 61.3cm, signed and dated 1922 at the bottom left of the picture. On the frame was visible the number '37'. This confirmed that this picture had been exhibited at Abbot Hall Gallery in 1976 and therefore had been in Somervell's personal collection at the time of his death. Also visible on the frame were the initials 'J M S', one of Somervell's grandchildren. The Yellow Band and perhaps even one of two of the pinnacles of the north-east ridge can all be seen.

A very similar picture exists, signed but not dated, that is almost identical to this one in size, 50cm × 57cm, as well as view. Both were very probably painted in that first week of May 1922, possibly from the same length of canvas. The similarity of the two pictures even suggests that they may have been painted at the same time.

In early 1926, the eight pictures reproduced in *The Fight for Everest: 1924* were, with 40 or so others, exhibited at the Redfern Gallery in London by Somervell's father. Two pictures of Everest were included, both catalogued

5. 'Height of Achievement', *Westmorland Gazette*, 27 April 1979.

'Gaurisankar', 1924 watercolour. *(Royal Geographical Society)*

as 'Mount Everest' (cat nos 23 and 29). One would have been the view of
Everest from Rongbuk reproduced in *The Fight for Everest: 1924*. The other,
possibly a watercolour dated 1922, is also a view of Everest from Rongbuk.
This was reproduced in *AJ* 2020.[6]

In his introduction to *After Everest*, Francis Younghusband refers to a picture of Everest by Somervell in the collections of the Royal Geographical
Society. So I wondered if one of the two pictures of Everest exhibited in
1926 now resided in South Kensington. Yet when I visited the RGS in 2005,
I was shown a watercolour of Gaurisankar dated 1924. The staff assured
me that this was the only picture by T H Somervell known to them. However,
I was left wondering whether a picture of Everest from Rongbuk by Somervell
might lie somewhere, forgotten, within that institution.

In 2021, a chance discussion with Michael Somervell, a distant relative of
T H Somervell, provided a clue. Some years previously, he had viewed a large,
damaged oil picture of Everest at the RGS. Could this be the picture reproduced in Norton's account of the 1924 expedition? In due course, I contacted
Dr Eugene Rae, principal librarian at the RGS and yes, he was aware of
a picture of Everest by Somervell that was in store. But which one was it?
Was it the one reproduced in *The Fight for Everest: 1924*? Or another painting
of Everest from Rongbuk? Or perhaps some other view of the mountain?

6. D J Seddon, op cit.

'Everest from Rongbuk', as reproduced in *The Fight for Everest: 1924*, 1922 oil, 80cm x 120cm.

Once the pandemic restrictions of 2021 were eased, I was able to view this picture and discovered it was indeed the version of Everest from Rongbuk reproduced in *The Fight for Everest: 1924*, signed and dated 1922 at the bottom right of the picture. At 80cm × 120cm, this is one of Somervell's larger pictures and is his largest known picture of Everest. A picture of this size would have taken many hours work to complete. So it may well have been painted after Somervell's return to the UK in October 1922. Regrettably, the picture now has a number of tears to its canvas and the colours are, I fear, irredeemably faded. It is seen at its best in *The Fight for Everest: 1924*.

Further Pictures and Thoughts
On 4 May 1922, and a week or so before they moved up to camp III, Somervell and Mallory climbed a peak of some 6,500m to the west of the Rongbuk valley. There is a picture in a private collection (oil, c22cm × 33cm), unavailable to reproduce, whose colours have also faded showing Everest and the Rongbuk valley below. In the upper left of the picture, the junction of the north and the north-east ridges are clearly seen. Although undated, I believe this picture to date from this excursion in 1922.

I suspect Somervell painted fewer pictures of Everest from Rongbuk in 1924 but he continued to paint this view of the mountain even many years later. One such picture, dating from 1957, and with the Rongbuk stream prominent in the foreground, was reproduced on the cover of *Everest: A Thousand Years of Exploration* by Michael Ward.[7]

It is a matter of great regret that of the 16 or so pictures Somervell painted in that first week of May 1922, perhaps only three of the six oils survive, the third image of this article and its pair, and the sixth image. None of the watercolours appear to be extant.

---

7. M P Ward, Everest: *A Thousand Years of Exploration*, Hayloft Publishing, Newton Stewart, 2003.

'Everest from Rongbuk', 1957. *(Hayloft Publishing).*

In his lifetime, Somervell may have painted perhaps 20 or so pictures of Everest from Rongbuk. In all perhaps just eight of Somervell's pictures of this view of Everest survive, seven oil and one watercolour. The titles given to these pictures vary. They include: 'Mount Everest', 'Mount Everest from Rongbuk'; 'Everest from North'; 'Mount Everest from the Rongbuk Stream'; 'Everest Base Camp, North Face' etc. This is somewhat confusing but all of these pictures show a view of Everest, its north-east ridge, Changtse and the Rongbuk valley with or without glacial moraines and streams, tents and yaks. There are other pictures showing the east face of the mountain as well as the more distant views I have referred to above and elsewhere.[8]

Acknowledgements

I wish to thank Michael Somervell for inspiring me to re-visit the RGS, and Dr Eugene Rae for allowing me to view 'Everest from Rongbuk' at the RGS. This is the fourth article I have written about T H Somervell. The others appear in *AJ 2005, AJ 2020* and *Himalayan Journal* 2006. A fuller account of his life is held at the Alpine Club Library.

8. D J Seddon, op cit.

DONALD M ORR

Picturing the Eiger

'The Eiger from Wengeralp' by Maximilien de Meuron.

Numerous artists over the years have attempted to affect the ideal mountain picture and in the 19th century many came under Ruskin's influence on art through *Modern Painters* and other works, which could be both formative and at the same time contradictory. Ruskin determined to experience the Alps at close quarters but his ascent of the Buet with the guide Couttet in 1844 was his first and last climb. The mental rigour and physical exertion necessary to gain that understanding eluded him. For Ruskin that renewal of self which was 'the goal of all their striving'[1] was not to be realised.

An early exhibition of mountain paintings was organised in London by D W Freshfield in 1894 when he was president of the Alpine Club, consisting of works by historical and contemporary artists, those who sought out dramatic mountain landscapes and those who also climbed them. In his

---

1. R Hubank, Evening Light, The Ernest Press, 2009, p250.

preface to the exhibition catalogue Freshfield stated 'the beauty of the Alps exists; poets have found it and painters will.' What was hoped for was a new enthusiasm for the Alps as a source of true and adequate feelings as opposed to 'rather foggy impressions'. A closer interaction between painters and their subject matter was called for. While the exhibition was a success Freshfield continued writing about 'the lack of beauty and interest of most of the paintings which were devoted year after year to the Alps and other ranges.'[2] Some of Freshfield's writing in his descriptions of mountain areas could easily rank among the finest in travel literature; his *The Exploration of the Caucasus* has been described as having 'a quality that would bring tears to the eyes of even the most blasé bibliophile.'[3] Yet he avoided trying to express his love of mountains or any aspect of mountain philosophy in prose. Only in some of his poetry did he approach the notion of a region of greater truth, of a sense joy and fulfilment in the mountains – 'to dwell in the elemental spaces, remote from Heaven and Hell.'[4]

By 1955 Winthrop Young was claiming that mountaineering literature 'had been inhibited by the repressive conventionalism of the nineteenth century'[5] but was also still advocating that 'an artist of mountains will devote his whole skill to painting them as they are.'[6] From someone who was highly literate this seems rather vague advice, especially given how innovative he was in climbing and organisational terms. If visual accuracy is being demanded, under what weather conditions or what atmospheric circumstances should it be delivered? These things vary daily, let alone through seasonal changes. As late as 1974, Merrick was still advocating that the 'art of portraying mountain peaks in a realistic and accurate manner'[7] was what was needed. For him 'only a few truly great artists have painted immortal mountain paintings.'[8] Yet he cites Turner as 'one of the few giants to turn his attention specifically to the Alpine landscape.'[9] Turner certainly painted many Alpine scenes but it was the scale of the light effects and atmospherics that attracted him, allowing him to create impressionistic views. When one considers his depictions of Skye, particularly 'Loch Coruisk'[10], we are beyond any impression and really are in the region of expressionism. That much desired realism seems to come in many guises.

What were artists to seek? 'A mystical light thrown over the universe'? '[A]n insight into the unknown'?[11] Freshfield wanted a more experiential foundation for mountain paintings but not all mountaineers wanted to lose themselves 'in the vast emptiness where there is nothing but sun, silence

2. C Engel, *They Came to the Hills*, Allen & Unwin, London, 1952, p162.
3. T Anderson, *Bread and Ashes: A Walk through the Mountains of Georgia*, Vintage, London, 2004, p227.
4. D Freshfield, 'The Song of the Himalayan Fairies'.
5. G Young, 'Courage, and Mountain Writing', *The Mountain World*, M Barnes (ed), Allen & Unwin, London, 1955, p11.
6. Ibid, p17.
7. H Merrick, *Companion to the Alps*, Batsford, London, 1974, p70.
8. Ibid, p76.
9. Ibid, p71.
10. J Turner, 'Loch Coruisk', watercolour on paper, 8.9cm x 14.3cm, 1831, Scottish National Gallery, Edinburgh.
11. C Engel, p63.

and solitude.'[12] The question as to what painters should paint is as wide and varied as trying to define what climbers should climb. A love of science or of nature, a sense of adventure or danger, ambition or escapism, or a quest for a vague mysticism have all been recruited as reasons for the development of mountaineering. For artists, the motives included a 'new' scene, an arresting panorama, technical difficulty in creating a three-dimensional illusion of complex topography and, for the most part, selling the production on completion. Scenes could be enhanced, valleys steepened, waterfalls heightened, rocky peaks augmented simply because the mountain was a model for a painting, an artwork, not a photographic representation. It may well have been that direct image, that unadorned depiction that Freshfield desired, but that was more for photographers. That isn't the way artists work and not what art is about.

Artists who climbed, who regularly visited mountain areas, travelled through them and experienced the weather conditions and physical effort required to ascend them were not common. More were content to work from the valley, to find a viewpoint and depict distant peaks. The four European artists selected here all committed themselves to mountain areas recording the landscape that fascinated them and, by that, revealing it to many who would never enter those regions at all. They come from different eras and schools of thought, their styles vary, but their subject is the same: the Eiger.

Maximilien de Meuron (1785-1868)

Born into an aristocratic family in Switzerland, his art lessons began in Neuchâtel with Matthieu Ricco but he later studied with the Giradet brothers who were noted for their etchings and engravings. Directed towards a diplomatic career he studied law in Berlin but continued to learn about art and develop his own work while in Germany. Returning to Switzerland in 1803 he took a position in the foreign affairs ministry but resigned in 1808 to go to Paris and further his artistic interests. In 1809 he and Gabriel Lory visited Italy as part of their continuing education and by 1812 he was back in Switzerland attempting to organise a national museum of art for the country. He petitioned the government for a building, organised public opinion, and offered some of his own canvases to start the collection.

In 1818 and 1819 he worked in the Bernese Oberland recording mountain landscapes which formed the basis of a major exhibition in 1822 in Paris. The success of this venture saw him elected to the grand council of the Canton of Neuchâtel the following year. By 1824 he was exhibiting at the Academy of Arts, Berlin where Friedrich Wilhelm III bought several of his works. This and the general appeal and quality of his work saw him made an honorary member of the academy in 1825 but he avoided the teaching commitment by declining the offer of a professorship. Throughout the latter half of the 1820s he organised several major art exhibitions, which greatly strengthened the standing of Swiss art.

12. Ibid, p142.

In 1835 the painter Louis Léopold Robert committed suicide in front of his easel on the tenth anniversary of his brother's suicide, to whom he had been much attached. Meuron had been supporting Robert financially and encouraging him in his work, and was greatly upset by his death. He organised a retrospective exhibition of his friend's work the following year. Soon after this Meuron's son, also Maximilien, died unexpectedly and threw the artist into a depression whereby he stopped painting altogether. He did some sketching in 1842 on a trip to Italy but never again went back to the industry of his previous habits. The rest of his life was spent organising exhibitions and promoting local artists.

'The Eiger from Wengeralp'[13] is a picture lying firmly within the German Romantic tradition. The few wandering cattle suggest that people rarely visit this area whose height and bleakness make it inhospitable. The colour in the lower half of the scene is a series of dark browns. Vegetation is sparse and it would imply that the only reason the cattle are there at all is to drink from the pool in the foreground; one can see little else to tempt them to this spot. The desolation is capped by the soaring verticality of the Eiger, creating a picture of two halves, which, while joined in the barrenness, are worlds apart. The horizontality of the lower portion is juxtaposed by the verticality of the upper. A hill-scape where occasionally there may be some green growth fronts a rock and icescape far removed from the world of men. This isolation is added to by a sea of mist rolling down from the south side of the mountain to circle around the north face, concealing the base and accentuating the difference between the two environments. The cattle in the foreground indicate that life is possible there but beyond that, on the mountain itself, nothing but rock, snow and ice prevail. While the summit of the Eiger was first attained in August 1858, Meuron's depiction is remote and isolated: an object of contemplation not a mountain to set foot on.

Alexandre Calame (1810-64)

Born in Vevey, Switzerland into an artistic family, Calame's father was a stone carver but he experienced a difficult childhood, including the loss of the family fortune. This ended his formal education and he worked in a bank from the age of 15. It was in his spare time that he continued drawing and painting mainly small, local landscapes. In 1829 he gained a patron who made it possible for him to study under François Diday whereby, after a short time, he determined to dedicate himself to art. By 1835 he was exhibiting his Alpine scenes in Paris and Berlin. In 1842 he went to Paris to show his mountain paintings including scenes of Mont Blanc, the Jungfrau, the Brienzersee and Mont Cervin. Partly on the strength of this he started teaching in Geneva and in 1844 visited Italy bringing back many studies that broadened his appeal with the public. Yet the Alps remained his speciality. Printmaking and lithography of his sketches allowed a greater awareness of his work and his 18 studies of Lauterbrunnen and Meiringen and 24 sheets of Alpine passes

---

13. M de Meuron, 'The Eiger from Wengeralp', oil on canvas, 51cm x 40.5cm, Institution Musée d'Art et d'Histoire, Neuchâtel.

'The Grand Eiger' by Alexandre Calame.

made him famous all over Europe. Writing a century later Arnold Lunn cited him, along with Lory and Linck, as a superior mountain painter.[14]

'The Grand Eiger'[15] is a fine example of the German tradition of Romantic painting and it too is based on the view from Wengeralp at the top of the Kleine Scheidegg pass. Calame knew of Meuron's painting, but his 1884 interpretation varies greatly from the one painted 65 years previously. The foreground rocks are an invention and in the mid distance the pool that Meuron also utilised. Perched on the foreground rocks is a bearded vulture, a lammergeier found in Alpine regions, intimating this is the abode of such creatures but also perhaps offering a warning to be wary in this environment. The darkness of these immediate rocks, the vulture scanning below, and the light across the chasm all contribute to this warning. Beyond rises an ethereal vision of the Eiger. Calame still accurately relays the soaring verticality of the mountain balanced at half height in his composition with the horizontally based foreground. The doubled perpendicularity fashioned by the foreground cliffs creates a sense of remoteness, of isolation whereby the sunlit sublimity of the mountain is ever out of reach: a sight to be seen, contemplated, even venerated, but at a distance.

14. A Lunn, *A Century of Mountaineering*, Allen & Unwin, London, 1957, p65.
15. A Calame, 'The Grand Eiger', oil on canvas, 106.2cm x 139.9cm, Kunstmuseum, Bern, 1884.

'View of the Eiger and the Mönch from the Wengeralp' by August Leu.

August Wilhelm Leu (1818-97)

August Wilhelm Leu was born in Münster in 1818 and trained under Johann Wilhelm Schirner, a landscape painter of the Düsseldorf School. Leu travelled to Norway in 1843 and again in 1847. The resulting paintings established him firmly in the Romantic tradition and effectively made his reputation. His mountain scenes of Norway and the Alps, usually produced on a large format, were firm favourites with the public and allowed him to travel regularly to the Alps. Strengthening his appeal, he moved to Brussels for a time before moving back to Düsseldorf. His fame broadened and he received acclaim at the Paris Exposition of 1855. This renown continued and in 1882 he moved to Berlin to become a professor of art and a member of the academy where he received several gold medals over the years. His prominence in mountain landscape painting saw him elected to the Vienna, Amsterdam, and Brussels academies where, at the latter, he was awarded the Belgian Order of Leopold, an honorary order of knighthood. He continued to paint Alpine pictures, dying in Seelisburg, Switzerland in 1897.

'View of the Eiger and the Mönch from the Wengeralp'[16] contains a small classic of human interest in the two young women collecting water in the

16. A Leu, 'View of the Eiger and the Mönch from the Wengeralp', oil on canvas, 81cm x 100cm, Gallerie Koller, Zurich, 1865.

left foreground but the scale of the figures and the state of the chalet easily avoid accusations of sentimentality. The mountain massif is the subject of the canvas. High summer in the Alps and bright sunshine reveals the peaks with a slight haze over them and cloud building over the north face of the Eiger. First climbed in August 1858, a year after the first ascent of the Mönch, this canvas would have attracted considerable interest in 1865 when it was painted where the balance between quiet agricultural activity and the looming verticality of the north face would not be lost to alpinists.

Henry Wood (1869-1944)

Best known as the founder of the Proms, which after his death became the Henry Wood Promenade Concerts, Sir Henry Wood was in his time a distinguished conductor and musician. His talent as a painter has almost been forgotten.

Winning prizes for music and art at school he entered the Royal Academy of Music at the age of 17, which was the start of his professional life. He claimed to have studied art at the Slade but he did attend painting classes at Heatherley Art School, one of the oldest independent art colleges in London, founded in 1845. While music was his profession, painting was his passion and wherever he went in the world his painting equipment went with him.

While Wood embraced the avant-garde in music furthering the work of Poulenc, Bartók and Stravinsky he did not aspire to nor reflect the concerns of the Impressionists or those of the Post-Impressionist Period. In 1911 at the Piccadilly Arcade Gallery, he organised a major exhibition of his paintings where the sale of some 50 oil studies raised a considerable sum for retired orchestral musicians. In an interview conducted by the *Guardian* in October 1938 he stated, 'Painting is my real love' and admitted 'but I have no talent whatever for portraiture.' He remained a life-long amateur artist concentrating on still life, domestic garden scenes, and landscapes from his travels.

'The Eiger, near Mürren'[17] has inscribed on its reverse side 'The Eiger from my hotel in Mürren'. It was a painting he was especially delighted with. In a letter to his daughter Tania he stated, 'I cannot tell you the inner joy and satisfaction looking at the Eiger, for four or five mornings, gave me – it is a living and life-long experience.' For a talented amateur the capture of the intensity of the vertical north face is a triumph. Sharpness and perpendicularity dominate the image creating a feature as dwarfing as the Matterhorn. The juxtaposition of the lush green of the alp below the starkness of the north face, and the almost black-and-white treatment of the rock and icefields determine a powerful aspect where the soft blue of the sky strengthens the overall dominance of this feature in the landscape.

Recording the image of the Eiger continues. Graphic art utilises the north face in post cards and posters, contemporary artists still document aspects of the mountain, and photographs of the mountain and its railway proliferate

---

17. H Wood, 'The Eiger, near Mürren', oil on canvas, 60cm x 44.5cm, Royal Academy of Music, London, 1931.

'The Eiger, near Mürren' by Henry Wood.

in Swiss calendars. Film too has examined the mountain as a setting. Clint Eastwood's *Eiger Sanction* (1975) was based on Trevanian's 1972 novel; the death toll could be linked to the attempts on the north face throughout the 1930s. Directed by Louise Osmand *The Beckoning Silence* (2007), from Joe Simpson's book of the same name, shadowed the 1936 tragedy as a part documentary, part enactment of the events of that year. Similarly, the German *Nordwand* (2008) saw director Philipp Stölzl utilise the Kurz and Hinterstoisser struggle from a different angle. Factually based yet still examining the loss of life on the north face *The Alps: Climb of Your Life* (2007) directed by Stephen Judson was a commemoration of the attempt by John Harlin II on the *Eiger Direct* by his son 40 years after his father's death. The visual appeal of the Eiger and the challenge of its north face have not diminished.

ROBIN N CAMPBELL

The Art of Everest

To celebrate this year's centenary of the first full expedition to Everest, the *Alpine Journal* chose to put together frontispieces that illustrate the art of Everest. It has to be said that such art is in rather short supply, understandably so. Besides the cost and difficulty of getting there, brushes, colours and fingers do not perform well in extremes of cold and altitude. Artists who have attempted plein-air work at high altitude are few and far between. Karl Blodig reported Edward T Compton's suffering and hardihood in working thus in the high Alps.[1] Edward Norton complained in his Everest diary about 'everything freezing'. Rob Fairley wrote to me that: 'The high altitude sketches were not done in a book but on individual sheets … in a book everything froze together making an interesting bookwork but useless topographically. Very high up I also carried water in a vacuum hip flask but even then the sketch freezing before drying was a constant problem … and freezing brushes also, even on lower peaks like Ama Dablam.' Howard Somervell made frequent use of pastels, presumably at least partly because the pastel sticks performed better than messy mixtures of colour and water or oil. I selected four works by Howard Somervell, two by Edward Norton, four by Rob Fairley, and one each from Elsie M Dixon and Philip MacLeod Coupe, and will make a few remarks about each of these artists and the works chosen.

The work of **T Howard Somervell** has been well described in the *Alpine Journal* by David Seddon[2] and readers consulting his excellent articles will be amply rewarded. Seddon sometimes describes Somervell's work as cubist but his paintings are all topographical in intent, without significant deconstruction of the depicted mountain. However, he did tend to use a restricted range of colours and tones, and to build up his images of mountains using a geometry of approximate triangles, rectangles and trapezoidal shapes. This restricted range is sometimes unhelpful. In his views of Everest from Rongbuk, for example p105, it is impossible to resolve Changtse in the middle ground from the background of Everest's north face, unless you know it is there. To some extent Somervell assumes the viewer of his work knows the structure of the mountain. In his pastel works we see a more uninhibited use of colour as in his 'Seracs on the East Rongbuk Glacier' (p281) rendered in spooky blues and purples, or in the striking 'Monsoon over Sikkim' shown below, using a full range of strong colours.

1. P Tallantire, *Edward Theodore Compton* (1849-1921), published privately, 1996.
2. *AJ* 2005, pp217-230; *AJ* 2020, pp87-104; and *AJ* 2022, pp86-91.

T Howard Somervell's 'Monsoon over Sikkim', 23cm x 33 cm, pastel, 1922. *(Alpine Club)*

Somervell showed considerable dedication to his art in trekking twice to the Rupia La (in 1922 and 1924) to paint Everest's east face and north-east ridge, see p287. However, I think the finest of the works used here is on p1, his view of the Everest group from the Singalila ridge, which perhaps shows some influence from his friend and hero Nicholas Roerich (1874-1947) in the strong perspective produced by the ranks of misty foothills and the reducing grain and tone of the sky as it recedes from the viewpoint. Although Roerich produced a few views of the Kangchenjunga range that are clearly topographical, he didn't set out to record mountain topography and didn't paint Everest, despite some works with hopeful titles given to them by others. He seems to have been a painter interested in showing the 'spirit of place' rather than particular mountains, very much as was his near-contemporary Lawren Harris (1885-1970) in his magnificent paintings of imaginary Canadian mountains.

Perhaps the strongest climber of the 1922 and 1924 expeditions **Edward F Norton** (1884-1954) held the height record on Everest for 30 years. He was also an amateur artist who sketched plein air in watercolour and gouache. The two Everest views from the Pang La (p49) and from Chogorong (p217), both drawn in 1924, are simple in execution but attractively rendered in his favoured harmonious colours of purple greys and reddish browns. He produced some other sketches that were in my view more effective, for

Edward F Norton's 'Chomolhari from Jebel La', 18cm x 25cm, watercolour and gouache, 1924. *(Courtesy of Norton Family Archive)*

example the well-composed and carefully drawn Chomolhari from the Jebel La shown above.

Based in Darlington, **Elsie Margaret Dixon** (1889-1980) was a very able amateur watercolour artist. She was born in Bombay to Robert Hume Gunion and Lilian Eleanora Cassels and married John Reginald Dixon in 1913. Dixon became MD and CEO of the Cleveland Bridge and Engineering Company which constructed a number of well-known bridges around the world, and this enabled Elsie to travel widely in Europe and the Antipodes, where she drew Alpine and New Zealand mountains. She exhibited her work locally, and at the Society of Women Artists and Royal Institute exhibitions, as well as at the Alpine Club. Her watercolour of Everest's northern aspect (p125) is as successful as any, yet it received criticism by the anonymous reviewer in *AJ* 1935, p131: 'Several drawings of the Everest district and of other Himalayan peaks by Mrs Stephenson, Mrs Dixon, Mrs Hartley Bibby and (in oil-colour) by Mr Harold Meyer were very well executed. All, however, were done from photographs, a form of art which, in our opinion, is hardly suited to a serious exhibition.' This was surely harsh, and unjustified. How could any woman get herself to Rongbuk in 1934 without male disguise and illegal visas? Besides, a mountain's structure can be known well through close examination of written accounts, maps and photographs. This is how we plot our expeditions after all. Why should an artist attempting a mountain portrait endure the suffering of plein-air work, or, painting a person, subject the sitter to countless hours of discomfort, if these can be avoided by using knowledge obtained by means other than the fetish of life drawing?

Brought up in Southport, **Philip MacLeod Coupe** (1944-2013) drew and painted from an early age but his father disapproved and he was obliged to study architecture. However, after election to RIBA in 1974, he turned to professional lute making before concentrating on painting and moving to Cumbria. He was elected to the Lake Artists Society in 1984 and was president from 1990 to 2005. He was known for plein-air painting in oil or watercolour, and visited Iona every year, authoring a book *Paintings of Iona: Peploe and Cadell* (Malvern, 2014), published posthumously. His powerful image of Everest's north face reddened by sunset (p151) hangs in the hall-way in the Club's rooms in Charlotte Road. He produced at least one other version of this painting, which was sold at Mitchell's of Cockermouth in 2014 for the paltry sum of £300.

The artist **Rob Fairley** (b1953) has been a member of the Club since 1991. His work was featured in the frontispieces for *AJ* 2016. He was educated at Edinburgh College of Art and has been a mountaineer and painter through-out his life, producing work of the highest quality in all media from pencil to oil painting, and climbing at a high standard in Scotland, the Alps and the Himalaya, which he first visited with Mal Duff in the 1980s. His exemplary watercolour of 'Everest Base from Rongbuk Glacier' (p335) features beauti-fully drawn Changtse and Everest, but my eye, which has had a varied his-tory, was pulled down to the bravura still-life painting of the blue storage barrels and the drapery of the tents. Fairley's other watercolours show Ever-est from the south, towering behind the Nuptse-Lhotse ridge. While 'The Burning of Tyngpoche Monastery' (p373) is another large finished painting, with every detail of rock and snow carefully observed, the final two works are unremoved A5 sketchbook pages. The top image on p391, with its fresh washes of beautiful colour recalls Edward Norton's sketches but the one below it, despite the small format, has a high degree of finish with the tree-crinkled middle-ground horizon and the triple-peaked Kusum Kanguru both meticulously painted. To my mind, Fairley is our foremost mountain-eer-painter, carrying on the splendid tradition established by Edward T Compton, Ernst H Platz, and of course Norton and Somervell.

Acknowledgments

In locating the images used as frontispieces, I am indebted to assistance from Tony Astill, Bernie Ingrams, Janet Johnson, Norman MacNab, David Seddon and Barbara Grigor-Taylor.

Science & Environment

'Everest from Rongbuk', T Howard Somervell, oil, 50cm x 61cm, 1922?.
(Courtesy of a private collector)

STUART A DUNNING

The Chamoli Disaster

During the morning of 7 February 2021, and without warning, a muddy mixture of rock, ice, debris and water with an unknown source rushed down the Rishiganga and Dhauliganga valleys in Chamoli district of the Indian Himalayan state of Uttarakhand. Both rivers feed ultimately into the Ganges from the Nanda Devi Sanctuary. The landslide scoured the valley slopes more than 200m above the river channel, sweeping away roads, bridges, valley-floor hydropower infrastructure worth an estimated $220m, and, beyond price, a current estimate of 204 people.

News of the disaster emerged in real time, with locals live-streaming the flood on social media, including footage of a group frantically trying to escape from a hydropower scheme only to be washed away. These images are shocking, the voices of those recording the video shouting warnings filled with fear. Some of it is hard to watch but perhaps necessary as we think about the often remote concepts of climate warming or transitions to greener hydropower in increasingly fragile mountain environments. At the end of this article there is a link to some of the footage. If you can, I'd recommend watching some of it first before reading on and with the sound turned up. It conveys the overwhelming noise, the dramatic suddenness and the helplessness of those caught up in such powerful events far more than any written description.

What followed in the days, weeks and months after the disaster was a mixture of what is truly good about science but also revealed complexities that are more difficult to imagine, requiring self-reflection for researchers like me. It is often this sort of devastating event that moves science forwards and makes individual careers. Yet we can often become lost in the excitement of an international team remotely unpicking a chain of events that occurred somewhere we may never visit.

In the immediate aftermath of the Chamoli event, there was an obvious working hypothesis for its cause. Sudden onset floods in the Himalaya are most often the consequence of what we term Glacial Lake Outburst Floods (GLOF), sourced from the ever-growing collection of lakes fed by retreating and thinning glaciers held back by moraines or even other glaciers. True, there was no long-term glacial lake at the snout of Ronti glacier, the ice overlooked by Trisul (7120m) and Nanda Ghunti (6309m) and popular with trekkers crossing the Ronti Saddle (c5200m) on the outer edge of the Nanda Devi Sanctuary. But it could have originated from a temporary impoundment with a multitude of causes: certainly not unprecedented.

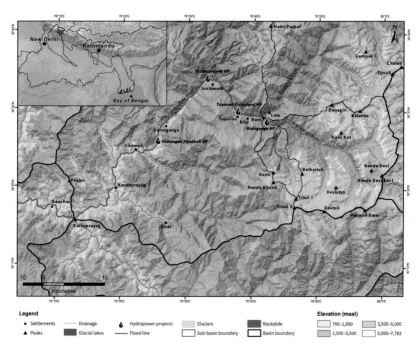

Map of the Chamoli hazard cascade Uttarakhand, India, and impacted hydropower schemes. *(ICIMOD)*

Then Dan Shugar from Calgary University leveraged something that has become more and more powerful in detecting and understanding events in distant places with few or no permanent human population: satellite imagery. The imaging company Planet Labs allows scientists access to daily, sometimes twice-daily images of Earth at a resolution of 0.5-5m taken by their network of 200-plus satellites. Dan spotted the source area for a massive ice-rock avalanche high up on Ronti Peak (6063m). More amazingly and purely by chance, the satellite image he used was taken as the ice-rock avalanche and resultant debris flow and then debris flood (jargon that tells us how the material moved) made its way towards people down valley. It is strange to look at this image taken from 475km away in space and then reconcile it with the footage taken from ground level as the flood swept people away. Witness accounts, both footage and statements, combined with various satellite data were critical to how our understanding of this 'hazard cascade' unfolded.

What follows is a piecing together of the story from a number of sources, including the 53-author paper I was involved with as part of the GapHaz[1] community, a scientific standing group of the International Association of Cryospheric Sciences/International Permafrost Group. Whilst this scientific effort went on, the authorities and locals were faced with the task of attempting

1. www.gaphaz.org

Satellite image from Planet Labs Ltd draped over 3D terrain showing the Chamoli hazard cascade as it happened with clouds of dust showing the path it took. The 'swash' up the slopes above the river is marked with a dotted line. *(ICIMOD)*

to rescue survivors and recover the dead from wet slurry that became more and more like concrete. The scenes chimed very much with the footage I show every year to undergraduates from the United Kingdom's worst landslide disaster, Aberfan in October 1966, when a debris flow from a colliery spoil tip buried a primary school, killing 28 adults and 116 children.

Landslides and rockfalls of all sizes regularly occur in the high mountains and they do so following a very logical relationship: there are many, many smaller events than the largest ones, what we term a magnitude-frequency relationship. The Chamoli landslide was not the largest of the large, even at an estimated 27m cubic metres of rock and ice, in a classic comparison some 10,800 Olympic-sized swimming pools, or more than six times the volume of Wembley stadium. What that landslide did is something that's becoming a real concern: it initiated a hazard cascade. The material became a debris flow and then a debris flood (wetter). Instead of just coming to rest in the valley floor with zero loss of life, it initiated a chain of events that massively increased the distance over which destruction occurred.

The size of the initial landslide was measured from space, using overlapping images to create 3D scenes, termed 'digital elevation models' (DEM), much like your eyes do. A global DEM is what Google Earth is draped on to visualise topography. DEMs for before and after the Chamoli event revealed the size of the hole left in Ronti Peak: 550m wide, 80m deep on average, with the top of this source occurring at an altitude of c5,540m. This slab

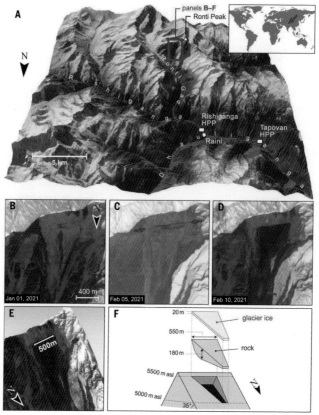

Overview of the Chamoli disaster. Fig A gives a 3D rendering of the local geography with labels for main locations mentioned in the text. ('HPP' indicates hydropower project.) Figs B to D are before and after satellite images of the site of the collapsed rock and glacier block and the resulting scar. Fig C shows recent snowfall in the region just before the event. The red arrows in C indicate the fracture that became the head scarp of the landslide. The arrow in Fig D indicates a remaining part of the lower eastern glacier. Fig E is a rendering of the scar. Fig F is a schematic of failed mass of rock and ice. *(Shugar et al 2021)*

of rock with a (debated) 20m of ice on top fell over 1,800m in around a minute to the valley floor at speeds reaching 200mph. If you've spent time on or around glaciers and high mountains, you'll know the crack of rockfall, that momentary sense of fear as you try to work out where it came from and where it is headed, followed by thuds reverberating through the ground you are stood on. Upscale that to a chunk of rock six times the size of Wembley weighing perhaps 49 million tonnes hitting the ground at 200mph and you can see why the Chamoli event provided an energy release equivalent to around 15 Hiroshima atomic bombs.

This energy was picked up by a seismometer network operated by the National Geophysical Research Institute of India, allowing researchers to pinpoint the event's time to the second: 14 seconds past 10.21am. As with so many disasters, timing mattered. If it had happened in the middle of the night people would have been in very different parts of the landscape; variation in exposure to hazard is such a strong control on the impacts of events. As it travelled down valley towards the region's hydropower schemes, the ice-rock avalanche became a slurry-like debris flow and flood, a mixture of broken rock, ice, melted ice and river water. After 15km it hit the Rishiganga hydropower scheme travelling at an estimated 55mph. After another 10km it hit the Tapovan Vishnugad hydro construction site at 35mph, already a massive 3,700m lower than where the landslide started. There was simply not enough warning for those working on the tunnels and infrastructure at Tapovan to escape. Of the current official number of 204 dead and missing, the majority were working at these hydropower schemes. Almost no fatalities were locals. The final death toll has been difficult to judge and it is unlikely that any trace of many of those still missing will ever be found.

The destructive power of the debris flood waned as it travelled down the valley, still stripping banks of vegetation and leaving a trim line that can be seen today. Yet that wasn't the end of its impacts. Twenty-four hours later, dirty water could be seen from space entering the reservoir at Srinagar (the one in Uttarakhand, not Kashmir), 150km away. Eight days after the landslide, the impact on the water quality in Delhi, which draws on a canal from the Ganges was notable and newsworthy in India, with suspended sediment spiking 80 times above permissible levels. Two and a half weeks later and now 900km downstream, the same plume of dirty water was still visible at Kanpur on the Ganges, still moving at around 53km per day.

'Build back better' has been a mantra in disaster recovery for many years. Perhaps don't build back at all is more reasonable for some hydropower schemes in some locations. It is never that simple of course. We want the world to move away from fossil fuels and to embrace green energy. Yet the reality is that damming has huge impacts on rivers, and dams are encroaching into higher elevation areas prone to Chamoli-type hazard cascades. Much has been written about these risks for some time but we can't act as colonial scholars telling Indians how to use their landscape and the risks locals face: so-called parachute science.

Locals in the Chamoli region are not disconnected from their landscape and its risks. The village of Raini sits above the Rishiganga hydro project and was the first major settlement impacted by the flow. Raini is where the Chipko movement originated in the early 1970s, a grassroots women-led environmental movement protesting unsustainable commercial logging. They were literally the original 'tree huggers', clinging to trees to protect them. ('Chipko' means to hug or embrace.) The movement spread and was instrumental in the creation of India's Forest (Conservation) Act of 1980. The settlements that make up Raini village sit above the confluence of the Rishiganga and Dhauliganga and as a result of the debris flow may now be uninhabitable as the flow destabilised the fragile balance of forces keeping the hillside from sliding into the down-cutting river: an issue throughout the Himalaya.

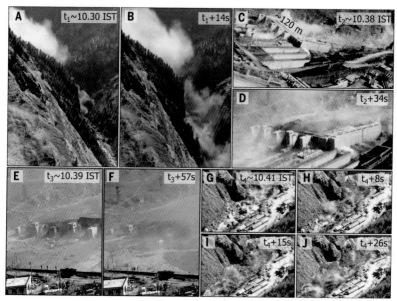

Sample video frames used to analyse flood velocity and discharge. Figs A and B: Flow front arrives and rushes through the valley upstream of the Rishiganga project. Fig C: Flow front arrives at Tapovan project's dam. Fig D: The reservoir is being filled quickly; spillways are damaged. Fig E: The dam is overtopped. Fig F: Collapse of remaining structures. Fig G to J: Flow front proceeds down the valley below the Tapovan dam spreading into the village. *(Shugar et al 2021)*

When it comes to climate change, residents of Raini, the Chamoli region, the government of India and the rest of the world are trying to balance energy needs, livelihoods, income and the landscape amongst feedback loops we still need to know so much more about. So what do we do about the risk of those still living within reach of hazard cascades in terms of new and existing in-river projects?

There are two really exciting avenues of research. The first is looking for precursors to failure. The second is live detection of future events to allow early warnings to evacuate. There were reports of locals hearing noise in the hours before the landslide, reports that seem to be verified by seismic records. In retrospect, this could have provided enough time to issue a warning but failures are common in the high mountains and most do not cause such widespread hazard cascades. Can we really evacuate everywhere each time? Looking even further back, it seems Ronti Peak has been no stranger to large ice-rock avalanches. Seasonal avalanches have pinched the river on numerous occasions, creating localised pockets of water. In 2000 and 2016 very large events filled parts of the valley floor for over six kilometres; they just didn't initiate a more far-reaching debris flow or flood. Several groups have characterised the source of the 2021 event opening up since 2016, using a time-series of satellite data. The crack at the top of the affection terrain opened and the block moved some 20m-30m prior to failure. Much promise

Looking up valley at the damaged Tapovan hydropower scheme in the Dhauliganga around 25km downstream from the source of the rock-ice avalanche that started the hazard cascade *(Sajjad Hussain)*

lies in this sort of work; regional deformation monitoring can and does already take place. The challenge lies in identifying the signal from the noise and in making decisions as to which moving mountains may be on their way to a catastrophic failure.

The Chamoli event once again showed the power of a relatively new science discipline termed environmental seismology. The work of practitioners Kristen Cook and Anil Tiwari ably characterised the timing and nature of the flow as it moved down valley. One obvious question that hides so much complexity is: 'can we use this method to live detect, locate and evacuate?' Scientists continue to push the boundaries of what is possible with existing seismic networks, and possibilities for more local systems in areas deemed high risk. In an ideal world a seismic detection would have given workers at Tapovan 20 minutes to escape. An interval of five to seven minutes is more likely in a simpler river-rise system. Early-warning systems are an entire research field but they are only effective if people are well drilled and practised and they respond as expected. Unlike earthquake response drills like 'drop, roll, cover', preparing to face hazard cascades such as Chamoli is not straightforward. This was especially true for the more than 30 workers trapped in the tunnels at the Tapovan hydro project. It is hard to imagine any system that would have allowed them to escape.

What role did climate change play in this disaster? There is a strong association of warming temperatures and large slope failures in the high mountains of the world. Permafrost is degrading; slopes are responding to ice removal; rain and snow patterns are changing. It is incredibly hard to link a

Planet Labs' satellite image of Srinagar (Uttarakhand) taken on 8 February 2021, one day after the event. The muddy plume that started 150 km away the day before can be seen arriving from the right, making its way through the reservoir for the hydropower project. *(Planet Labs)*

single massive ice-rock avalanche to a climate-change 'trigger'; there are so many interlinked factors in play. But it is likely in the opinion of the authors that warming-induced changes combined with geological structures on Ronti Peak caused the failure.

If you take away just one thing from reading this, let it be the understanding that there are no natural disasters. Landslides happen, debris flows and floods happen. What makes these events a disaster is the fact there are things we value being in the way, in this case expensive hydropower schemes with vulnerable workers. But there will certainly be more Chamoli-type events. They just may not make the western news.

Further Reading
There are more than a dozen academic papers dealing with the Chamoli hazard cascade but many are behind paywalls. Below is a selection of open-access articles.
www.icimod.org/article/understanding-the-chamoli-flood-cause-process-impacts-and-context-of-rapid-infrastructure-development
D H Shugar et al, 'A Massive Rock and Ice Avalanche Caused the 2021 disaster

at Chamoli, Indian Himalaya', Science, vol 373, iss 6552, 2021.
science.sciencemag.org/content/sci/early/2021/06/09/science.abh4455.full.pdf
available free from: *eprints.ncl.ac.uk/275391*
P Rautela, S Khanduri, S Kundalia, G C Joshi, R Jugran, 'Sequential Damming Induced Winter Season Flash Flood in Uttarakhand Province of India',
Journal of Environmental & Earth Sciences, vol 3 no 2, 2021.
ojs.bilpublishing.com/index.php/jees/article/view/3069
A Tiwari et al, 'Potential Seismic Precursors and Surficial Dynamics of a
Deadly Himalayan Disaster: An Early Warning Approach', Scientific Reports
12, 3733, 2022.
www.nature.com/articles/s41598-022-07491-y

Video Links
These videos give a sense of the catastrophic nature of the event and its
aftermath.
youtu.be/V2hH8hUAPuY
www.youtube.com/watch?v=h2g5BNbS_dM
The following video contains footage of workers attempting to escape from
the Tapovan dam before being washed away to their deaths. It is hard to
watch but underscores the human tragedy of that day and the lessons we
need to learn.
www.youtube.com/watch?v=NsS8SrvrojE&t=212s

CATH FLITCROFT

The BMC and Climate Change

Black mass. Two views of the summit trig point of Black Hill in Derbyshire 13 years apart, the first in 2004 and the second in 2017 after restoration by the Moors for the Future Partnership. Stopping peat erosion keeps carbon in the ground. *(Stephen Dawson/Moors for the Future)*

Unusually high temperatures, glacial retreat and collapse, wildfires, drought and the threat of war cast shadows over Europe this summer. With mountaineers first-hand witnesses to the impacts of climate change, it's not surprising that climbing federations around the world are looking at their own policies. The Alpine Journal invited **Dr Cath Flitcroft**, *policy officer for Access and Conservation at the British Mountaineering Council, to answer question on the organisation's aims and future direction in this area.*

How significant is the BMC's new Environmental and Sustainability Policy? What is the BMC trying to achieve?

Overall, this is a statement of our commitment to help reduce the impact of BMC activities on the environment (both as an office, as volunteers and across the membership) and it demonstrates a clear trajectory for the organisation to combat climate change and adopt more sustainable practices through actions and partnerships. In a nutshell, it's our own checklist to ensure we are doing all we can to help safeguard the mountain environment and tackle the climate and biodiversity emergency we are all faced with.

Amongst other things the new policy commits the BMC to consistently measure and publicise our annual climate footprint and progress in reducing our greenhouse gas (GHG) emissions (the first report will be out in late summer) and from this, we will develop a climate action plan to be actioned across BMC workstreams, demonstrating our commitment to reaching net-zero GHG emissions by 2040. This comes on the back of the BMC signing up to the UN Sports for Climate Action Framework in 2021. This is a cross-sport initiative which provides a clear structure to enable us to plan our work in this area.

Some aspects of the policy (for example, the promotion of sustainable transport and low-carbon travel options) will be a real challenge but we are committed to trying to find solutions and not shy away from the difficult issues. The BMC really is committed to tackling the climate and biodiversity emergency and hopefully the new policy demonstrates this.

You've been at the BMC for a while now. Are you aware of increasing interest for these issues from the membership? Or has the growth of indoor climbing blunted progress? Do you get any pushback?

Most definitely there's been an increase in interest. I think most of us have now woken up to the fact that climate change is real, and the landscapes we love and treasure are already changing, or are very likely to, over the next few years. The media interest around COP 26 in Glasgow, the flurry of reports from the Intergovernmental Panel on Climate Change, news of avalanches (most recently in the Dolomites and Kyrgyzstan) and gritters being brought in to try and reduce the impact of melting roads all demonstrate the fact that we're living in worrying times.

The growth of indoor climbing hasn't affected progress. I imagine the interest in the sport will only increase too as more of us seek shelter from the extreme weather that climate change is more frequently presenting us with.

I have had no pushback at all from our members or from the office. It can at times seem like an unsurmountable task. Smaller clubs for example, don't know where to start on their climate journey. But I'm excited to work with all sectors of the BMC and get individuals, clubs and partners connected to the right people.

**The BMC's Climate Project seems a major initiative.
Can you outline briefly what it entails?**

The public-facing part of our work on the sustainability and climate agenda is actually through our overarching Sustainable Steps Campaign: this is a host of useful information and advice varying from the BMC Lift Share site and our Recycling Centre to interesting articles on the carbon footprint of various travel and transport options.

The biggest part of our overarching campaign is the Climate Project. We wanted to find a way for members effectively to 'offset' their travel or personal carbon footprint and we wanted it to have real meaning (and be UK-based). We therefore decided to support the work of Moors for the

Future Partnership (MFFP) in the Peak District as they try to transform the moorland landscape and bring the underlying blanket peat into good condition – a healthy peatbog has a huge carbon sequestration capacity. So, at the point of joining the BMC or when members buy travel insurance, they can donate to this project. Specifically, the money is being used to purchase sphagnum moss, which is a key (and final) part of the peatland restoration story. So far, MFFP believe it has saved 62,000 tonnes of avoided carbon loss per year. We felt this project offered so much more then many of the traditional offsetting schemes: landscape restoration in the UK alongside tackling climate change.

You have a personal interest in peat. Can you explain briefly the extent of carbon storage in the UK's peat moorland and bog and how it's been impacted by air pollution and drainage?

By investing in peatland restoration these amazing landscapes can form some of the greatest carbon sinks in the world. A wet pristine bog locks up carbon dioxide (CO_2) in the ground and, unlike trees, has no time limit to the amount of carbon it captures. The UK's peatlands store over three billion tonnes of carbon, around the same amount as all the forest in UK, France and Germany put together. Not only that, but they are already part of the landscape (unlike new tree planting). Peat is the single biggest store of carbon in the UK, storing the equivalent of 20 years of all UK CO_2 emissions and according to DEFRA, one hectare of restored blanket bog avoids 19 tonnes of carbon loss per year.

Unfortunately, the moorlands of the Peak District and south Pennines are some of the most degraded in northern Europe. This is due to their unique geographical position at the time of the industrial revolution. In the 1800s, and into the early 20th century, the surrounding towns of Manchester, Sheffield, Bradford and Stoke-on-Trent were at the heart of Britain's industrial prosperity. However, the industries they relied on were also creators of massive amounts of pollution. This pollution fell as acid rain in the moorlands, wiping out the layer of vegetation that protected the moorlands, leaving the area covered with blackened, bare peat.

The loss of vegetation meant there was nothing to prevent erosion as rain washed the peat off the hills. This left carbon in the water, staining it brown, and also bringing with it the same chemicals that were present on the moors, making the rivers unfit for drinking water without heavy treatment, or wildlife.

The Moors for the Future Partnership are working to protect these moors, reverse hundreds of years of damage caused by human activity and transform the landscape back into a heathy bog (and active carbon sink). The BMC are supporting the Partnership's work to plant sphagnum moss back to where it should be. Peat is carbon-rich. Sphagnum moss – the moss that forms the peat in the Peak District and South Pennines – absorbs carbon to grow and locks this carbon up as it decomposes from its base. Sphagnum's unique root system means that it biodegrades from the bottom up, creating

Cotton grass on Black Hill and a gritstone pavement. Moors for the Future completed its seven-year MoorLIFE 2020 project in the summer of 2022 following a £16m investment. *(Moors for the Future)*

more peat as well as protecting and binding it. Sphagnum can hold up to 20 times its weight in water and in slowing the flow of water from the moors is essential in flood prevention. Bogs are amazing and we need to do more to protect and nurture them.

Biodiversity in the uplands is in a parlous state in the UK. How does Moors for the Future impact that?

Not only is the work of Moors for The Future helping tackle the climate emergency but it's also at the same time restoring the landscape, which has multiple benefits. It enhances habitats, helps reduce the risk of wildfire and flooding, and provides good-quality drinking water.

A healthy blanket bog has a wide range of plants and invertebrates. In addition to sphagnum and heathers, where there is no local seed source, the Partnership plants native moorland plants that have extensive roots to help stabilise the peat, increase the biodiversity of the moors, and provide important habitat and food for a wide range of wildlife. The young plants of each species need particular conditions, their 'niche', if they are to survive on the restoration sites. For example, crowberry needs to be planted at the top of a slope, cotton grass needs to be on a flat, wet area, and bilberry and cloudberry should be planted on the tops of peat 'hags'. Wading birds like dunlin, curlew and golden plover nest on the moors and raise their young. The invertebrates are an essential source of protein for their chicks. The approach by Moors for the Future is truly holistic in tackling the climate and biodiversity emergency.

A 'sitch' of sphagnum moss, which used to cover much of the southern Pennines before drainage and burning transformed them. Restored sphagnum improves biodiversity and slows water leaving the moor, as well as locking up carbon. *(Moors for the Future)*

**There are volunteer opportunities for the Climate Project.
What are they and how successful has that initiative been?**

Stabilising bare peat by adding heather and grasses halts the loss of peat by erosion. But for the blanket bog to begin actively creating new peat, more intervention is needed. In particular, finding sources of suitable sphagnum species to re-introduce onto restored sites. To do this, MFFP usually use cultivated sphagnum moss in the form of plug plants, which need to be planted by hand as they are so delicate. So far, about five million sphagnum plugs have been planted by hand: this is where volunteers are needed.

Unfortunately, Covid-19 and poor weather has meant that there hasn't yet been the chance for the public and BMC members to get involved as part of the Climate Project. There will be opportunities to do so each year going forward but these will be limited to November and March, which is the optimum time to plant the plugs.

One of our aims for this year is to also draw together a list of landscape restoration projects across the UK where volunteers are needed and then advertise these accordingly.

Energy costs around the world have spiked in the aftermath of the war in Ukraine. Is the Green Energy Deal still in place?

The BMC deal with Octopus Energy is currently running. Members can get £50 off when they change to them.

Transport in general and flying in particular are major problems in terms of climbing's carbon footprint. The MEF is looking at a tariff for carbon offsetting. Is the BMC considering anything similar, either for the mountaineers or competition climbers it supports?

Gross emissions are inherent in our business; travel will always be a part of our business model but there are smart ways to plan to get to net zero and make real meaningful changes to the way we and everyone else operates.

Currently we are asking members for a voluntary donation to the Climate Project but we are in the process of developing a specific carbon calculator so members can understand the footprint of their travel plans and donate accordingly. Similarly, we are working to make all of our events carbon neutral including climbing competitions as well as working with the GB climbing team to see if we can do the same here (this is a work in progress but everyone is very supportive).

In addition, the International Committee have recently changed their application process so that applicants must demonstrate the efforts being taken to reduce the impact of their expedition so that travel only happens when it has a carbon neutral impact. As such, the BMC will only support expeditions in remote environments that can demonstrate they are trying to minimise the environmental impact, have a plan to offset any carbon emissions, leave no trace behind, taking into consideration the waste management system of the local area and the end destination for any disposed waste, and recognise the need to respect (and where possible) the economic, cultural, social, religious, political, environmental and other beliefs of the local populations.

We also advocate various carbon calculators that can help individuals assess their own footprint under out Sustainable Steps Campaign.

What's the BMC's view of offsetting?

The BMC has offset its own operational footprint. Our view really is that it's part of the story now and a necessity but needs to be backed up with real changes and understanding of our behaviour and the emissions costs of our activities, and what we can change in the way we do business to have the most impact.

As more businesses and individuals move towards net zero, the reliance on such schemes should get smaller and smaller. I don't think we will ever be in a position to not offset given the nature of our business but each year as we tweak our operations, we will be relying on schemes less and less. We certainly aren't offsetting as a way to avoid changing the way we operate.

It's almost impossible to prove additionality with absolute certainty, as to the success or otherwise of many of these schemes. That is why we are supporting a project (with Moors for the Future) that's research based and where the impact can be clearly measured.

Do you track what federations abroad are doing with regard to climate change? Is there anything that's caught your eye?

As a signatory of the UN Sports for Climate Action Framework, we have access to a number of other sporting bodies across the globe who are also working on the climate emergency and have the chance to attend workshops, webinars and meetings on specific issues (and share good practice). This has been exceptionally useful.

In addition, we have representatives who sit on various committees within the UIAA and European Mountaineers (EUMA) both of whom are encouraging members to take more climate action. In particular, EUMA are encouraging their members to calculate their carbon footprint and take individual actions to reduce their impact by utilising goclimate.com. This website is well worth a visit and I like the idea of understanding the footprint of other mountaineering federations.

The DAV has also got a campaign called #doitsimply (act sustainably) and have some good advice on various topics including public transport links across Germany (very useful). Perhaps my favourite is 'Where is Roland', an initiative by the Royal Dutch Climbing and Mountaineering Club *www.nkbv.nl*. Their Climbing4Climate campaign follows a mountain guide, Roeland van Oss, who was climbing all 82 4,000ers of the Alps in a climate-neutral way this past summer (2022). Through the project (*nkbv.nl/c4c*), he drew attention to the climate problem in the mountains to inspire others.

How has the recycling project progressed?

The response to the initial article (and list of places you can get gear repaired, recycled or donate it to be re-used) has been fantastic (163,000 hits so far which is eight times the average BMC article viewing figure) and as soon as it was published, a number of other retailers got in touch to ask if they could be added to the list.

Ultimately, I would like to translate all of this information into a useful app and that's something we're going to look into later this year.

Memoir

'Everest and North Peak from Rongbuk', Elsie Dixon, watercolour, 35.5cm × 25.5cm, 1934?. *(Courtesy of Tony Astill)*

DENNIS GRAY

Joe Brown, Look Down

Memories of the Master

Balancing act. Joe Brown laybacks up a freestanding pole outside the Wall End Barn in 1951. *(George Kitchen collection).*

Joe Brown, look down from your pillar of fame, Almscliff tiger is my name.

Dennis Gray

In Langdale's green valley, where the lads are so pally,
As soon as they learn you have food, fags, or dough.
The climber retires, to the barn of Zeke Myers,
Crying ackers and shekels, alive, alive oh!

The Bradford Lads

A typical Wall End crew in 1951.
(Neville Drasdo collection)

Slim Sorrell picks up Joe Brown and Pete Cargill at Wall End.
(George Kitchen collection)

The door of the Wall End Barn was pushed open. Outside it was raining heavily, as it had been all that day and the one preceding it. Into the warm fug, created by the number of bodies laying about gossiping, cooking and sleeping, stepped two strangers. One was like an ox, tall and well built, the other smaller but of what was then medium height, both of them dark haired, both carrying huge packs and dripping wet. One of the barn regulars ventured a 'hello', wondering where they had come from, imagining they had got so wet walking from Chapel Stile, where the midday bus turned off to Coniston.

'Scafell,' was the single-word reply from the laconic ox.

This was 1951 and I was 15 years old and, I guess, a bit of a pain, since instead of going to school I spent a lot of time in the Yorkshire Ramblers' library in Leeds, reading journals and climbing books. Intrigued, I began to question the newcomers as to what routes they had done as they unpacked: they had climbed on Esk Buttress and Scafell's East Buttress. This seemed incredible to me in the conditions, but my questioning was obviously so annoying that I was bundled physically into a bag, which was tied up with slings, carried outside and placed on top of a wall on the Blea Tarn Road. I was scared stiff but despite the sharp stones of the wall sticking into me I daren't move in case I fell off.

After what felt a long sentence my jailers reappeared and the ox demanded if I had learned to shut up. Through the rain and cold I admitted I had, at which they carried me back inside, cut me loose and even made me a brew. To be fair to my young self, I was climbing with Peter Greenwood, Harold Drasdo, and more infrequently at that time Arthur Dolphin and none of them would have had the temerity to be on Scafell in such weather. I subsequently learnt that the shorter of the two, Joe Brown, was the best bad-weather climber I have ever tied on with, and that his partner, the ox-like Slim Sorrell, was his perfect foil, being, as I have intimated above, a genuinely strong man. And thus began two friendships that lasted until their respective deaths, Joe in his bed at 89, Slim in a macabre sequence of events that ended with his murder at the age of 47.

A few weeks later I met Ronnie Moseley and Ray Greenall, also at Wall End. They told of the formation of a new climbing club, the Rock and Ice, and that both Joe and Slim had joined. My loyalty was then to the Bradford Lads, just a loose-knit group of climbers who originally got together by visiting West Yorkshire outcrops; it was never a club but later I learned that was what Joe really believed in. It was his close friendships with many of those involved that meant he did sign up and with his membership the Rock and Ice became legendary, although within their ranks they had other climbers who were almost as adept.

I kept in touch with Ron and learnt that Slim was organising a Rock and Ice bus trip to Glencoe at Easter 1952, so I badgered him and was on board when it set off from the centre of Manchester late one evening. My seat companion was Don Whillans and I had never then met anyone so acerbic. I had met him once before as I jogged down the track having just completed my first route on Cloggy. 'Bloody stuck up,' was the epithet he hurled at me as I passed him, terrified by his aggression. I was pleased that more gentle souls were on board including Joe and his then girlfriend, Mavis Jolley. She had been to school with him, and she told me later he was known as 'that small Chinese boy'. Joe's schooling finished at 14 when the Nazis bombed the building flat and he was apprenticed to Archie, a one-man property-repairing business.

This must have been the slowest bus trip to ever brave Shap for it kept on breaking down and it took most of the four-day holiday to reach our objective. Brown and Whillans spent what time was left exploring the then unclimbed Creag a'Bhancair, whilst I joined in an ascent of the Clachaig Gully, which was rather more like swimming than rock climbing. An amusing aside: sometime after this I was climbing with Pat Walsh and we made the second ascent of *Carnivore* on Bhancair. I told Joe I had found the route 'bloody hard!'

'You must have been off form,' he replied. 'That crag's full of big holds.' Brown was not easily impressed.

By 1952 the Rock and Ice legend was the talk of the climbing world. There were no magazines, no internet; their standing spread by word of mouth, although some of the detail of their new routes was published rather belatedly in the long defunct BMC publication *Mountaineering*. It is a truth that after the Second World War it was the working-class climbers, mainly from the grime and poverty of the northern cities – the Creagh Dhu in Scotland, the Bradford Lads in the Lake District and the Rock and Ice in Wales – that dominated the sport. There had been working-class climbers before the war but they had been limited by a six-day working week or unemployment and lack of funding. The long-established clubs, with a mainly middle class membership looked askance at this flood of newcomers into a preserve they regarded as their own. That prompted this riposte from Slim Sorrell: 'When we met some of the members of established clubs at the outcrops they rather cold shouldered us until we started to climb, then they went all sheepish and moved away.'

Petrol rationing finished in 1950, although food was still couponed. I had found that as a schoolboy climber I was lucky hitch-hiking although there were few vehicles on the road. I had kept in touch with the Rock and Ice and joined them for my first visit to the Roaches, where we stayed in a barn close by. On the first evening I joined in the 'rough' games session. Every member had a speciality but Joe was the only one who could 'bum skip', literally sitting on the floor and skipping with a short piece of rope. That caused much hilarity.

Next day I was collared by Brown to second him on the *Sloth*. Recent to my visit, he and Whillans had pioneered this fearsome roof climb on the upper tier of the crag. They had spun a coin for who should lead and despite Joe's double-headed penny (a joke around the belief we held at that time), Don won the honour of the first attempt on one of the most famous outcrop climbs of that era. He did not waste that opportunity, and after a bit of a struggle, moving out along the flakes under the roof, managed to reach some good jams, hung down and pulled up. Seconding, Joe hadn't found it technically too demanding, but it rather rankled with him and he wanted to experience an ascent on the lead.

Next morning I climbed up to the pedestal under the roof whilst my leader readied himself. I then securely belayed Joe as he climbed up to a feature we called the Cheese Block around which he draped a sling. He then climbed up and launched himself across the roof, somehow reached round to find good jams, hung down and then with a heave was up and out of sight. The rope went tight between us and I started to climb, easily at first up to the Cheese Block but then my problems started as the rope was pulling me off. Remember also that in those days we tied directly onto it.

Yet I recalled how on the first ascent, Don, being small, had managed to wedge himself across the roof, his body fitting into the flakes. Somehow I managed to do the same. My difficulty was how to extricate myself from this position but suddenly from below me on the pedestal I was offered these instructions: 'reach out your full length, there you will find a jug and stonking jams, lower onto your arms and pull up.' It was Joe offering this sage advice; he had obviously descended at speed down the easier route on our left and I followed his instructions although as I climbed the rope remained slack. I imagined somebody else was up there holding the rope and I kept shouting 'take in!'. On reaching the top I was more than surprised to find the rope securely belayed but nobody there. Later, when I tried to remonstrate with Joe, he answered cheerfully: 'you were firmly belayed and couldn't have fallen far!' Being a *senpai* of the sensei was a real apprenticeship.

That same year of 1954 I travelled to the Llanberis Pass where I found shelter in the road menders' hut, set under the Cromlech boulder. There was a mixed group, mainly members of the Rock and Ice, and we had the door of our dwelling firmly shut with a large boulder stopping anyone we did not wish to allow into our midst. Just a few weeks before the police had arrested one of the Rock and Ice for staying there and we didn't wish to suffer the same fate. The weather outside was abysmal and we spent most of that rainy, cold day in our sleeping bags, playing card games. About five o'clock there came a hammering on the door and the high-pitched voice we all

A Brown study. Joe bouldering at the Roaches while the Rock and Ice look on. Dennis Gray is centre, cheering him on.

recognised: 'Let us in!' Joe was with a companion we knew as 'GG' White. They were wet through and the chorus was:

'Where have you been?'

'Idwal.'

'What on earth did you do there?'

'Suicide Wall.'

'You must be joking.'

'No,' answered Brown. 'It was hard.'

'What was it like GG?'

'Bloody hard, like Joe says!'

I doubt whether any other leader then active would have climbed that route in such conditions.

Shortly after we moved into a club hut, because so many of us crowded into the road mender's cabin that it became untenable. Slim decided the time had come for an eating contest. At that time he was the instigator of the wilder activities of the club, the stone fights up and down the Pass, the wrestling matches, and the demonstrations of how to fall gracefully (one of which at Dovestones Quarry went wrong and he damaged a leg). It took most of the day to make a suitable stew in a baby's bath we had found but initially Slim wouldn't let me take part, being too young and small. After an intercession from Joe I was allowed under sufferance to join the others and repaid Joe's faith in me by winning the competition, eating several bowls of stew, which was delicious.

Having reached the age of 18 I had to register for national service. I could have been deferred but the head of the printing college in Leeds advised I should get it over and then return to studying. I had strong views about this and registered as a non-combatant but was delighted when I was posted to the Army Pay Office on Manchester's Stockport Road. I lived in a civilian billet on Brynton Road, which led onto Dickenson Road where Joe then lived at his mother's. My very first weekend there we all went to High Tor pegging, the weekend after to Stanage, the weekend after that Wimberry and then up to Yellowsacks, followed by climbs further afield in Wales, the Lakes and Scotland.

Most of these trips were in the cold winter of 1954. I was used to roughing it with the Bradford Lads but this was a different world of dossing: in caves, at the foot of crags, in broken-down shooting cabins. Joe seemed inured to the cold and as I was by then his gentleman's gentleman, as long as he (actually his mother) provided good food to cook each weekend, I dared not complain but secretly planned as soon as I was able to buy a four-seasons sleeping bag: a rather wild dream given I only received 28 shillings each week from the army.

The Rock and Ice were the most together of any climbing club at that time. Mid week they would meet at Ron's parents house one night, the Palais at Levenshulme on another, and the YMCA in the city centre to finalise the venue they would meet up the following evening on the Thursday night. They drank gallons of tea, talked climbing and climbers, and I recall only Ray Greenall ever danced at the Palais. In between times Joe persuaded me to go twice to see Audie Murphy in *Ride Clear of Diablo*. He was a real fan of Westerns and his reading was dominated by Oliver Strange's 'Sudden' novels.

I used to attend the club's venues nearly always late although nobody ever asked why. I was a member of the Manchester Athletic Club and would first go to the Fallowfield track. When Joe returned from the successful ascent of Kangchenjunga in 1955 I ran into him in my running strip in Longsight as I headed home to change.

'What is a gentleman's gentleman doing running around like he's being chased by the police?'

'I have just met the greatest athlete in the world,' I confessed. 'Emil Zatopek. At the Olympic Games he won the 5,000m, 10,000m and the marathon. I doubt anyone will ever equal that.' But Joe remained unimpressed.

It was about that time that Archie retired through ill health. Joe asked me one day to give him a hand as he had now inherited the business. Our task was to break up a large concrete floor for which Joe used brute force and a sledgehammer. I kept having a go with another sledgehammer but after a few minutes was kyboshed and relegated to tea boy. It made me think: I could run many miles without tiring but Joe's fitness was of another kind. Watching with a sledgehammer, I realised he was super-fit; his work had given him an outstanding physique for climbing.

It was also around this time that some members of the group acquired nicknames. Joe became 'The Baron'. Ray Greenall was 'Anderl the Brew' because he looked a bit like Anderl Heckmair and could make a brew whatever the conditions. Whillans became 'The Villain'. The most inspired I think was 'Mortimer'. Joe Brown and Joe Smith had been climbing on High Tor, made illegal by the local council in the early 1950s for some reason unknown to us. Waiting at the top for them to finish was the police.

'What are your names?'

'Joe Brown and Joe Smith.'

The copper in charge rolled his eyes. 'Can't you do better than that?'

It took quite some time before they established they were telling the truth and were then free to go with a caution. In order to avoid any future confusion, and two Joes being one too many, Joe Smith became 'Mortimer', swiftly edited down to 'Morty'.

My two years in Manchester ended in 1956 but I stayed in touch with my friends there. In West Yorkshire, most of the Bradford Lads had moved away, taking advantage of the opening up of higher education. The only one remaining active in the region was the gentle giant John Ramsden. One weekend at Froggatt Edge we met Peter Biven, then from Leicester. He told of the magic land of Cornwall and its granite sea cliffs, of which Trevor Peck and he were pioneers. And so that summer, Ram and I decided to check this out. The ride down on his Royal Enfield Bullet motorbike was exciting and we climbed at Bosigran, Chair Ladder and Sennen. We saw no other climbers during the week we were there, although we did meet a very old A W Andrews, who could justly claim to be the original Cornwall sea-cliff pioneer. I reported all this to my Rock and Ice friends and in 1957 a large number of the membership decided to holiday down in the southwest, although Whillans, who was off to the Himalaya, chided that we should wait to visit such when we were 'old and past it.'

In 1957, Joe married Valerie Gray, a teacher and climber from Blackburn. Slim was their best man. As part of this change of status they joined the Cornish Riviera team. By that time they travelled in an Austin A35 van while I and my passengers drove an A40. They had a hunting horn and we had a bugle and as we passed each other we would give a blast on these instruments. To see the Rock and Ice at the seaside was a revelation. We had a dinghy and Joe exhibited his enthusiasm for fishing. We'd heard that off the coast was a basking shark and we set out to catch it. We spent several hours at sea, all of us were sick and we never caught the shark but we did a lot of climbing on the sea cliffs and all returned with happy memories of cream teas and superb granite.

A planned visit to the Alps in 1958 was almost undone by one of our games. Joe, Morty and I had been climbing on Clogwyn y Grochan and Joe challenged us to a race back to the tents when we had finished for the day. The descent was short but steep and we were all going hell for leather when Brown took a screamer. Turning back I saw him laid out in agony on the scree. Morty and I scrambled back up to him and pulled him back up to his feet,

The Rock and Ice, with Joe Brown turned towards Dennis Gray.

only to find he couldn't move unaided. We helped him down to the tents and he decided he had to go to hospital. But there was a problem. Neither Val nor Joe would countenance going to Bangor accident and emergency, which had a bad reputation amongst climbers at that time. So we laid Joe full length in the back of my van and Val followed driving their A35, Morty directing me to Withington Hospital, Manchester, where we discovered Joe had fractured his leg. I don't know why but Joe seemed to have a blind spot about running; he even had the confidence one weekend to challenge Eric Beard, one of the greatest fell-runners of his or any era, to a race up Catbells in Borrowdale. Beardie gave him a head start of half the fell but still beat him to the summit.

Joe made a quick recovery despite him limping badly on occasion and our plans for the Alps were still on. Val, Morty and I drove the A35 to the coast and left the car there, catching first the ferry then trains to Chamonix. Whillans was already there when we arrived, recovering from an epic ascent of the *Bonatti* on the south-west pillar of the Dru. For our first climb, Joe decided we – Morty, Joe and me – would ascend the north face of the Charmoz but though we made ready to start the weather turned against us. Back in the woods of the Biolay campsite, I shared a tent with Joe, Val having gone off on a journey with some French friends. All around us were British climbers, including other Rock and Ice members. We were our usual messy crowd and I remember one day being embarrassed when some of the Chamonix guides, Lionel Terray among them, visited us. They were dressed immaculately and had come to pay their respects to Joe Brown, leader of the Fissure Brown on his 1954 new route on the west face of the Blatière, the hardest free pitch in the western Alps. I used my schoolboy French to translate.

Don having recovered, he joined Joe and Morty for an ascent of the west face of the Petites Jorasses, which I backed off feeling ill. Down in Chamonix

Joe Brown leading the crack high on Kangchenjunga in 1955, photographed by
George Band. *(AC Photo Library)*

Muztagh Tower in the Karakoram, photographed by Vittorio Sella. *(AC Photo Library)*

I met Eric Beard who had hitched there by himself and went back to the woodcutter's hut, the famous Chalet Austria, which we made our base. He seconded me on an ascent of the *Ménégaux* on the Aiguille de l'M. We then met up with Whillans, Morty and Brown, I to climb the east face of the Capucin with Don, Morty and Joe the Dru via the *Bonatti Pillar*. The weather intervened and although Whillans and I succeeded we ended with a forced bivouac on our descent, whilst Joe and Morty had a less successful outing on the Dru.

Whilst we were in Chamonix we read that the Rock and Ice was to be disbanded. The reason, we learned, was that those currently the club's officers could not find others willing to take over these positions. Whillans was furious at this news; Joe was his usual sanguine self. I had never formally joined, just attended. But the club's demise marked seven years of achievement and a few years later, when I lived in Derby, Nat Allen and I reformed the club.

On the train coming home was in fact the only time I ever saw Joe lose it. There were no seats available so we were sitting in the corridor on our gear. A ticket inspector came down the train and Joe stood up to show him Val's and his ticket, at which the official called him something unprintable, grabbed his gear and threw it as far as he could. The next we knew, Brown had grabbed him and pushed him up against a compartment door. The day was saved by Val with her excellent French. She explained we were 'les alpinistes' on our way home from the Mont Blanc range, which is why we had so much equipment with us. We were not the idle dossers the inspector had believed us to be.

In 1959 Joe had his first taste of a professional film assignment, taking the role of climbing stand-in for the lead actor in *Hazard*, a steel-industry safety film being shot in the Dolomites. The director was Tom Stobart, who had made the successful 1953 Everest film. I received a message that if I managed to get out to the Dolomites I too could find work on the production. Deciding I had gone as far as I could working for a printer and publisher in Leeds, I recruited Eric Beard, Brian Fuller and Eric Metcalf to travel out with me in my van to share the cost and we met up with the film crew in Cortina. We spent over a month working on *Hazard*, and it was truly an education, mainly on how slow the filming process really is. It seemed that a few minutes of shooting took many hours of preparation. None of the 'stars' were climbers but Joe was in his element doubling as the hero, the beginning of his successful film and television work.

By 1960 I was administering a fine-art plate-gravure unit for one of the biggest printers in the UK. The unit was based in Derby. Joe contacted me in the spring to see if I would accompany him on a trip back to the Dolomites and Chamonix? Of course I would but the longest I could be away would be three weeks. That seemed ideal to Joe and our driver Claude Davies who was happy to go along for the drive. There was, however, a snag. Joe had developed a stomach ulcer (too many bacon butties), and so for the early part of our stay in the Dolomites we lived on Ovaltine and milk. So the mantra was start climbing late and finish early. Nevertheless we climbed half a dozen routes, including the *Spigolo Giallo*, the north face of the Cima Grande and the *Pilastro de Rozes* on the Tofana but had a rather gruesome time on the Civetta. We had not then started wearing crash helmets, and quite a way up the north-west face some stones fell, one of which hit Joe on his head while he was leading. His flat cap offered no real protection but for some reason he just kept on climbing and must have run out at least 300 feet of rope. When I finally joined him his face was covered in blood. The last sections of the climb seemed harder than we expected, but I think it was the conditions rather than the route.

Setting off for the western Alps I had the only disagreement I ever had with Brown. I suggested we went via the Eiger north face but he made it plain he wasn't interested and that it wasn't worth wasting our time on such a diversion. Arriving in Chamonix we were met with the news that it was the worst season ever and the snow level was down below Montenvers. We met up with Robin Smith and Dougal Haston and agreed that during the first break in weather we would try the unclimbed south face of the Fou. When it finally came, the four of us set out for the Envers des Aiguilles hut the very next day. Just to reach the refuge was a challenging climb in itself; the slabs leading up to it were covered in ice and snow and required an axe and crampons. I would have liked a rope but dare not ask this sort of company for one. Robin burnt us off as he started to sing, illustrating he had plenty of puff left. We were the first climbers at the hut for days and were away before light next morning. The way to the south face is via a couloir and we cowered on its left side as soon as we entered it as first rocks and then snow whistled down.

Joe Brown in the Caucasus in 1962. Dennis Gray (opposite) at work on his Austin A40.
(AC Photo Library/Dennis Gray)

'I'm going down,' I decided. 'This is suicide.' And as it was now getting light, that's exactly what I did. Before I'd reached the hut it had started first to hail, then snow. I had just snuggled down in a pile of blankets when the others came clattering back to join me. Retreating to Montenvers that day we were in a mood of high spirits, jollity and grip. Back at the Biolay we packed up and set off with Claude driving us home in style.

Joe stopped being a property repairer in 1961 to become an outdoor pursuits instructor and he and Val moved to live in a flat at the Whitehall Centre in Derbyshire. He became keen on canoeing and for some reason contacted me to make a trip with him down the Derwent. I was an absolute duffer at canoeing but agreed. All went well till we hit some faster-flowing water and Brown, who by then who saw himself as an expert, ran flat out into a bridge support. I could feel the 'bang' and followed on as carefully as I could to avoid the obstacle. When we finished, Joe had trouble getting out of his canoe; he had hurt his back in the collision. I phoned the next day to see if he was all right but Val answered. Joe had gone to hospital where the medics had to pass him through the window because his body had stiffened so badly they couldn't get him through the doorway. Typically, he was soon out and about again.

In 1966 Val and Joe moved to Llanberis to open his shop in its main street. One of the more lurid tabloids ran the headline 'Human Fly moves to Wales!' so I sent a card addressed simply to the 'Human Fly, Llanberis'. Of course, it reached him. In April 1966 the BBC had made their famous live broadcast of Joe and an all-star cast climbing Red Wall at Gogarth, so amusingly caricatured by Tom Patey in his article 'The Greatest Show on Earth'. I was a porter and part of the rigging team. In 1967, when ITV's World of Sport got in on the act with a broadcast from Tremadog,

Brown once again showed his calmness under media pressure whilst climbing *Vector*. I was in charge of recruiting the team of climbers who made this possible and was responsible for the camera operator's security. A memento I have of this is Joe singing his party piece 'The Sergeant Major' at the post-event party, recorded by producer Ned Kelly.

After the *Vector* climb Joe and I went our separate ways but we remained close friends. I visited him a few days before he passed away. We both agreed we had been so lucky, having lived the lives we had, starting out in the late 1940s. Joe was the outstanding climber of my generation and his record speaks for itself with over 600 new routes in the UK and so many first ascents abroad, especially Kangchenjunga, the Muztagh Tower and the Trango Tower. At the age 60 he was still able to lead *Suicide Wall* once again and summit Cho Oyu. Nobody I know remained active so long. But above all this he was good company. When I was with him we laughed a lot, except when we had to be serious. Fame never really meant much to him and he remained the same person as when I first met him as a 15-year-old in the Wall End Barn.

1966 and All That

The Year Time Stopped

Leo Dickinson with his camera tilted towards the Cima Grande. *(Leo Dickinson).*

As ill health kept him increasingly at home, I would phone Joe Brown regularly for one of our epic chats, which continued, I now realise, for around seven years. During one of these conversations, in the last year of his life, Joe told me that mountains alone were not interesting: it was the people that climbed them that were. That's why he had not climbed solo.

In 1966 I met the first of those interesting people; this story is about how they changed my life. I'd hitchhiked to the Tre Cime di Lavaredo and teamed up with fellow Prestonian Steve Suthorn. We were diametric opposites. Steve expected things to go wrong while I was more optimistic. He was often right.

After five routes we set off up the *Comici* on the Cima Grande. Like many Brits we had started too late but after several hours reached the last vertical pitch. Steve had been anxious he might damage his watch if he wore it so had given me that responsibility. I don't know why he thought I'd be any safer with it, but I was happy to oblige. Now, with the summit almost in sight and well over 1,000ft above the valley floor I glanced at my wrist and as I did so the strap broke. The watch fell.

I yelled to Steve 80ft below me to try and catch it: clearly, an overoptimistic impulse. He snatched at it as it whistled past and then yelled up at me.

'You bastard! You've broken my watch!'

'It's not broken,' I reassured him. 'It's still working. Still keeping perfect time.'

I thought of Emilio Comici, whose route we were on, and that wonderful line he had: *from the summit let fall a drop of water, and this is where my route will go.* And as it transpired, so did Steve's watch.

'Bastard!' Steve's rage brought me back to the present.

'Look, Steve, the watch is fine.'

And then, with the afternoon sun catching the face, his watch exploded in a diamond burst of glittering pieces.

'Now it's not working,' I added. Helpfully.

I hadn't realised how long it takes to fall such a long way. It was well over 10 seconds before it hit the ground, the time a skydiver takes to reach terminal velocity. After that each 1,000ft takes another five seconds.

Across the valley in the Locatelli hut we met a film team headed by the German alpinist Lothar Brandler – of *Brandler-Hasse* fame. Their route was the other classic north face line up the Cima Grande. Three years later with Brian Molyneux I would spend two and a half days repeating this superb creation but just then Brandler and his team were hard at work climbing and filming a new route named the *Saxonweg*. It relied almost entirely on hand-drilled bolts and seemed too ridiculous for words.

That said, the project was offering work to a wandering Brit: Denny Moorhouse, who within a couple of years had founded the equipment company Clog in Deiniolen. The Germans had a nickname for Denny, calling him 'Doctor Death' due to the epics he seemed to attract on his ascents. He would end up bivouacking in the most unlikely places, like waterfalls, and had fallen from Brandler's own route when several pegs ripped. Before Jumars and his own improved 'Cloggers', Denny's only option was to un-thread his shoelaces and prussik back up 50ft to safety having done nothing to dent his reputation.

I was fascinated by Brandler's lifestyle and in retrospect I realised it had some influence on my own future, although not entirely. (Brandler's career would swerve in a more 'adult-oriented' direction.) His lead climber was Werner Bittner who, like Raymond Lambert and Reinhold Messner, had continued climbing after losing most of his toes through frostbite during a winter ascent of the north face of the Matterhorn. Before that, he'd been part of the team that had made the first winter ascent of the *Brandler-Hasse*. Even after he lost his toes he did winter ascents of routes like the *Walker Spur*.

Brian Molyneux bivouacking on the *Brandler-Hasse*. *(Leo Dickinson)*

If you were pitching Bittner's most celebrated achievement to a film producer, and by most celebrated I mean in media terms, you'd describe it as *Bonnie and Clyde* meets the north face of the Eiger. His partner on the *Heckmair* route in 1964 was a 32-year-old secretary working for Erhard Junkers, owner of the Junkers aircraft company (think Luftwaffe). Daisy Voog had been born in Estonia in 1932 and fled to Germany with her parents during the war. A talented athlete as a young woman, she'd discovered climbing later in life and set about making her mark: but how to fund her ambitions? Sponsorship being more difficult in the 1960s, Daisy elicited a direct contribution from her employer's safe to the tune of ten thousand deutschmarks without first going to the trouble of getting his permission. Oh, and she 'borrowed' a company car to get her to Switzerland, also without permission. As the first woman to climb the Eiger Nordwand Daisy certainly made her mark but in 1965 she was put on trial for embezzlement and other charges and given nine months probation. Bonnie met a stickier end.

My final encounter that summer happened as we slipped out of a hut to quaff an illicit bottle of brandy to celebrate a climbing success. The sound of falling rocks behind us made me stop and turn round. Someone was following us up the hill. I waited anxiously for the figure to catch us but then he stopped a few feet below me. I remember being disconcerted because although he stood very much on the downhill side, he was looking me straight in the eye. Our pursuer was clearly extremely tall. He said he had overheard us speaking English and being an American wanted to introduce himself.

'I'm Layton Kor, from Colorado.' He was looking for a partner so I volunteered. He wanted to do a little-known grade VI on the Cima Piccola, the *Comici-Mazzarona*, first climbed in 1936. He would lead the aid with his newly developed chrome-molybdenum pegs and I would lead the free pitches.

At that point I hadn't done much aid climbing. I'd learned by watching Pete Crew climb Kilnsey's *Main Overhang* on the BBC and then doing it myself. I'd also raced up Malham's *Central Wall* twice in one evening, thanks to all the bolts being in. This was climbing? On the Cima Piccola, I was intrigued by a technique I had never seen or even heard about before – or since. Layton would quickly knock in pegs with a few blows and then tie them off with hero loops where they left the rock before moving upwards. When it was my turn to follow I found I could pull these pegs out with one hand. Except that every sixth peg was driven in harder to hold a fall. It saved so much time, he explained, when I quizzed him about it.

The previous winter, Layton had been part of the Anglo-American-German team that climbed the *Eiger Direct*, which after the death of John Harlin was called the *Harlin* route. It was fascinating hearing Layton's stories because they were so fresh in his memory. At the time I was an engineering student at Preston Poly. One of our tutors was a keen mountaineer and during one of his lectures had a radio tuned into the BBC to hear Peter Gillman's commentary. It was a thrilling story until the moment the rope broke. Now I was hearing from a man who was actually there.

Aid-climbing maestro Layton Kor on the Cima Piccola. *(Leo Dickinson)*

Kor adds his name to the summit register. *(Leo Dickinson)*

A month after I left Lothar Brandler, Werner Bittner, Denny Moorhouse and Steve's broken watch in the Dolomites, England beat Germany in the 1966 World Cup final.

Funny how life plays out. Fifteen years after that summer of 1966 I was, like Lothar Brandler, making climbing films of my own, including *Eiger Solo*, about the ascent of Eric Jones. For that film I recreated three of the most memorable epics that all mountaineers must know: the tragedy of Death Bivouac, the story of Toni Kurz and the Hinterstoisser and the moment the rope broke under John Harlin.

I remember that Tim Lewis, then editor of *Mountain* was none too impressed, thinking it was too Hollywood. But Peter Gillman went white. 'That's exactly what I remember.' Historian Audrey Salkeld justified it by saying, 'The *Eiger Direct* was a public media event.' Just to check, I did contact John Harlin III who gave the re-enactment his seal of approval.

I didn't see Layton again after that summer of 1966 until 40 years later. I was filming in Guam for Discovery Channel, following a salvage crew looking for sunken treasure. Apparently a Spanish galleon had hit a reef and the gold it was carrying, now worth $186m, sank to the bottom.

Denny Moorhouse packs a bag while Lothar Brandler looks on.
(Leo Dickinson)

A connection on one of my dive lights needed re-soldering so I left it at a local dive shop with my nametag attached. Next day I was surprised and delighted to find not only was it repaired but there was a note from Layton Kor who now lived on Guam and wanted to meet. I had a beer and being a Mormon he had a coke, although his faith did allow him a couple of wives. We had a lot of laughs reminiscing about the Eiger and the Tre Cime four decades later on a tropical paradise island from where, in those days, B-52s took off for Vietnam. Joe was right. People are interesting; mountains just exist.

ROB COLLISTER

A Cautionary Tale

Back in the day, when I was a pushy young alpinist but not yet a guide, Mike Esten asked me to be his deputy on a ski tour he was leading. My wife, Netti, who had not been skiing very long, came along too for her first tour. To cut a long story short, six of us met up in the Gnifetti hut above Alagna on the south side of Monte Rosa while another three waited for us in Zermatt. Apart from a hurried, viewless visit to the Signalkuppe, the weather kept us frustratingly pinned down in the hut. With two weeks to play with, the plan was to ski over to Zermatt but twice we turned back having slogged all the way up to the Lisjoch. On our third attempt the weather was still poor when the alarm went off but when we surfaced for a late breakfast it was to clear skies and no wind. It seemed our luck had finally turned and we hastily packed up and set off. Tim started with us but then turned back, feeling unwell. He agreed to return to Alagna and bring the car round to Switzerland. Had he stayed with us, I would not be writing this today.

Three hours of hard graft, breaking trail in deep wind-blown snow, brought us to the col. To our dismay, there was cloud in the valley below and the wind was picking up again. But at least it would be behind us, we reasoned, and with luck the cloud might dissipate or sink down. I know now that cloud in the valley is a very bad sign unless it is in the still calm conditions of a temperature inversion. At the time, however, the idea of turning back yet again was not appealing and besides, our friends in Zermatt were waiting for us. We decided to press on.

Skiing down, we lost some height but all too soon it became apparent that the cloud was rising to meet us. Approaching the first icefall, I was in front but the light was flat and I could see less and less. The Grentz glacier is notoriously crevassed and I became increasingly uneasy. It seemed best to turn back before we were commited. However, by the time we had put skins back on, it was already too late. The wind had become ferocious, blowing clouds of spindrift down the glacier, and it was soon obvious that making progress against it was no longer an option. We would have to stay where we were, in the open at 3,900m.

Our first plan was to dig a trench, roofing it with skis and cutting bench seats to sit on inside but it quickly became clear that this was not going to work. We only had a couple of shovels in the party and spindrift filled any hole as fast as we dug it. The wind had become so strong it was hard to stand upright and Mike recalls being blown off his feet. In the end, we created a crude windbreak with our skis and sat on our rucksacks in a shallow scoop,

Netti Collister arriving at the Gnifetti hut at the start of the tour.

our feet on the two ropes spread out as insulation. What saved our lives was the two-man Zdarsky sack I was carrying. I had long been sceptical of the orange poly bags that were de rigueur at the time but it was many years before the advent of KISUs (Karrimor Instructor Survival Unit) or bothy bags. Although intended for two it was just big enough for the five of us to pull the yellow nylon bag over our heads and sit down in a tight circle.

There we stayed for the next 24 hours while the wind lashed the fabric and we eyed the stitching anxiously. Often, we had to shout to make ourselves heard. At one point, someone straightened a leg convulsively with cramp and a split appeared in the nylon. Fortunately, Mike and Robin were able to adjust positions to sit on it or we would have been finished. Condensation on the inside of the bag created a layer of ice that was shaken all over us in a perpetual cloud of ice particles, making everything damp. We were not seriously cold; body heat saw to that. But it was hideously uncomfortable and claustrophobic. Even so, nobody whinged and Mike and Netti kept us entertained with stories and limericks. Netti remembers all five of us wordlessly bellowing 'Brindisi', the drinking song from *La Traviata*.

Our lunch food was soon eaten leaving only glucose tablets to pass around. Water in our bottles froze solid. It grew dark and, though we could not hear anything for the racket of wind and spindrift, frequent illumination of the tent made us aware that we were in the middle of a thunderstorm. The thought of our skis and ice axes outside became one more thing to ponder. Sometime in the dead of night, when morale was at its lowest ebb, Robin produced a fruitcake baked by his wife and for a few minutes we all cheered up.

Not until noon next day was there any hint the wind might be dropping and the mist thinning. We began peering hopefully through the ventilation hole every few minutes until, suddenly, we were rewarded by a glimpse of the north face of the Lyskamm 200m away and a patch of blue sky overhead. It was time to make a break for it but we were stiff and cold and packing up took an age. As soon as we emerged from the bivy sack our damp clothing froze solid so that we clunked around, like knights in armour; with frozen mittens doing anything with our fingers was problematic. Hypothermia was not far away. The ropes were so embedded in the ice that we had to hack them out with axes, cutting one so badly that we abandoned it. Although we knew the glacier to be dangerous, the idea of tying knots in the wire-like rope we had left did not bear thinking about, let alone skiing roped.

Eventually we set off. I was in front, Mike bringing up the rear, our route down the glacier now clearly visible. I started to struggle with iced-up glasses and Robin led the way for a while as we crossed the glacier to the far side. We could see crevasses ahead and I took over again, carefully skirting round one band of holes and then traversing a steep moraine wall to avoid another. At the end of the traverse I fell over with a thump, releasing a small wind slab avalanche that knocked Netti off her feet, though without burying her.

Soon after, we reached a point of safety where we could regroup before skiing on down to the Monte Rosa hut. By now, however, the weather was closing in again. Robin was agitated about the state of his toes and he skied off at once, without discussion. Netti, shaken by the avalanche, also wanted to get off the mountain as fast as possible. I was conflicted as there was no sign of Mike and John but the mist was about to envelop us and I was worried about finding the hut. We waited impatiently for several minutes and then set off, assuming they would not be far behind. In the event, we reached the hut without difficulty following Robin's track. Robin said later that he was guided to it by the smell of goulash cooking. But half an hour later, when we had wearily taken off our boots and outer garments and entered the cosy warmth of the living room, we realised that the others still had not arrived. I was berated by the guardian for not keeping the party together and I was just setting off back up the hill when, to our relief, they appeared. It transpired that John had cut a corner and fallen three metres into a crevasse, luckily landing on a snow bridge. Although he managed to climb out unaided it had all taken a long time.

Next day, Robin was flown out to hospital by helicopter and eventually made a full recovery. The rest of us skied without further mishap down to Zermatt where we learned that the storm had claimed the lives of 32 people across the Alps.

There are many lessons to be learnt from this epic but the most important has to be the value of carrying a group shelter. I am pleased to say it is now a standard piece of kit for British leaders at all levels from summer ML to IFMGA guides. The same is not true on the Continent. When seven people died on the Pigne d'Arolla three years ago, caught in a storm only 500m from the Vignette hut, they were found lying in the open with no shelter whatsoever. I rest my case.

History

'Alpenglow on Everest North Face', Philip MacLeod Coupe,
oil, 125cm × 176cm. *(Alpine Club)*

JOHN MIDDENDORF
'Engineered Beyond All Reason'
The Early Piton: 1870-1920

The cover of Fritz Schmitt's *The Mountaineer Today* (1937), with the piton's importance in 1930s alpinism clearly illustrated. Schmitt was a working-class climber who was fired from his job as a railwayman in 1933 for his opposition to the Nazis and went on to have a distinguished publishing career.

In the late 1800s, the Campanile Basso became one of the Dolomites' last great problems, one that Hans Barth, among the top free climbers of his day, dubbed the 'Dent du Géant of the Eastern Alps'. Part of the Brenta group, the spectacular sub-range of the southern limestone Alps in Trentino, Campanile Basso is hidden from the valleys below, so the sight of this wild 300m tower first appears at close range, drawing the climber's eye wistfully – and often fearfully – to its dramatic and lofty summit. Trentino was also home to the Società degli Alpinisti Tridentini, an organisation dedicated to reinvigorating Italian morale in the region as it chafed under the Austro-Hungarian Empire.

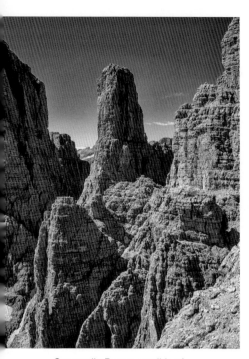

Campanile Basso, crucible of modern rock climbing.

Among their number was the wealthy photographer and innovative climber Carlo Garbari who wanted the summit of the Campanile Basso for Italy. In 1897, Garbari and his two guides made a spirited attempt, which involved intricate route finding and bold free climbing up exposed and difficult rock, spiralling up the south, east and west faces. After 300m, the team was stopped by a 20m headwall just short of the summit. At a small ledge later dubbed the 'Garbarikanzel', the Garbari Pulpit, the junior guide, Nino Povoli, boldly free climbed up this blank wall but was unable to commit to the final difficult and unprotected moves to easier ground.

Rope management had been evolving in the 1890s, especially in the eastern Alps, from the Alpine method where several people climbed together connected by a rope, all of them poised to support any slip of the team, to the system where a single climber led and another, the second, braced on the cliff, held the rope close in hand, perhaps wrapped around the arm for added friction. On Campanile Basso in 1897, without solid anchors on the small ledge of the Garbari Pulpit, a 10m factor-two fall on the static manila ropes of the day would either snap the rope against an edge or else the force would rip the trio from the mountain.

Nevertheless, in his book, *Half a Century of Alpinism*, the great Tita Piaz told a possibly tall tale of how, with the climbers perched among loose rocks covering the ledge, Garbari pulled a gun on his unwilling guides to force them on to the summit, an action, Piaz wryly noted, that 'saved Garbari forever from being bothered by unemployed guides.' Yet despite the urging of Garbari, it was not yet time for the summit of Campanile Basso and the team retreated.

Two years later in 1899, Austrians Otto Ampferer and Karl Berger followed Garbari's route to the ledge and were also stumped by the obvious direct route up the headwall. Instead, fearlessly, Ampferer made a blind and airy traverse around the exposed north-west corner, found a weakness up the middle of the imposing north wall and climbed onto the celebrated summit, 'a spacious plateau with a block altar in the middle'. The summit of what the Austrians preferred to call the Guglia di Brenta was won and the ascent became big news across the whole European climbing community. And in reporting their ascent in the 1899 *Mitteilungen des Deutschen und Österreichischen Alpenvereins* 'Reports from the German and Austrian Alpine Clubs', the Austrians acknowledged their use of pitons for the descent.

Subsequent ascents would add many more pitons to the route. In the 1907 edition of *Mitteilungen*, Hans Barth wrote:

> *As smooth as a snake, the wild rock tower rises an estimated 300m. It's a good thing that modern mountaineers have enough respect for these wild rock monsters that they don't kill them completely with wire cables, stairs and railings, [and only] mark vulnerable places with iron pins and rope rings.*

Barth noted that the second ascent of the Campanile Basso, made by two Munich climbers, had marked a number of these 'vulnerable places' with pitons. A fixed rope was also reported as being in place at one section. On Barth's ascent in 1901, made with the superbly named engineering entrepreneur and author Alfred von Radio-Radiis, he described bringing sharp steel pitons for the ascent and looking up from the base to a 'yellow-red overhang adorned with rope rings': slings and pitons. Later, unsure of where the route continued, he sees: 'A hook[1]! So it has to go this way.' At a tiny ledge, he notes:

> *Our predecessors once again had left their weapons in the body of this wild mountain, and we thanked them for their support.*

And again, on a section midway, where the route exits a chimney and moves out onto an exposed face:

> *The first climbers again tamed the stubborn rock with a hook, so one calms down about climbing the pillar.*

For the final bold climbing around the north-west corner to the final wall, he writes, 'an alcove with rusty hooks in it, above it a brittle outcrop with a hammered peg and a weathered hemp rope ring still seems to hold,' followed by a description of the committing moves above. In short, by the third ascent of Campanile Basso, the route had a good number of added pitons and safer belays. With increasing safety at precarious and exposed belays using piton anchors tied off with cord, short lead falls and swings onto the anchors could be risked. It was still a dangerous route for the time. In 1911, Eugen Prosch from Würtzburg fell while traversing the north-west edge at the Garbari Pulpit. Having disappeared from view, his companions heard a scream and there was a jolt on the rope, which then went slack. Prosch fell several hundred metres to the gully below and his body was cut in two on a sharp rock.

Yet despite such horrors, the arrival of pitons had transformed climbing

---

1. A direct translation of the German *Haken*, often used for peg. See later in the article for more on nomenclature. Barth also uses the word *Stift*, similar to the British English word 'peg' or 'pin', also German for 'pencil'.

on the Campanile Basso. In 1904, Nino Povoli (later written as Pooli) returned, redeeming himself by climbing directly up the headwall, presumably with a safer belay. (In 1907, Conrad Kain reported 'two iron spikes and a rope-off ring, and an anchor at the belay.') The mountain soon became a test-piece for the best climbers in the eastern Alps, including the Austrian alpinist Vineta Mayer with her husband and Joseph Ostler from the Kufstein, who made the eighth ascent. (A few years later, Vineta's sons, Guido and Max, helped pioneer their era's longest and hardest routes in the Dolomites). In 1908, the visiting American Oliver Perry-Smith led a bold new route up the south-west face, and in 1911 Beatrice Tomasson climbed the tower with Angelo Dibona and Michele Bettega.

Twelve years after the first ascent, Paul Preuss', solo first ascent of the east face of the Campanile Basso remains one of the most spectacular on-sight solos in climbing history, a 500m line that also became 'well-pitoned', according to the *AJ* 1961, despite its clean origins. One of the climbers that Tita Piaz most respected – along with Georg Winkler and Paul Preuss – was Rita Graffer, noted for her lead of the *Preuss* with her younger brother, presumably when the route was not yet 'well-pitoned'. She also put up a new 350m route on the south-west arête of Campanile Basso using 12 pitons in 1934. That same year, the *Alpine Journal* downgraded the original route to the status of 'classic', noting exactly 619 ascents to that point. In the later published 'piton debates' of 1911-12, Piaz argued that pitons for safety were justified, as life was more important than bravado, and regretted the 'double falls' of the time: when a falling leader also ripped the second to their death. Piaz deeply lamented Preuss' death, climbing solo on the north ridge of the Mandlkogel.

The early years of climbing on the Campanile Basso opened the eyes of many to new horizons in the vertical world. Yet it also illustrates that the story of alpinism's most inspiring climbs is also one of inventive minds: pioneers who realised the potential of new tools, refined them and then used them to venture onto ever more visionary lines up the most imposing vertical walls on Earth. But the process was always controversial, and nowhere more so than in the long and tortuous history of the piton. Its development drew on existing technology, advances in metallurgy, the design genius of a few visionaries and the never-ending debate among climbers about what constitutes an ethical ascent.

In 1880, A F Mummery declared the summit of the Dent du Géant 'absolutely inaccessible by fair means' after being turned back by a steep band of exposed slabs leading to the top. Several other teams had also tried and failed. Two years later, in 1882, Jean Joseph Maquignaz, his son Baptiste and nephew Daniel Maquignaz broke with Alpine tradition to forge a route up the slabs, over a period of days systematically hammering in a number of rudimentary pitons, described as 'stanchions', into cracks as hand- and foot-holds, fixing ropes as they went. Their clients, the notable Sella family, followed these ropes for the first ascent. The route, 'Sella's Staircase', is often said to mark the end of the Silver Age of alpinism. And with the extensive use of

The complexities of reaching the summit of the Campanile Basso became an ethical dilemma in the early 1900s.

mechanical tools for the ascent of the Dent du Géant, debate on the sporting limits of style and the use of tools in the mountains began in earnest.[2]

Eventually, hammered stanchions like those used in 1882 evolved and their name became 'pitons' in English while remaining Haken or 'hooks' in German. This article explores how this game-changing technology went from late Silver Age climbers using simple wrought-iron spikes to 1920 and the first 'modern' steel piton credited to Hans Fiechtl and other lesser-known climbers. It's a story about how ambition drives technological change, a never-ending cycle of one leading to the next, and how alpinism defines its own limits.

First Steps

The ice axe, the first iconic mountain climbing tool, was from the start used as it is today for both ice and rock, sometimes hooked on a high rocky ledge to assist vertical gain. As climbers moved onto longer steeper rock routes, ice axes were often in the way, and for a short time a metal hook became an alternative lightweight tool of choice. Edward Whymper, whose ascent of the Matterhorn closed the Golden Age of alpinism, carried a clawed hook attached to a short piece of rope. The 17-year-old Munich climber Georg

2. The second ascent was made less than a month later by W W Graham and the guides Auguste Cupelin and Alphonse Payot. Graham used all of the sieged ropes and pitons of the Sella expedition but also climbed to the other, slightly higher summit of the tooth. Soon after, he applied for but was denied membership of the Alpine Club, perhaps because of his use of what members considered unsporting methods to claim an ascent. The route up the steep slabs of the Dent du Géant is still to this day maintained with thick grabby fixed ropes; but even with the ropes, the route requires the skills and abilities of a 5.6 rock climber and very exposed climbing.

Edward Whymper's 'climbing claw'.

Winkler carried a hook attached to a rope, and occasionally used it for descent from the many rocky spires he climbed, perhaps even from his famous solo ascent of the Vajolet Towers in 1887. Sometimes called a 'grappling hook', the 'claw' could also be placed at the end of an alpenstock, according to Whymper though modern climbers might feel climbing on a blindly placed hook requires great faith.

As late as 1905, the Austrian alpinist and surgeon Günther von Saar described himself using a 'strong steel hook, in the form of a question mark, attached to a 10m rope' as a tool for descent. But after a few of these (as well as some ice axes) had to be left behind as rappel anchors, the straight hammered-in spike became a more logical and acceptable rappel anchor. For example, in addition to the short lengths of rope fixed on the Matterhorn from early in its climbing history, Hans Lorenz, writing in 1900, suggests that from 1870 stanchions were also being used for descent: 'And behold, there is a rusty broken *Stift* [pin] in the rock, hit more than three decades ago, a memorable sign of a memorable time.'

At the end of the 19th century, technical rock climbing began its branching-off from alpine mountaineering, which had become a popular activity by the early 1900s. The Deutscher und Österreichischer Alpenvereins (DuÖAV), created by merger of the German and Austrian Alpine Clubs in 1873, exploded in membership from fewer than five thousand members in 1874 to a hundred thousand by the 1910s. Memberships of the Club Alpin Français, Schweizer Alpen-Club and Club Alpino Italiano also expanded. Comfortable huts that could sleep 50 or more were constructed in the high meadows and on cliffs where there was once only a small shepherd's shack. New railroads allowed easy pan-European travel and tunnels bored through the Alps, like the Mont Cenis Tunnel completed in 1871, allowing easy transit under mountain ranges that had been a major expedition overland for the previous generation. The mountain dragons were being tamed.

The construction of an Alpenweg involving iron ladders and rods with wire cables for safety turned the Zugspitze (2692m) from a rarely climbed peak to a huge tourist draw, attracting thousands of what were known as Hochtouristen.

This infrastructure boom extended into the mountains. Existing routes were fixed with new equipment to aid a broader range of ability: these were the *Alpenweg*, with rungs and ladders fixed to overcome technical sections. A good example was the Zugspitze (2692m) in the Wetterstein range in the eastern Alps: modern Germany's highest mountain. A Bavarian army surveyor Lt Josef Naus claimed the first recorded ascent in 1820, but subsequent ascents were relatively few until an Alpenweg was constructed in 1875. A 15m slab was equipped with an iron ladder (the 1911 guide calls it the 'chicken ladder') and a series of drilled iron rods (*Eisenstiften*) with wire cables protected a slippery traverse. In 1897 a large refuge – the Münchner Haus – was built on its summit. The accessibility of Germany's highest mountain caused controversy in the Alpine clubs as thousands of *Hochtouristen* (high altitude tourists) swarmed the summit, with many alpinists lamenting how the 'Queen of the Bavarian Alps' had 'lost its horror.'[3]

The installation of metal bolts and wire cables[4] to protect exposed areas

3. The first cable car was constructed in 1926, from the village of Ehrwald in modern Austria, using technology developed by the mining history. Soon after, the mountain became a focal point for adventurous stunts and demonstrations of allegiance to the Nazis. Although it's worth adding that E L Strutt, in a 1942 *Alpine Journal* account of his adventures in the Eastern Alps in the 1890s, could still write: 'Even now, when the cliffs have been engineered beyond all reason, the climb from the Höllental still counts as a good expedition.'

4. The general use of hardware in the mountains increased rapidly in this period: Marmolada saw its first via ferrata up the west ridge in 1903, using Eisenstiften (iron rods) and wire cables to ensure safe passage for all Hochtouristen. Alpine clubs and militaries established new routes over passes between ranges, sometimes blasting steep gullies and cliff sides, also helping maintain control of the frontier, the natural defensive border between regions. Expanding infrastructure involved huge efforts to establish huts and rifugios in the

The south face of the Marmolada, first climbed in 1901 by a team including Beatrice Tomasson. The ascent was later downplayed by the influential historian Domenico Rudatis and faded from view until this century.

and provide steps and handholds in the mountains was referred to as *Anbringung von Versicherungen*, the 'Fixing of Security'. The phrase *Künstliche Hilfsmittel* (artificial aid) first appears in the 1880s, defined in the *Mitteilungen*. These included wooden ladders, ropes tossed over flakes and even rockets fired over summits[5], in addition to the iron rods and cables being installed on Alpenweg. (Bottled oxygen was also on the list.) Failure on a climb was often excused with the suggestion that the route was 'absolutely inaccessible without the use of artificial aids', as one report in 1891 put it.

For more than three decades after the time of Whymper, as climbing got steeper, lines on rock were primarily focused on major chimney features with 'windows': safe places often found in long deep cracks offering a good belay stance. But towards the end of the 19th century, climbers began venturing out onto the exposed faces of the Dolomites. To explore this wild new terrain, alpinism had to find a compromise between the wholesale equipping of Alpenweg (and similar but later via ferrata and Klettersteig) and a wholly pure free-climbing ethic. The debate of what constituted aid

deeper ranges. Metal rung ladders were drilled and cemented into stone slabs to avoid the need for any risky climbing in variable weather conditions, and more complex Alpenvereinsweg ('Alpine Club Trails') were designed and constructed: one project in 1910 on the western border involved 620kg of iron rods and 340m of wire rope, with 500 steps cut into the rock. In a single season, trail crews installed the 870 iron rods with expert rock drilling and anchoring techniques. The iron rods, weighing c1kg each and installed with chisel, soon evolved into lighter, more efficient tools for anchoring in rock.

5.   C T Dent wrote in his 1892 Badminton Library book *Mountaineering*: 'Climbers, more ingenious than prudent, have endeavoured, by means of rocket apparatus, to fire up a rope armed with a grapnel. This plan was tried unsuccessfully in an early attempt on the Aiguille du Géant.'

FIRST CLIMBING SHOPS

The indomitable Mizzi Langer (1872-1955), alpinist and rock climber, ski racer and entrepreneur, equipment designer and inspiration for a new generation of women alpinists.

The pre-First World War period in the eastern Alps was an era of heroic climbs up spectacular limestone cliffs that had once seemed unimaginable as climbs. As pitons were adopted from other industries, then manufactured for climbing purposes by local black-smiths, mass production and the ready availability of shop-bought hardware equipped a new generation of climbers pushing standards on big Alpine walls. One of the first dedicated gear shops, in business by 1900, belonged to Marie 'Mizzi' Langer (1872-1955), an Austri-an alpinist and rock climber, and med-al-winning ski racer. Mizzi's shop in Vienna offered all the latest equipment for the alpinist and skier, including well-designed and fashionable women's outfits for the mountains, advertised as 'sporty and functional'. Her catalogues showed women not just climbing but in the lead, inspiring a generation of women alpinists, such as Käthe Bröske and many others who were climbing at the highest levels. The main Klettergarten in Vienna is named after her.

Mizzi Langer's illustrated catalogues contained not only the latest equipment but also tips on the most modern skiing and climbing techniques. Gustav Jahn, an accomplished alpinist and artist, captured the Alpine zeitgeist with his seasonal illustrations: beautiful pristine ski fields in winter and the mountain experience in summer. Mizzi Langer catalogues were featured in the 1905 *Mittielungen*, a notable exception to the 'understandable rule' of the DuÖAV not to endorse businesses, thanks to the artwork of Gustav Jahn and technique articles by noted climbers such as Hans Barth.

The Austrian National Library has copies of Mizzi Langer's advertisements in the monthly periodical *Der Gebirgsfreud* (The Mountain Friend), which reported on a range of mountain activities from 1890 to 1941. Climbing gear listed for 1910 included rappel slings with ring (*Abseil-Schlingen und Ringe*), pitons (*Mauerhaken*), foldable candle lanterns for alpine starts and marking papers (*Marklerungsblätter*), which were sheets of red paper strips left at key spots of an ascent to mark a trail for descent. A pack of 50 were offered free to customers.

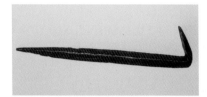 

Early wrought-iron *Mauerhaken* from c1880 and c1890 associated with the Zsigmondy brothers and Schmitt. Early pegs were simply metal-ware manufactured for other purposes that proved useful to alpinists. *(Messner Museum)*

in the mountains was further fuelled as new technologies brought alpinists more portable 'security' than heavy stanchions.

Twentieth-century climbing kicked off with Beatrice Tomasson's famous first ascent of the south wall of Marmolada in 1901, the largest steep big wall climbed at the time at over 500m. The wall had seen several attempts by then and several mountain guides had made solo reconnaissance. It was an obvious prize, a clear next step in big-wall climbing thanks to its size, altitude and prominence in the landscape. Beatrice, who was for a time the governess of E L Strutt, climbed the Marmolada with her regular guide Michele Bettega and Bortolo Zagonel.

The team used four pitons in key sections for their one-day ascent, although the ways and means of that ascent were debated for the next few decades. A description was never presented, so subsequent climbers had to figure out the route for themselves. The second ascent in 1902 by the German brothers Georg and Kurt Leuchs involved three days of initial reconnaissance, then two days on the wall in frosty conditions with a bivouac. Guido Rey climbed the route with Tita Piaz in 1910, describing his adventure in *Alpinismo Acrobatico* as the 'most difficult in the whole chain of the Alps.' Today, the route involves 27 pitches of climbing and has over 50 fixed pitons. Despite the route's significance and commitment, this landmark ascent was largely forgotten after the First World War, as its technical difficulty was eclipsed by a new generation of piton-assisted ascents in the Alps, and then written out of histories in the 1930s.[6]

In 1903, the Dresden climber Fritz Eckardt, philosophising in a series on the 'sporting side of alpinism', compared climbing to other athletic pursuits and noted how many sports depended on the tools as much as the capabilities of the sportsperson. (He also presciently discussed the problems of competition.) Eckardt noted how aids like wire ropes, pitons, bolts and handrails are called 'unfair means', using the English phrase presumably as a nod to British ethics, but that ice axes, ropes, crampons and snowshoes are tolerated. In the struggle of ascent, Eckhardt emphasised how it is nature that dictates the necessary equipment, those 'inventions of the human spirit'. It was clear by 1903 that for most leading eastern European climbers pitons could be described as 'necessary equipment'.

6. Italian historian Domenico Rudatis wrote two pages on how the Tomasson ascent was not a significant milestone. Thereafter, it disappeared from histories until this century.

From 1885, the term *Mauerhaken* ('wall hook') began appearing in the *Mitteilungen* as a hammered-in metal tool for security. Mauerhaken is not a term unique to climbing: it applies to any sort of masonry hook hammered between stones or into adobe dwellings and used for attaching lanterns, cooking gear, horse reins, signs and so forth. It dates back centuries: the double Mauerhaken was a common symbol on coats of arms representing security built into castle walls. Early electrical engineers adopted the term for insulators on telegraph poles (1886). Fire brigades included Mauerhaken as part of their climbing equipment for brick and stone structures well before it was ever used to refer to a piece of gear used for mountaineering (1877).

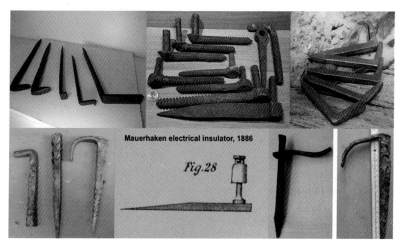

Mauerhaken electrical insulator, 1886

Fig.28

A selection of Mauerhaken.

In German, the general word for piton is still *Haken*, or hook. Among historical terms Mauerhaken is most common but *Stahlhaken* (steel hook), *Felshaken* (rock hook) and *Ringhaken* (ring hook) were also used, sometimes interchangeably. Karabiners were originally called *Karabinerhaken*. We also see *Eisenstift* (iron pin), used in the context of a hammered piton, such as the report on the ascent of the Dachstein (1876 *Mitteilungen*), which also involved fixing a ladder on the route. But Eisenstift as a bolt for a hole drilled with a drill or stone chisel soon became differentiated from Mauerhaken for cracks.

Steeplejacks (think Fred Dibnah) also used wrought-iron wall hooks, called 'iron dogs' (sometimes also called 'staples') for laddering up chimneys. The technique of connecting multiple ladders with hammered-in wall hooks to service tall industrial chimneys, designed to force pollutants high into the atmosphere rather than settling in local communities, dates back to the mid 1700s and was a burgeoning profession in the early climbing era.

Towards Lightweight Steel Anchors

Thus pitons were introduced, first as abseil anchor, then as belay anchor and eventually as aid for ascent on routes. For example, in 1894, Ludwig

Purtscheller reports on the first traverse of the Meije with the Zsigmondy brothers.

> *One of the most terrible abseiling points is located on the Zsigmondy ridge be-*
> *tween Pic Central and Grand Pic de la Meije, its height is thought to be around*
> *30m. The foot of the rock face, because it overhangs, is hidden from view. [We]*
> *overcame this obstacle by driving a Mauerhaken into a crevice in the rock slab,*
> *wedging it firmly with stones and attaching a Seilring [rope sling]. Such tricks*
> *with the rope are always a bit daring. They can only be justified in those cases*
> *where there are no other means.*

Seilring ('rope ring') can be an ambiguous term in the early journals as it applies to both metal rings, primarily used for abseil anchors (primarily called *Abseilring*), and also to a short sling of rope (also known as *Rebschnur* or *Repshuur* and later as *Seilschlinge*) used to connect the running rope to the pitons, called a 'running belay'. Note that well into the 1920s, a *Stahlhaken mit Seilring* (a steel piton connected to the running rope system with metre length of 5-7mm cord), was the standard system in the days before strong karabiners. Ropes slings, *Seilring*, were still the primary means of connecting rope and peg, and designers of the era discussed smoothing and rounding the piton eye to ensure there were no sharp edges to damage the attachment cord. Hence the standard technique of tying off a fixed

An unknown climber illustrating the use of *Seilring*, the method of tying the lead rope into a rope sling before the advent of karabiners.

piece of protection with a short loop of rope being the standard practice of the day; dynamic lead falls were not yet an option so a low-friction ring was not required and hemp on hemp does not have the same danger as later nylon ropes do with their low melting point. Early ring pitons used for climbing were made for other purposes and unless thick and heavy, a wrought-iron ring would have been a weak point in the system.

By the end of the 1800s, there are increasing references to three Mauerhaken being carried in a climber's pockets as standard equipment for many German and Austrian alpinists, along with rope slings to attach the pitons to the rope system. Fixed pitons were noted at crux sections in route descriptions, and by the early 1900s, climbers in the eastern Alps began to admit openly the use of Mauerhaken for ascent. During an ascent of the

What's he got in his pockets? The great Angelo Dibona (1879-1956), pioneering guide and ski instructor who claimed to have only placed 15 pitons when Luis Trenker asked him, six of them on the north face of the Laliderer. He was known to carry three or so in his pockets.

Watzmann, Germany's third highest peak, Wilhelm von Frerichs admitted in the 1903[7] *Mitteilungen* to driving a 'wall hook' to overcome an overhang: 'the rock became climbable, the terrible wall lay below us,' he wrote and then added, 'maybe this confession costs me my mountaineering reputation.' Controversy over the use of pitons would culminate in the Mauerhakenstreit debates of 1911-12.

The early *Mitteilungen* have frequent references to 'Haken mit Seilring', 'hook with rope ring', often in use as an aider for pulling on and also stepping into and sometimes referred to wryly as a noose, as climbers bypassed a section 'von Seilring zu Seilring', aiding up a line of fixed gear. It's easy to imagine the progression from using pitons with ropes slings as an occasional hand or foothold, to pitons providing protection for the roped climber a few moves past the piton.

Starting in the 1890s Oskar Schuster advanced piton-protected climbing to a high art on the sandstone crags of Elbsandsteingebirge. Schuster was one of the best all-around rock, ice and expedition climbers of the era and describes placing pitons (and bolts) 'of many sizes' on tricky leads.[8]

The game filtered south and climbers aimed initially to use pitons only for 'security' – belays and protection, and not for aid – and bolder free climbs became possible in the first decade of the 20th century. In a far cry from the rock engineering specialists busily establishing the early via ferrata at this time with literally tons of gear, the early Alpine rock climbers of the early 1900s were going light and efficient, from the ground up, with a minimum of tools to get the job done with a high standard of free climbing.w

The great Italian climber Tita Piaz made the sixth ascent of the Campanile Basso in 1902 and in the years after advanced the art to new levels on the limestone big walls in the eastern Dolomites[9], using pitons efficiently for

7. Von Frerichs wrote a 35pp retrospective of the Watzmann in the 1903 *Mitteilungen*.
8. Schuster made extensive explorations in the Caucasus but was caught there by the Russians at the outbreak of the First World War and died of typhus in an Astrakhan internment camp in 1917.
9. From the 1906 *Mitteilungen*: '[the Piaz-Wenter 1902 ascent], in particular, has become important for the future of the Guglia, because the first and still only authorised German mountain guide got to know and love this first-class climbing tour and since then, as a Guglia specialist, has climbed it many times.' Piaz was heavily involved with mountain rescue, including over 100 incidents in his career, and was known for his complex rigging when safe rope and anchoring techniques were required at a moment's notice. Throughout his career, Piaz adopted all the latest climbing tools.

Max Matthäus on the Winklerturm in 1911, illustrating how the rope lay across early pitons. *(Walter Hahn)*

rock-climbing belays and protection and mastering the use of a specialised piton hammer for faster and safer rock climbs up the steepest terrain.[10] He also had a technique to quickly attach a sling or a rope. While no one, frankly, has any idea of the design of these first steel pitons, I believe it was informed by pitons known from the Elbsandsteingebirge.

By 1911 Angelo Dibona with Luigi Rizzi and Guido and Max Mayer climbed an 800m route on the north wall of the Laliderer in the Karwendel range, equipped with six pitons, according to Dibona. The route required a bivouac and set new standards of difficulty on long routes. One section in particular required complex piton and rope work to overcome a tricky downward rope traverse.

Not much of the pre-1910 hardware survives, though perhaps some unidentified gear still exists in a local museum. By many accounts, they were not the round eyebolts depicted by Claude Wilson in 1893 and they were not all ring pitons, nor the L-shaped Mauerhaken. Available descriptions suggest instead they were likely flat blades of various lengths and thicknesses and thus probably custom made. While the definitive design of the first steel pitons is unknown, it was likely informed by bolts used in the Elbsandsteingebirge: a steel piton with an inline eye.

From Industrial Tools to Climbing Hardware

Most, if not all pitons used for climbing before 1900 were made of wrought iron rather than steel. Cast iron, with its high carbon content, is strong but too brittle for the purposes of climbing since it shatters when hammered. Wrought iron, as the name implies, can be worked thanks to its much lower carbon content and was a standard smithy material in the 1800s. The early climbing Mauerhaken were crafted from wrought iron in the forges of blacksmiths using hammer and anvil. Broadly speaking, impurities in the iron make it malleable; its internal structure appears almost fibrous, part of the reason it was aesthetically pleasing as well as structurally useful: think Crystal Palace or Eiffel Tower. Wrought iron can also be 'case hardened' by packing it in a high-carbon material and then heating it so that some of the carbon migrates into the iron. In the days before climbing hammers and

10. In the famous *Mauerhakenstreit* debates of 1911-12, Georg Leuchs commented on how Piaz was willing to use up to 30 pitons for an ascent, as reported by Hans Dülfer.

Top: 'The ghost of Hermann von Barth looks on in contempt at wall hooks and rope, the aids of modern climbing technology.' Above: 'There sits the indignant baboon. My dear gentleman. That's unfair competition!' Ring pitons illustrated, from *Der Alpinismus im Bildern*, 1911.

karabiners, these wrought-iron Mauerhaken, or 'wall hooks', were shaped like a 'L', and pounded into cracks with a suitable stone, then used as a hand or foothold, or rappel anchor. As a belayed point of protection for the next few moves past the anchor, climbers would make sure the rope ran over the wall hook but also often connected them to form a running belay using a Seilring, the knotted sling of cord.

We know also that pitons with an integrated ring were used before 1910. There is a mention in 1905 (of climbers being able 'to drive in a wall hook with ring very firmly, the rope is pulled through, we can finally calm down') and the influential mountaineering author Oskar Meyer mentions their use in 1910 as a point of abseil on the Brèche du Perron.[11] Most of these pitons are identical to tools used by loggers to lash log rafts together, called 'log dogs'. The rings appear to be spot rather than forge-welded, so would likely have been made in a factory rather than a local blacksmith's. But the term *Ringhaken*, 'ring hook', does not appear frequently in the old *Mitteilungen*.[12]

The evolutionary link between the original Mauerhaken and the modern piton was not, therefore, ring pitons but more likely a flat piton with a large inline eye that allowed the thick short cord of a Seilring to be passed through easily. In the pre-karabiner days, early articles on how to craft pitons emphasise the need to round out the eye in order to prevent damage to a cord under stress. In the days before electric welders in local shops,

11. The term also appears in the 1909 edition of Franz Nieberl's *Das Klettern im Fels*, with illustrations by Carl Moos, an excellent resource for studying climbing-gear evolution as updated editions appeared every decade into the 1950s.
12. Ring pitons, a flat blade of varying sizes with a hole and a welded steel ring, became more available from around 1910 with stronger steels, better welding shops and an expanding electric grid. The term Ringhaken became much more common in the 1920s when Sporthaus Schuster began selling flat pitons with welded rings, which were more commonly sold as rappel anchors. In the 1920s and beyond, the term 'Ringhaken' faded as climbers began primarily using the generic Haken, or Felshaken (steel hook).

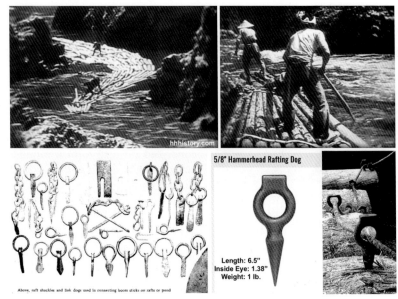

Log dogs or 'rafting dogs' used in the timber industry, compared to ring pitons.
The latter were difficult to manufacture before electric welding became available.

it would have been simpler to make flat pitons with a larger inline hole for cord, rather than a captive forged ring.

There were many designs of masonry wall hooks, some with rings for hanging items on walls or tying up a horse, but wrought iron rings would not be as strong as steel, unless thick and heavy. The earlier, wrought-iron Mauerhaken weighed at least 500g each (over a pound), and were long and thick. Case hardening wrought iron made it less malleable but it still wasn't practical for thinner pitons, which were required to protect cracks on the hard limestone routes being explored in the Dolomites and eastern Alps. A round spike hammered into dolomitic limestone would shatter the rock. A flattened wrought-iron spike would have been too weak with a tendency to bend and shear. What was really missing in the early 1900s was a thin piton that was strong and light. It was only in the early 1900s with the greater availability of hardened steel sheets, strengthened by the rolling process, that narrow pitons could be developed, coinciding neatly with this early era of technical rock climbing. The first published reference to steel pitons is from Hans Barth and Alfred von Radio-Radiis during their ascent of the Guglia di Brenta in 1901.[13]

13. *Ein Rebschnurgürtel, um sich gegebenen Falls buchstäblich aus der Schlinge ziehen zu können; scharfe Dolche für meuchlerische Verwundung in Form von Prima-Stahlhaken und den von den Erstersteigern verfaßten Steckbrief in der Brusttasche.* From 'On the Guglia di Brenta', Zeitschrift des Deutschen und Österreichischen Alpenvereins. Bd 38, 1907.

A PITON MYSTERY

It is interesting, perhaps ironic, that it may well have been Claude Wilson who coined the term 'piton' in the *All England Series: Mountaineering*, one of the first climbing instructional books in English and a 'practical guide for would-be climbers', published in 1893. Wilson, born in 1860 near Liverpool to a Quaker family, was among the most distinguished alpinists of his generation and a president of the Alpine Club. He climbed hundreds of the most difficult summits in the western Alps, including the first guideless ascent of the Grépon in 1892. In the *Alpine Journals* of his era, pegs were generally – and often disparagingly – referred to as 'iron stanchions' because that is exactly what they were in those early days.

In French mountaineering journals up to 1904, the word 'piton' occurs frequently, but only in reference to steep spires of rock and never as a metal stanchion. The *Bulletin Mensuel* of the Club Alpin Français' refers in 1883 to the anchors on the first ascent of the Dent du Géant as 'des coins ou pointes d'acier' (wedges or spikes of iron). The French alpine journal, *La Montagne*, first refers to a piton as metal hardware in 1918, specifically a 'piton de fer' (iron spike). In a 1916 report on the north face of Mont Aiguille, *le clou* (nail) appears as a 20 cm long metal anchor. Mont Aiguille's north wall was first climbed in 1895; the 1916 climbers removed *le clou* and proudly reported they did not use it for ascent ('sans l'aide'). It is one of the earlier references to a mechanical tool used for assistance on many ascents and descents of the era, yet generally ignored in the early French mountaineering literature.

In France, pitons gained greater acceptance when the great Armand Charlet acknowledged using them in the 1929 edition of *La Montagne*: 'soon we are at the chimney with *piton de fer* [iron peg]. This piton which until now I have always disdained, I am very happy to use today.' At the time, he was making the first winter ascent of the Dru and was in a storm at 3,500m, simul-climbing with his partner up a loose and icy chimney while an avalanche of debris was falling on them.

The British especially were reluctant to publish any reference to – or admit use of – pitons as a mountaineering tool in the early days of climbing, even the amazing routes in the Alps going up in the 1930s with the aid of pitons. A Cox read this before the Alpine Club in 1941: 'The piton, indeed, is in rather a different category, for it is never used, fortunately, as a mere convenience. Undoubtedly it possesses a power for evil, and it is healthy that it should be viewed with suspicion.' (Paul Pritchard recently remarked to me that 'avoiding pitons helped Britain push bold free climbing,' and it's true).

In Italian, *chiodi da roccia* (rock nails) is the name for pitons. The word 'piton' in Italian can be translated into English as 'to snape', a verb meaning to bevel the end of a timber. As early rock anchors for climbing were often wood wedges as well as iron stanchions, perhaps the Italian word for piton is the origin of Claude Wilson's reference. The word 'piton' also appears in French medical journals as a small peg hammered into bone in a surgical procedure so it's also possible Wilson, a distinguished medical man, borrowed the term from the French medical profession.

There was nothing new about steel, of course. The Japanese 'jewel' steel of a thousand years ago could, in the hands of a great sword smith, make a blade that was diamond hard at the cutting edge, tough on the surface but more malleable in the core. But until the mid 19th century steel remained prohibitively expensive for widespread use, made in small batches with charcoal or, later, coke: the various forms of crucible steel. Solving that problem, first through the Bessemer process and then the Siemens-Martin open-hearth system would be a turning point in industrial history.

Britain was the largest global producer of steel in 1850 with 50,000 tonnes per annum. By 1900, steel was made primarily with coke and output was measured in millions of tons per year. Germany, the world's second largest producer (after the US), was making four million tons of Bessemer steel and 1.5 million tons of Siemens steel per year. Wrought-iron production, largely from Sweden, dwindled to negligible quantities as wonders like Gustave Eiffel's tower were superseded by marvels like New York's Brooklyn Bridge, its steel made in Sheffield, and Manhattan's skyscrapers. The Iron Age had given way to the Steel Age.

The wider availability of stronger, harden-able steels required blacksmiths to broaden their skills, as industrial mass production reduced demand for locally worked metal-ware. Heat-treating metal was an evolving art and new steels required adaptation to find the right blend of heating, quenching and tempering. Given that blacksmiths were forging custom-made pitons, it's not surprising there are reports of bad ones, sometimes with the smith responsible identified in journals (on the Durreck, 1910: 'The first wall hook – from the blacksmith in Sand – bends. Only the second "real" one holds.').

The Modern Piton: the Fiechtlhaken

In the years prior to the first World War, a new piton design emerged, crafted from thin steel, which remains a standard design to this day. Hans Fiechtl[14] (1884-1925) a contemporary of Piaz, Dibona, Dülfer, Preuss and others, was a mountain guide from Münster in North Tyrol, and is credited with the first thin piton design with a larger offset-eye. Some histories credit his invention to 1910[15], but it is not until 1920 that the first published account of the Fiechtlhaken appears in the *Mitteilungen* in an article titled 'Das Versichern beim Klettern' (Security for Climbing), an overview of a basic protection system using rope, piton, karabiners and rope slings.

Reading the old journals it becomes clear that there was a marked increase in piton climbs – all considered 'artificial aid' ascents – from the turn of the century and by 1910 had become a boom. So it's likely that some climbers had access to versatile and lightweight pitons that could be quickly tied off safely prior to the Fiechtl design, but with its offset large eye, it was

14. In 1911, Fiechtl climbed a new route on the Zsigmondyspitze using thee pitons on a 'very smooth wall' for aid, and Fiechtl's route on the south wall of the Schusselkarlspitze with Otto Herzog in 1913 is recognised as one of the most difficult big walls of the pre-First World War era (it is also the climb where a karabiner might have first been used on an early big-wall pendulum.)

15. The date of the first Fiechtlhaken is unclear, but there is a reference suggesting Fiechtl might have still been using traditional wrought-iron Mauerhaken on the Rofanspitze in 1908.

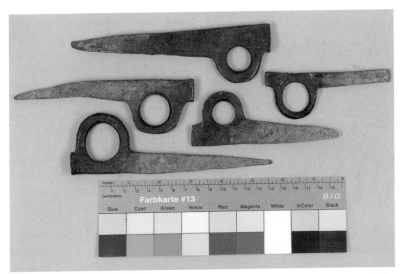

Fiechtlhaken, named for the innovative equipment designer Hans Fiechtl (1884-1925). These are likely not pre-First World War but typical of the pitons Fiechtl was manufacturing and sharing.

quickly realised as the most functional and became the new standard.

The early Fiechtl pitons were likely cut from sheet steel[16], then tapered (i.e. made thinner at the end) by hand, a hole punched, and then heat-treated to the desired hardness. To fabricate the larger holes for the eye so they could accept a thicker cord, the smith would use a stud or slot punch and then use a series or progressively tapered tools, called 'drifts', to get the hole to the desired shape and size.[17] The 1920 article explicitly recommends smoothing and rounding the piton eye to ensure there were no sharp edges to damage the attachment cord.

The offset-eye piton design has two major advantages: the eye, when nailed to the hilt, provides extra support in vertical cracks, and the offset-eye design reduces 'oval-ing' of the eye when the piton is being pounded, thanks to continuous material through the centreline. Limestone cracks are hard and brittle, but also can be very undulating, so the proper hardness of the piton – not too soft, not too hard – will allow the piton to thread deep into tricky placements without shattering the rock. Fiechtl and his blacksmith figured out the optimal hardness for a good limestone piton, and shared the new design widely.[18]

16. Rather than forged from a billet, as later Lost Arrow designs were, though horizontal Fiechtlhaken were also forged in the early 1920s from steel billets.
17. If you wanted the hole to swell below the centre-line of the stock, as with the eye of a piton to maintain a straight top line for hammering, you would make the hole offset toward the side of the stock, in effect the bottom of the placed piton, according to modern blacksmith Mitchell Goldman, via email correspondence, 2021.
18. According to Horst Höfler, Fiechtl's early pitons were made in Münster, where he lived at the time, between the Karwendel and Wilder Kaiser ranges, where technical big-wall rock climbing began. Note Fiechtl's name is often misspelled as Fichtl in the literature. Mühlbacher is still the name of a large local engineering business.

The fatal 'double fall', illustrated in an oil painting from 1880 by Munich artist Ernst Platz (1867-1940).

US Army piton from 1950, made to Fiechtl's design.

Awareness of better protection systems increased as piton-craft became more accepted. The 1920 'Security for Climbing' article with its first Fiechtl piton image was written in response to a sad accident witnessed by the author when the second was killed after the leader fell, known at the time as a 'double fall', and mentions that finding 'pleasure in danger' is fine but only if going solo. Optimising security, especially for a belay, for a team is perfectly justified for those who value life.[19] In the pre-Great War period, there were some who had developed good protection technique with pitons, and many who did not either out of principle or lack of access to the new tools, but the teams that adopted the new protection devices put up some incredible big walls. The original Fiechtl design has stood the test of time and remained popular well into the 1960s. The US Army made thousands of this design, and even today titanium versions are still available.

Flat Fiechtlhaken are good in vertical cracks, but poorly loaded in horizontal cracks. Necessity breeds invention and sometime before 1922 horizontal pitons also appeared, with the blade at a right-angle to the eye, a design generally known as 'Lost Arrows'[20] in Yosemite. Horizontal Fiechtlhaken are more versatile as they work for both vertical and horizontal cracks; the added torque on the blade when loaded in vertical cracks is often beneficial to its holding power. Despite the varied designs and means of manufacture, all early pitons with the characteristic offset eye became known as Fiechtlhaken.

19. The author describes the piton as a 'wrought-iron pin used as a Mauerhaken, whose head is forged into a fixed ring, combining all the advantages of strength, suppleness, and equity', but it's clearly a description of steel, not wrought iron. Climbers and authors were still mistakenly referring to pitons in this way into the 1930s and even today, calling the early mild steel pitons as "soft-iron" (they are steel not iron). Wrought iron has a maximum hardness of about c100 Brinell. I recently tested a mild steel US WWII Army piton at c200 Brinell, and the mild steels of Fiechtl's era would have been hardenable to this hardness as well. By comparison, modern 4130 chrome-moly knife-blades are equivalent to c375 Brinell.

20. To make a 'horizontal' piton from a flat Fiechtl design, a blacksmith would hold the blade of the piton over the face of the anvil with the eye of the piton pushed against its side and with repeated blows 'set down' the material with the hammer, changing the profile of the steel to be less narrower and wider, make it more suitable for a horizontal placement.

Perhaps the finest Fiechtlhaken ever made, crafted by Bugatti engineers for the king of Belgium, c1930. *(Società degli Alpinisti Tridentini)*

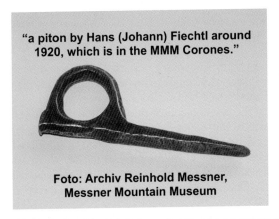

"a piton by Hans (Johann) Fiechtl around 1920, which is in the MMM Corones."

Foto: Archiv Reinhold Messner, Messner Mountain Museum

Y_ROUTE in Northface of Sekarlspitze, FA: H.Fiechtl/E.Schmid, 1923 Piton from Hermann Huber Collection (found in 1964 on route)

In the early 1920s, the brand August Schuster München, sold in Schuster's Rosenstrasse shop, began mass producing pitons.

Larger cracks were sometimes protected with wood wedges until the 1940s and the invention of angle pitons that required new materials, principally chrome-moly steel, and manufacturing techniques. It should be remembered that the best climbers of the early 20th century were exceptional layback, off-width and chimney experts, even by today's standards, and boldly ran it out on wider cracks and chimneys at a time when anything longer than a three-metre fall on the ropes of the day was a dice roll. Pitons were generally carried in coat pockets, and tales and tips were shared on awkward tricky placements on run-out leads: deftly placing a good anchor with one hand.

Flat pitons with welded rings were also produced in various sizes in the 1920s and beyond, but considered less versatile. They were less safe in horizontal cracks because of awkward loading on the ring and best employed as rappel anchors. Long serrated Fiechtlhaken were introduced as ice pitons. But flat and horizontal pitons with the offset eye were the two main designs for the next several decades, and both designs have ever since been referred to as Fiechtlhaken, with many variations of the blade.

Some time in the 1920s the brand ASMÜ (August Schuster München), sold in Schuster's shop on Rosenstrasse, began 'mass producing'[21] flat and horizontal pitons with blacksmiths in Bad Oberdorf in the Allgäu mountains.

21. Hermann Huber clarifies: 'having seen the workshops in Bad Oberdorf, I can only say it was not a real industrial mass production but they must have been quite busy meeting demand. The ASMÜ pitons were more or less a monopoly in Germany for a while.'

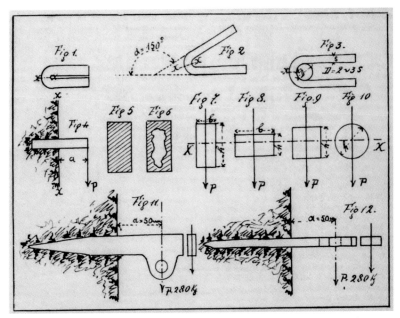

By 1926, the design and heat treatment of thin steel mountaineering pitons had become a science.

ASMÜ's pitons were shipped worldwide, finding their way into mountain ranges all over the world – and into the history books. By the 1930s, mountaineering journals around the world were sharing the art of piton-craft; the art of rock climbing had been transformed.

ERIC VOLA

The Devil's Needles

How Raymond Lambert Lost His Toes

The Aiguilles du Diable suitably lit. *(Alamy)*

In the telling of this story, I could not stop thinking of our late-lamented Doug Scott. Raymond Lambert and Doug had so much in common. Both were stars who did not behave as stars. They also had the same 'mountaineering spirit' and, if Raymond had lived long enough, he would have loved to help Doug when in 2007 he promoted the Spirit of Mountaineering commendation within the Piolets d'Or. Replace the 'Devil's Needles' with 'The Ogre' and you will find the same superb mountaineering and human qualities in both men and in their friends who did more than their best to bring them down safely. Raymond, who was so proactive in helping Tenzing with his Himalayan Mountaineering Institute in Darjeeling, would have responded positively if Doug had asked him to participate in his Community Action Nepal activities. So, I hope readers will view this story as a tribute to the unique mountaineers Doug and Raymond were.

In March 2022, Victor Saunders, the Alpine Club president, sent the following letter (but in French) to the Androsace Club in remembrance of the feat on Everest 70 years ago by their members including Raymond Lambert who teamed up with Tenzing for the summit assault in 1952. He also thanked them for their contribution to the successful 1953 Everest expedition.

[To t]he president and members of the Geneva section of the Swiss Alpine Club.

Seventy years ago, climbers from Geneva reached their highest point on the south-east ridge of Everest. Their achievement was quite remarkable because most of their route had been exploratory.

Initially following Shipton's expedition of the previous autumn through the Khumbu icefall they were the first to cross its final huge crevasse to gain entry to the Western Cwm from where they reached the South Col alongside l'Éperon des Genevois. They [Tenzing and Lambert] then succeeded in placing a tent at about 8,400m where they spent the night without sleeping bags or even a stove with which to make a drink, and the following day reached their high point of about 8,595m. From there they were able to confirm that the route onward looked feasible as far as the South Summit. The information they gained was generously passed to the British expedition of the following year, greatly helping them to take the final step in the journey to the summit, making it the achievement of a succession of expeditions.

In the words of Dittert in Les Avant-premières à l'Everest, 'Les expéditions montent sur les épaules les unes des autres. Nous sommes montés sur les épaules de Shipton, lui sur celles de Houston, ceux qui viendront après monteront sur les nôtres.'

Those climbers of the Swiss expedition in Spring 1952 all came from Geneva and were members of the Androsace Club. It is interesting to note that the climbing team of the British expedition of 1953 were also all members of a single club (including the New Zealanders), namely the Alpine Club. It therefore gives me the great pleasure as president of that club to send our very warmest congratulations to climbers from Geneva on the 70th anniversary of their quite extraordinary achievement.

Victor Saunders

Many older climbers will remember the name of Raymond Lambert, the powerful and renowned Swiss guide from Geneva who with Tenzing reached a height 200m or so short of the summit of Everest during the 1952 Swiss spring expedition, a new level of achievement that contributed to the success of Hillary and Tenzing the following year. Most will also remember that Raymond climbed on Everest in specially made shoes, the size of a child's, after losing all his toes during a storm in the Mont Blanc range and

Raymond Lambert and Tenzing Norgay on Everest in 1952.

how this did not prevent him climbing extensively in the Alps and later in the Himalaya and Andes. But few will know the events that caused the loss of his toes, which ended with a rescue that will remain unequalled in the history of the Chamonix guides.

At the time Raymond was 24 years old and at his best. In 1937, he graduated first from the guide school of the Valais and before that, at the early age of 19, he had discovered the joy of winter climbing with a traverse of the Grépon. The year of his graduation as a guide, with his pal Marcel Gallay, about the same age, he made the first winter ascent of the Caïman and the Crocodile, two of the Aiguilles of Chamonix and quite a significant ascent at the time. Two years before, in 1935, with Giusto Gervasutti climbing with Renato Chabod and Raymond climbing with Loulou Boulaz, a top climber with quite a few first female ascents, he had made the second ascent of the Croz spur on the north face of the Grandes Jorasses, unfortunately learning on their way down that the first ascent had been done two days earlier by Rudolf Peters and Martin Meier. In 1936, also with Loulou, he made the second ascent of the north face of the Petit Dru, opening a variant to Pierre Allain's crack, the first grade VI in the Mont Blanc range, which became famous as the Fissure Lambert. In 1938, Raymond was already considered to be one of the best climbers and overall mountaineers of the time.

His next target with Marcel would be the first winter traverse of the Aiguilles du Diable, the 'Devil's Needles', up to Mont Blanc du Tacul, a traverse first done in the summer of 1928 by the famous French Chamonix guide Armand Charlet with another guide, George Cachat, and two American clients, Miriam O'Brien and her future husband Robert L R Underhill. At the time it was considered one of the best routes in the Mont Blanc range with five dramatic tops over 4,000m.

Les Aiguilles du Diable vues de la Brenva   Photo André Roch

A visual glossary of the Diable ridge.

Raymond Lambert and Marcel Gallay prepared very well. During the summer they discussed thoroughly the use of snowshoes, skis, sleeping bags and the terrain (glacier, snow and rock). Raymond had done the traverse in the summer 1933 with Loulou Boulaz so knew the route well. Then, in December 1937, Raymond told Marcel that the party would now be three. Erika Stagni had become a regular client and that summer of 1937 Raymond had done a dozen significant routes with her in the Mont Blanc range including a first ascent on the Pointe de Nantillons. She was aged 22, was pretty, energetic and climbed fast: the perfect client for an ambitious young guide and her mother was a wealthy lady of Geneva, Mrs Amstutz.

In those days – no cable car of course – it took two days to reach the foot of the climb, stopping overnight at the nearest refuge, the Requin (2516m) four hours from the top of Montenvers railway. An attempt in early January, without Erika who is ill, is abandoned when the weather turns, so they wait for another opportunity.

Day One

Monday 7 February 1938. The three climbers leave Geneva by car at 5am, an early start as they want to stay not at the Requin that night but at the La Fourche bivouac hut, then known as the Borgna, at 3,600m on the French-Italian ridge between the Tour Ronde and Mont Maudit. The following day they intend to make tracks up to the col du Diable. But on the road a heavy wet mist slows them down and they only reach Chamonix at 8am, stopping at the Hotel des Alpes to collect the special sleeping bags they ordered from Pierre Allain's Paris shop. They then stop at the Hotel des Tines to prepare their rucksacks, leaving behind anything unnecessary. At 10am they set not for La Fourche but the Requin hut. The weather is perfect,

An image from summer illustrating the complex terrain of the Diable ridge.
(Ed Douglas)

their spirits very high, but Raymond has a bad cold or flu. As soon as the snow allows, they put on their skis. When they reach the Requin hut at 7pm, Raymond goes straight to bed having swallowed a cup of tea and several aspirin. Marcel and Erika make a good soup before joining him.

Day Two

Tuesday 8 February. They leave the Requin at 10am. Raymond's illness has gone, the weather is magnificent: not a single cloud. The glacier is in perfect condition, better than expected, so they easily overcome the Géant seracs and reach the foot of the Capucin du Tacul where they stop briefly to drink. Right above them, the Aiguilles de Diable are lit up by the strong sun. It's warm and they take off their jackets.

They leave their skis at the foot of the slopes coming down from the Gros Rognon and a rucksack with some food, which they intend to take on their way down, and put on their snowshoes. They want to reach La Fourche before night falls. The snow is hard, the way up easy and they comfortably navigate the crevasse zone until a snow bridge breaks. Marcel is out in front and he falls in. Lambert, solid as a rock, soon has him back on solid ground like a package. They laugh like kids and Marcel in those few minutes realises that Erika Stagni knows her way in the mountains and that Raymond is as strong as ever.

At last, having overcome La Fourche's bergschrund, they are on the ridge and at the small Borgna hut (3600 m) fully covered by snow. After clearing snow off the door, which overhangs the void, they enter the hut. It is tiny, just three mattresses with some blankets and cooking equipment. The weather is clear, the view magnificent and the night superb.

Day Three

Wednesday 9 February. They wake at 5am and after breakfast prepare their feet against the frost, putting camphor cream on their feet, then mustard flour and newspaper around the inner shoe. At 6.30am they start on the ridge and reverse quickly their way up the previous evening, thanks to the steps they have cut. The day is perfect, the five aiguilles are silhouetted against the sky: the Corne du Diable, Pointe Chaubert, Pointe Médiane, Pointe Carmen, l'Isolée and then Mont Blanc du Tacul.

They re-cross the La Fourche bergschrund and traverse the Maudit cwm, heading straight towards the Diable gully, climbing up its right side to reach the base of the aiguilles. Up to this point, the snow and rock conditions have been perfect; they did not need either to use their crampons or cut steps. For Raymond, such conditions are better than summer. At 10am they are at the col du Diable (3951m). The air is fresh. Following an easy crest and ledges, they reach the gap between the Corne du Diable and Pointe Chaubert. The day is warming up and they rest a few minutes.

They bypass the Corne du Diable and start on Pointe Chaubert, without gloves. Raymond leads. At each belay, Marcel joins him first and then they both lift the heavy rucksacks before Erika follows. The climb is on dry and

A Francis Marullaz photo of the Aiguilles du Diable. Marullaz was the lodestar of the Androsace, the Genevois climbing group of which Geoffrey Winthrop Young wrote: 'Mountaineers could not hope for a better guarantee for the future than that the younger generation of Swiss.' He was also the stepfather of distinguished neuroscientist Krešimir Krnjević, whom he introduced to climbing. *(Francis Marullaz)*

warm rock but the rucksacks seem to hit every snag and the snowshoes from one fall into space and down the gully. They reach the top of the Chaubert at 2pm. The weather is magnificent. They have now in front of them the Pointes Médiane and Carmen. Two 25m abseils get them to the gap (4017m) at the foot of the Médiane, a splendid 80m vertical wall of strenuous V.

The difficulty increases but Raymond is fully fit again and his two companions climb well and fast. But the sun has turned and they need their gloves now. Marcel takes the lead and night is coming when they reach the top of the Médiane at 6pm. They look for their planned bivouac site, 10m below the summit. They have done three-quarters of the route and most of the difficulties are now behind them. They clear snow from their bivouac site against a wall. Everything seems fine, the view is magnificent and they all feel in perfect condition. They sleep peacefully in their sleeping bags.

Marcel opens one eye and sees the moon with a halo. He says nothing, goes back to sleep but with a little pinch in his heart. At midnight they are roused by an unusual sound: their kitchen is shifting from a gust of of wind. Within a few hours, the sky is covered in clouds and snow starts falling. By 3am they are trapped in a storm.

Day Four
Thursday 10 February. Morning comes but the bad weather continues. Around 50cm of snow has fallen on the rocks and they themselves are covered with a layer 20cm thick although, thanks to their equipment, they have not yet felt the cold. Their night has almost been comfortable.

At 7am they are ready to go. Their situation is serious and there seem to be three options. The first is retreat but climbing back over the Pointe Chaubert is impossible. The second is dropping down the gully between Chaubert and Médiane but the avalanche risk is far too great. They would be swept down like wisps of straw. The last and only realistic solution is to finish the

Climbing the Isolée. *(Francis Marullaz)*

A view down the ridge showing its exposure.
(Rémi Thivel)

traverse and reach the summit of Mont Blanc du Tacul where they know the way down will be easiest.

Raymond reaches the gap below the Pointe Carmen and traverses to its foot. The climbing is only mild IV but the rock is now white with falling snow and icy in places. Their ropes are frozen, their clothes wet and now they feel the cold. Marcel belays Raymond and at last he reaches a stance. It has taken two hours to climb 30m. Erika reaches Raymond and then Marcel, still on the Médiane and higher than Raymond and Erika, slides the rucksacks on a tight rope towards his partners. One arrives too fast, splits open and its contents, their food, disappear into the abyss. This will have a dramatic impact for their future bivouacs.

When Marcel joins the others, it is noon and the snow continues falling. They are also surrounded by fog. Soon after, they reach the summit of Pointe Carmen. Now they can see the last aiguille, l'Isolée, surrounded by grey clouds. Two abseils later they are at the gap beneath l'Isolée (4054 m) comprising overhanging cornices. The void beneath is masked with heavy cloud. From time to time, they catch fleeting glimpses of the Tacul ridge. They avoid the Isolée, crossing its foot to step onto the snow-covered ridge leading to the summit of Mont Blanc du Tacul. The needles are passed. But it snows continuously, a thick blanket of treacherous powder. The first slope is steep and nothing to make a proper belay. Before, on the traverse, the wind could not get at them. This is no longer the case. The maelstrom throws snow in their eyes, blinding them, and it is now bitterly cold.

Overcoming this slope takes a long time but they believe that once up it they will be at the summit and safe. But when they reach the ridge below the summit, the storm has become an awful hurricane. The cold is terrible, and they have had no food since the previous night. They blindly follow a rocky ridge covered with ice. The strength of the storm is such that at one stage, Erika, two metres below the ridge on a tight rope between Raymond and

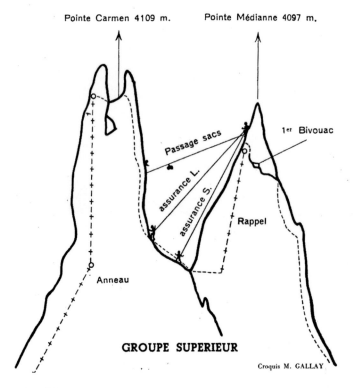

Schematics of the team's descent from the Pointe Médiane and the second bivouac.

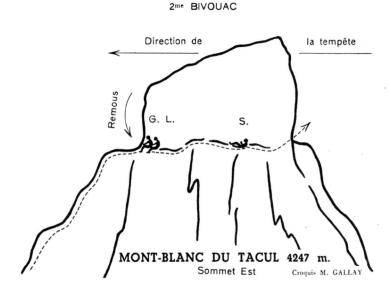

Marcel, is lifted and blown to the other side of the ridge.

At 3.30pm, they reach the summit of Mont Blanc du Tacul. They try to descend but blasts of wind throw them down in the snow. Visibility is now zero; it's impossible to find one's bearings, impossible to walk against the storm. The wind is so strong that they must hang on in order not to be swept away; they cannot breathe through the nose. Raymond fears their lungs will freeze if they continue.

In fact, to insist means certain death and so Raymond decides to bivouac. They look in vain for shelter. On the south side, they finally find a tiny ledge that will make a precarious niche where the wind is not blowing so strongly. Raymond and Marcel do their best to improve its defences for Erika. They tie her off to the rock. She will be able to spend the night well protected from the wind and the snow. But the shelter is small and only Erika benefits. Raymond and Marcel remain on a slanting slab facing the full blast of the storm. The wind is freezing them; the snow infiltrates their sleeping bags. Their long night is terrible.

Day Five

Friday 11 February. At around 8am they get going again. Visibility is not good but they can't stay where they are. The temperature has fallen to -40°C. They decide to get down to the col du Maudit (4051m) following a ridge that should give them some protection from the wind. They are roped together with Raymond leading. Erika is picked up by a blast of wind and then starts slipping but manages to stop herself. They are constantly brushing ice from their eyelids as it totally blinds them within seconds. They go further down the ridge hoping to reach a point where the storm relents but when they reach the altitude of the col they are swallowed whole by the storm. They are separated by only five metres of rope but even so, they cannot see each other. The wind and snow blind them. Each feels as if they were totally alone in this freezing whiteness. Marcel catches Raymond to speak to him but is frightened by the sight of his totally white face.

'Raymond, we cannot get down further. We must find a shelter, if not we are lost!'

They have now reached the Maudit pass and are headed towards a slope that appears steep. By chance, Raymond discovers a small crevasse where they will spend their last two bivouacs. The hole is two to three metres long and at its end they discover a cavity. They start enlarging this until they have enough room for the three of them and then close the entrance with blocks of hard snow and ice. Outside the temperature is still -40°C but inside it's not much below 0°C. However, the crevasse is watery, so everything becomes wet quickly. Their first action will be to take care of their feet by rubbing each other. Marcel's left foot is already frozen. Raymond feels that both his feet are frostbitten and some of his fingers too from climbing the Pointe Carmen. Erika, thanks to her excellent circulation is still okay.

They are both hungry and thirsty, having consumed nothing for the last two days. Looking in their rucksacks, they discover only some bits of chocolate,

Model illustrating the final bivouac in the crevasse on the col du Maudit, taken from Marcel Gallay's account of the ordeal, *Une Tragique Aventure au Mont Blanc* (1940).

three dried fruits, a Maggi soup bag and aspirin tablets. Nothing else. They try in vain to light a fire. Everything is far too wet. They shave the wooden shaft of an ice axe into small pieces but even these remain frozen solid. With their last match they manage to light paper they had laid down. A small flame burns for a while but before they can melt any ice it sputters out. They still mix the Maggi soup tablet with snow and swallow that instead. They then cut each dried fruit in three and chew them slowly. Erika gives hers away.

Inside their shelter the darkness is complete. They use their rucksacks to block the entry. Night comes. The wind is still so strong that snow invades the crevasse and settles on their bodies. They finally manage to seal the entry with a pair of snowshoes. While Raymond and Marcel discuss the possibilities of being rescued, Erika promises that if they all get out alive, she will take care of all expenses for treating her companions' frostbite. She says she will buy a place where all three can live together and asks them to kiss a religious medal that she wears around her neck as if to sanctify this oath.

Raymond will name their shelter: 'the hotel of slow death'.

Day Six

Saturday 12 February. When they wake up, trapped inside the crevasse, they think that the weather has relented, but when Marcel pierces a hole in the wall with his ice axe, they realise the storm is still raging.

They are thirsty and hungry. To eat, they have only the aspirin tablets left. To drink, ice cut with an axe that burns their throats. Raymond and Marcel take out their leather rock-climbing slippers to cut off small pieces to chew. When Erika sees Marcel's knife she screams.

'You're not going to kill me and eat me, are you?'

Marcel laughs. 'We're not there yet.'

Marcel and Raymond are convinced that rescue parties must have started looking for them. But will they find them? Usually storms last a maximum three days and then relent. Two days have gone, so maybe tomorrow the storm will cease? All they can do is wait. Raymond is overwhelmed by his responsibility. Marcel encourages him.

'You'll see! The weather will improve. We must hold on.'

Their thirst is atrocious. They will end up drinking their own urine using a cigarette box. The thirst and the need to absorb something warm are stronger than their revulsion. Erika tells them that her mother will do everything to have her rescued, so they must hope. The wind blows ceaselessly, the ice around them cracks and they do not even know exactly where they are. Night comes. They rub each other to make sure none of them will fall asleep to avoid numbness. This will be their third night without sleep.

Day Seven

Sunday 13 February. When daylight arrives, they can no longer hear the storm. It's 8am. Marcel punches a large hole in the door letting in the still strong wind but he also sees… the sun! He shouts:

'We are saved!'

They swiftly decide to go down but first they must dig their way out of the crevasse. This takes a lot of effort. Once outside, they recognise their position, near the Maudit pass and facing Mont Maudit. The altitude is 4,051m. The cold is so intense and the wind so strong that they have to go back to the shelter of the crevasse, which they can now see is on the edge of a 1,300m drop. After a long wait, they are ready to go again and leave most of their unnecessary equipment in the crevasse.

They don't get far. Advancing slowly, like drunken men, they suddenly find themselves in a thick mist: impassable! Raymond realises that with his two companions going so slowly, they do not stand a chance. They go back again to their shelter again and start enlarging it so they can stand but in doing so, part of the ceiling falls down, letting in the intense cold. They try to repair it but in vain. They throw much of their previously abandoned equipment outside in the faint hope that rescuers may see it. But in the crevasse, their hope is gone. They seem lost.

Their last chance would be to reach one of the rescue parties that must be looking for them. Descending as three would take too long and be too complex. But they do not want to leave Erika alone. So it falls on Raymond, the guide, and by far still the strongest, to go. It is his duty. He must, at all costs, find the rescue party and tell them where his companions are, even if he loses his life in doing so. Marcel embraces him, convinced he will not see his friend again and Raymond leaves.

Marcel and Erika start a long wait. Twice they will try to go down but in vain, the clouds are much too thick. Their last attempt leaves them without any strength. Marcel never stops rubbing Erika lying in her sleeping bag. Slowly they enter into nothingness. Marcel is certain he will die but still he encourages Erika.

'Has Raymond succeeded?'

Although convinced otherwise, Marcel tells her he is certain that Raymond made it.

'Do you think my feet are frozen?'

'No. Not at all. You just don't feel them.'

'You're not going to leave me, are you?'

'No way.'

Erika asks Marcel to pray with her. She is obsessed with her feet, which Marcel continues to rub.

'I prefer to die than to have my feet frozen.'

Each time she says something desperate, Marcel reacts to boost her morale. Erika promises that if they survive, she will take care of Marcel and his young wife as well.

Night comes. Their fifth bivouac begins. Their clothes and sleeping bags are wet. All night, Marcel goes on rubbing Erika who has bouts of delirium about her feet. Since Raymond left, no one has taken care of Marcel's feet. He has nothing dry to put on them, particularly the heel of his left foot which is in contact with the ice as he braces himself to rub Erika's feet properly. Their thirst is atrocious and even Marcel becomes delirious at times.

Raymond meanwhile has been showing his best qualities as a mountaineer, finding his way down despite the fog. Tired, frozen, tortured by lack of food and sleep, he has only one fixed idea: get down at all costs and find the rescue party. He has left his two companions whose lives fully depend on him. He must succeed.

Several times he has to climb back up to find the route, crossing for a second time many crevasses. During one bright interval of clear weather, he sees the Chamonix valley in the sun. Two hours later he is back at his high point, a few metres from his companions' shelter, lost for three hours because of the heavy fog. He could let them know he's back, but he thinks it would have a disastrous impact on their morale and so he starts back down again.

Finally, he finds the normal route and seven hours after his first departure, he climbs down the bergschrund and reaches the col du Midi, continuing towards the Gros Rognon on the way down to the Requin hut. His tracks are those of a drunkard. He is wading now through snow that reaches his knees. His feet have no feeling. He could stop, and his ordeal would end, but no, his companions are counting on him, he must go down, always down: get to the Requin hut and the rescue party.

Walking towards where they left their skis, he sees one of the rescue parties that have come up from Geneva. Skiers! He shouts, but they do not hear him and continue down. He gesticulates and shouts again as loud as he can. At last, the skier leading them points his arm towards him; they turn around and come towards him. The rescuers have just decided to abandon their search.

They had looked for them in vain and were going down to the Requin hut. It's Loulou Boulaz, René Dittert, René Aubert, Muller, Robert Gréloz, Bader and Bonnant: his dear friends from Geneva.

They give him some cognac that burns his insides. Raymond tells them where the crevasse in which his companions are and the others help him ski down to the Requin. It is late now and they are exhausted, so they pass the burden of rescue to another party. When Raymond finally reaches the Requin hut, he faints. He wakes the following day in pain. His friends have been taking care of him all night, waking him every so often to make him drink warm soup and tea. But he only thinks of his companions, his mind tortured with the idea that one more night and the crevasse will become their icy grave.

At around 9pm, three guides from Chamonix arrive: Paul Démarchi, Arthur Franchino and Michel Payot. They had been on their way to explore the Mont Mallet area when they crossed paths with Loulou Boulaz and Robert Gréloz who told them to go to the Requin hut. Raymond tells them where his companions are. They ask him the same question many times as they believe he is delirious. They want to be certain. He tells them they must reach his friends before daylight, if not they may believe he has failed and attempt to come down by themselves, which would mean their certain death.

Raymond warns them of the terrible cold but that doesn't stop them. They leave at 11.30pm. At the Requin the temperature is -31°C; on Mont Blanc du Tacul it must be -40°C. They reach the crevasse at 6.30am plunging through snow up to their bellies from the Midi pass onwards. Raymond's tracks have already been covered by fresh snow. During the night 20 more guides and friends from Geneva arrive with Armand Charlet at their head and the personal doctor of Mrs Amstutz sent to take care of Erika. He examines Raymond's frostbite. They plan to leave in the morning, to take over from the first rescue party of three, with orders to get Erika down and take care of Marcel Gallay.

Day Eight
Monday 14 February. At 6.30am, Marcel and Erika hear noises, then voices. One, two, three heads appear in the crevasse's opening. The Chamonix guides, Payot, Démarchi and Franchino have found them. The first thing they do is to give Erika and Marcel a one-litre bottle of rum that they drink in seconds, like it was water. Then the guides give them some dry clothes and blankets.

Their orders are to rescue Erika, so they start down with her. She leaves without even looking at Marcel who remains behind alone with some sugar lumps, some dry prunes and what is left of the rum. The Chamonix guides tell Marcel that at most he will have to wait two to three more hours before a second rescue party comes up to take care of him.

At noon he's still there, alone. He shouts and shouts and finally, after waiting six hours, the Chamonix guide Jérôme Bozon appears. Marcel gets himself out of the crevasse to the guides' astonishment. Armand Charlet arrives with Luc Couttet, Walter Marcuard and Francis Marullaz, the last two being Marcel's friends from Geneva. An avalanche has covered the previous party's tracks and they have lost a lot of time. They cut off Marcel's wet trousers, tie him in blankets like a bundle and start the 3,000m descent. One of his friends tells him:

'Lucky, we didn't listen to the party taking down Miss Stagni. They had told us: "Don't go up. It's useless! Gallay is done for."'

Marcel learns that the first rescuers who took care of Erika came directly to their crevasse while the party that saved him had been looking a long time and may not have found him if he had not shouted. It takes three hours for the party to reach the col du Midi (3544 m) where more rescuers are waiting.

Some other friends from Geneva are there. They tie Marcel on skis and the descent continues until they reach the Requin hut at night. Raymond has refused to be taken down until he was sure Marcel had been rescued and was safe. Then five friends have started down with him on a sledge to the Tines, before he is taken by ambulance to the La Colline clinic in Geneva where he is soon joined by Erika Stagni, the Chamonix guides, Paul Démarchi, Arthur Franchino, Jérôme Bozon, Michel Payot and his friend from Geneva, Francis Marullaz and then the following day, Marcel Gallay.

Raymond writes later: 'The hotel of slow death could not keep its prey.'

Aftermath

Erika Stagni left the clinic after three weeks totally unscathed, thanks to Raymond but most of all thanks to Marcel's constant attention during their last two bivouacs. She continued climbing all her life, particularly with Robert Wohlschlag, (nicknamed 'Pellebrosse', because of his thick red hair that was hard as a brush) a powerful climber from Geneva who eventually married her. Among the top routes and first rock ascents Erika did with him was the first female ascent of the *Brandler-Hasse* in 1964. She was certainly one of the best lady climbers of the years between 1940 and 1960, and the richest: lucky Pellebrosse!

Several Chamonix guides who suffered frostbite were treated at the same Swiss clinic in Geneva, their expenses covered by Mrs Amstutz. Paul Démarchi and Jérôme had all the toes of their right feet amputated. Paul lost two from the left. He had been so badly frostbitten that he was brought down on a sledge from the Requin hut. A third Chamonix guide lost one joint on each toe of his right foot and two others suffered less severe frostbite that kept them in hospital for three weeks.

Raymond lost all his toes, three joints on fingers of his right hand and one of his left. That didn't prevent him from becoming the most famous Swiss guide of his time. 'I am now equipped with the hooves of a chamois,' he said when he wore his custom-made new shoes the size of those for a 12-year-old kid. As a guide, he was very much like Gaston Rébuffat, taking clients up hard routes, but as a climber (and as a character) he was much more like Lionel Terray: powerful, daring and very friendly. A unique combination!

Raymond and his friends from the Androsace performed incredibly well during the spring 1952 attempt on Everest, considering they effectively climbed without oxygen. The apparatus they had could only be used properly at rest and was only used by Raymond and Tenzing above the South Col. Their friendship with the Sherpas and particularly Raymond's with Tenzing was unusual at the time but typical of 'the best mountaineering spirit'. After the 1952 attempts, Tenzing did not want to join John Hunt's expedition, preferring to wait for the Swiss to return. Jill Henderson, secretary of the Himalayan Club in Darjeeling, tried to convince Tenzing but to no avail. So she wrote to Raymond Lambert asking for his help. Raymond wrote the following letter to his pal Tenzing:

Hop Tenzing, ça va bien?

My life is back to normal in my quiet Switzerland, far from Everest where we have lived those intense moments. No day goes by since that I don't think again of the moment we turned around, with our finger touching the summit. But at least we are here to talk about it.

Miss Henderson told me of your hesitation about returning to Everest with the British. You would be too tired; you would not want to go back without us. You, Tenzing, tired? I find it hard to believe it … In case, here is a jar of Ovomaltine to perk you up. As far as we are concerned … After the English, it is the French who got the permit, whatever happens. For me, the summit of the world will remain forever a dream. But for you everything is still possible: your quest has not ended. The mountain that no bird can fly over is waiting for you. And if you get to the top, my friend, a part of me will also be on the summit. So, we will not have given, risked everything in vain.

After receiving this letter Tenzing went to see Miss Henderson and told her that he agreed to join the British team. On their return, after their success, John Hunt's expedition made a stop at Zurich where the whole Swiss team, Raymond Lambert at their head, toasted them with champagne and Tenzing gave back to Raymond the scarf he had taken with him to the top of the world.

Tenzing returned to Switzerland several times, each time staying with Raymond, his dearest friend, who trained him for his new job as director of Himalayan Mountaineering Institute in Darjeeling. This comradeship between Tenzing and the Swiss was very different from his relationship with the more hierarchical British. (Tenzing had been to Garhwal with André Roch's Swiss team in 1947.) The Swiss considered Tenzing to be like them: a mountain man and their equal.

After the Swiss expeditions in 1952 to Everest, in 1954 Lambert made an unsuccessful attempt on Gaurisankar and then went to Cho Oyu with Claude Kogan, another great female climber. What happened there was typical of Raymond's mountaineering spirit. Arriving at base camp, they discovered a small Austrian expedition was already there and had already made a first attempt on the summit. Exhausted, they were resting before their second try. Raymond's companions wanted to press ahead after the Austrians refused to join forces. But Raymond told his companions:

We will not! In the mountains there is a law, an unwritten moral code that does not allow competition to take over even between rival parties and even if those are from different nations! And there also is a principle of anteriority!

Despite his team insisting, Raymond didn't budge and with support from Claude Kogan he decided to let the Austrians have two attempts before making their own. The Austrians duly succeeded but by then the weather had worsened. Raymond and Claude Kogan reached 7,730m before turning around. In 1955 he finally succeeded in the Himalaya, making the first ascent of Ganesh Himal (7429m), again with Claude Kogan and Eric Gauchat. There were further expeditions, to the Andes in 1957 and an attempt on Distaghil Sar (7885m) in 1959. After that Lambert started a new career as a famous mountain pilot.

In his tale of their ascent of the Aiguilles du Diable and the subsequent rescue, published in the journal of the Swiss Alpine Club, Raymond ended thus:

*I have the feeling I did my duty despite everything and I am happy that Miss Stagni has been brought back safe and sound to her family. Time, the great healer, will help us forget those painful hours, but in the bottom of our hearts, we think: **long live mountaineering!***'

For Marcel, the ordeal was longer and more damaging. Erika's promises of help, particularly with medical expenses, were brushed aside by her mother on the grounds that Marcel should have had insurance. So Marcel was moved from the private clinic to a public hospital in Geneva. He was well looked after but in those days frostbite treatment was quite crude, particularly when the damage was so deep as it was for Marcel. His toes and the heel of his left foot were so badly frozen that all these were amputated and he never climbed again. His misery was accentuated by the feeling he had been abandoned by Erika but in fact it was only her mother who was able to dispose of the family's wealth. Marcel expressed his gratitude to his rescuers:

I am indebted to the guides and my friends, who risked their lives to rescue me, and I express once again all my gratitude.

But he added:

They, at least, did not bargain with their dedication. What I have never understood is the cruelty of the fate which since the arrival of the first rescuers separated me from my companions, always keeping me apart, with no aid or encouragement, even from my partner Erika who, as far as she is concerned, got out unscathed from this adventure.

Marcel Gallay showed unequalled courage but was psychologically as badly injured as physically due to the attitude of Mrs Amstutz.

One final questions remains. Considering the extreme weather conditions, why did Chamonix guides agree to a rescue party? Their past and future behaviour shows that in such horrendous conditions and with so many hazards, they ordinarily refused to risk their lives, particularly in winter. Why in this case did they show so much bravery and such unique mountaineering spirit? In my opinion, the answer is threefold.

First, Mrs Amstutz promised double pay to all the guides agreeing to rescue her daughter. Second: Armand Charlet. He was at the time the leading Chamonix guide and his word and moral authority with the Chamonix guides were paramount. The money alone was not enough, since in almost all other cases it was offered to no avail. Armand had great panache and the Aiguilles du Diable were his domain. Finally, Raymond and Marcel had many climbing friends in Geneva and the Valais. Those friends shared gallantly the burden of the rescue with the Chamonix guides. They all showed real boldness and true mountaineering spirit despite the premium wages offered to the guides. All his life, Raymond felt deeply indebted to all the rescuers, the Chamonix guides and his friends from Geneva. As he wrote:

I cannot find strong enough words to express my gratitude.

Bibliography

M Gallay, *Une tragique aventure au Mont-Blanc*, Coopérative d'Imprimerie Genève, 1940.
R Lambert, 'La traversée des Aiguilles du Diable en février 1938', Bulletins annuel, Club Alpin Suisse, 1939.
R Lambert, *A l'assaut des 'quatre mille'*, Editions Jeheber, 1953.

J G R HARDING

The Mountain Life
of Freya Stark

Herbert Arnould Olivier's portrait of Freya Stark, painted in 1923 when the explorer was 30. She began travelling in 1927, following the death of her sister Vera. *(National Portrait Gallery).*

Dame Freya Madeleine Stark, who died in 1993 having reached her centenary, achieved a degree of fame as a traveller that few other British women have rivalled. Showered with medals and awards from learned societies and academic institutions, she was awarded the CBE in 1953, created a dame in 1972 and latterly became a friend of the Queen Mother. She was also an honorary member of the Alpine Club. Widely travelled, she had an unquenchable restlessness that saw her pony-trek aged 77 through Nepal and the Himalaya, albeit supported by a BBC television team. Her name is still familiar even to those who have never read a single page of the two-dozen books of travel and autobiography she intended as her epitaph.

As a desert traveller, she was compared with 19th century women pioneers like Lady Hester Stanhope, Jane Digby El Mesrab, Lady Anne Blunt and Gertrude Bell: 'intrepid solitary Englishwomen exploring the far-flung corners of the East'. *The Telegraph's* full-page obituary blithely portrayed her as 'journeying into the wildest parts of Syria, Turkey, Persia, Afghanistan and the Himalayas' while that in *The Times* described 'a woman who travelled the hard way in male lands,' although she did once ask her publishers to send her a tin bath.

Freya Stark's courage, steely determination and scholarship are undeniable; she also possessed literary genius. But she never made desert journeys of any significance and her claims as a pioneer traveller must rest not on two over-hyped south Arabian journeys in 1935 and 1938 but the three she made through the mountains of Persia between 1930 and 1932 and her ride from Hakkiari to the Tigris some 25 years later. Janet Adam Smith's timely corrective in her *AJ* 1994 obituary of Stark – 'long before she had made her name as a traveller and writer she had made her name as a mountaineer' – lends useful perspective. For mountains were always the metier that guided her paths and provided the stage for her most challenging adventures.

That Freya achieved national treasure status within her lifetime reflected an exceptional determination and force of character driving her to attain the fame she craved. Born in Paris in 1893 to Bohemian artistic parents, their peripatetic lifestyle and unhappy marriage ended in a separation that left Freya confused, insecure and miserable. Her rootless teenage years in provincial Italy were blighted by the ill health that forever dogged her. Although her adolescent years never lacked for intellectual and artistic stimulus, she was a shy, gauche and awkward girl ever conscious of her face having been permanently disfigured by an accident when she was thirteen: her hair was caught in machinery and her right ear torn off, requiring skin grafts. These inauspicious beginnings only steeled her resolve, strengthened her instinct for self-preservation and developed a highly competitive and ruthless streak buttressed by sublime egotism.

As a child brought up at Asolo, where she lived in a house belonging to the artist Pen Browning, the looming shadow of the Dolomites imbued in her 'the love of hills in the years before memory'. When her parents moved to Drogero, a mountain village ringed by the Maritime and Cottian Alps with Monte Viso dominating the eastern skyline, their sight 'filled me with a strange yearning and has done ever since'. To seek solace from an unhappy marriage, her father was wont to retreat to a tiny mountain hut called La Messigliera where he found the company of smugglers and chamois hunters more congenial than the domestic hearth. Freya often came along as his companion and together they would trek all day through the Piedmont foothills with the glittering snowfields beckoning above.

Freya's early setbacks were cast aside in 1911 when at 18 she enrolled at Bedford College, London. Here she renewed an adolescent acquaintance with William Paton Ker ('WP') a distinguished scholar and later the Professor of Poetry at Oxford. Ker early recognised Freya's unusual intellectual

The Macugnaga or east face of Monte Rosa, which Stark climbed in 1924. *(Alamy)*

qualities and became the friend, mentor and adopted godfather 'who taught me all I know about English literature.' WP was also a member of the Alpine Club, elected in 1908 aged 52 with a reputation for exceptional physical strength and endurance. On the regular annual Alpine visits he made until the outbreak of the Great War, his delight in the company of the young included Freya whose mountain yearnings he transported to a higher plane in 1913 when he introduced both she and her sister Vera to 'the hazards of mountaineering' in Italy's Gran Paradiso range. Here, the sisters did their first roped climb on the Petit Pousset and then went on to climb the Grivola, Gran Serz, Herbetet and Torsiva with WP and guides.

Freya's promising mountaineering career was interrupted by the First World War and in 1916 her private life shattered when her fiancé, the 39-year-old Italian artist Guido Ruata, broke off their year-long engagement and married his former mistress. To restore her self-esteem, Ker suggested she enrol as a nurse in G M Trevelyan's Italian ambulance unit. She served for eight weeks in a Voluntary Aid Detachment near the Italian-Austrian front based at the Villa Trento forward HQ where Geoffrey Winthrop Young, severely wounded by shellfire while driving his ambulance four days before Freya's arrival, was about to have his left leg amputated. He survived this traumatic operation on 7 September. Freya later recalled in *Traveller's Prelude* (1950) 'creeping in and hearing Geoffrey Young playing to himself on the piano.'

In the immediate post-war period, impoverishment, illness and domestic disharmony further tested Freya's resolve. However, by 1919 she had recovered sufficiently to join Ker in Courmayeur from where they completed the circuit of Monte Rosa, trekked up to the Brouillard glacier, and traversed the Cima Blanca and Betta Forca. They also climbed Freya's first 4,000m peak, the Zermatt Breithorn, a 15-hour day which ended disagreeably when WP adjudged their guide so incompetent that he refused to shake the wretched man's hand after paying him off. Before leaving Courmayeur an incident presaged trouble to come when, on climbing to the col du Géant hut (now the Torino), WP experienced minor heart troubles. Undeterred, they moved on to Macugnaga, the alpine village under the shadow of Monte Rosa, which Ker had always regarded as his 'holy of holies'. Their successful ascent of the Pizzo Bianco, Ker's 'special mountain', was the first by a woman.

For the next couple of years Freya was subsumed in her family's complicated domestic affairs, but in 1921 her decision to take up Arabic (rather than following WP's bizarre suggestion that she learn Icelandic) marked a signal

Freya Stark in Jebel Druze, Syria, in 1928. *(RGS/Alamy)*

turning point. Mountaineering was resumed two years later in 1923 when Ker invited her to join his family party at Macugnaga, selecting the Pizzo Bianco as a first objective with Ker, two of his granddaughters, Freya and his guide Tofi. Ker was now 68 and although 'very strong and happy that day', was struck down by a heart attack; he sank to the ground murmuring 'This is my mountain,' and expired. While Tofi raced down for help from the valley, the three women waited besides WP's body for seven hours.

After Ker's burial at Macugnaga's churchyard, Freya decamped to Zermatt to join her mother taking with her Tofi. From Zermatt, the two of them crossed into Italy via the Cima di Jazzi before embarking on a traverse of the Matterhorn from Zermatt to Breuil. While descending fixed ropes on the Italian side Freya's frozen fingers lost their grip and she fell. Left dangling at the end of Tofi's rope she quickly recovered and they returned to Zermatt across the Theodul pass having completed the traverse in the fast time of 17 hours. Later that year, Freya visited the Pyrenees with Venetia Buddicombe, an adventurous aristocrat whose cool elegance Freya much admired. After wandering about the hills, making a leisurely two-day ascent of Canigou, Freya observed that the Pyrenees were 'wilder than the Alps'.

The following year, 1924, Freya returned to Macugnaga with her mother, ostensibly to join a Ker family visit to WP's grave. Her covert object was to climb Monte Rosa's east face by its greatest route, the *Marinelli* couloir, notorious for its length and avalanche danger. The team consisted of a Belgian and his guide, Freya, Tofi and a porter. After a seven-hour hut march they began the climb that same night at 11pm as a very early start is essential to negotiate the couloir: a 'highway for the avalanches of Monte Rosa which pour down with a dull soft sound as if they were milk.' At one point, Freya disappeared into a crevasse to the horror of her mother who was watching progress through a telescope below.

Having safely exited the lethal couloir, they still had to climb the Lys glacier, near vertical in places, with Tofi cutting steps continuously for five hours. They reached Monte Rosa's summit after 12 hours but took another four to find safe haven at the Margherita hut. The following day, the Belgian was so sick with altitude that his guide rushed him down to Zermatt while Freya, Tofi and the porter returned to Macugnaga by the Italian side. Freya's accounts of this magnificent expedition, only the second by a woman and 'the only really big climb of my life' were written many years after the event: 'all detail forgotten.' She had originally intended to return and put up a new route with Tofi 'but illness intervened and the longer climbing was over,' leaving her to repine 'the loss of mountaineering more than most things'.

In 1927 Freya enrolled at the School of Oriental Studies (SOAS) in London to advance her Arabic. The following year she embarked on her first journey to the Near East, again with Venetia Buddicombe. Intent on exploring the volcanic Hauran plateau in south-west Syria (now the Golan Heights) this mountain tramp, accompanied by a local guide, a mule and two donkeys, almost ended in disaster due to Freya's insouciance in blithely disregarding official warnings that this dangerous Druze territory was under strict martial law. Eventually arrested as spies, they were lucky to be released after only three days' detention. Venetia described the experience as 'a grim little journey'. For Freya it was a magical *entrée* to the Oriental world.

While at SOAS Freya had learned Farsi as well as Arabic and now looked eastwards to Persia. After centuries of decline, a country that boasted three thousand years of civilisation was undergoing radical transformation under its dynamic new leader Reza Khan. Appointed shah in 1925, Reza instituted a crash programme of industrial modernisation, social change and the brutal re-settlement of Persia's nomadic tribes. This had one positive effect: making areas previously blighted by internecine tribal warfare, brigandage and extortion comparatively safe for travellers. Both the Elburz mountains and Luristan fell within this category and Freya was determined to visit both.

For Freya the Elburz held a special fascination as the site of several reputedly inaccessible Assassin castles secreted within its mountain fastnesses. The history of this Ismaili sect whose suzerainty over much of 10th century Persia and Syria had been secured by a network of strategically sited fortresses, was coloured by their unsavoury reputation. Revisionist historians have re-evaluated the Assassins as cultured and devout rather than hashish-crazed fanatics, but Freya's romantic nature inclined to the older tradition. Moreover, as few Europeans had penetrated their Elburz redoubts, she was determined to be the first woman to reach the most famous of them all – Alamut. Built by Hasan-i-Sabah the 'Old Man of the Mountains', on a massive rock overlooking a remote valley, here he trained his *Hashishin*, 'hashish eaters', in the dark arts of assassination with the promise of an eternal afterlife in a paradisical garden where lubricious houris satisfied every fleshly need.

Panorama of the Takht-i-Sulaiman massif, photographed in 1956. Left to right: Alam Kuh (4826m) from north-east ridge; Sarchal glacier; and Takht-i-Sulaiman (4665m). The massif's glaciers are largely gone. *(J G R Harding)*

In May 1930, she set out from Qaswin with two muleteers in search of Alamut and duly attained the goal that only one European, Lt Col Sheil in 1838, had achieved before her. Amidst its ruins, she ruminated on the fate of nations and how in 1256, Hulagu, grandson of Genghis Khan, had wantonly destroyed both the castle and its priceless library. Pressing on up the Shah Rud to Garm Rud, she undertook a hazardous climb of over 4,500ft to reach the ruins of another legendary Assassin castle, Nevisar Shah to become its first European visitor.

Freya now headed north to the Caspian coast by an ancient trade route across the spine of the Elburz. On breasting the Salambar pass her sight was arrested by a group of striking peaks to the east. Having correctly identified one of these as Takht-i-Sulaiman, the Throne of Solomon, her imagination was seized by the ancient legend of how the wily King Solomon had lured Bilquis, the Queen of Sheba to share his bivouac or freeze to death on its summit. But it was the throne's distinctive pyramid which she fancifully likened to Switzerland's Weisshorn, the 'Queen of the Alps', that fired her ambition to be the first European to attain its summit.

Freya's research was generally meticulous but apparently not as regards the exploratory history of these genuinely alpine peaks. Under winter snow, the 4,619m Takht-i-Sulaiman, the Throne of Solomon, undoubtedly bears resemblance to the Weisshorn, yet an immediately adjacent mountain Alam Kuh, significantly higher at 4,826m with a magnificent north face and six-kilometre glacier at its base, had already been climbed in 1902 by the Austrian botanist brothers Bornmüller from the upland southern basin of

Hazarchal where, in 1843, another Austrian botanist, Theodor Kotschy had spent several weeks on scientific research. That no European had made a serious attempt to climb Takht-i-Sulaiman was due to local insecurity, problems of access and the Caspian mist that envelope these mountains in summer. Nonetheless, Capt J B L Noel (later photographer to the 1922 and 1924 Everest expeditions) had spotted them in 1913 en route to India to make his covert Everest reconnaissance. Curiosity prompted him to strike inland through Mazanderan's deciduous jungle to reach the Kalardasht valley from where Takht-i-Sulaiman is visible on a clear day and accessible within two days' hard trekking. But Noel went no further. Freya had read his account in the *Journal of the Royal Geographical Society* for June 1921 but drew no conclusions.

In August 1931, Freya left Qaswin on her second Elburz venture with the Throne of Solomon her prime objective. But whereas her previous year's journey had been in May with the high peaks still snow-covered, she now chose the hottest and unhealthiest month for travelling. Initially retracing her 1930 route, she bagged her third Assassin castle at Lamasar, but then contracted a series of illnesses in the malaria-ridden Shah Rud valley. Grounded for a week in the village of Kandichal 'slipping from coma to coma' with malaria and heart trouble, she got word through to a young doctor who gallantly interrupted his own family holiday to make a five-hour journey to offer aid. After diagnosing malaria and dysentery, he injected a cocktail of camphor, emetine and quinine, allowing her to continue on muleback while he meekly bowed attendance. A second bout of illness enforced another week's halt at Bara Rud where the selfless doctor administered quinine injections three times a day while fortifying himself with opium and *arak*.

Alam Kuh's north face and north-east buttress (centre) from the summit
of Takht-i-Sulaiman. *(J G R Harding)*

On reaching Garm Rud, she hired a second guide, Hujjat Allah, 'the refuge
of Allah', to lend support as her regular muleteer Aziz was faltering.
Weakened by illness, she found the mule-back climb to the Salambar pass
'steeper than the way from Zermatt to the Hornli Hut', but recovered enough
to descend the spectacular Gelza Rud gorge and then swing south up the
Sehazar Rud to Darigan, the last village in the valley. Here, to her chagrin,
she discovered the tearful, homesick Greek wife of a Hungarian engineer
commissioned by Reza Shah to investigate the area's potential for shooting.
Put out by having to accompany this miserable lady the following day to the
hot springs of Abigarm, Freya was further dismayed by the unwelcome
presence of a dozen men and women up from the coast taking its sulphur-
ous waters. Copying Balqis' example after her night with Solomon, Freya
took a surreptitious dip in its murky waters before spending a cheerless night
in her tiny tent.

Next morning she retraced her steps down the valley to Mian Rud from
where the Throne of Solomon was barely five kilometres away up the narrow
Barur Rud valley. According to a local shikari she had hired as a guide, it
was now easily accessible but when she, Aziz and the shikari pressed on up
the Barur Rud, the shikari suddenly made off with her binoculars in search
of ibex. 'Guideless and lost', Freya and Aziz carried on to a point from
which both Takht-i-Sulaiman and the great wall of Alam Kuh (Freya's Siah
Kaman, the 'Black Carder Bow') were clearly visible. But at this *moment
critique* Freya's courage failed her: 'Though there appeared no difficulty for
an able-bodied mountaineer … still weak from my illness … no path appeared
for a mule to follow … I judged the thing to be a ten-hour effort.'

Descending Takht-i-Sulaiman with Haft Khan (4539m) behind and the north-west glacier below. *(W J E Norton)*

Freya estimated the Throne to be 15,300ft, actually 1,252ft more than its correct height. Nonetheless, to have covered the five kilometres from Mian Rud to its base would have involved climbing 4,778ft in dehydrating heat, crossing a crevassed glacier and 'an endless grind of scree'. At 38, Freya should have been at the peak of her powers, but she had done no serious climbing since the Marinelli eight years earlier and had been travelling on muleback as an invalid for most of the past few weeks. She decided that the Throne was a peak too far though later blamed the Hungarian engineer for telling her errant shikari that if a foreign woman climbed the Throne, Reza Shah would punish all who had helped her. She also surmised that had they only continued up the Sehazar Rud beyond Abigarm 'an easy mule track would have led us to a possible distance of the summit.' Freya was mistaken. Precipitous peaks bar approaches from the upper Sehazar Rud; the Barir Rud had offered the easiest route to the Throne.

To have had this glittering prize snatched from her grasp was a bitter blow. But Freya was ever resilient and took the advice of an old shepherd to continue her journey to her next objective – the Kalardasht valley – by a high-level mule route traversing the massif's northern outliers. That she only just managed to cross the 14,000ft Kalau pass after experiencing severe altitude sickness for the first time in her life vindicated her earlier decision.

Dropping down through the dense Mazandaran forest, her reception at the Kurdish village of Rudbarek from its bullying headman was hostile. She tamed his rudeness with resolute charm and after a desultory investigation of the site of the legendary city of Kalar, completed the final stage of her Elburz trek after swinging south up the Chalus gorge to follow another high-level trade route with tantalising views of Takht-i-Sulaiman to the west and thence to Tehran.

Here, at the British legation, she bumped into the 25-year-old diplomat Douglas Busk, a former leading light in the Oxford University Mountaineering Club who had done some serious Alpine routes with the great Chamonix guide Armand Charlet. Though later a pillar of the establishment as chairman of the Mount Everest Foundation, thrice an ambassador and a knight of the realm, the youthful Busk had been a prominent member of the 'Young Shavers', a ginger group of young Alpine Club members determined to adopt modern mountaineering methods. Before Busk left England, Brig Ernest Gueterbock, an AC grandee, had mentioned that an unclimbed peak called Takht-i-Sulaiman existed in an unmapped section of the Elburz.

Busk's chance meeting with Freya, who generously showed him her Elburz sketch maps, spurred his ambition to climb this mystery mountain that same autumn. His reconnaissance from the south with a legation colleague failed to locate its precise location due to misleading local information and lack of time. However, in 1933, accompanied by two other legation members, muleteers and mules, a four-day approach march took them to Hazarchal where both Kotschy and the Bornmüllers had made their base. From here, Busk and his head muleteer Ni'matullah attained Alam Kuh's heavily indented east ridge to see, across a wide glacier, the Throne of Solomon barely two kilometres away. Busk realised immediately that his chances of reaching it from this side were negligible due to Alam Kuh's seemingly impassable two-mile-long north face dropping 700m plumb. He pressed on alone to make the second (and first British) ascent of Alam Kuh's teetering summit.

With the group's topography now unveiled, Busk saw that the key to climbing the Throne of Solomon was from the north. But once again, time constraints left him with no alternative save the southern approach. In 1934 he gave it his last shot and after meeting up with the German explorer-scientist Hans Bobek who was making a comprehensive geological and cartographical survey of the area, they climbed Alam Kuh together. In 1936 Bobek returned with a powerful German mountaineering team to make first ascents of Takht-i-Sulaiman and Alam Kuh's north-east buttress, but a 17-hour expedition that so impressed its lead climber Ludwig Steinauer, fourth to climb the Grandes Jorasses' central spur, that he named it the 'Persian Jorasses'. Bobek's definitive map *Karte der Takht-e Sulaimangruppe* published 22 years later in 1956 to celebrate the Vienna Geographical Institute's centenary, is reproduced in *AJ* 1958.

Subsequent British climbing history in the Takht-i-Sulaiman massif is short in telling. The Cambridge North Persian Expedition 1956 led by Bill Norton made the first British ascent of the Throne of Solomon and several other peaks. In 1963 Richard Isherwood and Henry Day, members of another Cambridge expedition, repeated Steinauer's north-east buttress climb in five hours. In 1964, while attempting Alam Kuh's north face direct, Trevor Jones was lucky to survive a stone fall that split his climbing helmet, left him badly concussed and peremptorily ended the expedition. Leyla Pope, a president of the CUMC, has since described Steinauer's route as 'an easy day for veiled ladies'.

For Freya, the 150-mile Elburz journey in 1931 was the longest and most demanding she ever undertook, though her failure to climb the Throne of Solomon was probably her greatest disappointment. Early in the following year 1932 she embarked on her last Persian adventure: a covert, unauthorised journey to explore the remote highlands of Luristan while ostensibly searching for Bronze-Age figurines. Travelling up from Baghdad, she slipped over the Persian frontier with a Lur guide who didn't even have a passport. Covering some hundred miles on horseback, amongst the wild and anarchic Lur nomads 'untainted by civilisation' who would have 'murdered for a toman'. This hazardous venture yielded no treasure and ended in another fiasco when the Persian mounted police eventually caught up with them. Freya was escorted to the Iraq border and deported as an illegal entrant. The fate of her guide is not recorded.

In 1934, *The Valleys of the Assassins* was published by the impressionable 22-year-old Jock Murray. Promoted as 'travels in unexplored Persia' it was an immediate bestseller with a freshness and clarity that in her later works is sometimes submerged in an overworked tapestry of language and historical allusion. Almost overnight, Freya became a celebrity. Although already awarded the Royal Geographical Society's Back Grant for her Persian cartographical work, the Royal Asiatic Society now presented her with the Burton Memorial Medal. Ten years after her Marinelli triumph, Freya was awarded honorary membership of the Ladies' Alpine Club without having been an ordinary member. Save for Janet Adam Smith, she knew few if any of the Club's distinguished literary members such as Dorothy Pilley. Similarly honoured was the veteran traveller-explorer Gertrude Benham, who had climbed over 300 mountains in all seven continents alone, save for native guides, and had once walked across South America. Freya's record might not have compared but she counted her honorary membership as 'a rare honour which could not have given me more pleasure.'

Emboldened by her literary success, Freya now turned her attentions to the legendary wadi Hadhramaut in south Arabia to trace its ancient incense routes and to become the first European to visit the ruins of fabled Shabwa. In 1935, a six-day donkey ride from Mukalla with an armed escort took her to the wadi where she recorded in meticulous detail domestic life in its sky-scraping, mud-brick cities. Suddenly struck down by illness, she was evacuated from the wadi by the RAF at considerable cost to the Aden government, with neither objective realised.

On her second Hadhramaut venture in 1938, she attached herself to an archaeological expedition led by the formidable Gertrude Caton Thompson.

Freya had no professional qualifications for the arduous fieldwork involved, took no active part in the expedition's organisation or excavations and was frequently ill. Caton Thompson was not impressed. Freya resented the snub, quit the expedition early and made her own way back to the coast after deliberately disregarding official instructions not to do so for political and security reasons. This three-week journey, punctuated by stops for illness, was completed after she joined an armed camel caravan travelling only by night. These abortive Hadhramaut trips, fulsomely recorded in *The Southern Gates of Arabia* (1936) and *A Winter in Arabia* (1940), in which Caton Thompson is never referred to by name, only cemented her reputation as an intrepid traveller.

During the Second World War, Freya was employed by the British government to promote anti-Axis propaganda and undertake intelligence work in Aden, the Yemen, Egypt and Baghdad. In 1942, she was awarded the Royal Geographical Society's Founder's Medal for her Persian and south Arabian travels. In March the following year, Lord Wavell, then viceroy of India, invited her to stay. Having persuaded him to give her special permission to drive a government car to Baghdad on the clear understanding that it would then become part of the embassy's carpool, she enlisted a high-ranking airman as her chauffeur. Their circuitous, 1,200-mile sightseeing journey through Persia ended prematurely in Tehran where Freya sold the car for a 500 per cent profit and pocketed the proceeds. When her host the ambassador Sir Reader Bullard got wind of it, she was never again offered work by the British government.

In 1947 Freya married her erstwhile Aden boss Stewart Perowne, a distinguished colonial civil servant and brilliant classical historian. It only lasted five years. Freya later maintained that she had no idea he was a homosexual. In 1951, she was awarded the Royal Society for Asian Affairs' Sykes Memorial Medal and switched her main travelling interests to Turkey's southern shore, including one journey by private yacht. Her final Turkish venture, a hundred-mile horseback ride from Kurdish Hakkiari to the Tigris along the fringes of the Taurus, (*Riding to the Tigris*, 1959), ranks as one of her most original and was her last of consequence.

In 1972, her eightieth year, Freya was appointed a Dame of the British Empire and continued to travel as a distinguished tourist in the Middle East, Central Asia and the Himalayan foothills, her reputation as 'one of the most famous of all Arab and Asian travellers' seemingly unassailable. However, in 1993, Molly Izzard's biography Freya Stark burst the bubble. Izzard, an adventurous journalist long resident in the Middle East whose husband Ralph had been the *Daily Mail's* ostracised correspondent for the 1953 Everest expedition, had been commissioned by Jock Murray. However, the deeper Molly delved into Freya's life, the more she disliked her subject, concluding that she was sly, hypochondrial, ruthlessly manipulative and self-centred. When Murray insisted that changes be made, Izzard refused and switched to Hodder & Stoughton. On the book's publication, Freya's many friends and admirers damned it as spiteful, nit picking and debunking. But others, including

Stark at the reception following her wedding to the historian and colonial civil servant Stewart Perowne. The marriage proved shortlived. *(Alamy)*

Colin Thubron, were impressed by Izzard's meticulous research while Wilfred Thesiger dismissed her journeys as no more than those of 'any moderately enterprising secretary'. This was ungallant, to say the least. Her three Persian journeys and ride to the Tigris were brave and imaginative ventures.

My own path crossed with Freya's several times, in the Elburz, Hadhramaut and Turkey, and in 1973 I happened to meet her for real. There might have been much to chat about and she graciously signed my copy of her *The Valleys of the Assassins*. But that was it. Freya Stark was neither a saint nor a pioneer explorer but rather an acute observer whose genius as a writer and photographer illuminated landscapes and the lives of those with whom she empathised. Above all, mountaineering was to her 'the key to a world a little above the human world and beyond it'.

Bibliography

D Busk, *The Delectable Mountains*, Hodder & Stoughton, London, 1946.

D Busk, 'Climbing and Ski-ing in the Elburz Range, N Persia', *Alpine Journal*, vol 45, p334, 1933.

D Busk, 'Climbing in the Takht-i-Suleiman Group, N Persia', *Alpine Journal*, vol 47, p299, 1935.

D Busk, 'The German Expedition in the Elburz Range, N Persia', *Alpine Journal*, vol 49, p245, 1937.

D Busk, 'A Map of the Central Elburz', *Alpine Journal*, vol 63, p207, 1958.

M Izzard, *Freya Stark*, Hodder & Stoughton, London, 1993.

M Ruthven, *Freya Stark in Persia*, Garnet Publishing, 1994.

F Stark, *The Valleys of the Assassins*, John Murray, London, 1934.

F Stark, *The Southern Gates of Arabia*, John Murray, London, 1936.

F Stark, *A Winter in Arabia*, John Murray, London, 1940.

F Stark, *Traveller's Prelude*, John Murray, London, 1950.

Re-Remembering Maestri

Cesare Maestri. *(Leo Dickinson)*.

In the *Alpine Journal* last year [1], Alan Heppenstall gave a balanced and generous account of the life of the Italian climber Cesare Maestri without avoiding the issues that put Maestri among the more controversial figures of 20th century mountaineering. Given the assistance Heppenstall received from Maestri's son Gianluigi, the editor is happy to publish Gianluigi's rebuttal (in italics) to specific passages and our response.

On p80, Heppenstall wrote: '*El Arca di Los Vientos*, as it was called, presented extremely difficult climbing on rock and ice, and showed no signs of any previous ascent.' Maestri says:

---

1. A Heppenstall, 'Remembering Maestri', *Alpine Journal*, vol 125, 2021, pp65-83.

What you have written does not correspond with the truth, because up to a certain point signs were found of the ascent by Cesare and Egger. Further the first ascent of 'El Arca' did not follow the exact line that Cesare claimed to have followed. This is to leave aside the fact that the weather conditions on that mountain are such that visible signs of the passage of others can easily not be discovered.

Also on p80: 'Some who knew the circumstances thought that it might help his mental state if Cesare could be persuaded to reveal the true events of that period in 1959, but he remained stubborn to the end.'

These 'deductions' of yours appear to be out of place. You start from the premise that the events of 1959 were not as Cesare described them, and the fact that he remained stubborn to the end underlines the supposition that he was lying.

On p81: 'During the interview (with Charlie Buffet) Cesare slightly changed his story, but the true circumstances of Egger's death were not revealed.'

Here again you seem to be starting from the premise that Egger's death was not as Cesare has always described, and as I told you several years ago that is a serious accusation, which I must contest totally.

On p81: 'The full story of Cerro Torre died with Cesare on 19 January 2021.'

You continue to insinuate that the story of Cerro Torre in 1959 was falsified by secret information that Cesare was unwilling to reveal, thus stating as a fact that he was a liar, rather than presenting this as your opinion, and the opinion of others.

Editor's note: In his first comment, Gianluigi is presumably referring to the gear found comparatively low on the face, on the ledge below the triangular snow patch. This cache was discovered in 1974 by Jim Donini and others, barely 300m up a 2,000m climb, long before *El Arca di Los Vientos* was climbed. Nothing whatsoever, as far as we are aware, was found above this point and *El Arca* really begins above the col of Conquest. Cesare Maestri claimed to have placed 60 hand-drilled bolts above this cache. None has yet been found to corroborate his claim.

That Cesare was suffering in his latter years from some form of mental distress was based partly on Cesare's own writings, but also on the word of neurophysiologist Prof Marcello Costa who spoke to Cesare on the phone and reported that he seemed disturbed. Gianluigi asks: 'How do you imagine Cesare reacted to the death of his climbing companion and the endless controversies surround the climb that have continued until this day?'

We don't say in the article that Cesare was lying but the fact is Cesare himself changed several aspects of the story over the years. For example, the first version Cesare gave of Egger's death said he was lowering him at the time the fatal avalanche struck and the rope parted. In the Charlie Buffet interview, he contradicted himself, saying that Egger didn't need lowering and was in fact abseiling. Since we have different versions of the story we cannot be sure which to believe. (Gianluigi says these discrepancies were a consequence of the passage of time and a fading memory.) The configuration of ropes discovered with Egger's body doesn't support either of these versions, looking more consistent with a crevasse rescue, although Gianluigi disputes this.

It is often overlooked that there were two men on the historic attempt in 1959 to climb Cerro Torre. So while the continuing controversy may seem a burden on the family of the recently deceased Cesare Maestri, it was agony for the family of Toni Egger. His mother and siblings never knew for certain what had happened to him. Maestri visited them soon after returning from Patagonia but Egger's sister Steffi (unlike her mother) did not believe the version of events he gave. Toni Egger was an assiduous diarist but his journals were never returned to his family. Even at the end of her long life, Steffi hoped that Cesare Maestri would explain why. He died a few months before she did, without that explanation.

PETER FOSTER

One Hundred Years Ago

The balloon goes up. The 10 members of the 1922 Everest expedition in
Darjeeling before setting out for Tibet, posing for a picture postcard.
Back row, left to right: C G Crawford, A W Wakefield, G L Mallory,
T H Somervell, E F Norton, H T Morshead. Front row left to right: E L Strutt,
C G Bruce, T G Longstaff, G I Finch. *(AC Photo Library)*.

To the members of the Mount Everest Expedition; gratus gratulabundus[1]

Pope Pius XI

1. 'Beloved best wishes.' Pope Pius XI had been elected at the conclave in February 1922. Formerly Achille
   Ratti, he was an accomplished alpinist. In 1890 he had opened the route to Mont Blanc via the Dôme
   glacier. In May 1922 the AC offered him honorary membership, which he declined. On their return from
   Everest, the members of the expedition presented him with a fragment of rock picked up at the highest point
   reached, mounted as a paperweight on ebony and with the names of the party on a silver shield, which
   apparently had a permanent place on the papal desk.

Everest is not yet climbed. Nor do we know for certain that it can be climbed. But we may see how much nearer we are to a solution as a result of this year's expedition.

George Mallory

Just you wait, old thing, you'll be for it soon!

Geoffrey Bruce

On 7 June 1922 disaster struck the first expedition trying to reach the summit of Everest. Earlier that day George Mallory and Howard Somervell, accompanied by the transport officer, Colin Crawford, and 14 Sherpas had started up the slopes of the North Col of Everest when about 180m below the col they were startled by an ominous sound 'like an explosion of untamped gunpowder' and in a moment the entire party was engulfed by avalanche. Nine porters were swept over an ice cliff into a crevasse and seven were killed; the climbers and remaining porters were unscathed.

Mallory blamed himself for misjudging the snow conditions; Somervell felt guilty that only porters had perished: 'why, oh why could not one of us Britishers have shared their fate? I would gladly at that moment have been lying there dead in the snow, if only to give those fine chaps who had survived the feeling that we shared their loss'. Lt Col Edward Strutt, deputy leader of the expedition, observed disdainfully: '[a]s to the British Public, the middle classes, shop-keepers, gillies etc., who alone show a real interest in the expedition, these rather welcome the accident (dead bodies always appeal to them) and think us real 'eroes in consequence.'

The decision to launch this last attempt had been controversial with both Strutt and Tom Longstaff arguing against. At the beginning of the expedition Longstaff had announced: 'I want to make one thing clear. I am the expedition's official medical officer. I am, as a matter of fact, a qualified doctor, but I feel it my duty now to remind you that I have never practised in my life. I beg you in no circumstances to seek my professional advice, since it would almost certainly turn out to be wrong. I am however willing if necessary to sign a certificate of death.' But now he felt it his duty to voice his concern about the physical condition of the climbers: all who had gone high, except Somervell, exhibited signs of exhaustion and varying degrees of frostbite. 'Must put my foot down,' he wrote in his diary, 'there is too little margin for safety.' Mallory considered he was fussing: 'Longstaff … is in one of his moods of bustling activity, when he becomes tiresome, interfering, and self-important.'

The go-ahead was given by expedition leader Brig Charles Bruce, who had come under pressure from the Mount Everest Committee to deliver results. Throughout the expedition Bruce had been fielding missives from South Kensington. Responding to a telegram from Sir Francis Younghusband, president of the Royal Geographical Society and chairman of the MEC, he wrote, with characteristic levity: 'To tell the truth from the terrific strafes we have been receiving, we thought that the expedition was not considered to

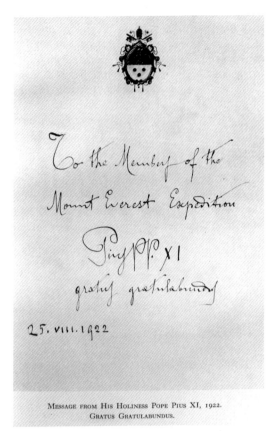

The glittering prizes. Congratulations from Pope Pius XI, the 'climbing pope' Achille Ratti, whose papacy began in February 1922; the gold medal awarded to T H Somervell at the 1924 winter Olympics. *(AC Photo Library/Ed Douglas)*

MESSAGE FROM HIS HOLINESS POPE PIUS XI, 1922.
GRATUS GRATULABUNDUS.

be a very great success, in fact I was contemplating a flight to South America.'

The expedition had ended in failure but much had been learned, albeit at a cost. On 21 May, Mallory, Somervell and Edward Norton had set an altitude record, reaching a height of 8225m, and a week later George Finch and Geoffrey Bruce, using supplementary oxygen, went higher still (8323m), thus settling the question of whether humans could function and survive at these altitudes, and both Mallory and Finch were confident that a feasible route to the summit had been found.

Such was the performance of the high-altitude porters, which had exceeded expectations, tactics could be altered to increase the chance of future success. Previously no porter had carried above 7,165m but now they had carried from the North Col to 7,775m, some repeating the ascent on successive days. There seemed no reason not to believe that they could carry even higher, making the placement of several camps above the col a practical plan.

Prior to this expedition the need for oxygen and its benefit had been theoretical and controversial; now at least, practical experience provided a basis for decisions on its future use. By climbing higher and at greater speeds Finch and Bruce had demonstrated some increase in performance, but as important was the discovery of oxygen's value in counteracting the onset of hypothermia and frostbite. After a day of storm and intense cold endured at Camp V (7775m), Finch experienced 'a dead, numbing cold creeping up [his] limbs. Something had to be done. Like an inspiration came the thought of trying the effect of oxygen ... A few minutes after the first deep breath, I felt the tingling sensation of warmth and life to my limbs.' The 1922 Everest expedition was defeated not by any climbing difficulty but by oxygen lack, cold and exhaustion, a combination that would thwart subsequent Everest expeditions in the 1920s and 1930s.

In 1924, and for the first time, Olympic medals were awarded for mountaineering. Each British member of the expedition received a medal and, as an afterthought, medals were given to two porters. The International Olympic Committee justifiably declared that the Everest expedition of 1922 had been 'the greatest feat of alpinism in the preceding four years'.

Area Notes

'Everest from Chogorong', Edward Norton, watercolour and gouache, 18cm × 13cm, 15 June 1924. *(Courtesy of Norton Family Archives)*

The Alps 2021

The east face of Mont Blanc. (GP) Grand Pilier d'Angle. (S) The rock buttress of the Red Sentinel. The Red Sentinel route climbs the mixed spur immediately above. (1) *Cascata Major.* (2) *Route Major. (Lindsay Griffin).*

Late winter snow that took longer than normal to clear, on-going Covid-19 restrictions in the first half of the year and a surprisingly cool summer when the mountains mostly escaped the intense heat-waves that plagued the rest of Europe characterised the Alps in 2021. This report showcases a representative selection of the year's major adventures on rock and ice in both the western and eastern Alps.

Ice and Mixed

A notable ascent took place on **Mont Blanc** on 20 November 2021 when Francesco Civra Dano and Giuseppe Vidoni pioneered a partial new line on the historic Brenva face, the first new ground to be climbed there for many years. *Route Major* (TD, Graham Brown-Smythe, 1928) is one of the great classics of the range but is climbed far less frequently these days. Although the approach is extremely exposed to serac fall, once on the spur the route is relatively safe. In 1971 Pierre Mazeaud and Roberto Sorgato traversed left from a point low on the *Major* and climbed the right spur of a buttress between the *Major* and *Pear* (V and V+), eventually finishing up the left edge of the final buttress (V+) below capping seracs, well left of the line followed by the normal *Major* finish or the *Gobbi-Ottoz* and *Seigneur* direct variants. This route is highly dangerous, ED, and is thought never to have been repeated.

Immediately left of the *Mazeaud-Sorgato* on the lower buttress is an open depression at over 4,000m and Vidoni, who lives in Courmayeur, saw in November that it was now a steep, 170m icefall. Starting early from the col de la Fourche bivouac, in excellent weather and snow conditions, the Italian pair followed the approach to the *Pear* until they could climb directly to the start of the smear, which they reached at dawn. They found the ice to be good quality, but thin, with even short stubby screws not penetrating fully at times. They completed this section in five pitches, then slanted across the snow slope above to finish up the *Gobbi-Ottoz* direct variant to the Major. From here they continued to the summit and down to the Gouter that night, naming their route *Cascata Major* (1300m, VI, 5).

The north face of **Pointe Migot** (3311m) was first climbed in 1964 by the crack British team of Bonington, Brown, Ford, and Patey. These four slanted up right, parallel and left of the start of the *Rébuffat-Terray* to reach a ramp cutting back left and leading to the crest of the north spur. Just before the start of the winter season of December 2001 François Marsigny and Thierry Renault climbed a difficult parallel ramp to gain the north spur, from where they rappelled into the couloir on the left and followed it to the col supérieur des Pélerins, completing a route they named *One Step Beyond*. Little has happened here since, though in 2006 Malcolm Bass, Dave Johnson and Simon Yearsley made the first winter ascent of the 1964 route, finishing via the couloir on the left.

High up on the face to the right of these routes lies a conspicuous rock scar overlooking the upper half of the *Rébuffat-Terray*. In late April, John McCune and Will Sim climbed around 250m of the winter version (*Carrington-Rouse*) of the *Rébuffat-Terray*, then broke out left towards the rock scar. Four pitches of difficult mixed led to a great arcing roof – the crux section – where McCune changed into rock shoes and climbed around it in two pitches. Easier climbing led out to the north spur, from where the pair traversed to the top of the *Rébuffat-Terray* and descended it via the fixed anchors. The new line has been named *Above and Beyond* (6b+, M6).

On the showpiece of the Valais Alps – the **Matterhorn** – there were two impressive ascents of the legendary 1965 *Bonatti* route (1000m, ED3) on the north face. On 31 March three of Italy's most active alpinists, Matteo Della Bordella, François Cazzanelli, and Francesco Ratti left the Hörnli hut at 5am and reached the summit at 9pm. They continued in the night to the Carrel hut on the Italian ridge, arriving at 11.30pm.

More impressive was the ascent by Simon Messner and regular climbing partner Martin Sieberer, who on 17 October took the 4am train from Täsch to Zermatt, and then walked all the way to the Hörnli hut. Arriving at the base of the route at 9.15am, they found conditions good and decided to continue despite the late hour. Climbing the upper face in the dark (they could find no bivouac site), they reached the summit just before midnight, and by 2am were sitting outside a crowded Solvay hut on the Hörnli ridge. Their exhaustion, due to 3,000m of ascent, had been accentuated by all water bottles freezing solid early in the day, making it impossible to take a drink throughout the entire climb.

Walter Bonatti's ascent, solo, over five days in deep winter and with temperatures down to -30°C, marked the end of extreme alpinism for this great Italian climber. Although his route was repeated over the next few years in both summer and winter, it subsequently had little or no attention until the mid 1990s. The crux of the route is considered the seven-pitch Traverse of the Angels. Bonatti needed this section to be relatively dry in order to negotiate the technical rock terrain, but nowadays, with a good plastering of snow and ice, it can be climbed quite fast using mixed climbing techniques.

One-day ascents are becoming less of a rarity, though remember that in September 2010 the Swiss Patrick Audenblatten and Michael Lerjen-Demjen completed the route on sight in an astounding seven hours and 14 minutes, making the round trip from the Hörnli hut in less than 10 hours.

The Dolomites continue to be explored for ephemeral ice and mixed climbs, for which there still appears to be great potential for those with good knowledge and able to snatch conditions when they arrive. One of the foremost protagonists is the Italian Emanuele Andreozzi, who with various friends climbed three big new lines in the spring.

On the first day of April, with Matteo Faletti, Andreozzi tackled the north face of the **Cimon della Pala** (3184m), an elegant spire in the Pale di San Martino group that is often referred to as the Matterhorn of the Dolomites. The pair followed a logical line up an obvious series of chimneys, gullies, and ramps to create *Elements of Life* (900m of climbing, AI5 M6). Ice was in excellent condition: the face still receives no sun at this time of year, keeping the localised temperature well below freezing even when warm elsewhere.

The new route, to the right of *Via degli Allievi* (AI5 M4, Colomba-Vidoni, 2019), begins with a 100m icefall first climbed by an Italian team in January 2020. Above, it links lines of weakness and, at one point, traverses a spectacular shark's-fin snow crest in the middle of the wall. The pair reached a notch on the summit ridge only 20m below the top but, disappointingly, conditions prevented further upward progress: it was, after all, April Fool's Day. They rappelled and down-climbed from this point along the left side of the north face.

Matteo Faletti on the tricky fifth pitch (WI5 M5) of *Pazzione Primavernale*, north-north-east face of Cima Tosa. The spire behind is the Campanilo Basso. *(Santi Padros)*

The end of May and winter was long gone, yet the Dolomites were still covered in deep snow. On 20 May, taking advantage of these unusual conditions, Andreozzi, Faletti and Santi Padros (Spain) climbed a huge ice-mixed line on the north-north-east face of **Cima Tosa**, at 3,173m the highest peak in the Brenta Dolomites. This is the rock wall left of the famous *Canalone Neri* (AD, Neri, 1929, skied from time to time). After camping below the face, the three left at 2.15am and took 16 and a half hours to complete *Pazzione Primavernale* (1000m, 19 pitches, AI6, M7, 90°+) to the great summit plateau. They slid and down-climbed the *Canalone Neri*, regained the tent and skis, and were back at the road by 11pm.

The first half of the route follows the 1933 *Castiglione-Detassis* (IV and V) then traverses left to cross the *Piaz* route (IV+/V, Michelson-Piaz, 1911) before leaving it to climb the right-hand of two huge and previously untouched chimneys. No gear was left on the route.

This was the first time all three had climbed together but it was certainly not the last. Ten days later Andreozzi and Padros were below the north-west face of the **Cima de Gasperi** (2994m) in the Civetta group. They had walked up to the Vazzoler hut in relatively warm temperatures above green valleys but when they stepped out of the winter room at 2.15am they encountered a hard frost. The goal was a huge gully-depression left of the north-west arête (750m, Andrich-Bianchet-Zancristoforo, 1935) and they were surprised

Santi Padros dry-tooling pitch 18 (M7) of *Pazzione Primavernale*. *(Emanuele Andreozzi)*

Emanuele Andreozzi looks for protection in the upper chimneys of *Pazzione Primavernale* on Cima Tosa. *(Santi Padros)*

to be able to climb the first 300m unroped. Things then became more intense with a few hard and sometimes unprotected pitches. The climb finished up a large chimney, which proved to be easier than it had appeared from below. At the exit, they traversed left across the 1934 *Benedetti-Zanutti* route for three pitches to a col on the north-east ridge, which they reached after nine and a half hours climbing. From there it was a straightforward descent on snow to the hut. The route was named *Alchimia* (800m, 11 pitches, AI5+, M6+).

The Fanes group is a large and complex region northwest of Cortina that is known for its ski touring and for difficult adventurous rock routes on peaks such as Cima Scotoni and Sas dla Crusc. In recent years it has become more or less the backyard of talented South Tyrolean Simon Gietl. A cabinetmaker turned professional alpinist and mountain guide Gietl was honoured with an award in 2016 for being Italy's foremost mountaineer.

Monte Sella di Sennes (2787m) is a popular ski ascent from the east but in early January Simon and his brother Manuel decided they should 'take a look' at the south-west face. After one false start, they began a line that almost immediately proved challenging. By the time they had completed pitch three, a serious bit of WI5+, the face was in full sun and the pair thought it best to bail. They returned somewhat earlier the following day and by 10am had already reached their highpoint. More superb pitches of mixed led to the summit plateau. *Sorijina* (700m, M6, WI5+, 50°) was completed in just

Pazzione Primavernale on the north-north-east face of Cima Tosa. The large gully to the right is the *Canalone Neri*. *(Santi Padros)*

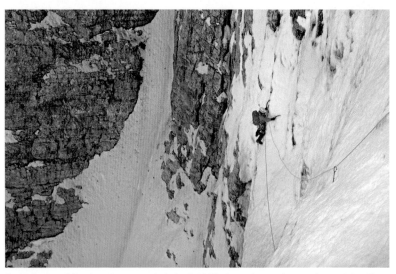

Santi Padros following the second pitch of *Alchimia* on the north-west face of the Cima de Gasperi. *(Emanuele Andreozzi)*

seven and a half hours, and when the two regained their car at 5.30pm, the thermometer recorded the same temperature as when they had left it 12 hours previously: -23.5°C.

West of the Brenta Dolomites, the Adamello-Presonella range still has considerable scope for hard ice and mixed climbing but lines are very dependent

The excellent goulotte on pitch four of *Alchimia*, Cima de Gasperi. *(Santi Padros)*

Spectacular scenery on the north-west face of the Cima de Gasperi. *(Emanuele Andreozzi)*

on conditions and favour inside knowledge. In the final days of the year, on the north face of 3,325m **Cima Busazza**, west of the 3,556m Presanella, Andreozzi and Faletti, this time accompanied by Francesco Nardelli, created the demanding *Strapazzati dalla Luna Piena*. Although relatively short by their standards (470m, 10 pitches), the climbing was sustained and time-consuming, following thin smears through steep granite. Protection was poor and the difficulties substantial (M6, AI5, 90°). Climbing well into the night, the three reached the west summit, traversed east and then embarked on a previously equipped rappel descent, in many places having to add new anchors. This allowed the collection of their skis at the base of the route. Twenty-three hours after leaving, the three regained their car, parked near the Passo del Tonale.

Ski

Steep skiing gains an ever-increasing number of exponents while improved equipment has greatly augmented the potential for big, bold, and new ski descents. Arguably, no one is as prolific, or extreme, as the Dutch mountain guide and French resident Paul Bonhomme. His goal during the 2020-1 season was Project X, to complete 10 first descents, each more than 500m and 50°. All were completed, including the east face of the 4,135m **Combin de la Tsessette** via a 1,200m line called *Les Piliers de Bagnes*, the 900m *Merci Mamans* on the south-west face of the **Bietschhorn** (3934m), and his last, on 28 May: the 950m south-west face of the **Täschhorn** (4491m), which he named *X*.

With his regular skiing partner Vivian Bruchez, he first climbed the proposed ski line on the Täschhorn and then the pair skied from the summit, replacing skis with crampons near the base to down-climb a narrow five-metre section. After descending the top part of the east face and *Mischabelgrat* (south-south-east ridge), the pair dropped into the south-west face from the brèche at 4,350m and followed the line climbed in 1956 by Erich Vanis and Hans Chval-Kremslehner, moving west near the bottom to finish down the 1935 *Biner-Taugwalder* start. Apart from near the bottom of the face, the ski line lies to the east of the historic 1906 original route, often cited as one of the greatest mountaineering feats of all time. Climbed by guides Franz and Josef Lochmatter and Josef Knubel with Valentine 'VJ' Ryan and Geoffrey Winthrop Young, and rarely since, it is seriously exposed to rock fall in summer, and still graded TD+ today.

Rock in Summer and Winter

Cyril Dupeyré, Benjamin Ribeyre (France) and the American Erin Smart are three active guides based in La Grave on the north side of the Écrins. Over three consecutive days in August 2020 and a fourth, 26 August, in 2021, they opened the first new route in six years on the south side of the **Meije** (3984m). *Athée Pieds* (970m, 20 pitches, 7c, 6c obl) lies entirely to the right of the historic but infrequently climbed south face of the 3,973m **Doigt de Dieu** (700m, TD+, 5+), though the latter's original finish contains, remarkably for the era, a short section of 6b, climbed in 1951 by Victor Chaud and Jean Walden. This last-named route, of mixed quality rock, was soloed in 2016 by Ribeyre.

A large terrace that slants up from the right cuts the south face at around half-height and is referred to as the Snow Band. It can provide an escape

The south-west face of the Täschhorn with (1) the historic 1906 route, an ascent well ahead of its time and still rarely climbed today and (2) the ski descent by Bonhomme and Bruchez. *(Lindsay Griffin)*

The south face of the Meije above the Etancons glacier. (A) Pic du Glacier Carré. (B) Grand Pic. (C) Doigt de Dieu and the line of *Athée Pieds*. (P) Promontoire Ridge, the normal route up the Meije, reaching the left side of the hanging snowfield – the Glacier Carré – then climbing the left skyline ridge of the Grand Pic. *(Lindsay Griffin)*

Il Regalo di Berna on the south face of the Grandes Jorasses. The top of the pillar is connected to the snow plateau of the normal route by a short ridge of IV. *(Lindsay Griffin)*

from the lower section or access to the upper but it also marks a delimitation of two rock types: granite below and gneiss above. The new route weaves up the steep compact wall below the shoulder immediately right (east) of the Doigt de Dieu. Most of the belays are bolted and around 40 protection bolts remain in place, of which 14 were placed in the compact rock of the crux sixth pitch. And so 'Athée Pieds', or atheist feet, now reach the finger of God.

On the south face of the **Grandes Jorasses**, left of the *Hypercouloir*, stands a fine triangle of rock, its right edge a perfect pillar of seemingly compact granite. It is known variously as the South Pillar, the Pilier du Glacier Suspendu and the Ghiglione Pillar. Piero Ghiglione and Arthur Ottoz made the first ascent in 1948, climbing more broken ground left of the true pillar but working right toward the top to finish near the crest (TD, VI). There have been few repeats, possibly none of the original line, and the long access to the base has become objectively dangerous in recent decades of warm, drier summers. In May 2019 Jon Bracey and Enrico Bonino climbed an ice-mixed line that is probably quite similar to the middle-upper section of the 1948 route (5b, WI5+, M6+).

The true crest of the pillar, such an obvious and logical line, had been considered by many over the years, including more recently Matteo Bernasconi, who throughout the last decade has been a regular climbing partner of Matteo Della Bordella. In 2020 Bernasconi perished in an avalanche and Della Bordella was motivated to complete one of Bernasconi's dreams.

On 23 February, Della Bordella, Giacomo Mauri and Luca Schiera skinned up to the Boccalatte hut and set off at 4am the following morning and in four hours had reached the foot of the pillar. Two 60m pitches (6a and 5+) on the left side of the initial buttress took them to the start of the

more compact pillar crest. Contrary to expectations – they were carrying bivouac gear expecting a two-day ascent – the granite was extremely weathered and well featured and the three were able to climb fast over moderate difficulties (4+ to 6b). The pitch below the summit of the pillar was completely vertical but with great holds and with temperatures throughout warm enough for bare-handed rock climbing it proved no obstacle. From the top, an easy ridge led to the glacier plateau and the Grandes Jorasses *Normal Route*, which they descended to the Boccalatte hut, arriving at 7pm. The 450m route (excluding the approach) was named *Il Regalo di Berna*.

The west face of the **Petit Dru** now has a hard new free route. Four members of the Groupe Militaire de Haute Montagne, Thomas Auvaro, Léo Billon, Jordi Noguere, and Sébastien Ratel took four days to complete the climb (18-21 February) and a fifth to descend to the valley. The ascent was live streamed on social media by a cameraman filming from Montenvers.

With the Grands Montets lift closed, the team had to make the more arduous approach via Montenvers, choosing to ferry loads to the bottom of the face a week earlier. When the four set off up their chosen route, which approximated the former Harlin-Robbins *American Direttissima*, they were unaware that in winter 2015 two Spanish, Josep Maria Esquirol and David Palmada, had spent 14 days on this line before bailing a little over 300m from the top, though they still gave their attempt a name: *Abdruits* (6a, M5, A5, 70°). The French followed the Spanish attempt for the first third of the face and then made a variant before rejoining for its last seven pitches. Almost immediately above the Spanish high point, they found the crux to be a dangerously loose pitch of 7a. A further five pitches of sustained 6b and 6c led to easier ground and eventually the summit. The rock was generally sound and the climbers felt the hard dry-tooling pitches would have been very much harder climbed conventionally with hands and rock

On the first complete ascent of a new traverse at the north-eastern end of the Aiguilles Rouges. *(Florent Pedrini)*

shoes, perhaps 7c. The route was largely protected with nuts and cams and named Base (1000m, 7a, M8+).

There is still potential to discover fine new rock routes of an adventurous yet technically less demanding nature in the wild corners of the Mont Blanc range, notably on the Italian side. Returning to one of their old haunts in September, Simon Richardson and Michel Rinn, operating from the Comino hut above the roadhead in the Italian Val Ferret, climbed the east pillar and ridge of **Mont Vert du Gruevettaz** (2810m). The 6b+ crux was an overhanging chimney-crack, and the name – *Bella Vista* – reflects the outstanding views into the Triolet glacier basin from the upper half of the climb.

Rather novel is a new traverse in the **Aiguilles Rouges** created by Alexandre Henot, Florent Pedrini and Emmanuel Ratouis. After three years of exploration and preparation, the three eventually made a complete crossing over two days in September 2021, with a pre-placed bivouac by the Aiguille Morris.

The route, which features around 40 previously unclimbed pitches, starts towards the north-east end of the range in the vicinity of the Aiguille de Praz Torrent, where it climbs a 400m pillar (6b, 5c/6a obl) to the top of a formation the ascensionists have dubbed the Aiguille de la Tempérance (2722m). The traverse continues south-west along the chain, past the bivouac, to the col de L'Encrenaz, from where a second pillar, named the Pilier de la Deuxième Naissance (around 400m, 4b-6a) leads to the Aiguille de l'Encrenaz (2887m). The traverse finishes with the north ridge of the Aiguille de la Persévérance. Passages have been equipped (and sometimes re-equipped) to make them possible for an ascent with 50m ropes but a good rack of cams is essential to protect the climbing adequately. Count on taking 10-12 hours

During the new two-day traverse of the north-eastern section of the Aiguilles Rouges with Mont Blanc visible distant left. *(Florent Pedrini)*

each day for the walking, climbing, and traversing. With the continued ravages in the Mont Blanc range due to climate change, this new traverse adds to the armoury of long mountain routes available from the Chamonix valley, giving a wild experience but always with stupendous views towards Mont Blanc.

Climbers are still squeezing lines into the facets of the **Matterhorn**. In 2018 local activists François Cazzanelli, Marco Farina and Francesco Ratti, with Emrik Favre and Roberto Ferraris, climbed *Diretta allo Scuda* on the rock wall – the Scudo or Shield – on the south face below Pic Tyndall. Sadly, one year later, Ferraris, a guide, mountain rescuer and prolific new router, died in an avalanche while skiing in the Valtournenche. Cazzanelli, Farina and Ratti wanted to dedicate a new route to Ferraris and so over two days in September 2021 they climbed a pillar, now with the proposed name the *Pilastro Roberto Ferraris*, on the left side of the triangle of rock climbed by the 2002 Gabarrou route *Padre Pio* and further right, the 1970 Calcagno-Cerrutti-di Pietro-Machetto route. The pillar ends on a spur of the south face, well below Picco Muzio, from where a rappel descent was made. The 650m, 16-pitch route, with difficulties up to 6c, was named *L'Amitié* to celebrate the close friendship between the three ascensionists and Ferraris.

Two notable free ascents of Alpine rock routes took place in the summer and autumn, both in Switzerland. The steep, monolithic north face of the **Petit Clocher du Portalet** (2823m) stands opposite the Orny hut at the east end of the Mont Blanc massif. It has always been a forcing ground for free climbing. In 1989 Philippe Steulet climbed the old *Darbellay* aid route at 8a, the first time a climb of the eighth grade had been established in the western Alps. In 2001 Didier Berthod and François Mathey climbed a fantastic splitter crack on the orange wall left of the fourth pitch of *État de Choc*, the Remy brothers' 1983 strenuous crack feast (280m, 7a). Graded 7c+, this pitch was traditionally protected but ended in the middle of nowhere. Twenty years later Fabian Borter and Bertrand Martenet bolted a continuation on or close to the left arête of the north face, and with the help of Berthod, recently returned to climbing after a long absence living in a monastery, climbed the line but were not able to free it. This fell to the Belgian Sébastien Berthe, who redpointed the route in one day on 6 August. After the first three pitches (6b+) of *État de Choc*, the seven new pitches of *Histoire sans Fin* are graded 7c+, 7c, 8b+, 7c, 8b, 8a+, 6b+. His partner on this ascent was Siebe Vanhee, also Belgian, who returned on 9 August for his successful redpoint. The two feel it is probably the finest multi-pitch granite route of that level in Europe.

The **Dündenhorn** lies above (and north-east of) Kandersteg in the Bernese Oberland. Exploring little frequented corners in the early days of Covid-19 was understandably desirable, leading Peter von Känel and Silvan Schüpbach to investigate the mountain's previously unclimbed west face. The Swiss pair established an eight-pitch route on excellent limestone protected entirely by traditional means. Schüpbach came back in the fall of 2020 to look at a better and more direct finish, checking out the final pitches from the top.

The north face of the Petit Clocher du Portalet and the superb left arête taken by *Histoire sans Fin*. Immediately to the right, the prominent right-facing crack and corner system is *État de Choc*. *(Claude Remy)*

Tradündition on the west face of the Dündenhorn, Bernese Oberland. *(Vladek Zumr)*

He returned several more times and in September 2021 equipped the route with fixed ropes so he could work on a redpoint ascent. This took place on 15 October when, with the support of von Känel, Schupbach completed the sustained route *Tradündition* (8a, 7b+ obl), climbing the final pitch (6b) for the first time: the first free ascent was therefore also the first ascent of the route. Apart from cams and nuts, a few pitons and peckers were used, and the climbers feel their new line is probably the most difficult purely trad multi-pitch route in Switzerland. They would like to see the Dündenhorn remaining a bolt-free zone.

In the first week of March stable high pressure sitting over the Dolomites prompted a flurry of activity on the vast north-west face of Civetta. Lorenzo d'Addario and Nicola Tondini made the first winter ascent of *Dulcis in Fundo* (c400m, IX-, de Blasi-dal Pozzo, 1988) on the **Torre di Alleghe**. Neither had previously climbed the route but they completed it in a day. On **Punta Civetta**, Titus Prinoth and Alex Walpoth made the first winter ascent of *Chimera Verticale* (600m, IX, Bau-Beber-Geremia-Matteraglia, 2008). The pair required two bivouacs. Walpoth had previously repeated the line, situated between the classic *Aste* and *Andrich* routes, in summer 2014. In 2001 Venturino de Bona, climbing alone, put up *W Mexico Cabrones* (1150m, 33 pitches, VIII-) on **Punta Tissi**. Alexander Bau, Thomas Gianola and Giovani Zaccaria had all climbed this route at various times in summer but combined forces to make the first winter ascent with two bivouacs.

Bau and Tondini, together with Alessandro Beber, are some of the most prolific Dolomite pioneers. Between 2009 and 2012 the three established the 1,200m *Colonne d'Ercole* on **Punta Tissi**. They spent days on the route during the course of three years before making a two-day (25 hours climbing)

Silvan Schüpbach on pitch one (7c+) of *Tradündition* on the west face of the Dünden-horn. After a bouldery start on mediocre rock, the climbing quickly becomes excellent. *(Vladek Zumr)*

free ascent. In keeping with many of their other major ascents, this team climbed emphatically without bolts, overcoming difficulties up to 7c. In mid August 2021, Léo Billon and Enzo Oddo climbed the route on sight and in a single day from the Tissi hut, completing the 29-pitch route itself in just under 12 hours – an impressive achievement.

In February, after his ascent on the Sella di Sennes, Simon Gietl returned to the Fanes to make a roped solo ascent of the famous *Central Pillar* on the **Sas dla Crusc**, a legendary route first climbed in 1968 by Reinhold and Günther Messner. Reinhold made a committing lead of a four-metre, off-vertical wall of friable rock above an ankle-snapping ledge to create the first 'alpine' VII+ in Europe. Hans Mariacher, thinking he was on the original line, climbed around this section in 1978 to make the second ascent of the route.

Silvan Schüpbach on the crux pitch six (8a) of *Tradündition* on the Dündenhorn. This pitch is mainly protected by short knifeblades and a couple of peckers, all left in place to facilitate repeat ascents. *(Vladek Zumr)*

The *Mariacher Variant* (VII) is the one mostly followed today. Until the mid 1990s Messner's original route had only ever been repeated on a top rope. Even today, opinions still vary on the grade, though the majority lean toward VIII- or 7a. Gietl took only eight hours to make the ascent, which was likely the first winter solo.

Gietl returned to the **Sas dla Crusc** a week later for another Messner route, *Grosse Mauer* (VI+/VII-). This time he dispensed with bivouac gear and simply took a lightweight paraglider. He dispatched the route in just four hours (first pitch in crampons, the rest in rock shoes) and after a quick flight was back at the car by 2pm.

Another notable Gietl ascent took place in May, this time on the attractive formation of **Torre del Lago** (2654m). Gietl was astonished to find that the crest of the conspicuous south-west pillar was still unclimbed. He rectified this with Andrea Oberbacher, the pair creating the 12-pitch *Zero* at mostly V and VI with a crux of VII/VII+. As Gietl reported, 'it's nice to climb a difficult new route, to have a hard time and then be rewarded with the redpoint, but it's also just as satisfying to establish something that's a bit more relaxed.' Given the well-protected, good-quality climbing, it ought to become popular.

Apart from free climbing *Histoire sans Fin*, the Belgian Vanhee also made a notable ascent in the Tre Cime, where he repeated Dave MacLeod's *Project Fear* (8c) on the north face of the **Cima Ovest**. Macleod (with Alan Cassidy) climbed the 1968 *Bauer-Rudolph* aid route until he could continue direct via few new pitches to reach and climb the 8c crux of Alexander Huber's *Pan Aroma*.

Vanhee only briefly practised the route before making the redpoint but decided to link Macleod's 7b+ and 8a+ pitches, and the *Pan Aroma* crux, into one long 50m roof-pitch. Belayed by Italian Nico Cad and hampered by the cold conditions of late summer, Vanhee took two falls, returning to the belay each time, before finally making the continuous redpoint. The pair then continued up the upper section of the *Cassin* to summit.

In retrospect, Vanhee felt a couple of the pitches, including the *Pan Aroma* crux, might originally have been slightly overgraded (maximum difficulties of 8b) and therefore kept with an overall grade of 8c for the more difficult link-up.

Thanks to Rodolphe Popier and route authors for help in compiling this report.

SIMON RICHARDSON
Scottish Winter 2021-22

Mark Robson on the first ascent in early December of *Princess Cut* (VI,6) on Glas
Leathad Beag on Ben Wyvis. The climb is exceptionally steep for a turf-based route
and Bulldogs were the most effective form of protection. *(Simon Richardson)*.

The Scottish mountains were battered by almost continuous storms from
December to February, but despite the challenging weather there were some
exceptional performances. Greg Boswell had an excellent season with five
outstanding first ascents and during the second half of February. Tom Livingstone climbed 14 difficult routes up to Grade IX in as many days whilst visiting
from Chamonix.

Winter made a half-hearted appearance in late October but climbing opportunities were few and far between and only a handful of snowed-up rock routes in the Northern Corries were completed. November was remarkably mild but all this changed on 26 November when Storm Arwen swept in. Whilst the east of Scotland was battered by hurricane-force winds, Mike Lates and Tilly Cottrell took advantage of relative calm on the west with the first ascent of *North Buttress Gully* (III) on Bla Bheinn on Skye.

It was cold at the start of December and Liam Campbell, Macauley Wood and Jamie Whitehead visited Creag Loisgte on the south-west ridge on Ben Lawers and made the first ascent of *Lucky Sunday Arete* (III,4). The same day, Steve Kennedy and Stan Pearson climbed the 420m *Diamond Crossing* (III) between *Helter Skelter* and *The Ramp* on the east face of Aonach Beag. Further north, Greg Boswell, Hamish Frost and Graham McGrath made the first ascent of *Take Me Back to The Desert* (IX,9) on Beinn Eighe. This route goes directly up the wall near the left-hand end of the Eastern Ramparts starting just right of *The Modern Idiot*.

Four days later, Oliver Skeoch and Ryan Balharry made the first winter ascent of *The Jester* (V,7) on Stob Coire nan Lochan in Glen Coe. This small but impressive pinnacle lies at the foot of Pinnacle Buttress and is well seen on the approach to the corrie. The following day, Mark Robson and I visited Ben Wyvis and climbed *Princess Cut* (VI,6) on Diamond Buttress situated on Glas Leathad Beag. The climb is exceptionally steep for a turf-based route and Bulldogs were the most effective form of protection.

Overall, January was another disappointing month with limited snowfall quickly taken away by sudden thaws. The month started off on a cold note and on 5 January, John Higham and Iain Young made the first ascent of *Geologists' Ridge* (IV,4) on the 450m south-west face of Conival. This 11-pitch route was one of the mountaineering highlights of the winter and an intelligent choice in the early season snowy conditions. Two days later, Neil Adams, Nathan Adam and Garry Campbell visited the newly developed Jacobite Buttress on Sgurr Ghiubhsachain above Loch Shiel and made the first ascent of the excellent looking *Raising the Standard* (V,7).

The finest climbing day of the month was 9 January when an east-west split resulted in a wonderful winter day on the Cairngorms, with the hills frozen and white with fresh snow. Four parties visited The Stuic on Lochnagar and Stuart Macfarlane and Di Gilbert made an early repeat of *The Stoee Chimney* (IV,6). Ascents were made of *First Light* and *Daybreak Corners*, and *Forrest Templeton* and I made the first ascent of *True Grit* (V,7), the steep depression between *Bonanza* and *Twilight Groove*.

The band of cold clear air that day also extended across to the far north-west and three teams were in action on An Teallach. Doug Bartholomew and Graham Wyllie made an early repeat of *Lord Berkeley's Seat* (VI,6). Erick Baillot and Andy Sharpe also had their eye on the route, and as consolation, made the third ascent of *Monumental Chimney* (V,7). The most impressive climb on An Teallach that day was Guy Robertson and Adam Russell's second ascent of *The Wailing Wall* (IX,9). This outstanding line up the left side

Neil Adams in early January on the first ascent of *Raising the Standard* (V,7) on Sgurr Ghiubhsachain. This excellent looking climb lies on the recently developed Jacobite Buttress above Loch Shiel. *(Nathan Adam)*

of the upper Hayfork Wall was first climbed by Martin Moran and Murdoch Jamieson in December 2010.

February started warm, but the temperatures gradually dropped. On 6 February Forrest Templeton and I visited Corrie Farchal in Glen Clova on a hunch that it had been cold enough to freeze the turf above 700m and the cliff would be white with new snow blown over the plateau. The gamble paid off and we made a beeline for the two-tiered buttress left of *Seven Ages of Man* on the left side of the cliff. The first tier is cut by a deep chimney and was relatively straightforward, but the second tier, a vertical wall capped by an overlap, only succumbed to a brave and forceful lead by Forrest. In keeping with the Shakespeare theme, we called the route *All the World's A Stage* (VI,6).

Forrest Templeton on the crux pitch of *All The World's A Stage* (VI,6) in Glen Clova's Corrie Farchal on the first ascent in early February. The route climbs over the icicle-draped roof with bold climbing on blank powder-covered slabs above. *(Simon Richardson)*

Three days later, Huw Scott, Tom Fullen and Nathan Adam added a couple of good new mixed routes to Raw Egg Buttress on Aonach Beag. *Old Yoker* (VI,7) starts at the base of Ruadh Eigg Chimney and takes the obvious slim turfy left facing corner in the wall right of *Blackbeard*, and *Youthful Enthusiasm* (V,6) climbs the crack and off-width corner right of *Old Yoker*. The same day, Tim Miller and Matt Glenn climbed the short and bold *End of Ethics* (VII,7) on the wall right of *Thea* on The Garadh on Ben Nevis.

Greg Boswell returned to Scotland in the middle of the month after two months of high standard ice and mixed climbing in the Alps. He put his fitness to great effect on 21 February with the first ascent of *Last Crusade Winter Variation* on Church Door Buttress with Guy Robertson. This bold IX,9 is a winter version of the summer E3 and finishes up the impressive ice smear of *Gates of Paradise*.

Huw Scott on the first pitch of *Old Yoker* (VI,7) during the first ascent in early February. This excellent looking technical route lies on the left wall of Ruadh Eigg Chimney situated high up on the west face of Aonach Beag. *(Nathan Adam)*

Dave Riley and Andy Harrison had an excellent day on Lurcher's Crag on 25 February climbing a continuous run of ice between Central and Diamond gullies resulting in the 365m *An Ice Surprise* (IV,4/5). Parts of this route may have been climbed before but there is no record of approaching the upper cliffs from directly below via the icefalls, so this section is likely to be new. Further north the same day, Mark Robson and I ploughed through deep snow to *Bianasdail Buttress* (V,6) on the west flank of Beinn a' Mhùinidh above Loch Maree. This gave an excellent four pitch mixed route with success in doubt until the very end.

On 6 March, Greg Boswell succeeded on one of the most prized objectives on Ben Nevis when he made the first ascent of *The Fear Factory* (VII,7), the prominent hanging icicle on the Little Brenva Face with Guy Robertson and Hamish Frost. The upper part of the ice fang had previously climbed by Dave MacLeod and Andy Nelson in February 2013, but they ascended steep rock further right to gain the ice, so the prize of the complete ice feature remained. For Boswell, the main difficulty was dealing with the delicate icicle

Greg Boswell stepping out on to the huge hanging icicle of *The Fear Factory* (VII,7) on the Little Brenva Face on Ben Nevis in March. This magnificent feature was the last great, unclimbed icefall on Ben Nevis. *(Hamish Frost)*

and the lack of protection: it was too dangerous to place screws in case the ice shattered and detached. In the event, Boswell made a 20m run out up brittle vertical ice to reach the safety of the easy ground above.

The weather became very warm during the second half of March and most winter climbers hung up their axes and crampons with the apparent early onset of spring. Winter returned at the beginning April however, and Greg Boswell and Guy Robertson made the first ascent of *The Reckoning* (X,9) up Hayfork Wall on An Teallach. Boswell's enthusiasm meant he was climbing until the very end of the season so it was appropriate that his persistence paid off with the final new route of the winter. *Fear of the Unknown* (VIII,9) takes the steep featureless wall between *Migrant Direct* and *Nocando Crack* on Number Three Buttress in Coire an Lochain and was climbed with Jamie Skelton on 9 April.

IAN WALL

Nepal

Himalayan weather is created by prevailing winds that roll in from the Bay of Bengal and winter winds from Central Asia. A sudden change in conditions in those regions will always have a huge impact on the environment, communities and tourism in Nepal and especially if those winds from the Bay of Bengal are held by the high Himalaya.

Cyclone Hudhud, which struck Nepal in October 2014 originated from a low-pressure system that formed under the influence of an upper-air cyclonic circulation in the Andaman Sea. Shortly before it made landfall in Andhara Pradesh, it reached its maximum speed of 115mph before moving further inland to Nepal and Uttar Pradesh, pushing the fading monsoon back into Nepal. Unlike most of these storms, which dissipate quickly over land, Hudhud reached as far north as the Himalaya with fatal consequences. It was a harbinger of things to come.

Over the last few years the predictable four-season weather pattern has changed, the edges of these seasons becoming blurred. Unusual weather is now increasingly common out of season. Situations like Hudhud are becoming more likely, associated with global warming. The monsoon brings less rain but more intensively, threatening worse flooding.

One such event happened in June 2021 when the Helambu region was affected by an early spell of monsoon weather with storms and flash flooding that inflicted major damage to the long-awaited Melamchi water supply into Kathmandu. The project was luckily only somewhat damaged and repairs were swiftly completed. The first supply of water reached the reservoirs on the outskirts of the Kathmandu valley in April 2022. However, in the last days of June 2022 the authorities have expressed concern that there are insufficient mechanisms to restrict the large flow of water and that there is a risk of flooding.

The autumn season 2021 also saw bad weather and unusual snowfall in the mountains while the winter period produced some extremely low temperatures. Spring 2022 provided a good and stable weather pattern but once again May saw regular storms in the middle-hill regions and flooding in Kathmandu and other low lying regions attributed to early pre-monsoon weather patterns.

Unsustainable Development in Nepal's Mid Hills
There is an increasing trend of erecting 'viewing towers' on established natural viewpoints. These are, in my opinion, destroying the natural beauty of those locations in the name of tourism. Kathmandu now has its own

The latest 'development' craze in Nepal is for hill-top towers, which critics say is disfiguring the country's natural landscapes.

Road building has accelerated in recent years in Nepal, where the JCB franchise was briefly the busiest in South Asia. But projects are often started without proper engineering or environmental impact assessments disrupting water supplies and causing landslides.

new viewing platform. Although the skeleton structure has only just been completed it has caused a public outcry for the inappropriate use of land originally acquired by public donation at an estimated cost of seven billion rupees, a government priority that seems misplaced for a country like Nepal. The federal government has allocated money to build similar structures across the country, with the former prime minister K P Oli allocating an estimated Rs1.5bn to construct an 18-storey tower in his constituency of Damak, Jhapa, which will soon be completed.

Nepal has always regarded itself as the premier adventure tourism destination but in the light of global competition does Nepal still deserve that accolade? Visitors and trekkers expect to see wildlife, traditional architecture and a pristine environment but these qualities must be managed to meet the expectations of local stakeholders. Without access to modern facilities more and more people will migrate to Kathmandu and large cities leaving their villages to fall into ruin.

One significant problem is road construction. Without doing the appropriate technical work, building roads in the mid hills leads only to environmental disaster. Sadly, there are people in high places that see road development as providing financial perks and enhanced political standing. As a result of poor environmental impact studies, the first monsoon often results in landslips, rendering the road impassable and with no funds left for maintenance. Tourist appeal has also been dented and the damage to watercourses is well documented. However, there are short-term benefits for local communities as many find temporary employment in road construction, including people formerly involved in the trekking industry seeking alternative income during lockdowns.

New road construction in Solu Khumbu is one such high-profile project. The road into Salleri and Phaplu has been is several years old but more recently it has been pushed closer to Lukla. This latest section, from Salleri to Lukla, will be 104km long. At present the road is near Kharikhola village and the completion date to Lukla is intended to be December 2022. The road into Jomsom will eventually become more vehicle-friendly, linking the China- Mustang road to the central regions of Nepal and beyond. At the moment the surface is graded stone but the road from Kagbeni to Muktinath is already black-topped.

Today, pressure on the principles of sustainable tourism principles is extreme and without a planned approach and monitored development, Nepal is in grave danger of shooting itself in the foot. The loss of trekking trails to road development, high permit costs, the migration of wildlife and misplaced development strategies along with all the associated light, noise and air pollution could result in trekkers and other visitors looking at alternative locations and destinations. There is also the possibility of different forms of tourism that are less environmentally aware than trekking, like off-road vehicles.

Helicopter Boom
Nepal has faced challenges in the past to attract 'top-end tourists', looking enviously at Bhutan, but now that it is happening, some communities are regretting the fact. Helicopters are a popular way for the wealthy to get around. Helicopter sales to Nepal have consequently boomed with more than 20 new machines being delivered over recent years to the airlines of some of Nepal's top agencies: Shree Airlines, Simrik Air, Fishtail Air, Air Dynasty, Heli Everest, Mountain Helicopters, Altitude Air and Manang Air. Airbus has reported they expect to hand more than 30 helicopters by 2025. Khumbu is the busiest destination in Nepal for helicopter tours. Local residents now complain these flights create unbearable noise pollution in an otherwise quiet and sensitive environment. While there are undoubtedly advantages in having helicopter services, for rescue and medical emergencies, rubbish collection and disposal, the overuse of helicopters is creating evergreater problems and pressures.

Autumn 2021
There was a reminder early in the season that honesty and transparency are critical if ascents are to be taken at face value. The first headlines of the autumn concentrated on **Manaslu** when in October Jackson Groves published images taken by his drone that clearly showed where the lines of rope fixed by commercial expeditions really end: way below the summit.

Drone footage from Manaslu has lifted the lid on commercial expeditions not fixing ropes to the peak's summit, bringing into question many claimed ascents.

In the background, Mingma G Sherpa can be seen clearly leading his team to the true summit. Groves' images prompted statistician Eberhard Jurgalski and his team at *8000ers.com* to start looking closely at claims to have climbed Manaslu and in doing so reopened the enormous can of worms of whether those who have claimed all 14 8,000m peaks really have been to their true summits. When Jurgalski was done, he pronounced that just three on the list of around 36 had actually been to the top of all the peaks: Ed Viesturs, Veikka Gustafsson and Nims Purja, although not on his Project Possible round, going back later to tag Manaslu. The question is, does it really matter? Reinhold Messner, Jerzy Kukuczka and Erhard Loretan might be off Jurgalski's list but most mountaineers who understand the sport won't be discounting them.

Tom Livingstone and Matt Glenn succeeded in climbing the north pillar of **Tengkangpoche** (6500m) over a seven-day period in October 2021. They called their route *Massive Attack*. Livingstone reported hard mixed climbing, difficult aid sections and a long exposed snow ridge to the summit. The climbers used some equipment cached by a previous abortive attempt by an American team, which prompted controversy. See this edition, pp16-31.

In mid October, Slovenian alpinists Luka Stražar, Nejc Marčič, Marko Prezelj, and Matija Volontar visited Rowaling, their main focus being **Chobutse** (6686m). The mountain was first climbed in 1972 by a German team via the north-east ridge and more recently, in 2015, Mingma Gyalje Sherpa soloed the west face, but the north-west face is a real step up. The Slovenians split into two teams and on 28 October Marčič and Stražar started up Chobutse's north-west face. They faced steep, exposed climbing in the central part and

The line of *Massive Attack* on the north pillar of Tengkangpoche.

The line of the Slovenian route climbed in October 2021 on Chabutse (6686m).

despite unfavourable terrain they found two really good bivy spots before topping on 30 October. The climb was accompanied with low temperatures and strong winds, creating frequent spindrifts. To avoid confusion, the pair visited both the central and east summit before rappelling and descending the southern side of the mountain to reach base camp. Prezelj and Volontar tried a line up the mountain's south face but were forced to turn around because of the high winds.

An eight-person French team from the Groupe Excellence d'Alpinisme National led by the well-known veteran Stéphane Benoist and comprising Thomas Arfi, Louis Pachoud, Gabriel Miloche, Pierrick Fine, Pauline Champon, Anouk Felix-Faure and Pierrick Giffard acclimatised with an ascent of **Cholatse** (6440m) before making the first ascent of the north-east ridge of **Nare Ri Shar** (6005m), a satellite peak of Kangtega, (700m, D), which they named *Sugar Ridge*, presumably a comment on the snowy terrain that was broken up with the occasional rock section.

Fully acclimatised, the group split into two. Thomas Arfi, Louis Pachoud, and Gabriel Miloche went for **Mingbo Eiger** (6070m), a satellite peak of Kangtega south of Ama Dablam. Having spent two days at the base of the peak's west face checking conditions, on 26 October they climbed the couloir on the left side of the face. A little after 5pm, they reported from their bivouac site that all was well. Sadly, that was the last anyone heard from them. The French Federation of Mountain Clubs made every effort to locate the three and helicopter pilot Claudio Mittner spotted tracks on the summit ridge suggesting they turned around at 5,900m. An avalanche fracture line was spotted above and it's assumed the trio was swept away.

While this trio were on Mingbo Eiger, the rest of the group – Fine, Champon,

The route *Brothers in Arms* on Cholatse (6440m), climbed by a French team over five days in October.

Giffard, Felix-Faure and Benoist — started up a new route on the north face of **Cholatse**, facing 'six days of bitter cold and verticality'. On their last day up, 29 October, they learned the fate of their compatriots. They subsequently called their route *Brothers in Arms* (1600m, ED, VI, M5+, WI5).

Earlier in October, another French team featuring Charles Dubouloz and Benjamin Védrines climbed an impressive new route up the north face of **Chamlang** (7319m). The peak was most recently in the limelight thanks to the new route on its north-west face climbed in 2019, the work of Marek Holeček and Zdeněk Hák. That year, Védrines attempted the mountain's north-east couloir with Nicolas Jean, reaching a fore-summit at 7,240m before descending. In the autumn of 2021, Védrines and Dubouloz reached base camp with Damien Tomasi, Fanny Tomasi-Schmutz, Symon Welfringer and Aurelien Vaissière who planned and subsequently failed to climb the mountain's north pillar. The team acclimatised on **Mera Peak** (6476m) before Védrines and Dubouloz set off, early on 9 October, climbing fast up steep and difficult terrain. They needed just two bivouacs to reach the summit and one more on the way down the west ridge, reaching base camp again on 12 October. *À l'Ombre du Mensonge* (1600m, ED, M5+, 90°) was, Vedrines said, 'the most demanding climb I've ever done, both for the nights under spindrift and for the pitches we had to climb. I am very happy to have succeeded with Charles, in this ambitious challenge for both of us. I return having learned from the experience and happy, happy to have intensely enjoyed the Himalayan mountains.' The route name, which translates as 'shadow of a lie', refers to the claims made earlier in 2021 regarding summits on Manaslu.

Another impressive new route from the French on Chamlang (7319m), *À l'Ombre du Mensonge*, a north face direct with just two bivouacs on ground with vertical ice. *(Charles Dubouloz)*

In October, the Spanish Mountaineering Team (EEA), under the leadership of its director Mikel Zabalza, arrived at the south face of **Dorje Lhakpa** (6966m). Other members of the team included Javier Guzmán, Rubén San Martín, Mikel Inoriza, Ander Zabalza and Iker Madoz. The team spent a few days acclimatising and looking at the west ridge as a possible descent route. They then climbed a fore-summit of **Urkimang** (6197m) with two bivouacs. Bad weather then stopped them for a week but a brief weather window opened before a forecast of strong winds. Mikel Zabalza, Madoz and Inoriza headed for the south face while the others looked at the south-west face, both teams sharing a common approach to 5,800m. The route up the glacier was tortuous and they needed a second camp at 5,700m before accessing their routes. The south-west face team left at midnight but abandoned their attempt in the face of heavy snow and bitter cold. The south face team continued to a camp at 6,100m and from there they reached the summit on 25 October at 4pm. It was the first ascent of the south face. Difficulties were snow and ice around 55° to 65°.

The ascent of the season and perhaps of the last decade was the success of the Ukrainian team on **Annapurna III** (7555m) in October-November 2021. The team consisted of Nikita Balabanov, Mikhail Fomin and Viacheslav Polezhaiko. They achieved what many regard as one of the last great goals of alpinism in the Nepal Himalaya, reaching the summit via the inspiring and notorious south-east ridge on 6 November, exhibiting the core ethics that many of our readers may believe mountaineering is all about. The route was completed in a single 18-day push from base camp armed with only the knowledge the team had gained from a previous attempt in 2019. They descended to 5,400m, the base of the west ridge, via an unknown route

The legendary south-east ridge of Annapurna III, finally climbed after four decades of attempts by a Ukrainian team. *(Nikita Babanov)*

enduring a three-day nightmare in high winds before walking down to 5000m and the flatter area of the glacier from where a helicopter picked them up. Mikhail Fomin later described the climb stage by stage.

The lower snow-ice section, between 4,600m and 6,100m was easy snow climbing followed by a series of snowy chutes and short sections of hard mixed climbing leading to a snow ridge. The prominent rock buttress between 6,100m to 7,100m was the technical crux of the route. At 6,250m came the crux chimney, which Formin described as 'one of the most rotten technical pitches I have ever climbed.' This was followed at 6,500m by a feature known as 'the knife': a huge, snow-covered ledge visible from Pokhara. Until this point, the team managed to find decent bivy sites where they could build ledges for their tent. Above the ledge to the summit, 7,100m to 7,555m, there were no technical difficulties but the climbers were very exposed to the elements.

'In snow terrain, you had to take your shovel to lead, because otherwise, it was so unconsolidated that you did not have solid footholds to progress,' Fomin reported. 'And in the mixed terrain, you're dealing with lots of loose rocks covered by fresh snow, so you have to be creative in finding ways to move forward.'

Back in Ukraine, Mikhail Fomin reported he was safe with his family and during the first days of the war with Russia they fled to Italy. The whereabouts of his partners Viacheslav Polezhaiko and Nikita Balabanov are unclear. Their social media presence was confined to sharing posts about fundraising or from those seeking material for the cause. Fomin himself is busy collecting funds. 'Now it is time for [the] many Ukrainian climbers to wear soldiers' helmets instead of super-lightweight BD or Petzl stuff and to protect Ukraine,' he was reported as saying.

The impressive new combination climbed by the Czechs on Ama Dablam. *(Zdeněk Hák)*

Opposite page: Cho Oyu from Gokyo. *(Ian Wall)*

Zdeněk Hák and Jakub Kácha climbed a combination of the *American Direct* and *Smid* on **Ama Dablam** (6812m) over three days to give *Lancmit Direct* (TD+/ED, V, WI4, M4-5). 'The conditions changed, depending on the altitude and which side of the pillar we were on,' Hák told *Explorersweb*. 'It was better to climb on the south side of the pillar, where the snow was starting to turn into firn. On the other hand, a northern exposure meant tricky climbing in unstable snow conditions.' The route was named for Czech legend Miroslav Šmíd, who was known as 'Lancmit'.

Autumn into Winter Season

A Nepali team set out to establish a new line up the south face of **Cho Oyu** as another option for commercial expeditions climbing the mountain from the Nepal side. As with all the other expeditions during the autumn 2021 season they were hampered by poor weather conditions and the expedition came to an end below the summit. The exact line followed by the expedition is vague at the moment, but from the expedition file it appears that the team split into two groups each looking at alternative lines. Seven Summit Treks announced that they would support Gelje Sherpa on a new attempt in November 2022. Mingma G of Imagine Nepal announced he will attempt the route started by Pioneer Adventure up the south-south-west ridge, starting on 1 October 2022 and supported by a commercial expedition with 10 Sherpa guides and clients 'with appropriate previous experience'.

Jost Kobusch accompanied by Nicolas Scheidtweiler did two first ascents, as of Kobusch's acclimatisation plan for his Everest winter 2021-2 expedition. This he did in the Annapurna region, where his main goal was unclimbed **Purbung** (6500m). He then soloed unclimbed Peak 6125m, still unnamed.

Redpointing Everest?

Kobusch's 2021-2 Everest project began on 22 December with the aim of finishing before the end of meteorological winter on 28 February 2022. Kobusch was attempting the west ridge but with no specific aim to reach the summit in 2021-2 but he had set himself the target of reaching 8,000m at the base of the Hornbein couloir. This was his second winter season on Everest, solo and without supplementary oxygen, his previous high point of 7,300m coming in 2019-20, part of a three-year project at the end of which he aims to solo a combination of the Yugoslavian and American lines in winter. On this occasion he faced continuous strong winds, very low temperatures and a particularly dry line, which didn't allow him to push any further than 6,464m.

In the era of commercial expeditions there is a fine line between duty of care and meeting the expectations of often demanding clients. In 2020 Garrett Madison called off his Everest expedition, judging an ice serac perched high above the Icefall as unjustifiably risky. He was subsequently sued by one of his clients for failure to deliver his contract. The court decided the client was not entitled to a refund and that guides should not fear lawsuits when making decisions about safety. The judgment is being hailed in guiding and outdoor-adventure circles.

Winter into Spring Season

In mid February a Czech canyoning outfitter arrived in Nepal for a three-month expedition. The company had made previous descents in the Annapurna region varying in length from one to six days. During this season they attempted to descend the **Seti Khola** but inclement weather raised water levels to an unacceptable extent and warm temperatures caused serious rock-fall risk in the canyon, thwarting their plans, according to expedition leader Olda Stos.

Toshiyuki Yamada and Takeshi Tani made the first ascent of the north-west face of Kangchung Nup (6090m). *(Toshiyuki Yamada)*

The first success of the spring 2022 season was the ascent of the north-west face of **Kangchung Nup** (6090m) by two Japanese guides, Toshiyuki Yamada and Takeshi Tani. The line is very similar to that attempted by a Czech expedition that reached 5,900m in 2014, from where they retreated due to dangerous conditions. Japanese alpinist and Buddhist monk Daijo Saito and Shigenobu Akihiro made the first ascent of **Saula** (6235m) on 3 May 2022. Saula is located in the Manaslu Himal, lying on the Nepal-Tibet border, east-north-east of Samagaon.

The new British route on Jugal Spire (6563m), climbed in eight days. *(Tim Miller)*

In April 2022 Paul Ramsden and Tim Miller climbed the steep and sweeping granite north face on an unclimbed peak in the Jugal Himal subsequently named **Jugal Spire**. *The Phantom Line* (ED+, 1200m), climbed over an eight-day period with five days spent on the face featured thin ice and mixed climbing across several blank sections of hard rock sections with the greatest problem an a snow-free section of rock in the centre of the wall that was overcome via a hidden squeeze chimney that was climbed inside for about three pitches. See pp1-15.

An expedition team of five climbers from the Korean Kyung Boc High School Alpine Club made the first ascent of **Phu Khang Peak** (6694m) on 4 May 2022, a peak located near Nar Phu, Manang district. The team leader Kim Migon, who had previously ascended all 14 8000ers, was accompanied by Kang Sin Won, Jang Daeboo, Kim Minsoo, Lee Kunjin along with Nepali guides Tshering Sherpa and Dawa Tshering Sherpa.

It was announced that Peter Hamor would try to traverse from **Yalung Kang** (8505m) to **Kangchenjunga's** main summit, with Romanian partners Horia Colibasanu and Marius Gane. However, in the end the Nepal authorities decided to charge the expedition for an additional peak permit for Yalung Kang and so the team modified its plans and subsequently only Horia Colibasanu summited Kangchenjunga.

Makalu (8485m) was climbed without supplementary oxygen in 17h 18m by Karl Egloff (Swiss) and Nicolas Miranda (Ecuador). They also climbed without the usual down suit as they felt the weather, which was relatively warm, would justify them using a multi-layer clothing system allowing greater freedom of movement.

Himalayan veteran Marc Batard recently announced he wanted to set up a new, alternative route into Everest's Western Cwm avoiding the Khumbu Icefall. Assisted by a small group of French guides, they started opening this new variation in 2021, planning to fix it with metal cables and bolts, like a European via ferrata. Nepal's tourism ministry decided his route was not strictly on Everest but on Nuptse, so they issued him a permit for the latter.

Marc Batard's concept of a new route on the southern Everest route aimed at reducing risk in the Icefall.

If he wanted to climb Everest, officials told him, he needed another permit. 'The mountain is not respected anymore, it's about the money, and helicopters,' Batard said. Considering many expeditions now train on local trekking peaks and use helicopters for dropping loads into higher camps, Batard has reconsidered his project, wondering if it's worth the expense and effort.

Under existing Everest rules, the Sagarmatha Pollution Control Committee fixes the route up to camp two. The task of fixing the rope to the summit from camp two falls to the Expedition Operators' Association. There was a significant drop in numbers of Everest climbers for the 2022 climbing season, mainly due to the war in Ukraine, Covid-19 in China and global economic woes. With a potential drop of nearly 100 climbers, the Nepali government stands to lose up to $1 million in royalties. It also means fewer jobs for mountain guides, support staff and local hotels and teahouses.

Everest saw another slew of 'records', including several climbers claiming speed ascents. Kristin Harila, a 36-year-old professional athlete from Norway climbed her first mountain in 2015 when she trekked up Kilimanjaro. Now she wants to climb all 14 peaks above 8,000m in a shorter time than Nims Purja and climbed five of them in Nepal this spring in just 29 days. By early July she had increased that number to six with Nanga Parbat but was injured by rockfall as she descended to base camp. Individually these ascents are of little mountaineering significance but taken together they are testimony to the power of focus, strength, endurance and mental stamina.

There has been a weather station positioned on the Balcony since 2019, $30,000 of precision instruments designed to measure wind, humidity, temperature, solar radiation and barometric pressure. It was one of five such automatic weather stations placed as part of a partnership between the National Geographic Society, Tribhuvan University in Kathmandu, and the

Tenzing Gyalzen: mountain guide and world's highest electrician.

Nepali government, with funding from Rolex. However, with gale-force winds, extremely low temperatures and exposure to solar radiation, the technology suffered and it stopped transmitting on 20 January 2020. In the spring of 2022 a technical team including 12 Sherpas climbed to a spot known as Bishop's Rock, approximately 50 vertical metres below the summit, to install a new and improved station. For IT specialist Tenzing Gyalzen Sherpa, a 31-year-old electrician and mountain guide from Phortse, this involved climbing to work at approximately 8,810m, which he has done for the last three years to service the automated weather stations.

The new station at Bishop Rock saw Tenzing Gyalzen complete the wiring barehanded, in -40°C wind chill. By the time the team had returned to base camp the station was already sending back essential data that would not only help guides plan expeditions and keep clients safe but would provide information related to changing weather patterns, snow melt and the potential impact on all those communities that rely of Everest and the Himalaya for their drinking water. As the 2019 and 2020 data continues to be analysed, it's yielding surprising conclusions across a diverse field of studies, from human physiology to questions of long-term water supplies and seasonal crop cycles.

One issue that appeared in the spring of 2022 was the role that modern communications play in reporting issues on the big mountains. Connectivity is possible from most points these days and as a result as soon as a team member reaches the summit the fact is relayed back to base camp and in turn broadcast over social media. This haste to make the news public is all part of modern commercialism but fact checking with the people concerned is way down the list of priorities. Consequently some ascents turn out to have been misrepresented in the rush to publicise. Sadly, when the true facts emerge they rarely get mentioned. I don't think there is a deliberate move to blur the truth but haste can lead to misinformation.

While we're on the subject of technology, in April 2022 the Nepali authorities announced the compulsory use of GPS in mountaineering. Although this was initially planned two years ago, implementation was delayed. Now the tourism ministry has announced it will test this initiative. Officials stated that GPS is being implemented to make mountaineering more transparent. (It also implies the ministry doesn't trust the system of liaison officers.) Mohan GC, director of the department, said it had procured 20 devices in July 2018.

Guiding Issues

Nepali guides have in recent years had the opportunity to become members of the International Federation of Mountain Guides Associations (IFM-GA). This requires them to train under common international standards: gaining experience in the appropriate environment and being certified by an official institution recognised by the IFMGA. Training can take up to five years and guides are always taking new courses to keep up to date with the latest standards and techniques. It's a major achievement for Nepal to be involved and has undoubtedly raised standards.

Nepal now has 72 IFMGA guides but on Everest alone there are more than 1,500 support workers, often referred to as guides by their clients. Of that number, only around 10 are actually IFMGA certified, through their local member, the Nepal National Mountain Guide Association (NNGMA) but attempts to increase the number of internationally accredited guides is stalled by a curious anomaly: liability insurance.

The IFMGA has a professional code of conduct outlining the role and obligations for mountain guides towards their clients. According to this code, mountain guides need to assess the skill level of their clients, as well as their previous experience, encourage an attitude of respect for the environment, make sure clients have the proper equipment and raise their client's awareness about hazards and risks. They also need liability insurance bought in their home country. And here comes the weird anomaly. Because in Nepal insurance companies issue insurance to expeditions, not individuals.

So the bottom line is that according to IFMGA criteria, certified Nepali guides can't work independently in their own country because they can't buy liability cover there. They have to appear on an agency's block insurance cover. Meanwhile experienced but unqualified Nepali mountaineers continue to work in Nepal as 'guides' because there is no statutory professional body with similar criteria.

There has always been friction between IFMGA guides and experienced Everest 'guides' who are not IFMGA-qualified. Kami Rita Sherpa has now climbed Everest 26 times but was dismissive in an interview in March 2021:

> *I'm not a certified international mountain guide, I never have been and never will, but people still come and ask me to guide them to the top. Nepal Mountaineering Association members (guides) only work in Nepal, the rules and laws must be made taking them into consideration. If they want, the 'international' guides should go abroad to guide. They are international guides, right?*

The number of Nepali guides who aren't accredited and work predominantly on 8,000m peaks has increased sharply in recent years to meet client demand, despite this group not having done any accredited training, relying instead on ad hoc courses and long experience of the big mountains in challenging conditions and hazardous situations.

In 2019 tourism authorities in Nepal announced a new law that would recognise holders of the 'red book' issued by the Nepal Mountaineering Association

Waste not. Work is needed to manage human waste in the Everest region.

(NMA) as mountain guides. The NMA hands out three colours of books (essentially licences) to mountain workers for data and insurance purposes, although for not third-party liability. The first is black and given to kitchen and support staff who work at high altitude. If a person works and renews this book for two years in a row, it's upgraded to a blue book, which recognises the holder as a support climber. This can be upgraded to a red book, which gives the person the title of sirdar (expedition leader), the person who manages all the other Sherpas on a climbing expedition or trekking group. The red book is also given to all Everest summiteers, irrespective of their other experience.

The NNMGA welcomed the government's plan of recognising these climbers and their contribution to the mountaineering industry but most of its members say that red-book holders should be called 'expedition guides' and not 'mountain guides' as the term 'mountain guide' implies something different. If anyone who has summited can claim to be a guide, it argues, then in the long run clients will be confused and their IFMGA qualification will be undermined. The NNMGA took their case to Nepal's supreme court and the law was overturned. The NMA resented this and has issued veiled threats to NNMGA guides about retaining their status as NMA members.

In the Mire
We should not allow this to happen anywhere especially a national park dedicated to Chomolungma, 'goddess mother of the world'. The Nepali name, coined in the 20th century, is Sagarmatha, mean's 'ocean's brow', a nod to the ancient Tethys Sea. Disposal of human waste in the Sagarmatha National Park near Kala Pattar causes environmental damage and a threat to the health of local communities as it slowly filters into the ground. Would this be tolerated in the grounds of Westminster Abbey? There is technology to deal with this problem and I hope this is something the Alpine Club could involve itself.

TIMOTHY ELSON & ED DOUGLAS
India & Pakistan 2021-22

Rohit Vartak climbing pitch three of *Trishul Direct. (Shivam Aher).*

The Indian Himalaya section was missing from the 2021 *Alpine Journal* because, as far as the author is aware, there were no permits issued by the Indian Mountaineering Foundation in 2020. The one climb that I have found information on is a winter attempt on **Baljuri** (5922m) near Nanda Kot in the Kumaon Himalaya during the second and third weeks of December by a team comprising Aniket Mitra, Rivusoumya Das, Ashish Chanda and Anindya Mukherjee. They turned back several days into their attempt due to the high avalanche conditions.

In 2021 the Indian Mountaineering Foundation issued 64 permits to a variety of objectives. All the permits issued were to Indian teams as foreigners were not allowed to travel to India in 2021. As of 27 March 2022, international flights to India are running again, the government is issuing visas and the Indian Mountaineering Foundation is issuing permits to international teams.

Shoshala Peak with the line of *Trishul Direct*. *(Shivam Aher)*

There are three climbs from 2021 which stand out: the first documented ascent of **Kang Yatse IV** (6130m); the second ascent and first Indian of the north ridge of **Manda I** (6510m) and the second ascent and first Indian ascent of *Trishul Direct* on **Shoshala** (4700m).

The Atal Rohtang tunnel opened on 2 October 2020, linking Manali with Keylong and cutting out the Rohtang pass, significantly reducing the time it takes to drive between the two. Of course, the wonderful view from Rohtang pass will be missed if the tunnel is taken. There are future plans to tunnel the other four major passes on the road between Manali and Leh.

In September 2021 Team Shivdurga, comprising Rohit Vartak, Yogesh Umbre, Sameer Joshi, Onkar Padval, and Bhupesh Patil, made the first Indian ascent of the *Trishul Direct* on **Shoshala** (4700m), a 750m big-wall route. Shoshala is in the Baspa valley of the Kinnaur region of the Indian Himalaya

Team Shivdurga on the summit of Shoshala Peak. *(Rohit Vartak)*

and was first climbed in 2011 by Elie Chevieux, Yannick Boissenot, and Giovanni Quirici over 10 days by the *Trishul Direct*. Team Shivdurga had their plans for a repeat of this climb postponed by the Covid-19 outbreak. Eventually, on 7 September, they started up to the base of the face and over the next 20 days pushed the route out while contending with consistently bad weather, with only 11 of those days climbable. They fixed ropes on the route and commented on the quality of many of the pitches, with difficulties up to 7a+/7b and a bit of A2. On 27 September, Rohit Vartak, Yogesh Umbre, Onkar Padval and Bhupesh Patil summited with Sameer Joshi summiting the next day. This climb is considered a milestone for Indian big wall climbing.

On 1 August 2021, a team of three Indian alpinists, Sonam Yangjor, Stanzin Wangial and Anindya Mukherjee made the first documented ascent of **Kang Yatse IV** (6130m) in the Ladakh Himalaya. **Kang Yatse I** (6400m) and **Kang Yatse II** (6175m) are both popular peaks approached from the Nyimalang Chu but after careful research Anindya Mukherjee identified that Kang Yatse IV was unclimbed and would best be approached from the Langthang Chu valley to the west of the Nyimalang Chu.

In 2021 Anindya Mukherjee made three attempts on Kang Yatse IV,

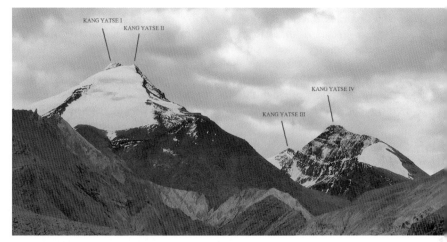

The Kang Yatse group from Hangkar. *(Sonam Yangjor)*

The map of the ascent route on Kang Yatse IV. *(Anindya Mukherjee)*

the first in February and March was with Aloke Kumar Das but a broken plastic boot thwarted their plans. In April, Anindya returned with Sonam Yangjor and Stanzin Wangial but climbing to 5,400m they sat out 27 hours of bad weather before retreating. The team returned on 24 July for the successful climb and summited on 1 August via the north ridge via three camps and graded the climb AD.

On 18 September 2021, a team from Giripremi, a mountaineering club from Maharashtra, made the second ascent and first Indian ascent of the north ridge of **Manda I** (6510m). Manda I is in the Kedarganga valley of the Gangotri region of Garhwal and was first climbed in 1981 by an Indian team. The north ridge was climbed in 1983 by a Japanese team. The Giripremi club first tried the north ridge in 1991 but retreated from c6,000m. Umish Zirpe, a veteran of that trip, organised the 2021 expedition. The mountain had changed significantly since 1991 with major glacial retreat and loss of snow cover. Over three days the team of Sumit Mandale, Vivek Shivade, Pawan Hadole, Mingma Sherpa and Nim Dorje Sherpa climbed the ridge through the night to reach the summit at 9.30am. On 14 September, other members of the Giripremi made the second ascent of **Bhrigu Parvat** (6041m), a peak situated north of Manda I. The summit team was Anand Mali, Varun Bhagwat, Rohan Desai, Ruturaj Agawane and Ankit Sohoni.

In August 2021 a five-member team from the Himalayan Club made the first ascent of **Peak 6065m** in Spiti's Kharcha valley. They named the peak Fyanlabte, which translates as 'butterfly' in the local Lahauli language. The team approached via the Kharcha nala and the Bara Shigar glacier. Rajesh Gadgil, Rajendra Shinde and Atin Sathe summited on 26 August.

In January 2021 there was the first Nubra valley ice climbing festival; the festival is the brainchild of Rigzin Tsewang, a local mountain guide who has developed many water-ice climbs in the Nubra valley. It is hoped that this will become an annual event.

Tim Elson

It's likely there will be much more climbing to report from India for 2022 and as these notes were finished news arrived of the first repeat of the iconic route on the west face of **Changabang** (6880m), first climbed by Pete Boardman and Joe Tasker in 1976. It was at the time among the very hardest climbs in the Himalaya, climbed in a lightweight capsule style: a route that signalled the big changes underway in Himalayan alpinism.

Kim Ladiges and Matthew Scholes from Australia and Daniel Joll from New Zealand arrived in India in early April and reached base camp on 11 April. Having acclimatised and established an ABC on the col beneath the west face, they climbed to ABC on 24 April for their attempt. On 25 April, they climbed to 5,900m and put up a tent and portaledge that they used for a couple of nights, fixing ropes to 6,150m on 26 April. They then made slow but steady progress over the next few days, sleeping on portaledges and working their way up the face to reach the summit at noon on 2 May. Their ascent was dogged by low temperatures and afternoon snowfall, as Joll reported: 'I can honestly say that I had the coldest hardest days of my mountain climbing career on that face. Leading through the rock tower with temperatures around -30°C was one of the hardest days climbing I've ever done. It wasn't the difficulty of the movement that made it hard; it was the cold.'

As the *Alpine Journal* neared deadline, the state government of Uttarakhand announced the opening of what it claimed were 30 unclimbed peaks and 10 more high-altitude trekking routes in a bid to boost tourism. Included in the list were significant peaks like **Rishi Pahar** (6992m) in the Nanda Devi area, first climbed in 1975 by a Japanese team but previously attempted by Eric Shipton and Bill Tilman, and **Devtoli** (6788m) in the same region, climbed by a team from Mumbai by Harish Kapadia in 1974. It will take further work

The Australian and New Zealand team on the second ascent of the *Boardman-Tasker* on the west face of Changabang.

ROUTE INFORMATION

Place: Karakorum (Pakistan)
Peak: Sani Pakkush (6,953m) virgin south face.
Grade: 2,500m., ED+/ 90° / M4+/ WI4+.
Date: 16-20/10/2020
By: Pierrick Fine and Symon Welfringer

Sani Pakkush (6953m), showing the 2020 French route up the south face and upper south-west ridge, and the upper section of that ridge on summit day. The climbers spent a second night at their high camp before descending the route.

to see which if any on the list are still unclimbed but making more peaks available is always welcome.

Covid-19 severely restricted climbing in Pakistan as well as India, although one ascent from October 2020 unreported in the *Alpine Journal* was a new route up the south face and upper south-west ridge of **Sani Pakkush** (6,953 meters) in the Batura Muztagh of Pakistan, from French stars Pierrick Fine and Symon Welfringer. Their route, which took five days, was called *Revers Gagnant* (2500m, WI4+ M4+ 90°) and it was the second ascent of the mountain.

The line of ascent and ski descent of Yawash Sar II, showing where Baranowski waited (B) and Bardiel's exit point on the ridge (A).

It was a similar story for 2021, where Covid-19 restrictions again reduced activity. In the spring, a Polish expedition climbed **Yawash Sar II** (6176m), previously attempted by Krzysztof Wielicki in the summer of 2019. The team established base camp in the Ghidims valley in late April and a day later reached an ABC at 5,160m, where the North Ghidims glacier splits. On 30 April at 4am, Jedrzej Baranowski and Andrzej Bargiel left for the south-west face of Yawash Sar II, carrying skis. Although hot during the day, temperatures at night were falling to -15°C and the pair was able to move unroped.

At about half-height Baranowski, struggling with the altitude, elected to stop and wait as Bargiel, famed for the first ski descent of K2 in July 2018, continued across the top of a large slab avalanche track and then climbed steep snow to the left side of a rocky rib to reach the south-south-west ridge, reaching the summit at 11am but stopping just short of the large cornice on top following advice over the radio from drone operator Jakub Gzela. Donning his skis, Bargiel descended the west-north-west ridge but the angle and the thin layer of snow over ice required him to make an abseil before he was able to ski diagonally across the upper face to meet his ascent route. Reaching Baranowski, the pair skied to the bottom of the face and were back in base camp the same day. On 1 May they returned to Shimshal and transferred to Skardu for the next phase of their expedition.

On 10 May, Baranowski and Bargiel, having left camp at 4.30am reached the summit of **Laila Peak** (6096m) at 1pm, having left their skis 150m below the top because of difficulties. They were able to ski the north-west face from this point to their starting camp at 4,400m above the East Gondogoro glacier. Their descent took two and a half hours. It was not the first descent of the north-west face, which was made by a French team in 2018 that included Tiphanie Duperier: see below. The first known ascent of the peak was made in 1987 by a British team that included Andy Cave, Tom Curtis, Sean Smith and Simon Yates. The Poles experienced good condition in the spring and suggested that spring and autumn might now offer the best seasons.

A French team comprising Tiphaine Duperier, Boris Langenstein, Aurelia Lanoe and Guillaume Pierrel had to wait for a week in Islamabad for their skis to catch up with them before flying to Gilgit on 2 June. Their ultimate goal was a ski descent of Gasherbrum II but not wanting 'to get bored going up and down on the same route for acclimatisation' they chose to do so in two different areas. Their first plan was to explore the Chiantar glacier in the Hindu Raj, but a transport strike ended that so they went instead to the Bagrot valley, north-east of Gilgit, on the south side of **Diran** (7,266m). Half a day's trek up the Burche glacier, they made a base camp and, for a recce, skied a peak of 4,800m directly above it. From its summit they spotted two more likely objectives around the 5,000m mark. In a four-day round trip, the team climbed and skied these peaks: **Darchan** (c5347m) and then a neighbouring unnamed summit to the south: Peak 5040m. They then skied the exposed west ridge, 55° at the top, with views of the Bulche Peaks and Diran. They then returned to the Hindu Raj.

The French left Darkot village with only five days before their scheduled departure for the Baltoro. Dry conditions were initially disheartening but they climbed the north-west couloir of **Garmush Zom I** (6244m) from a camp at 5,142m, finishing up the north ridge. Huge cornices blocked them from seeing into the Chiantar glacier and cold temperatures forced them off the top sooner than they wished for their 1,100m descent back down the couloir at angles of between 55° and 45°. This success encouraged them to move camp to below Garmush Zom South (6180m) where a couloir curved leftwards up the south-west face. This proved more difficult than the previous day's,

The French ski descent from high on Gasherbrum I. The peak above the skier is Masherbrum. *(Tiphaine Duperier)*

with avalanche debris on the lower route and above that a 200m icy section. Near the top was a short section of mixed they had to rappel on descent before skiing back down in the complicated snow conditions.

The team now transferred to Skardu and trekked up the Baltoro glacier, reaching Gasherbrum base camp (5040m) on 26 June. The plan was to climb the rarely climbed central spur on the south face of **Gasherbrum II** (8035m). After an acclimatisation climb in late June, the team climbed to 6,500m on 8 July and the following day were forced to camp early at 6,949m before reaching the plateau, slowed by deep snow and technical difficulties. The following day, 10 July, they reached the plateau via an icy 50° couloir and then continued up to camp at 7,321m. They reached the summit the following morning at 11.30 despite deep snow and a strong westerly that buried the tents. They spent two hours on top before skiing down through 'horrible' snow to their tents. Opting to continue, they rappelled the couloir off the plateau and continuing skiing down to their camp at 6,949m, reaching base camp next day.

Despite all this success, Langenstein and Duperier then made a lightweight attempt to ski the Japanese couloir on **Gasherbrum I** (8080m), attempting an optimistic summit push of 1,600m but turning around after an immense effort at 7,720m from where they skied down, with one 30m abseil, to reach base camp next day.

In late June, the French alpinist Mathieu Maynadier and Tom Livingstone arrived at base camp on the Yutmaru glacier, south of the Pumari Chhish massif, for an attempt on **Pumari Chhish East** (6850m). Poor weather hampered their acclimatisation, but on 9 July the weather improved and having waited a day for the mountain to shed recent snow, they started up the glacier, managing to avoid the worst of it via a snow gully. Having bivouacked under the south face they started up the south-east ridge, tackling steep ice, mixed ground and all of it buried in powder, making the route time-consuming. At the end of the second day they camped beneath a

The Anglo-French attempt on the south-east ridge of Pumari Chhish East showing camps and high point at around 6,700m. *(Tom Livingstone)*

James Price near the top of Darmyani on the south ridge with the Passu glacier below. *(James Price)*

serac at 6,500m but the last day of good weather forecast didn't materialise. At 11am, with snow falling and conditions deteriorating, the pair bailed, just 150 vertical metres below the summit. They abseiled the route, reaching base camp at midnight. Livingstone warned that they were hampered by difficulties with porters at Hispar.

The Batura Wall rises more than 4,500m from the Hunza valley, running for 40km without ever dropping below 6,000m. British climber James Price had been in Pakistan in 2020 during a season curtailed by Covid-19 but returned to explore the Batura in 2021. On 11 July Price and Hassan Aljabbal walked west up the Batura glacier to climb **Darmyani** (aka Maidon Sar, 6090m). Having gained Passu Cwm via a new route on the north ridge of **Hiriz** (5550m), price continued alone up the east ridge of Darmyani, turning around at 5,900m in difficult snow conditions. The following day he tried the unclimbed south ridge of Darmyani, gaining its crest at 5,200m via a snow and rock gully and up mixed ground to a final delicate pitch of IV and the summit.

Approaching the final seven-pitch ice slope of the north ridge leading to the summit of Peak 6032m. *(Kazua Hiraide)*

A few days later he attempted **Bublimotin** (6000m), the rock tower above Karimabad in the Hunza valley. Starting early from a camp on the Hasanabad glacier to the west, he climbed 1,400m on 60° ice, reaching 5,800m by daybreak. Caught out by the Karakoram sun, he was forced to seek shelter as ice turned to water and lacking bivouac gear opted to descend 200m below the summit.

On 1 September and now well acclimatised and equipped, he set off for **Passu Diar** (7,295m), which has seen few ascents. Using skis, he approached up a complicated icefall to reach the Upper Passu glacier to a high camp at 6,500m. On 11 September, he reached the Passu Terrace and continued to the saddle at the start of the south-east ridge of **Passu Sar**. He then headed back up the north-west face of Passu Diar, climbing a 70° pitch of snow and ice over a serac and then continuing 300m up easy ground to the summit. A day later, he skinned up the gentle southern flank of **Passu North** (6884m), a probable first ascent of this remote peak. Price concluded: 'The Batura Muztagh has phenomenal climbing potential with many unclimbed summits and new lines to explore. The proximity to the Karakoram Highway and the kindness of the local population make it even more desirable.'

Two more climbers who were eager to return to Pakistan as Covid-19 allowed were the Japanese Takuya Mitoro and Kazuya Hiraide. The summer season being finished, they chose to try some winter ascents in the Karun Koh area. (For more on the 2021 season in the Karun Koh region, see V Saunders, 'The Murkhun Valley', on p39.) Hiraide had made four attempts on **Shispare** (7611m) before succeeding on his 'dream mountain' and from the summit had seen **Karun Koh** (7164m or 6977m) but preferring the 7,000m contour had not thought of climbing there before. With winter approaching, the region made much more sense.

Researching the area, he discovered Japanese climbers had made two attempts on **Peak 6032m**, also known as **Maqbul Sar** and four kilometres north of Karun Koh, the second ending in tragedy with the death of Pakistani climber Sami Ullah Khan. The pair left Japan on 3 December and trekked up the Unakin-i-Gur valley to a base camp at c4,200m near the end of the Unakin glacier. Although it was not yet calendar winter, temperatures were already -20°C and below. Over the next two days they acclimatised by climbing the peak to 5,500m before sitting out a spell of bad weather at base camp.

On 16 December the Japanese left camp with three days of food and fuel, following the route of previous Japanese teams and camping not far below the north ridge. They started their summit push at 5am and reached the ridge at 5,800m at sunrise. The final steep slope to the summit had 20cm of snow on hard ice. They climbed this in seven pitches in temperatures below -30°C. They reached the top along a final corniced ridge at 12.45pm. Descending the same day, cold injuries scotched the same day, but unfortunately some frostbite injuries sustained during the climb prevented an attempt on Karun Koh. They proposed calling the peak Sami Sar in honour of Sami Ullah Khan.

Ed Douglas

South America 2021-22

Extremo Huanacuni Norte. *(Julieta Ferreri).*

Bolivia

In the summer of 2021, Argentine Julieta Ferreri and Brazilian Marcelo Motta Delvaux were active in the **Nevado Huancuni** (5798m) region. First they explored the area over two expeditions during June and July and then a climbing expedition that took eight days. They established base camp by Lago Nube and camp one at 5,000m, near the entrance to the south-west glacier. During an 18-hour push, the pair ascended the normal route, the south-west ridge of Huanacuni, first crossing the summit of **Extremo Huanacuni Sur** (c5450m). They then continued to the main summit finding powder snow above 5,500m. They were forced to stop 20 or 30m below the main summit. The ridge between Huanacuni and **Nevado Nube** (5710m) had snow at 65° but because of the poor powder conditions felt steeper. They descended the route of ascent and rated it AD/D.

Topo of ascents Nevado Huanacuni. *(Julieta Ferreri)*

Afterwards they crossed a pass (5250m) descending to a glacier below the west face of Huanacuni, establishing their next camp at 5,100m at the glacier's base. They then climbed **Extremo Norte de Huanacuni** (5400m) via a glacier on the edge of the west face that started at a moderate angle but steepened to 55° grades near the top. The route was rated as PD/PD+. This beautiful summit has no definitively recorded climbs but Lindsay Griffin reports that some peaks at the northern end of the Huanacuni massif were climbed by a German expedition in 1969. After descending, Ferreri and Motta Delvaux walked to the nearby road and took a bus to La Paz.

Meanwhile, in the **Cordillera Real**, Fiona Tummon and Alexander von Ungern left Peñas on 7 August to arrive close to the Paso Mullu col (4730m), just short of Lago Jankho Kota. From there they trekked west, crossing a pass a little over 5,300m below **Wila Lloje** (5596m), camping after four hours in the middle of the glacier plain beyond. Next day at first light they approached the long north-north-west ridge of Wila Lloje, which starts from a col south-east of **Peak 5604m**. They chose to climb all the gendarmes on this ridge, although they reported that most could have been passed on solid névé. Until the first significant summit – **Peak 5580m** – the rock was solid. Continuing over two more forepeaks, mainly on hard snow, they reached a steep rocky section below Wila Lloje itself. Progressively deteriorating rock on this 100m passage made for delicate climbing. From the top they descended the south-west ridge (55° in the upper section) to the col they'd crossed the previous day and regained their tents less than six hours after leaving.

Next day they opted to climb a gully on the east face of **Warawarani I** (5542m) that had caught their attention the evening before. They started at sunrise on an initial pitch of dry tooling to reach the bottom of a large cave and comfortable belay below what proved to be the crux. Taking a line around the left side of the hollowed rock formation, the crux 10m were vertical and very delicate, with compulsory tool placements in thin, shallow cracks, often hidden by moss, and thin edges for the crampons. Protection was poor. Above was a snow gully of c50° with steeper steps. From the top they descended the north ridge, then down-climbed a snowy gully to the east and were back at the tent before noon. The first ascent of Warawarani I was made in August 1975, by four Italians, via a gully on the east face. Glacier heights and snow cover have changed here dramatically.

On 10 August the two climbers left at dawn for one final climb. The mountain at the head of their glacier is **Jankho Peque** (5604m), 'white head' in local Ayamara, and they climbed its south face at around 50°, although snow conditions were poor, leaving them up to their waists at times. 'From the summit, we had the impression we were a little lower than both Warawarani and Wila Lloje, making us feel the map altitude for Jankho Peque is too high.' They descended the west ridge, packed up camp, and walked down to the road. The first recorded ascent of Jankho Peque was in 1998 by a four-man French party, which climbed the south-east ridge at F.

Peru

The **Cordillera Central** is located between the regions of Junín and Lima. It's very little visited, with many wild areas that remain untouched. All the 5,000m peaks here have had very few ascents. This allows an old-time version of mountaineering similar to that of the pioneers. During July 2021, the Peruvian Edward Saona and Frenchman Steve Meder, who has spent 17 of his 44 years living in Peru, explored access to the south-west face of **Nevado Sullcon Sur**. The pair ascended the north summit of **Nevado Sullcon** (5500m) to get a good view of the unclimbed face of Sullcon Sur (5650m). In August they drove 130km and six hours from Lima to Yurak Mayo (4300m), where the road finishes, and then trekked to base camp at the nearby Sullcon glacier at almost 5,000m. On 9 August they put up a new route on the south-west face of Sullcon Sur, 700m of mixed ground described by Meder as 'an interesting and sustained route with ice and rock of good quality, with climbing up to M5 and WI3+.' It took 10 hours to reach the summit ridge and after a rest they continued, passing lots of penitentes on the way to reaching the summit at 5.30pm, just in time for a superb sunset over the Pacific Ocean and a nice view of the Cordillera Central. They reached base camp after 17 hours of activity.

Steve Meder is very active with new routes in Peru. For his next expedition, this time in the **Cordillera Blanca**, he was joined by Peruvian friends Silio and Antonio Chinchay. Departing the town of Pashpa (3450m), they ascended the Uruscocha valley, camping near the second Uruscochas lake at about 4,335m, below the possibly unclimbed north-west face of **Urus Oeste** (5450m). On 4 September 2021, Meder and Silio Chinchay climbed the moraine to the lake at the base of the face (4800m) and continued climbing

Edward Saona on the second pitch of the south-west face of Sullcon Sur (5650m) in Peru's Cordillera Central. *(Steve Meder)*

View of the Cordillera Central from Sullcon Sur. *(Steve Meder)*

Cordillera Central - Peru
4to ascenso absoluto
Nueva ruta : Cara Suroeste directa
TD 700m M5/WI3 + /AI3
9 de agosto 2021
Steve Meder, Edward Saona

60/65°

M5
80°
70°

Topo of the south-west face of Sullcon Sur. *(Steve Meder)*

decomposed rocky terrain for 300m, with vertical steps of around III. They reached a suspended glacier and traversed left, climbing some 45°-50° ice slopes to reach easier snow slopes and penitentes and the summit pyramid. It took them 5 hours from camp and they rated the 600m climb at AD, 50°, III. The pair opted to descend via the eastern sub-peak (5350m, M3) and the south-eastern slopes of the 1963 normal route from Ishinca base camp and then the rocky north ridge, which they had attempted the year prior, and descended easier slopes from a col (5100m) to the moraine lake in the Uruscocha valley.

The Basque mountaineers Eneko and Iker Pou have made plenty of contributions to Peruvian climbing in recent years. The summer of 2022 was no exception. In late June, to-gether with Peruvian alpinist Micher Quito, they climbed two new routes on the Urus Oeste peaks that lie be-tween the Ishinca and Uruscocha valleys. The first was on **Urus Oeste** (5450m) from the Urus Oeste glacier. *Hanan Pacha* (425m, 90°) was climbed in an 11-hour round-trip from a base camp at 4,900. Three days later they

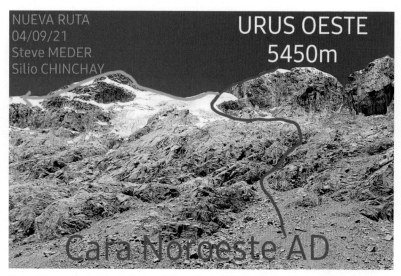

New route on the north-east face of Urus Oeste (5450m) in Peru's Cordillera Blanca. *(Steve Meder)*

High on Urus Oeste. *(Steve Meder)*

added a route to **Urus Oeste III** (5270m), likely the first on this feature climbed in 12 and a half hours. *Emmoa* (M6, 75°) is named in honour of the Basque mountain museum. The Pou brothers had already made an acclimatisation trip up **Huarapasca** (5418m) and done a free ascent of their own 2019 route *Aupa Gasteiz* (160m, 7c+). Yet they were far from done.

A few days after these ascents, they put a fabulous new mixed climb on the north face of **Cashan** (5716m) in the nearby Rajucolta valley, leaving

The line of *Hanan Pacha* from the prolific Pou brothers and Micher Quito. *(Iker Pou)*

Below: Iker Pou and Eneko Pou making the first ascent of *Bizirik* on the north face of Cashan (5716m). *(Iker Pou)*

On the first ascent of *One Push* on the south-west face of Pumahuacanca (5563m). *(Iker Pou)*

The line of *Bizirik*. *(Iker Pou)*

their bivy at 5,000m on 21 June and taking eight hours to reach the summit. They called their route *Bizirik* (980m, M6, 85°), which translates as 'alive'. They descended the opposite side of the mountain and were back at their base camp in a 13 and a half hour round-trip.

These were only warm-ups compared to what came next. Still in the Cordillera Blanca, above the Rurec valley, the Pou brothers and Quito climbed a new route on the south-west face of **Pumahuacanca** (5563m), a 'brutal' 1,000m line they called *One Push* (V, 85°, M7), named for the intense continuous effort required to climb it. Leaving their high camp at 5.15am on 12 July, their route culminates in an inspiring and perpendicular goulotte just below the summit, which they reached at 5.45pm, just in time for sunset. Pumahuacanca is a complex mountain with no descent straightforward and it took the trio another nine hours to reach safety on steep grass slopes, where they waited for dawn, reaching base camp 26 and a half hours after setting out. They described the route on social media as 'the hardest high mountain of our career', some claim given their extensive track record. The pair still weren't done,

The line of *Reino Hongo* on the east face of Jirishanca (6094m).

The line of *One Push*. (Iker Pou)

The meandering and difficult line of *Ànima de Corall* on the east face of Siula Grande (6344m).

climbing a 14m 8c+ rock route and reaching the summit of two 6,000m peaks, **Tocllaraju** (6034m) and **Ranrapallca** (6164m).

In the **Cordillera Huayhuash**, Alik Berg and Quentin Roberts climbed an impressive new route on the famous peak **Jirishanca** (6094m), a name that translates as 'bill of a hummingbird'. This spectacular mountain has a storied history, from the first ascent via the east ridge in 1957 from Toni Egger and Siegfried Jungmair to more recent new routes on the east face including Nick Bullock and Al Powell's *Fear and Loathing* and Aymeric Clouet and Didier Jourdain's *Tambo, Churros, y Amigos*, both climbed in 2003. However, there was still a huge amount of unclimbed real estate to the left of the face, which this summer attracted Berg and Roberts. During a three-week expedition in July 2022 Berg and Roberts managed to climb a new line on this east side of the mountain. More details next year, hopefully, but Roberts told *Planetmountain* that they called the route *Reino Hongo* after the South American mushroom kingdom in Super Mario, a nod to the complex snow mushrooms they met on the route. They rated difficulties at 5.8, 90°, M7 and quoted an elevation gain of 1,100m, 'although the numbers in no way represent the complexity of the climbing' and the height gain doesn't reflect the length of the route. Also on the mountain were Josh Wharton and Vince Anderson who repeated the 2003 Italian route *Suerte*, which controversially used dozens of bolts.

Staying in the Cordillera Huayhuash, Spanish climbers Bru Busom and Marc Toralles made the first ascent of the formidable east face of **Siula Grande** (6344m) in Peru, in a six-day effort starting 11 July. Despite numerous previous attempts, the east face had not been climbed in its entirety before, although in 2016 Max Bonniot and Didier Jourdain climbed the east pillar and south-east ridge. The two Spaniards had tried the face before in 2019 with Roger Cararach but abandoned the attempt when Cararach was injured by rockfall. Having bivied under the face on the night of 10 July, they set off on a meandering journey of 'great tension', the mountain's compact limestone low down exposed to rock fall. The pair was forced to climb after the sun had left the face in the afternoon or at night using big-wall tactics low down before reverting to alpine style higher up. They called their route *Ànima de Corall* (1100m, 7b, A3, AI5, M6) and described what must have been a harrowing descent on loose abseil anchors.

Expedition Reports

'Seracs on the East Rongbuk Glacier', T Howard Somervell,
pastel, 21cm × 29cm, 1922. *(Alpine Club)*

Expedition Reports

SUMMARISED BY ADAM BUTTERWORTH

Mount Everest Foundation (MEF) Expedition Reports

The Mount Everest Foundation (*www.mef.org.uk*) was established as a registered charity following the successful ascent of Everest in 1953. It was initially financed using the surplus funds and subsequent royalties from that expedition. It provides financial support for expeditions of an exploratory nature in mountain areas, and is administered by trustees appointed by the Alpine Club and the Royal Geographical Society.

The exploration is mainly of a geographical nature but may also cover disciplines such as geology, botany, zoology, glaciology and medical research. In return for funding the MEF requires only a comprehensive report, and copies of these reports are lodged with the AC and the RGS. The reports can be consulted at these establishments or alternatively online.

The MEF has made total grants of well over £1m to more than 1,600 expeditions with members from the UK and New Zealand. Donations to allow us to continue this work are always welcome. We particularly encourage donations from former beneficiaries of MEF grants. In 2021, due to lingering travel restrictions caused by the Covid-19 pandemic, only three MEF-supported expeditions were able to go ahead. The following notes summarise the reports from these expeditions.

GREENLAND & THE ARCTIC

Structural Glaciological Analysis of a Calving Glacier – Nathaniel Baurley and Chris Tomsett (July 2021)

This research expedition aimed to undertake a complete structural glaciological analysis of Fjallsjökull, an active, calving glacier in south-east Iceland. Due to time and weather constraints, the team decided to focus their efforts on using a UAV-mounted laser scanner to conduct surveys of the glacier. This novel methodology allows for the accurate delineation of glacial surface change and it is hoped that this will contribute towards a better understanding of glacial calving. In total the pair were able to carry out seven survey flights over four days in the field. Processing of the resulting data is ongoing, but due to the novel nature of the surveying method, it is expected that the results will prove to be of significant interest.

MEF Ref 21-07

CENTRAL ASIA

Alpine Club Kyrgyzstan Expedition 2021 – Tom Davis-Merry, Tom Simpson, Alex Metcalfe, Sam Davis and Sam Mace with Wayne Auton providing support from France (July-August 2021)

The team gathered in Bishkek before transferring to Kuiluu via Karakol. Here they established their basecamp with a view to climbing a number of virgin peaks off the East Bordlu glacier. Due to problems with acquiring insurance for the expedition, Wayne Auton was unable to meet the rest of the party at base camp as planned. The team was further reduced to just four members when, shortly after arriving at basecamp, Sam Mace was evacuated by helicopter due to an infected ingrowing toenail. Despite their reduced numbers, the remaining team members succeeded in establishing a new route on their acclimatisation objective; **Peak 4788m** on 13 August. The mountain was climbed via its west flank and summit ridge in alpine style at an approximate grade of PD+. The following day, the same team achieved another first ascent on the same mountain, again via the west flank, at a grade of AD+. On their return to base camp, the team discovered that the expedition cook had been threatened by a local farmer who had also damaged a number of the camp tents. The fallout from this event cut short the remaining climbing time and no further summits were achieved.

MEF Ref 21-09

EUROPE

Izvor Licanke 2021 Expedition – Christine Grosart, Richard Walker, Mark Burkey, Louise McMahon, Fred Nunn, Anton Van Rosmalen and Velimir Vrzic (August 2021)

The renewed exploration of the Izvor Licanke cave in Fužine, Croatia is now into its sixth year. Covid-19 forced a hiatus in 2020, but this 2021 expedition was able to go ahead as planned. Unfortunately one of the expedition's push divers became unwell early in this year's expedition, rendering them unable to dive. A standby diver was requested at short notice and the team were eventually able to conduct an exploratory dive. In total, they explored a little over 100 meters of new cave passage, both above and below the water. This took them to the completion of Sump 4 and beyond, where they identified another sump (Sump 5). In addition, the party were also able to survey the passage between Sump 2 and Sump 3, conduct a centre line survey of the dry cave between Sumps 1 and 2 and re-equip the line in Sump 1.

MEF Ref 21-22

Reviews

'East Face of Everest from Rupia La', T Howard Somervell,
oil, 49cm × 74cm, 1924. *(Alpine Club)*

Reviews

Imaginary Peaks
The Riesenstein Hoax and Other Mountain Dreams
Katie Ives
Mountaineers Books, 2021, 301pp, £22.

As the author Jonathan Raban is sailing north from Seattle on his absorbingly discursive *Passage to Juneau* (1999) he takes an irreverent broadside at the Northwest school of nature writers and poets, singling out, in particular, Barry Lopez, author of the celebrated *Arctic Dreams*. Raban, like me, is an admirer of Lopez's intent, his lyric passages and the microscopic particularity of his writing. But sometimes the prayerful tone can be too much for this self-exiled Englishman:

> *Reading the Northwest nature writers, I found myself an agnostic in their church; embarrassed, half-admiring, unable to genuflect in the right places. I wished there were more jokes.*

Raban's observations came back to me several times while reading *Imaginary Peaks*, and like him I sometimes felt unworthy of the earnestness of the words in front of me. For Katie Ives has written a beautifully crafted elegy to a seemingly more innocent past in mountaineering, unsullied by excessive commercialism and information overload, a time when a dream peak could not be digitally fact-checked.

Ives is editor in chief of *Alpinist* magazine; *Imaginary Peaks*, her first book, is already amassing accolades from the high priests of American mountain literature. But as Raban would have noted: there are no jokes. This absence of humour (I wasn't looking for belly laughs) is ironic in that the whole book is set around a joke – the Riesenstein Hoax – and its principal character is a jester fond of mocking fame-fixated climbers.

Instead *Imaginary Peaks* reads with a wistful melancholy, Ives seeming to echo those yearning lines from Joni Mitchell's song *Woodstock*: 'we've got to get ourselves back to the garden.' It's the garden of childhood wonder and possibility: Edenic. And above and beyond its hazy bowers rise knobbly ridgelines that Ives follows in her dreams up broken staircases spiralling to ancient tower walls.

If this suggests to you the influence of Thoreau or

Katie Ives, editor of *Alpinist* magazine, author of *Imaginary Peaks*. (Chris Weidner)

J R R Tolkien you would not be wrong. A New Englander, Ives grew up only a short walk from Thoreau's cabin and would swim in Walden Pond. Tolkien though cast the more powerful spell. Between elementary school and high school young Katie read the *Lord of the Rings* trilogy more than a dozen times and would carry the books along during early hiking trips in the White Mountains of New Hampshire.

Constellations of *Diapensia lapponica*, the pincushion plant, white and yellow flowers that grow only in alpine zones, reminded her of elanors, the golden star-shaped blossoms of Tolkien's elven forest of Lothlórien, where the passage of time seems to slow to near standstill. Eventually, though, Ives realised what she yearned for 'wasn't in the books' but related to a feeling experienced in the cold air above the tree line.

That sentence brought a knowing smile. A good many years ago I was having an immersive browse along the eastern religions shelves in the dusty labyrinth of the old Pilgrim's Bookshop (before the fire) when an elderly Nepali whispered over my shoulder: 'The answer's not in the books.' Nor, ultimately, does it lie in the mountains – real or imagined – though that is where Ives and the cast of this wonderful book spend years looking.

Ives plainly pondered hard over her title, pointing out in an author's note that the common definition of 'imaginary' by no means captures the nuances of all the ways that mountains intersect with human minds. Woven into this textured exploration are a hoax, supported by a photo of very real rock towers, false claims, fabulous mountains in fiction, others presumed by early makers to exist but on no hard evidence, and the alluring mountains of our dreams. Layered on these broad categories are differences of perception; in the mind's eye a mountain might be the abode of deities or a climber's project. The same physical features will be re-imagined according to the beholder.

The Riesenstein Hoax began with a photograph in the June 1962 issue of the since departed American magazine *Summit*. Reproduced at the opening of Ives' book, the photo shows imposing steep walls and towers soaring above glaciers to a jagged, snow-flecked ridge. Two route lines are pecked out but do not reach the summit. Route lines on lower peaks to either side of the so-named 'giant stone' do appear to have reached their summit goals.

The photo was accompanied by an unattributed article describing the adventure of three Austrians who thrashed through a forest wilderness in British Columbia until, from a high col, they gazed across a vast glacier to unfamiliar peaks. Their attempts on the main summit were repulsed by avalanche, storm and finally a fall that ripped two pitons and left one of the Austrians with minor injuries.

A caption located the unclimbed summit of approximately 8,100ft in the region of Prince Rupert. Though isolated, it could be reached in two days bushwhacking. Then came the challenge: 'Who will be the first to climb it?'

Who indeed? The Riesenstein Hoax is so little known among British climbers and Ives teases out the tale so well that it would be almost a spoiler to go into detail here. Who were the hoaxers? Where was the mountain? Who, eventually, climbed it? There are names here *Alpine Journal* readers will be familiar with – Fred Beckey and David Roberts were among the many who joined the hunt – but most will be strangers. All are caught up in a tale of the unravelling of a mystery and of days of toil through forest and over glaciers that echoes the Tolkien-esque quests of Ives' youth.

So I'll leave the Riesenstein itself hidden beyond the chilly mists. Hidden, that is, to all but the knowing handful. The hoax was rumbled by 1966 but it was more than a decade before the identity of its perpetrators was revealed: three mountaineers living in Washington state: Austin Post, photographer and glaciologist; Ed LaChapelle, glaciologist and author of *Secret of the Snow: Visual Clues to Avalanche and Snow Conditions*; and Harvey Manning, author of popular north-west guidebooks.

Manning, who edited early editions of the classic textbook *Mountaineering: the Freedom of the Hills*, emerges as both the likely mastermind of the hoax and the guiding spirit of Ives' narrative. He too was steeped in Tolkien. As a boy scout he had hiked out alone from camp in the Olympics and had what amounted to a life-defining epiphany on Marmot Pass. Though only 30 miles from his home in Seattle, the wild landscape was a revelation. He remained at the pass until sundown, watching transfixed as the edges of mountains dissolved, forest stretched into dark wildwood and the valley sunk into chasms of shadow. This was 'the-World-as-it-Should-Be,' he thought, 'the World-as-it-was Promised-in-Storybooks.'

Manning spent much of the rest of his life – he died in November 2006 aged 81 – trying to preserve 'the world as it should be.' The influence of his writings and activism contributed to the establishment of the North Cascades National Park and other protected areas in Washington. Passionate but by no means pious, Manning and his friends dreamt up their hoaxes on self-aggrandising climbers and the burgeoning gear industry amid home-brew-fuelled laughter.

Ironically the first team to set off for the 'Riesenstein' once its location had been unmasked came from a band of New York climbers who revelled in the name of Vulgarians. Scornful of stodgy club hierarchies – notably those of the Appalachian Mountain Club – the Vulgarians were the Merry Pranksters of the climbing world. Indeed their spheres overlapped; Ken Kesey was an honorary 'Vulgarian fellow traveller'. In June 1965 five Vulgarians confronted the reality of the hoax mountain and learnt a salutary lesson: in the words of one of the participants, 'to always be humble in the face of Nature.'

Ives began studying the Riesenstein Hoax and other 'imaginary' mountains in 2011 and finished her book as a Covid lockdown project. Over that decade several of Manning's co-conspirators and friends who shared their stories have died. Perhaps it is appropriate that *Imaginary Peaks* reads with a certain melancholy for it marks the passing of a generation fortunate enough to have been able to approach the mountain with a wonder unconditioned by Google Earth and other digital fog. (Ives, I guess, is some two generations younger than the hoaxers.)

It is primarily a book for an American audience; many of the cast of characters and places will be unfamiliar to British readers. However the broad themes of dubious claims, quests and a yearning for some kind of prelapsarian paradise are universal. Ives writes of her mountain dreams and emotions with a beguiling beauty, though she admits to being unsure what her own dream mountain represents.

All I know is that my longing for something nebulous and unnamed persists. If I had to pick a word, the closest one I can think of, now, is hope.

Here I sense Raban raising a quizzical eyebrow. Hope? Is that hope as a general emotional capacity or for something more particular? Though Ives italicises the word, this isn't a book that exactly brims with hope. Those of us young and active in the 1950s and 1960s certainly felt then that we were living in a time of hope. Jack Kerouac, as Ives reminds us, had one of his *Dharma Bums* calling for a 'rucksack revolution'. And it seemed on the brink. Manning, his friends, the Vulgarians and countless of their contemporaries all wanted a better world: less corporatised and environmentally rapacious, less warlike and socially repressive. Pockets of wild land have indeed been preserved and for that we must give thanks to the likes of Harvey Manning and his fellow hoaxers. As for the rest of those fine ideas, well, as Joni sang: 'that was just a dream some of us had.'

Stephen Goodwin

Everest 1922
The Epic Story of the First Attempt on the World's Highest Mountain
Mick Conefrey
Allen & Unwin, 2022, 320pp, £20.

I do like endpapers. They give a book that little bit of extra value and show that the publisher has taken some trouble, in this case splashing out on semi-gloss paper to enhance the rich tones of John Noel's 1922 team photo. And, significantly, it's not one of the usual hackneyed group shots, but a less familiar panoramic pose of the entire team (65 in all I counted) stretched across the desiccated landscape of Rongbuk, tweedy sahibs heavily outnumbered by a huge supporting cast of mainly Sherpa helpers.

In his centennial re-telling of the first ever attempt on Everest, Mick Conefrey pays due tribute to that supporting cast, naming many of the individuals who all too often in past accounts have remained anonymous shadows. Likewise some of the lesser known sahibs, such as Crawford and Wakefield: I never realized that they plotted their own unofficial crack at the summit, before admitting reluctantly to themselves that they were barely fit to go beyond the North Col.

The detail is good, but so too is the broad narrative. Conefrey devotes nearly half the book to the 1921 reconnaissance, which in many ways was far more exciting than the actual attempt of 1922. He reminds us just how involved were the political machinations to make that reconnaissance happen at all, and – despite all the petulant bad-mouthing from Mallory – what an impressive leader Howard-Bury was. The extended 1921 preamble will also familiarise readers new to Everest with the geography of the mountain and it introduces some of the key 1922 players, including the appalling, meddling expedition secretary back in London, Arthur Hinks.

That meddling was at its most shameful in the treatment of George Finch, excluded from the 1921 expedition on spurious medical grounds and only accepted reluctantly in 1922 (then shunned again in 1924), despite the obvious fact that he was by the far the most competent and experienced mountaineer on the team. Finch didn't get a very good press in Walt Unsworth's 1981 Everest history and it was only when Finch's son-in-law, Scott Russell, began to put the record straight a few years later that his reputation began to recover, boosted more recently by Robert Wainwright's excellent biography. Conefrey continues the process, examining the whole vexed question of the oxygen equipment championed so vehemently by Finch, making one marvel at the scientist-climber's determination not only to get the hideous Heath Robinson contraption to function at all, but then actually to use it successfully to establish a new world altitude record, only stopping when he was forced to turn back, nobly, to save his ailing companion Tejbir Bura.

As a non-climber, Conefrey brings a fresh eye and a grasp of the big picture. He has delved deep into committee minutes, diaries and letters to illuminate, for instance, the dire financial problems faced by 1922 expedition leader Charles Bruce, and the pressures of having to deal not only with his media sponsors back in London but also the infernal micro-managing of Hinks at the Royal Geographical Society. As a media man himself Conefrey is good on the whole convoluted business of presenting a great national event to the public. When it comes to topography, though, the layman has made a few mistakes. The south-west face of Everest is not the Lhotse face, the north ridge does not overlook the Kangshung face and whatever his Sherpas may have told him, it was not from the Nup La that Mallory gazed down into the Western Cwm in 1921. (I think it was the Lho La; the Nup La is a long way further north and the first westerners to cross it – illegally of course – were George Lowe and Ed Hillary in 1952.)

We will forgive the author those minor technical slips in what is otherwise a thoroughly engaging narrative. The epic first attempts on Everest have been retold so many times that all too often modern authors – myself included – have tended to stick to a few salient incidents and characters. Another tendency has been for the tedious cult of Mallory worship to obscure other perhaps more interesting characters. But for Conefrey this is a story 'of all the talents', including the fascinating John Morris, the irascible Longstaff, the appallingly snobby Strutt and the genial Norton, all of them somehow muddling along against the odds, to establish several new records on the world's highest mountain.

I thought that I was quite familiar with the detail of the actual climbing but this book really brings home just how strung out they were on the north ridge. It recreates vividly the miserable chaos at camp V, the forlorn attempt to reach 'The Shoulder' and the subsequent desperate retreat by Mallory, Norton, Somervell and a badly frostbitten Morshead. It also emphasizes the sense of attrition after Finch's attempt had also failed to reach the summit, with many of the team now too weak to go back up. Of course, the fitter ones did go back for that final fateful attempt to regain the North Col, with its lea slope heavily laden with new snow. Sifting through the diaries, letters and official reports, Conefrey comes to the uncomfortable conclusion that Somervell's guilt was justified: they were rash to try it and they were ultimately responsible for the deaths of seven Sherpas in a huge slab avalanche.

It was a sad end to an epic journey into the unknown. In the final pages, Conefrey does not neglect to describe the return journey to Darjeeling, the winding up of the expedition, and the discussions of a possible return to Tibet for another attempt. There is a sense of an unfinished story so I look forward to seeing what Conefrey makes of the 1924 denouement.

Stephen Venables

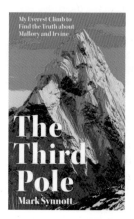

The Third Pole
My Everest Climb to Find the Truth about Mallory and Irvine
Mark Synnott
Headline, 2022, 448pp, £11.

Phineas T Barnum did not invent show business but he did give it an almighty kick up the backside. So explosive was the American's impact on popular British culture in the 1840s that his method became known as 'Barnum-ism', largely deplored in respectable publications but wildly popular with the public. Tom Thumb dressed as Napoleon? Bring it on. For Barnum, there was no difference in the quality of his spectators' perspectives, only in their ability to pay. Every 'show' had a bit of 'humbug', from religion down, something his friend Albert Smith understood very well when he adopted Barnum's presentation and marketing élan for his Egyptian Hall lectures on the ascent of Mont Blanc.

I thought frequently of Barnum-ism reading Mark Synnott's bumper new Everest book *The Third Pole*, the latest attempt to solve the mystery of Mallory and Irvine. For example, early in 1923, George Mallory arrived in New York on a disappointingly limited and only partly successful lecture tour. He drew large audiences for two nights in Philadelphia and rave reviews but in New York City on 4 February, despite leaving the audience 'fizzing', half the seats were empty and the show lost money. Synnott suggests that Everest's failure to capture the American imagination was a consequence of competing attractions: the Roaring Twenties and so forth. The *New York Times* certainly knew where the juice was for its readers. Its review next day ran with the clunky headline: 'SAYS BRANDY AIDED MT. EVEREST PARTY; A Swig 27,000 Feet Up "Cheered Us All Up Wonderfully"'. This was three years into prohibition and many Americans might have fancied a tipple, even if it meant a trip up Everest. I suspect Mallory's failure was because his agent hadn't prepared the ground in the way Barnum would have. Either way, America has made up for it since. I think it's correct that Mallory's fate and that of his companion Sandy Irvine now generates even more interest in the United States than in their homeland.

On the Barnum principle that more, not less, is more, Synnott offers a prodigious bill of fare in this book: history, biography, memoir, reportage, travelogue and speculation are crammed into its pages. And it's a congenial banquet, this Everest smorgasbord, cooked up in that moreish American magazine style that slips down easily, even if it does sometimes lack spice. One reviewer judged Albert Smith's show 'an agreeable rattle', and while Everest these days is more tarnished than agreeable, Synnott does his best to imitate Smith. Though he isn't much helped by the blurb on the back cover, pitching *The Third Pole* as the best book on Everest since *Into Thin Air*, published a quarter of a century ago. My immediate reaction was that the blurb's author can't have read many because off the top of my head I can list at least ten I'd rather read than *Into Thin Air*, some of which, inevitably, do better on the history and biography angles than Synnott does: Wade Davis' *Into the Silence*, for example, or Peter Gillman's *The Wildest Dream*. (Synnott does make some startling and dark revelations at the end of the book, more of which later.)

Synnott claims he had no intention of getting caught up in the Everest show but nonetheless the mystery of Mallory and Irvine lures him in and soon he is rummaging through what's left of the two British climbers, looking for clues about their fate. He is best, I think, on Sandy Irvine, who, I concluded, was a man after his own heart: optimistic, forceful, with a can-do spirit, quite American in fact. And Irvine, unlike Mallory, lacks that whiff of snobbery around matters technical: he liked tinkering, making things better. Synnott does something similar in explaining the complexities of the modern drone technology that is transforming so many aspects of our lives, not just filming in the mountains. Just as Irvine made the 1924 oxygen sets workable on Everest, so Synnott's companion, the brilliant cinematographer Renan Ozturk, gets his flying machines hovering roughly over the spot where Irvine's body was supposed to lie, knowledge of which provided the trigger for Synnott's journey. I found myself, a technophobe, compelled by these accounts in a way I wouldn't expect.

He is on less certain ground when it comes to teasing apart the complexities of British society and culture. He talks often of the British climbing establishment as though it were a homogeneous blob reacting predictably as one entity, rather than a complex of individuals of structures that were and are often at odds with each other. This lack of dexterity springs, I think, from a sort of Barnum-ism, reaching for the colourful snap judgment that moves the story briskly on. For example, he spends time in the company of veteran Irvine hunter Tom Holzel: always good value, never short of an opinion but not always right. (Synnott says in the depths of his notes that he tried to get a perspective from Audrey Salkeld, a more thoughtful source, but heard nothing back, without wondering why that might be.) It says something about Holzel that to test the idiom of 'eating crow' he once actually caught and ate one.

All books have errors and omissions but a few of Synnott's really should have been avoided. He does dig into what Noel Odell saw in 1924 but this was more complicated (and literally nebulous) than he allows; the whole trick springs from those moments and it needs proper scrutiny. You can't just take Odell at face value because the human mind often confects reality from what it expects to find, not what is actually there, especially when it's hypoxic. The reaction to Odell from the Mount Everest Committee was more complicated than simply a cold-shouldering from the 'establishment', another case of taking Holzel at face value. He mangles the relationship between Mallory and the Bloomsbury group. And I'm not sure that the British climbing establishment, whatever that now is, 'reveres' Mallory. The negative reaction, which was far from universal, to the discovery of George Mallory's body was a consequence of having a photograph of his corpse plastered on the front page of the tabloids, not because he was 'revered'. In saying no foreigner went to the north side of Everest in over 20 years before the Chinese in 1960, he forgets the curious exception of Earl Denman. Tenzing Norgay didn't move to Darjeeling after climbing Everest in 1953, he did so in the mid 1930s. The circumstances of the discovery of Mallory's body and the publicity around it could have been more balanced. The section on modern Everest and the training of local guides was superficial and misshapen and should have been omitted.

It's in the climax of the book that things really darken. Synnott's own climb to the summit reveals the polluted nature of modern Everest, impressions that are only reinforced in the documentary film produced from the same expedition by National Geographic and featuring Ozturk's ravishing imagery. It all looks beautiful from a distance but close up we see the ravaged portrait in the world's attic as Synnott unpeels the motivation and fate of a few of the other summit hopefuls around him. All of it seems a bit desperate and best avoided.

As it turns out, the spot that Holzel swears blind is the last resting place of Sandy Irvine turns out to be empty. This is where the book takes a nasty turn. Synnott hears later via the expedition's organiser Jamie McGuiness that the Chinese long ago removed Irvine's body, which is now, allegedly, being kept in storage in Lhasa, along with other artefacts, including his camera. This scenario seems improbable to me, although this is Everest so anything's possible. More likely though, I think, Irvine's body was unceremoniously tossed off the mountain. That also seems to have been the fate of George Mallory, whose remains no longer seem to be where they were interred. Perhaps this will proved to be a mistake. I hope so.

The purpose of this desecration is unclear, although Synnott argues that the Chinese weren't going to allow any possibility that their primacy on the north side of the mountain might be challenged. It's a depressing conclusion to the book and emblematic of the mountain's fate. Yet I doubt these dark revelations about the mortal remains of two genuinely inspirational men will make much difference to this dystopian circus. Because, as Phineas T Barnum once said, there's no such thing as bad publicity. But good heavens, what a freak show.

Ed Douglas

Searching For My Brother: John Syrett
Iconic Rock Climber of the 1970s
Pol Syrett
Blurb, 2021, 174pp, £74.

John Syrett was central player of the Leeds University Union Mountaineering Club in the early 1970s, despite being among a group that would go on to be widely known in their own right: Roger Baxter-Jones, Brian Hall, Angela Soper (née Fowler), Alex MacIntyre and Al Manson to name but a few. The reason is that John had something to teach us: pure style. And something also to show us: pure genius. None of us had either at the time.

I first saw John in action on the iconic Leeds climbing wall in the autumn of 1969 having just returned from the Alps. I arrived for a training session when Bernard Newman stopped me at the beginning of the wall's long corridor.

'Watch this kid.' A curly-haired youth in white shirt and flared trousers wearing sneakers was cruising up and down the wall effortlessly on problems I would soon be flailing on. 'He's just joined the club. Looks like we've found a good 'un.'

And so this shy, soft-spoken demigod entered our midst. By the time I returned to Leeds for post-graduate studies in 1972, Syrett was a major player on the UK rock scene. And two of his close friends, Al Manson and Pete Kitson, were also making names for themselves, especially on Yorkshire grit with bold new routes, all graded HVS and all now regraded mainly in the middle E grades. We all loved to climb with John. His calm confidence ran

Shooting star. John Syrett in his trademark white shirt at Almscliff. *(John Stainforth)*

Brian Hall and John Syrett at the top of Malham Cove's Terrace Wall after making the first ascent of *Midnight Cowboy* (E3 5c) in March 1972. *(Bernard Newman)*

up and down the rope. It was even possible to copy some of his unlikely moves if you watched him closely. He interpreted the rock in ways very few could, an early version of Johnny Dawes. As John Gill might have commented, for those of us not skilled enough to climb boulders, and were forced to find our challenges on big mountains, what we took with us from John was an understanding that a pure style on rock could also apply to unknown big mountain walls. Alex MacIntyre spent many cold days at the bottom of grit and limestone crags as John worked new routes, part of the learning curve he took with him into 'the art of suffering'.

When my friend Henry Barber came from New Hampshire to visit us at Leeds in 1973, John and Henry

Ron Fawcett, John Syrett and Pete Livesey in Yosemite in 1974. Syrett made many first British ascents during that season, climbing with legends like Jim Bridwell and Steve Wunsch. Livesey recalled how at one point Syrett disappeared into the High Sierra, having decided he needed to lose weight, 'wearing just shirt and shorts to reappear several days later having existed solely on water.' *(Jill Lawrence)*

immediately hit it off with their shared passion for ground up, on-sight ascents. Ironically, the one failure of style in John's life was the pre-inspection of *Wall of Horrors*, the climb that made his name. But that pre-inspection enabled him to climb the route in short shrift during a gale on a cold November day. It was too cold for his second John Stainforth to even attempt to follow. After that, John became a purist and set an example at a time when there were whispers of other well know rock stars pre-inspecting routes and arranging fixed gear.

After slicing a tendon in his little finger while trying to open a tin with a knife at a party at my house in the Lakes, John refused to go to the hospital immediately, and that led to the tendon never properly reattaching. I will never forget sitting in my kitchen with John the morning after his accident and hearing him dismiss his injury as trivial and not worth a visit to the hospital. Even the best of times can be so very cruel to the best among us.

His accident came at the end of his time in Leeds but he was already finding a life elsewhere back in the north-east of England working first as a physio and then offshore on oil rigs. He still climbed and according to the hard men of the north-east scene, the disability did not inhibit him as much as we all imagined. He did many new routes and repeats of the ferociously graded crags in Northumbria.

But John had entered a spiral of depression that led to heavy drinking and morose self-isolation. He blamed himself unfairly for the death of a colleague on the Brent Delta oilrig despite a court completely exonerating him at the enquiry. On the same day John committed suicide jumping from the top of Malham Cove after sharing a bottle of whisky with Pete Livesey in the village. His parents refused to believe it was suicide but his sister concludes that it was, citing John's propensity to blame himself for other's deaths and misfortune, and for putting their safety above his own.

You need not have known John Syrett or even to have heard of him to enjoy and learn from this book. Pol Syrett has immaculately researched the life of her missing brother, travelling on pilgrimages to Britain, Europe and America to meet John's friends and to see the crags and mountains where John climbed. In so doing, she brings back the community and the spirit of those early days of harder on-sight grades. John's biography is engaging, unusually intimate and full of the detail that only a sister could bring to his story. As with many good biographies, John's early family life and letters home when away tell us a lot we did not know about him. He had a passion for other challenges, like growing cacti for which he and his father built a greenhouse. A remarkable and plentiful selection of photographs from the era helps further enliven the telling of John's story.

The book concludes with a chapter of stories and tributes from many of the most notable climbers of his generation and Pol Syrett draws together all the threads that lead to John's early death in a remarkably frank concluding chapter:

Those who excel at any activity are often driven to their limits in order to achieve their goals, thus taking greater risks than the rest of us. … Mum once suggested that John's inability to settle in life was because he achieved too much at a relatively young age. … John certainly suffered when, after the accident to his hand, he was unable to climb at the same standard. He did regain his ability, but this injury, unlike others he had sustained, had a long-term impact, probably on his mental health as well as his physical ability.

John Porter

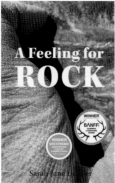

A Feeling For Rock
Sarah-Jane Dobner
Dob Dob Dob, 2021, pp268, £13.

Time On Rock
A Climber's Route into the Mountains
Anna Fleming
Canongate, 2022,
pp239, £17.

A *Feeling for Rock*, winner of the climbing literature award at the 2021 Banff Mountain Book Festival, is an edgy collection of 113 pieces of prose, poetry, technical advice, photographs and cartoons which explore a multiplicity of climbing-related topics. Climbing is considerably more than 'a bit of exercise' for Dobner: it propels her into 'the existential sphere' where 'we are stripped down and questions are asked.' Indeed, Dobner is as fearless and direct in her internal interrogations as she is on rock: she lays bare long-held assumptions, particularly about the place of women in the climbing community, and delivers thoughtprovoking 'kicks to the beehive' in areas not commonly prioritised in writing about climbing, notably hierarchy, colonialism and discrimination. She asks questions of readers, spotlighting those areas of the sport she feels merit scrutiny.

She is clearly in love with the climbing experience, embracing the intimacy of 'the heartfelt connection' to the physical features of rock and of the climbing community that the sport affords her. Section headings are different emotions, illuminating what being on rock gives her, with love a constant thread through the fabric of her writing – spiritual, sensual, metaphorical – but always candid and often imbued with a sense of fun. She 'married' the rock, became obsessed with her 'queer love interest' and remains faithful to the partnership. Climbing is both her love affair and her life, laced with the inescapable and addictive frisson of risk.

Of necessity the act of climbing generates a mix of intense feelings and Dobner writes about them confidently, illustrating what lies at the centre of her art. This has the welcome effect of stripping away the sport's mystique, thus opening the sport to non-participants. Her verbatim interviews with a group of young women who are just beginning to climb indoors demonstrate that their initial anxiety about the need for strength and fearlessness at the expense of all other qualities was unexpectedly quelled by their joy in simple achievement, trust and co-operation. This early recognition of what climbing offers is pinpointed in her later interviews with established climbers such as Johnny Dawes and Niall Grimes: 'how your emotions feel – that's what keeps me climbing.'

Dobner's writing crackles with energy: she sweeps the reader along with the force of her convictions. The non-linear form and the unpredictability of her choice of topics stimulate, entertain and amuse. There is a challenge here to look beyond what is expected to what is revealed: an unravelling of stereotypes, challenges to outmoded beliefs and behaviours in order to make the climbing community in which she has joyously found her sense of self and her home an easier place to be for everyone who wishes to join it. *A Feeling For Rock* emphatically communicates the all-consuming passion Dobner has for climbing, from its 'little unquantifiable wonders' to the undeniable conviction that for her 'rock is the earth's truth.'

In Time On Rock, Anna Fleming leads the reader on two parallel paths to her self-discovery: the development of her climbing skills and subsequent 'journey into the rock' through a series of encounters both with geological time and the human stories enshrined in it. When she recounts these stories – for example the 1932 mass trespass on Kinder Scout or the 4,000 year old rock etchings on Ilkley Moor – she draws the reader in to share the enrichment of landscape knowledge she experiences. As she becomes more proficient as a climber her awareness of that landscape and her place within it gradually crystallises, bringing a total immersion of self in the rock: 'The self is poured into the stone and the rock flows through the body.' This echoes the writing and practice of Nan Shepherd, the belief that to enter a mountain 'is a slow process of becoming, of allowing the self to soften and mingle into the environment.' There is no sense of 'conquering' the challenges presented by the rock, or climbing to try to prove one's prowess but instead of entering into a partner dance or play, an essential state of being, free from the preoccupations of the self.

The menu of rock Fleming brings to the reader is broken down into chapters, each type with its own distinctive qualities and challenges, each with its accompanying personal anecdotes and broader historical perspectives relating to the geographical area in which they are found. Fleming writes lyrically about the minutiae of surfaces, holds and progression through difficulties and dangers to becoming 'fluent in the rock', able to read its patterns, 'mapping body to stone.' When she broadens the narrative to encompass the vista from the top of a completed climb the 'dizzying expanses of space' propel the reader from acute sensitivity to the smallest of details to an appreciation and understanding of the broader landscape, which has been shaped both by geology and the many lives played out within it.

The two chapters which describe her two attempts to complete the Cuillin ridge, four years apart, are particularly engrossing since they chart a distinct progression not only in ability and experience but in her awareness of differences in scale and challenge. On her initial, ill-prepared ascent she spent 13 hours traversing less than a third of the ridge. On her second attempt she was humbler, having known the power of the environment and learned how to absorb its stresses and difficulties so that they became 'part of us, written into our muscles and memories.'

Fleming's writing is permeated with a deep love of the natural world, not just the rock she climbs on, and she has 'a searing intimacy' with the fells and mountains she walks and wanders. She describes her surroundings beautifully, homing in on telling details – a 'ruffling black loch', 'buttery light' and, pulling back to a wider view, 'the sweeping glacial trough of Ennerdale'. This acutely observant painter's eye adds another layer to the interplay of distance and shift of perspective which she experiences on the rock, the long and intensely pleasurable process of losing self to a greater and more profound awareness.

Val Johnson

The Vanishing Ice
Diaries of a Scottish Snow Hunter
Iain Cameron
Vertebrate Publishing, 2021, pp216, £20.

On 30 September 2017 Iain Cameron hiked into Garb Choire Mòr high on the southern rim of Braeriach in the Cairngorms. By whichever approach – over the plateau from Loch Einich, across from the Sugarbowl on the ski road above Loch Morlich, or from upper Deeside – it is a long and arduous flog.

This was the fifth time that year Cameron had entered Garb Choire Mòr, each time driven by a compulsion that many folk, mountaineers not least, would find a touch insane. He was anxious to know (to say 'curious' would be a gross understatement) whether any snow had survived the summer in this wildest of cliff-girt recesses.

It had – just. Cameron had arrived in time to conduct the last rites. So small and light was the remaining patch that he was able to lift it up.

It felt odd to be holding this lunch-platter-sized piece of old, dirty snow that had fallen from the sky late in 2006, eleven years previously, the oldest relic of its type in Britain. For some divine amusement, the weather gods laughed at us as we stood by the dying patch, sending a few derisory flakes downward.

The 'platter' would soon be gone: the fourth complete disappearance since 1996. Yet hitherto the only record of a snowless Garb Choire Mòr over the previous 300 years was in 1933 and 1959. It was the same story in 2018. Cameron had been keeping watch. On 29 September 2018 he peered over the hollow where the snow usually lies and saw 'not a lick of anything white'.

It then occurred to me that I had been one of only a very select few who'd stood on this hallowed piece of [so rarely snowless] ground. It felt like a little comfort, but my overriding feeling was sadness.

Reading this, a mental picture forms of Cameron, stood in this forlorn place, weary after his toilsome hike, head bowed, gazing blankly at the spot where on so many occasions he had exulted to find snow on a summer's day. He may not exactly have held cap in hands, but the scene evoked is that of the graveside. Think perhaps of the chilly cemetery moments in Carol Reed's *The Third Man* or innumerable westerns.

And perhaps we can people the stage with other mourners: Christopher Nicholson, poet and author of the beautifully meditative *Among the Summer Snows* (2018) would definitely be there, though he suffered agonies on his own pilgrimages into Garb Choire Mòr; Charlie English, author of *The Snow Tourist* (2009) perhaps, and poet Nancy Campbell, whose lyrical *Fifty Words for Snow* (2020) really should include a word for venerable snow patches. Present too, in spirit, would be the ecologist and doyen of snow studies in Scotland, Dr Adam Watson, who died in 2019 and to whom *The Vanishing Ice* is dedicated.

Indeed, as the graveside gathering grows so does the impression that books about snow are proliferating in inverse proportion to the rate of the white stuff's disappearance from the mountains. The fact that I'm writing this review in Braemar in February as the sleet hammers down and skis stand idle in a corner of the cabin only adds a personal element to this sense of loss.

Nicholson comes to recognise that death is closely linked with his fascination with summer snow, and he muses on the equivocal relationship between snow and time. On the one hand, snow is ephemeral, a model of transitory existence, a fact painfully underscored for Nicholson by the death from cancer of his wife Kitty. On the other, snow is capable of checking the onward rush of time, 'or at least of giving that illusion. Heavy snowfall brings the modern world to a temporary halt. Roads are blocked, airports shut down…'

Cameron is not much given to such philosophising. He is an electrician by trade and, being a good deal younger than the poet, more a creature of the social media age and the sharing of data.

However in his slightly gauche way he shares Nicholson's tendency to anthropomorphise snow patches and likens his visits to long-lying drifts, whether on Braeriach, Ben Nevis, Aonach Mòr or Aonach Beag, as akin to visiting an elderly relative: 'you hope that things will be good when you get there, but if the person turns out to be in poorer health than you anticipated, then your own feelings are correspondingly negatively affected.' Moreover, his going back to the same spots year after year is a demonstration that these 'elderly relatives have family that care for them.'

The strength of Cameron's book however lies in the extent of his researches into the arcane business of snow-patch recording and his obsessive enthusiasm for his subject. Each year, on 1 July, he can be found on the summit of Meall Odhar, overlooking the Glenshee ski area, for the annual Scottish snow survey; in 2010 he unilaterally postponed his honeymoon in order not to miss the survey. At 922m, Meall Odhar is, according the Cameron,

Vanishing trick. Only certain frequencies of light can penetrate snow, amply shown here in a magnificent snow tunnel near Drumochter in the Cairngorms National Park. *(Vertebrate Publishing)*

one of the finest vantage points in Scotland for the number of hills one can see that still carry snow. (The view down into the glen is less impressive, the scarred hillsides and skeletal ski pylons, accompanied by a soundtrack of motorcycles revving over the A93.)

Adam Watson initiated the annual survey in 1974 since when the decline in snow patches has been both remarkable and worrying. The mean total of patches visible from Meall Odhar has more than halved from 1,218 in the period 1974-89 to 465 in 2004-19. Cameron points to the correlation with NASA figures which show the 10 warmest years on record have been some of the most recent. One wonders what this year's count will be?

The snows of Garb Choire Mòr disappeared again in December 2021, their absence sending a timely Scottish message to COP26 delegates assembling in Glasgow for the climate change jamboree. (A message that like many others from around the warming globe was more heard than heeded.)

Cameron became the media's go-to expert. He had watched a patch known, from the rock shape above it, as the Sphinx as it dwindled from the size of an A4 piece of paper to nothing. 'How ironic and prescient it is that our longest-lasting patch of snow melted for the third time in five years, right on the eve of COP26,' he said. 'Before 2000 it had melted only three times in the last 150 years.'

This is, of course, disturbing stuff for those of us for whom the snow and ice of the Highlands are winter essentials, whether for climbing, hiking or ski mountaineering. According to a 2019 assessment *Snow Cover and Climate Change in the Cairngorms National Park*, the long-term trend is towards greatly reduced snow cover with the possibility of some years of very little to no snow by 2080. How soon before we're scraping around for the last patch on which it is possible to inscribe a couple of linked turns?

It is hardly credible to square this almost snowless vision of the Cairngorms – and the Highlands more generally – with the winters Watson enjoyed in the 1950s and 1960s. Cameron devotes an affectionate chapter on Watson, a mentor with whom he shared data and friendship, yet the portrait, for me, is incomplete and misses some of the broader appeal of Watson as a Cairngorm pioneer. Sadly, many of Watson's impressive forays on Nordic skis over the Cairngorms – often solo – will soon be unrepeatable, if not so already. In April 1962 he made a celebrated round of the six main tops of the Cairngorms; there are contrary spikes in the trend of diminishing snow cover so I guess the chances of repeating this traverse are not quite yet simply a dream, but you'd have to be fast into your bindings.

In conclusion let's head south and consider an example of the instances of serendipity that make *The Vanishing Ice* much more than statistics. Though born and brought up in Port Glasgow, Cameron doesn't share the disdain of many of his countrymen for hills south of 'the Wall'; one of his favourite groups of hills in the whole of Britain is the Quantocks, though this has little to do with snow.

One of the best documented hills in terms of snow-related events turns out, to my fascination, to be Cross Fell, hulking giant of the north Pennines and within clear sight of my home in the Eden valley. This record exists thanks to climatologist Gordon Manley, earlier in the field than even Watson, and described by Cameron as 'the snow researcher *par excellence*'. During the 1930s Manley spent many days walking or cross-country skiing in upper Teesdale and Weardale, just over the watershed from Eden.

Cameron picks up on Manley's finding that 'the indigenous use of skis by the lead miners in the northern Pennines has died out since 1900.' This suggested to Cameron that it was no longer practical to use them because of reduced snow cover, but he adds that Manley observed it might equally have due to the demise of lead mining on the Pennines.

'It is a delightful thought to imagine lead miners in Alston or some other North Pennine village setting off from their houses after breakfast on skis,' writes Cameron. Aside from the fact that the folk of Alston would point out that theirs is not a *village* but the highest market *town* in England, this is a distinctly romantic picture.

Lead mining was a hard life and a short one. Breakfast, as like as not, would not be had in the comfort of a house in the valley but in a stone hut high on the moors close to the mines. Here, in cramped conditions, men and boys would spend the long working week. As for skis, here I turned to the Gordon Manley's papers held at the University of Cambridge and came across the following gem:

Nothing is more enjoyable than to take quick advantage of a cheerful windy and bright February Sunday up Teesdale. It may be added that formerly in Teesdale and Weardale up to the end of last century [19th] the lead miners made use of what they called 'skees' – I have spoken with one of the last local men to use them, above Stanhope; they made them out of barrel-staves and it seems fitting that the most snowy district in England should be the only one I know of in which a 'native' development of 'skees' was found.

So my own, probably still over-romantic image is of miners, released from the hell of their working week, strapping on their barrel-stave skis and whooping down to the villages of Nenthead and Garrigill. Surely a run even less likely to be repeated than Watson's epic traverses of the Cairngorms.

Cross Fell, at 893m, is the highest hill in England outside the Lake District. Stalwarts of Carlisle Ski Club reportedly skied a large patch of snow near the summit on 1 July 1979 and a local farmer observed two tiny white dots in the same locality on 18 August that same year. This is the latest Cameron has ever heard of snow lying on an English hill in the current era. 'It is very hard to imagine that date being beaten in my lifetime, alas,' he says. I fear he's right, but I'll be keeping a weather eye out nonetheless.

Stephen Goodwin

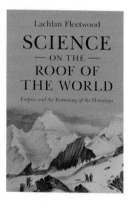

Science on the Roof of the World
Empire and the Remaking of the Himalaya
Lachlan Fleetwood
Cambridge University Press, 2022, pp294, £75.

Conducting science in the 19th century was truly hard work, especially in rugged mountain environments such as the Himalaya. For Europeans this vast region of mountains was a 'blank space' on the map, but it was by no means an invisible space. In particular, for the British East India Company (EIC), looking up from the lowland plains of India, it appeared to be a very visible and formidable barrier. An unacceptable geographical lacuna, the Himalaya presented itself as both a troublesome and a challenging prospect to the military minds that staffed the Great Trigonometrical Survey of India, the men tasked with measuring and mapping the entire subcontinent. It was both a physical and a political frontier demarcating the northern limits of the EIC's imperial vision. Psychologically tainted with the ever-impending threat of Russian military encroachment, which might descend otherwise unseen from the north. For the indigenous communities who had long lived in the region, of course, this space was far from being a blank. It was home. A place they knew and understood well. Consequently, in order to comprehend and quantify this region as a globally comparable space, European explorers realised they would need to utilise indigenous networks in strenuous efforts

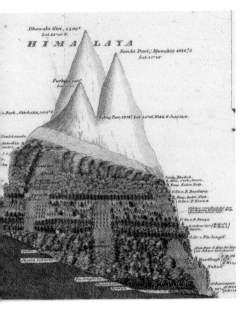

A detail, featuring the Himalaya, from the map 'Umrisse Der Pflanzengeographie', 'outlines of plant geography', from the monumental work *Physikalischer Atlas* (1838-45) which was used to illustrate Alexander von Humboldt's *Cosmos*. 'Umrisse Der Pflanzengeographie' was the work of the appropriately named geographer and cartographer Heinrich Berghaus. (*David Rumsey Collection*)

to measure these mountains and fit them into the hierarchical purview of western science, a fact that many of these heroically self-styled individuals subsequently downplayed.

At the start of the 19th century, as Lachlan Fleetwood shows in *Science on the Roof of the World*, contrary to our present-day perception, the Himalaya stood in the shadow of the Andes. Alexander von Humboldt's famous scientific explorations, particularly his ascent of Chimborazo in 1802, occluded the true stature of the Himalaya. It was not until 1856 that Mount Everest was found to be the world's highest peak. However, this book is not about the contest for achieving summit records. As Fleetwod says, 'mountaineering as a sporting pursuit, shorn of scientific pretensions, was still decades away from reaching the Himalaya when this study takes its leave'. Instead, this book is more intimately concerned with the ways in which a new concept of a 'vertical globe' was first mapped out. The guiding tenets of this project were very much rooted in, and facilitated by, imperialism. As such, it was a project that only really became feasible as a result of the Anglo-Gurkha War of 1814-1816, which gave the British greater access to the region.

The recent 'spatial turn' in historiography has prompted historians of empire to utilise geographical features such as oceans, islands, rivers, and, in this particular case, mountains to examine previously unseen 'transnational, transimperial and translocal stories'. Simultaneously, seeking to find and amplify the role of indigenous and subaltern voices who played a crucial part in assisting or resisting such efforts to broaden the horizons of western imperialist interests in frontier zones is also an important part of such histories. Hence, contemporary historians such as Fleetwood are increasingly drawing upon the more expansive scholarly resources of a transdisciplinary toolkit to re-write the history of exploration. For instance, utilising the allied perspectives of anthropologists, historical geographers and historians of science, to better inform their enquiries, reassessing primary source materials, and thereby shaping new and transformative histories of empire. In this respect, Fleetwood builds upon the previous work of exemplary scholars in this field, such as David Arnold, Christopher Bayly, Felix Driver and Sujit Sivasundaram.

Over the course of six fascinating and richly detailed chapters, Fleetwood contends that scale was a key criterion in assessing 19th-century scientific engagement with the Himalaya. As already noted, it was also one of the main reasons why the region's pre-eminence remained comparatively unrecognised for such a long time. While efforts to know and understand the region were initially overshadowed by the likes of the Andes and the Alps, the most useful and familiar comparisons to hand at the time (such as Mont Blanc and Snowdon), were simply dwarfed by both the conceptual and the physical reality of the Himalaya.

As a vast and culturally diverse region, the Himalaya was a space over which it has always been difficult to exert imperial or state power, something that has been a substantial focus of recent scholarly interest since the publication of James C Scott's *The Art of Not Being Governed* (Yale University Press, 2009). In terms of both culture and climate, this vast region is a multilayered zone of both mutually distinct and interdependent frontiers. And, as the first two chapters of *Science on the Roof of the World* demonstrate, this is why the Himalaya has always managed to resist easy quantification. Many of the scientific instruments available during the early decades of the 19th century were simply not robust enough or sufficiently calibrated to contend with the intense rigors of the region. It was these difficulties which scientifically-minded travellers set out to overcome, aided by parties of locals who acted as guides, porters, and collectors, but whose names were all too often left unacknowledged in the official records of such expeditions.

The central portion of the book (chapters three, four and five) examines the medical topographies as well as the materiality of mountain environments. Looking in depth at early understandings of altitude sickness and the different physiological ways in which mountain environments adversely affected the human body in terms of the physical and mental capacities of explorers to observe and record their findings under extreme conditions. This neatly flows into an examination of social hierarchies and the role of labour, as well as the ways in which material specimens, such as fossils and plants, were moved from the uplands down to the lowlands. Such material was circulated, used and interpreted in a variety of ways; valued either as medicinal or ritual objects by indigenes, or as purely scientific or commodifiable specimens by western scientists; for instance, informing geological interpretations of mountain formation, or providing the seeds for distribution to a network of botanical gardens across the British Empire. Here Fleetwood gives a special focus to the lesser known and somewhat neglected

'Junnoo [Jannu (7710m)] 24,000 ft from Choonjerma Pass [Mirgin La (4640m)] 16,000 ft, East Nepal', from Joseph Dalton Hooker's *Himalayan Journals* (1854). *(Wellcome Trust Library)*

gardens located in the Himalayan foothills where such specimens were first sent, to be commercially developed by indigenous staff. As Fleetwood discovers, these persons could be highly skilled and knowledgeable men who were already in post at these institutions and whose roles had been retained and continued from previous ruling hierarchies, thereby giving us a tantalising glimpse into the continuities and cross-overs involved in such processes of knowledge exchange between indigenes and imperialists.

The book concludes with a sixth chapter that very neatly surveys and sums up the highly detailed findings already outlined in the preceding chapters, reflecting upon the 'vertical limits' mountain environments imposed upon the creation of various 'imagined geographies', utilising Peter Bishop's *The Myth of Shangri-La* (Athlone Press, 1989) as a notable datum peg for previous cultural-scientific interpretations of the Himalaya. However, rather than being a region set wholly apart, Fleetwood demonstrates that the lowlands and the uplands were simultaneously both separated and conjoined in the contemporary colonial consciousness of British India. Thereby showing that while the mountain regions of the Himalaya ultimately remained marginal and peripheral spaces to the British Empire as a whole, they were nevertheless still intimately tied to, and thus in many respects helped to define, the imperialist appropriation of the Indian subcontinent. In essence, science was undoubtedly a tool of empire, but the Himalaya was the pre-eminent region that pushed the limits and defined the boundaries of both.

Science on the Roof of the World is a meticulously well-crafted scholarly monograph which has been very deftly derived from Lachlan Fleetwood's PhD thesis. Examining and reflecting upon a good range of scientific and geographical traditions, as they were first practiced in the Himalaya,

Fleetwood writes in an admirably lucid and engaging manner, which gives depth whilst remaining accessible. As such, *Science on the Roof of the World* should appeal equally to academics as well as to informed lay readers who are interested in the history and exploration of mountain environments alike. This book is an excellent and fascinating addition to the growing literature on early scientific and imperialist engagements with the Himalaya, one which views the region from the twin perspectives of both the local and the global, and one that shows the many ways in which each is intimately interlinked with the other.

Tim Chamberlain

Hamish MacInnes
The Fox of Glencoe
Edited by Deziree Wilson
Scottish Mountaineering Press, 2021, 366pp, £30.

The heart of the bibliophile mountaineer will surely beat a little faster on first handling this beautifully presented volume, cloth-bound in its smart slip case. It does indeed suggest something special.

Hamish MacInnes needs no introduction to readers of the *Alpine Journal* – his obituary appeared in last year's edition – and you would be forgiven for thinking this is a biography. Rather, it is a collection of MacInnes' memoirs in 33 chapters, some quite short, some running to 3,000 words or so and some mere musings, illuminated by several short, pertinent pieces from old friends with whom he had worked and climbed. (I must confess to being one of them.) It's well illustrated with photographs of his own, buttressed with others from several known photographers. Each chapter is a self-contained piece telling of an epic climb, an incident, an adventure perhaps or just an interesting happening that he felt was worth recounting and although those of us who knew him will realise that much is missing, by the time you have read this book you will have a pretty good picture of an extraordinary man.

Hamish was 90 and a well-established author when he died in 2020, with dozens of articles, several expedition books, a series of guidebooks, an internationally acclaimed mountain rescue handbook and even several whodunit novels to his credit, but canny Scot that he was, he had always organised his papers with a view to some sort of biography. Over the years he had written much that was applicable and doubtless he had expected to complete it himself but it was not to be. As an elderly man in his eighties the disgraceful misdiagnosis of a urinary infection saw him forcibly incarcerated in a psychiatric hospital, which together with the resulting memory loss, denied him valuable time in his few final years. Nevertheless, delving into his archives he did manage to reconstruct most of his life, and with BBC Scotland he produced a visual, semi-biographical pull-together for television, a fascinating miscellany of film rushes and photographs hung around his own commentary. Alas, it proved to be his public obituary, albeit only a transitory one, for unlike a book, things visual are here today and gone tomorrow.

Thus this book is selective and in no way definitive, and as the chapters are arranged in only approximate chronological sequence, and not formally dated, it recounts only segments of the MacInnes life story. There are several inaccuracies in material that presumably was written or completed in those final years after his recovery from memory loss. I hardly recognise his recounting of the filming of Clint Eastwood's *The Eiger Sanction* though I was with him the whole time, and there is much unsaid elsewhere that readers might have expected. But after all, the completion of the book was posthumous.

The chapter titles are typically MacInnes and suggest an intriguing and probably exciting text to follow. 'Misadventure on the Charmoz-Grépon and a Drainpipe' recounts an early escapade from which he was rescued by none other than Lionel Terray and Raymond Lambert. 'Perambulations on Mount Cook' explains why he is a notable figure in New Zealand, while 'Uncommon Men' is essentially a short history of the Glaswegian Creagh Dhu Club, with whom his time spent climbing 'was probably the most memorable in my life.' The reader will soon discover why. There is a vivid account of his lucky survival with Mike Banks in an avalanche on Rakaposhi, and of his epic 13-day traverse of Shkhelda on starvation rations.

It's is not all gripping adventure though. MacInnes tells the story of the legendary Glencoe School of Winter Climbing and of the development of the famous Message – the first all-metal ice axe – and how it evolved into the Terrordactyl. 'A First Ascent in the Frosty Caucasus' describes how prototype Terrordactyls proved their worth climbing a desperate new line on Pik Shchurovsky deemed impossible by the Russians. And few appreciate that besides his mountain-rescue expertise and the safety innovations to which several chapters are devoted, MacInnes was also something of a Rider Haggard character. Early on, while in New Zealand, he had learnt how to pan for gold and the chapter 'Not All that Glitters' chapter tells how he, together with Joe Brown and Yvon Chouinard roamed the Ecuadorian jungle on the trail of a lost cache of Inca gold, not just once but three times. Not surprisingly the famous ascent of the Great Prow of Roraima, complete with Don Whillans, Joe Brown and Mo Anthoine as jokers, warrants no less than 26 pages in 'The Lost World'. And let's not go into the contents of Chapter 31: 'The Y-Front Rescue'.

Of course the gist of some of the hair-raising happenings will be familiar to well-read mountaineers but reading of them in MacInnes' own words, telling it as it was, enlivened with his frequent wry asides and his fine sense of the ridiculous, brings them to life. He is often introspective and always aware of far more than mere difficult moves, overhanging rock and manky pitons: a hard man, yes, but a genuine aesthete. It is interesting to compare his rather folksy style with the more eloquent prose of his close friend Tom Patey, whose brilliant account of the first winter traverse of the Cuillin appears as Chapter 18, the only complete chapter from an outside contributor and too good to ignore. Each chapter is an easy and enjoyable read, and being complete is ideal for bed time reading and happy dreams of exciting adventures.

Some books are a pleasure to handle and the Scottish Mountaineering Press, the modern manifestation of admired guidebook publisher the Scottish Mountaineering Trust, has done Hamish MacInnes proud with this unusual volume. His friends especially will be touched by the excellent, specially commissioned pencil portrait of the man himself on the final page. Arranging his manuscripts, editing his text and designing such a book required much work and considerable talent. Deziree Wilson and the SMP production team are to be complimented on what must be the most attractive volume of its genre, at such a price, to appear for many a year. It is a worthy memorial and Hamish would surely have been delighted to see the finished volume.

John Cleare

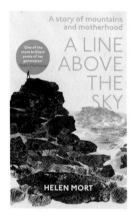

A Line Above the Sky
On Mountains and Motherhood
Helen Mort
Ebury Press, 2022, 268pp, £17.

Remember Messner's definition of mountaineering? 'If no risk has been taken, no climbing has taken place.' Remember Robert Burton on danger and what he calls 'a bitter jest' in *The Anatomy of Melancholy* (1621)? 'A bitter jest, a slander, a calumny, pierceth deeper than any loss, danger, bodily pain or injury whatsoever'. Helen Mort is the victim of at least two 'bitter jests', but she is also a risk taker. Halfway through this reflective memoir she catches herself 'taking liberties with a story that isn't mine to tell [...] I have no right to narrate this, embellish it, just as I have no right to delve into Alison Hargreaves's innermost life.' In this book Mort is intimate and unsparing in examining her experience of pregnancy, giving birth and the first years of motherhood as a climber and fell runner fascinated by the experience of Alison Hargreaves who sits on her shoulder throughout as her 'ghost companion'. It is a risky writing project. We know that Alison's story, and that of her son Tom, did not end well. But Mort is up for the challenge: 'If there is no risk in my writing, no fear, there is no pleasure. I have to make myself feel uncomfortable, take chances in the way a mountaineer does, calculating and recalculating, pitching their frail body against the wind. In risk, we feel most alive.'

There have been other books by women on climbing, the outdoors and motherhood, perhaps most notably Lilace Mellin Guignard's *When Everything Beyond the Walls is Wild* (2019), but none so frank, so visceral and so layered in meanings. Teased at school as a 10 year old for being fat – the first bitter jest – Mort turned herself into an athlete. 'All my life I'd wanted to be a line,' she writes, giving the book's title one of its meanings. The others are in a life as a writer of lines, a climber, a runner and 'underlining the desires of others'. 'Then there is the line of the pregnancy test' and the renunciation of lines, together with individuality. With her pink-cropped hair, Mort is uneasy at first in joining NCT classes with the other expectant mums: 'I did not feel like a mother. I barely felt like a woman.' But after their babies were born they 'began to know each other as women as well as mothers.' She writes: 'Together, we formed a shield.' The result of this new-found female kinship is a desire, when Alfie is a year old, to climb with a woman, something Mort had barely done before. The return to leading on Stanage with Anna Fleming as the only women climbing together that day is a reminder of how pioneering this can still feel at a personal level, for all our assumptions about progress.

Of course, the Alison Hargreaves narrative inevitably leads towards the death of her son, Tom and here the parallel 'ghosting' story might get uncomfortable. Mort recounts watching reports of Tom's disappearance and search efforts hourly through the night whilst breastfeeding three-month-old Alfie. Her emotional investment is clear. Later, while Alfie is safe at pre-school, there is a knock at the door. 'I could not shake the instinct that something must have happened to him.' In fact, it is an acquaintance calling to warn her that her face has been superimposed on a body on a porn site – the second bitter jest and the ultimate crossing of the line of her own body. In writing about this Mort 'takes back control.' Women, she says, have always been judged by the world by more than their subjective selves, as in the duality of mother-climber in Alison Hargreaves' case. Mort's conclusion to this book is to reflect upon the multiple roles of the women who came before her, her present friends and, as poet and novelist, her fictional characters: 'If women are always to be doubled, surveyor and surveyed, then let us be multiple. Let us stand so close that we seem to merge together, the dead and the living, the real and the fictional.'

In the final lines of the book Mort sees, with her eyes closed, a mother and son climbing on Stanage in the winter sun. A male reviewer might be forgiven for seeing, with his eyes closed, other lines above the sky, yet to be written. But that would not diminish his appreciation of this extraordinary revelation of what is also ordinary. The book belies its teasing assertion that to find meaning in climbing is to find meaning in life. Clearly it is not true for Mort to say that, 'You love it precisely because it means nothing.' Any reader will come away from this book profoundly enriched by the knowledge of why the opposite is the case.

Terry Gifford

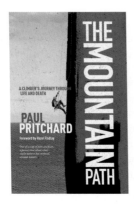

The Mountain Path
A Climber's Journey Through Life and Death
Paul Pritchard
Vertebrate Publishing, 2021, 192pp, £24.

Live it up, fill your cup and be merry, sow your wild oats whilst you may, for the toothless types of tomorrow, they were the tigers just yesterday!
Tom Patey

This is the most unusual mountaineering book I have ever read, a combination of the philosophy of risk, the psychology of why we climb and how it may unexpectedly change our whole being. I should have been prepared for Hazel Findlay's outstanding introduction; a committed climber she confessed that she finds most climbing books rather boring, too full of machismo, but not the writings of Paul Pritchard.

In the style of Dylan Thomas, let us begin at the beginning. Paul grew up rather hedonistically on the moors of Lancashire, setting fire to them being among his favourite occupations, along with spitting competitions and cutting school, but a teacher introduced him to the life-affirming activity of rock climbing in the local quarries of Wilton at the age of 16 and he was hooked. From then on climbing was to dominate his life. I know from personal experience what a vibrant climbing scene there was at that time in the rather low-key climbing environment of those quarries: Anglezarke, Houghton, the various Wiltons and that boulder-freakies' delight, Brownstones. Paul quickly became one of the area's leading pioneers.

In 1986 Paul moved to Llanberis, to what was to be one of the most innovative scenes of British climbing history, with totally committing new routes on the sea cliffs of Gogarth and desperately run-out climbs in the Llanberis slate quarries. There was besides the climbing scene the wild partying and this unfortunately led some of its participants to the dead end of drug use and a promising climbing career snuffed out. Fortunately Pritchard was not to be one of these. It was the time of the Thatcher revolution, the running down of heavy industry and the coal mines leading to mass unemployment, but Paul, who had happily sacrificed a joinery apprenticeship, became a full-time climber on the dole. Going climbing every day, the standard of these dole boys went through the roof. I recall giving a lecture in Sweden at that time and being asked at the end why there were so many hard, free rock climbs in the UK. The reply – 'we have to thank Mrs Thatcher for this!' – rather confused the questioner.

Paul was to experience the first of his brushes with death at this time whilst repeating a route on the back wall of the Wen Zawn at Gogarth. When he reached what he expected to be the crux it was seeping water, but he was not too worried for he believed he had good protection below him. The inevitable happened and he slipped off, but to his surprise the wired nut

Paul Pritchard, on the profundity trail. 'When I was first recovering, I never thought I'd be able to travel again, never mind pedal all the way to the highest mountain on Earth.' *(Sharyn Jones)*

just below him broke and this led to a chain reaction as his whole line of pro failed and he landed in the sea. The fall rendered him unconscious and he was under water for many minutes before his partner, the Australian climber and photographer, Glenn Robbins managed to climb down, fish him out and pull him onto a ledge above the high-tide mark. Glenn then gave him mouth-to-mouth resuscitation and Pritchard came back from the dead, although still injured in the fall. Robbins then tried to climb out but failed and things were looking serious when another climber appeared at the lip of the zawn. Alerted to Paul's predicament, a rescue helicopter was eventually summoned. But you cannot keep a man like Pritchard off the crag for long.

A few years later Paul was winter climbing *Centre Post Direct* on Creag Meagaidh, when he came upon a section of eggshell ice: frozen on the outside but soft snow underneath. In trying to climb this he was soon in difficulty and was sinking up to his armpits, breaking through the surface ice into the powder beneath. He tried to retreat but the inevitable happened and he took a monster 50m fall severely injuring his back. Fortunately fellow guide Nick Kekus was on the mountain that day and arranged a lower to the valley floor and the eventual arrival of Lochaber MRT and a helicopter that deposited him in Fort William's hospital. Besides his back injuries the ice hammer he was carrying hit him in the face as he was falling. Once again, instead of seeking solace on the couch, he was soon off to Patagonia and the Himalaya, and was still wending his way up extreme rock climbs.

Paul had begun to write about his climbs and journeys, and from the start his articles he received wide acclaim. His 1997 collection *Deep Play* won the

Boardman Tasker Prize and though this was richly deserved, it set in motion the most challenging of Paul's mishaps. Using his prize money to fund a world climbing tour in 1998, he arrived with Celia Bull on Tasmania for an ascent of the needle-thin sea stack the Totem Pole. What happened that day, when a rock struck him on the head and left him close to death as Bull hurried to get help, was described in *Totem Pole*, which also won the Boardman Tasker Prize.

In *The Mountain Path* we learn that though this left him hemiplegic, he has somehow crafted a life of adventuring and doing, albeit of a different style and standard but nonetheless worthy. In fact he writes in his latest book that his life has been enhanced and enlarged spiritually by this tryst with the grim reaper.

After a long period of rehabilitation in the UK, learning to deal with his reduced physical ability, he returned to Australia and to Hobart in Tasmania where he now resides, having married and become a family man; but his spirit of enquiry and his wide reading on every subject from psychology to philosophy fill the pages of *The Mountain Path*. Recovering myself from a stroke and a serious infection, I have also found one lives in thought rather than physicality. It's hardly surprising that Paul became enamoured of this exploration, especially whilst practising intense periods of vipassana meditation.

One chapter I found particularly interesting was 'Pilgrimage'. This describes the train journey from Chengdu to Lhasa and then Paul's challenging journey by tricycle first to Everest Base Camp then on to Kathmandu. The final chapter is about Paul's return to climb the Totem Pole, 18 years after the accident which nearly cost him his life. A jolly team assembled on the promontory opposite and belayed by Steve Monks he set forth. Steve, once a stalwart of the south-west climbing scene before discovering Arapiles and emigrating, led with his usual flair while Pritchard followed on Jumars, managing one arm pull-ups with his one good hand and a clever rigging system. Two long pitches and the summit was reached; Paul could finally put to rest his Totem Pole ambitions though he was, as we say in the north, completely banjaxed physically.

The Mountain Path is, like the writer, unique. I would recommend it to all who love and aspire to climb in wild places. But I would also place it on a list by anyone studying the psychology or philosophy of risk. The reading list at the end of this volume illustrates where the author is coming from and is comprehensive. Vertebrate, its publisher is to be thanked for the courage in publishing such an impressive work.

Dennis Gray

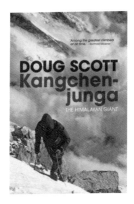

Kangchenjunga
The Himalayan Giant
Doug Scott
Edited by Catherine Moorehead
Vertebrate Publishing, 2021, 272pp, £24.

Kangchenjunga: a strange yet catchy name. Wasn't it that high, mysterious mountain of my childhood, beyond the lake where the Swallows and Amazons enjoyed their adventures? Literary researchers have suggested Arthur Ransome's original was probably Coniston Old Man but my mother told me the real mountain stood in the mighty Himalaya range in India, so I knew of it, as did geographers for centuries past. Indeed it was the best-known mountain in the Himalaya before the epic of Mallory and Irvine focused interest on Everest.

Visible from afar, known together with its massed satellites as the 'Five Treasuries of the Great Snows'[1], venerated by several religions and until 1849 thought to be the world's highest mountain, Kangchenjunga proved awkward to explore and a feasible climbing route difficult to locate. Nevertheless, standing a mere 46 miles (74km) from the Indian hill station of Darjeeling, itself served by a railway, the massif's eastern, Sikkim flank, where access was controlled by the Raj, was relatively well frequented from Victorian times. The western approaches meanwhile, rising in Nepal, remained, with a couple of notable exceptions, forbidden until 1949 when Sikkim itself, from 1950 an Indian state protectorate and later absorbed into independent India, became difficult to visit.

With its long history and ranking as the world's third highest peak, Kangchenjunga was an appropriate subject for a major biography, a task which has been shouldered by an author who knew the mountain better than most, having made its third ascent and that by a challenging new route. Sadly it is a posthumous publication and was to be his final book. That it actually appeared is due to the sterling work of its editor Catherine Moorehead, a notable author herself and an authority on the mountains of Central Asia.

Not surprisingly much has been written over the years about the Sikkim Himalaya and the occasional clandestine journey into far eastern Nepal, and Doug Scott delved deep in his research. The book comprises four parts, the first describing the geography of the region and explaining the various ethnic groups who inhabit it and something of their history, then in part two the missionaries, traders, explorers, scientists and artists who came to Sikkim are covered in some detail. He suggests that the first European sighting of Kangchenjunga was possibly by a pair of Portuguese missionary

---

1. 'Treasuries' or 'Treasures'? The local Lhopo folk considered the mountain to be the hiding place of mythical treasures hidden among the snows: gold, turquoise, precious stones, grain, salt, medicine and sacred scriptures, the latter rendering of the Tibetan was by those who held that it referred to the massif's five prominent summits.

Last words. Doug Scott at the snow cave at camp four (c7350m) on Kangchenjunga's north ridge in 1979. This third ascent of the mountain features in Scott's book *Kangchenjunga*. *(Doug Scott)*

friars in 1627, although later he postulates that it could well have been the English trader Ralph Fitch (1550-1611) who must certainly have seen the Himalayan snows from northern Bengal. As geography and history all this is a worthy addition to the works of Kenneth Mason and John Keay.

The third part is titled 'Climbs and Attempts' and is essentially the stories of the pioneering Victorian and early 20th century artists, writers, mountain travellers and serious mountaineers who penetrated into the inner recesses of the Kangchenjunga massif, explored, attempted and sometimes climbed outlying peaks, crossed difficult passes and searched for possible ascent routes, until eventually the boldest attempted to climb the mountain itself.

Many of these forays are described in the words of those who made them, with excerpts from the writings of the botanist Joseph Dalton Hooker and Edward Lear of nonsense fame, to Douglas Freshfield and Howard Somervell. Ten pages are devoted to the still on-going controversy over W W Graham's claimed first ascent of Kabru, an important Kangchenjunga outlier, in 1883. Had it been verified, this would have remained for many years the highest summit ever reached. In 1905 Aleister Crowley's team made the first attempt to climb Kangchenjunga itself. As it so happened the route selected by Crowley, later notorious for his dabbling in the occult, was that taken by the British first ascent team in 1955 after all attempts elsewhere by others had failed. Naturally the heights quoted in these pre-Second World War extracts are mostly in feet, while throughout the text all heights are rendered in metres, making it difficult to recognise the location mentioned. Unable to swiftly convert one to the other in my head, I found this omission exasperating. Why not include both?

Of particular interest were the exploits of Kellas, Raeburn, Tilman and Smythe, the latter on Dyhrenfurth's 1930 attempt on the very quadrant of the mountain by which Scott's team finally succeeded nearly 50 years later. It was Bauer's three gallant German attempts on the Sikkim flank, almost reaching the north col in 1931 that paved the way to the second ascent of the mountain by an Indian Army expedition in 1977. The old maxim that on a major peak the first ascent party climbs on the shoulders of previous attempts is particularly true on Kangchenjunga.

The fourth part is titled 'Ascents'. The first three are covered, each from a different direction and by lines identified many years earlier. The first two, well described elsewhere, occupy few pages, but Scott's own lightweight oxygen-less ascent of 1979, dealt with in some detail, is accompanied by a good map and his own fine atmospheric photographs, though initially the narrative first-person treatment seems incongruous in the context of a history book. Occupying considerable space, it is very much a personal account, typically à la Scott, and is, I suspect, much condensed from the original manuscript. For a detailed report of the climb it is worth re-reading Joe Tasker's succinct 550 word account in *AJ* 1980. The book concludes with a useful tabular summary of parts three and four and an exhaustive bibliography.

There are two picture folios containing 38 photographs, well reproduced, 18 of them from Scott's own expeditions. However, I would consider this as no more than adequate coverage for the sort of 'biography' this sets out to be. Were expense no object, what a fine opportunity it could have been for the lavish use of illustrations: maps, ethnic work, paintings (two are included) and the work of photographers such as Sella, Smythe and Brenner. In an appropriate format this could have been *the* definitive biography, a valuable collector's volume. The recent MacInnes memoir shows what is possible at a reasonable price.

However, my major criticism concerns the two most crucial of the four full-page maps in the text. While the art work is good, only the main Nepal-Sikkim watershed north and south of Kangchenjunga and its immediate glaciation is depicted; the forest of peaks and passes beyond to east and west, their names and heights, is blank paper. The important peak of Siniolchu, 'the world's most beautiful mountain' and prominent in the text, is nowhere to be seen. Thus, despite knowing the area personally, it was impossible to follow most of the exploratory itineraries mentioned without having my own maps to hand. The superb line drawings in Baume's *Sivalaya* and Evans' *Kangchenjunga: the Untrodden Peak* also proved useful reference for the later chapters.

It seems evident that the author envisaged a rather more comprehensive volume that he was, sadly, unable to complete. He was, I understand, already a sick man by the time he concluded his exhaustive research. To fit the publisher's requirements the editor was forced to cut some 80,000 words from the original manuscript, a challenging yet unavoidable task completed with great skill and only occasionally discernible. Nevertheless, whatever its faults, this is an important book from the pen of one of the giants of Himalayan mountaineering.

John Cleare

The Complete Rainbow
For Alan Rouse on K2

Knowledge never fits
or competes with symbols.
This perfect rainbow,
the arch of life, spans
from my motorway to your
distant mountain camp
where I should be
had work not made me pause
and leave before.

It completes those weeks
high up that made life seem
a world suited for atomic engineers
and mathematicians
on the unclaimed heights.
Its fragility gives beauty, shape
and ownership no home
but the knowledge shared
that you are no more

John Porter

Alan Rouse, who would have turned 70 at the end of 2021.
John Porter, who had been on K2 with Rouse in the fatal summer of 1986,
includes this poem dedicated to Rouse in his new collection *A Path of Shadows*,
published this summer by Little Peak Press. *(Bernard Newman)*

Mountain Republic
*A Lake District Parish: Eighteen Men, The Lake
Poets and the National Trust*
Philippa Harrison
Head of Zeus, 2021, 740pp, £35.

This history of a single large parish in the Lake
District will be of particular interest to ice climbers. It will prodigiously improve both their historical knowledge and the strength of their wrists.
It weighs 2.5lb and contains more detailed information than you can shake an ice axe at. The parish of Crosthwaite is: north of Dunmail Raise;
east of Sty Head, Newland House and Whinlatter pass; south of Skiddaw;
and west of Helvellyn. It therefore includes Borrowdale and Thirlmere.
Its market town is Keswick and just north of this is the church of St Kenti-
gern's, which was the keystone to the parish, ordained around 533. At 90
square miles it is by far the largest old parish at the centre of the Lake District, its boundaries crossing the summits of Helvellyn, Great Gable and
Skiddaw. This really is the glorious heart of a landscape whose real social
legacy remains little known despite the Romantic poets' popularisation
of the district. Philippa Harrison uses the phrase 'the indigenous people' in
seeking to bring alive their story through fascinating detail from 533 to the
First World War.

I confess to intending to skim this tome for the benefit of alpinists, who,
like me, tend to take the long history of indigenous people for granted. But
I got hooked on the telling details and the unravelling family stories. There
are over 200 pages of parish life, governance, mining, forest clearance, sheep
hefting and timber protection laws before we get to part two and the arrival
of poetic strangers, 'laiking' among the surprisingly sophisticated and regulated life of the rustics, to become known as 'The Lake Poets'. In fact, the
three themes of the subtitle are the highlights of the book's four sections.
From 1400 and for nearly 500 years, 18 local men regulated parish life,
adjudicated in disputes and raised a tax for the school and poor relief, per-
sisting in this role into the 19th century. Although about the lives on isolated
hill farms, this book emphasises community. In the later Middle Ages peas-
ants' improvised huts were replaced by 'clay daubins': clay and straw making
walls between oak beams. Building such a house took two days and was a
community event celebrated by a party at which all the neighbours helpfully
danced on the new clay floor to bed it in.

The parish is slightly 'expanded' in the second section of the book to include Wordsworth in Grasmere, but the interest is much more upon Robert
Southey who settled at Greta Hall long-term. He organised a bonfire party
on the summit of Skiddaw in August 1815 to celebrate the final defeat of
Napoleon. A cart reached the summit with fire barrels for rolling in flames
down the mountain, but also with beef and plum puddings, plus prodigious

amounts of punch. Wordsworth accidently kicked over the punch kettle and tried to slink off. But Southey identified him and set up a chant pointing him out. (Sounds like familiar euphoric summit behaviour.) What we miss today are facts like this: in 1800 eagles from Eagle Crag, Borrowdale and Eagle Crag, Thirlmere caused 'carnage' in the breeding season, taking a lamb a day in Borrowdale.

In 1856 the New Parishes Act reduced the parish from 90,000 acres to 9,200 and in 1874 the Endowed Schools Act removed from the 18 men the governance of their free grammar school. It is only at the end of the large parish story that Philippa Harrison sums up the way the enclosed mountain environment has sustained human qualities of fraternal solidarity, social restraint and independence for over 500 years. Landowners and lords of the manor may come and go but the inherited tenancies of the statesman system had led to what Harrison calls 'the special statesman community – to whom the mountains lent their strength'. In 1883, Hardwicke Rawnsley became the young new vicar of Crosthwaite's new smaller parish, the same year he founded the Lake District Defence Society and he would later co-found the National Trust in what, for Harrison's book, is an 'Afterglow'. (Harrison, drawn from a family of Furness farmers, now lives in Rawnsley's old vicarage.) But Wordsworth's claim for this community as a 'mountain republic' is endorsed by Harrison's characteristically finding the telling detail: 'the indigenous sense of equality, largely caused by the demands of nature and the mountains, as the hill farmer went about his everyday life, is exhibited in the wills of the time, which demonstrate a strong ethic to provide equally for every son and every daughter'. Anyone who thinks they have an intimate knowledge of the Lake District will enjoy discovering how much this fascinating book will prove them wrong.

Terry Gifford

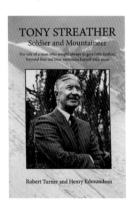

Tony Streather
Soldier and Mountaineer
Robert Turner and Henry Edmundson
Fastprint, 2021, 144pp, £13.

This co-authored memoir records the life of a very remarkable man: the soldier Col H R A Streather OBE, MBE and the mountaineer Tony Streather.

Streather's career as a professional soldier spanning some 37 years between 1945 and 1981 was unusual, variegated and distinguished. After joining the Queen's Royal Regiment from University College School, London where he was head boy, he was commissioned into the Indian Army to complete six years of active service with local tribal forces on the North-west Frontier as a participant in the closing chapter of the Great Game and witness to the creation of Pakistan after its partition from India.

Transferring to the Gloucestershire Regiment, ostensibly for the opportunities it afforded his passion for hunting, he served successively in Korea and in Cyprus where, in recognition for his leadership during the inter-communal riots between Greeks and Turks, he was awarded the MBE. He then went on to raise a new regiment for the Malaysian army during the communist insurgency; saw active service with the Gurkhas in Borneo and commanded the Gloster's Battalion in Berlin and Northern Ireland. Having done spells as an instructor at the School of Infantry, the Royal Military Academy, Sandhurst, the army's Outward Bound School at Towyn (and subsequently given unstinting support for the Duke of Edingburgh's Award and Endeavour Training) he completed his professional career as deputy commander, Sennelager, north Germany where he trained British units to support NATO in the event of military confrontations with Russia.

This meritorious record of military service would have sufficed for most men but it was Streather's achievements as a mountaineer that mark him out as exceptional. His transition from being the equivalent of a high-altitude fell runner, ridge-hopping the high passes of the Hindu Kush with fleet-footed tribal soldiers to becoming the first climber to ascend two peaks above 25,000ft with no previous alpine climbing experience is unique and extraordinary.

The fairy-tale of Tony Streather's ascent to mountaineering's pantheon in the space of a mere nine years from 1950 to 1959 is the book's main theme as neatly summarised in the eulogy Chris Bonington gave at Tony's thanksgiving service and reproduced herein. It began improbably when Tony joined the 1950 Norwegian expedition to Tirich Mir, at 7,699m the highest peak in the Hindu Kush, as its liaison officer. It soon became apparent that his strength, stamina and ability to perform seemingly effortlessly at high altitude qualified him for the summit team. On duly achieving their objective, Tony managed to unfurl on its windswept summit an enormous Union Jack, the only size available in Chitral.

Turned down for the 1953 Everest expedition for his lack of any Alpine experience, he was snapped up by the Americans as transport officer for their attempt on K2. Once again, his powerful performance at altitude promoted him to the eight-man summit team whose forced retreat after sitting out a seven-day storm at 7,700m would have ended in total disaster had not Pete Schoening's miraculous ice-axe belay held all seven on a precipitous ice slope. Tony survived this first near-death encounter though Art Gilkey perished. He was now a natural for selection to Charles Evans' brilliant 1955 Kangchenjunga 'reconnaissance' expedition, and with Norman Hardie became the second pair to summit after Brown and Band had shown the way.

Two years later, he agreed to lead the 1957 Oxford University Mountaineering Club's expedition to Haramosh. High on the mountain, against his advice, two members of the team Jillott and Emery pressed on up a suspect ridge and were swept down 300m by an avalanche into a remote snow basin. Tony's repeated attempts to rescue them over four days and three nights without food or shelter was, in Stephen Venables words: 'a tale of misfortune, catastrophe and heroic sacrifice almost unparalleled in the history of mountaineering'.

Two of those young men died on the mountain and a third suffered terrible frostbite injuries. No proper account of the Haramosh disaster was published in standard mountaineering literature until Ralph Barker's *The Last Blue Mountain* (1959). The recollection of the tragedy haunted Tony for the rest of his life.

In 1959, as a founder member of the recently formed Army Mountaineering Association, Tony led an army team to explore the remote Tirich Gol area in Chitral where they made the first ascents of the Malubiting East (6000m) and six smaller peaks including the aptly named Gloster Peak (5880m). In 1976, it was only appropriate that Tony's mountaineering career should close as leader of the AMA's Everest expedition on which Brummie Stokes and Bronco Lane, two SAS corporals, made the summit.

Although Tony was never to climb seriously in the Alps, on the strength of his Tirich Mir ascent and 'several years of scrambling in Baluchistan, Waziristan, Gilgit and Kashmir', he was elected a member of the Alpine Club in 1951 having accepted that it was not quite the moribund gentleman's club he had first imagined. Thereafter, he was to make valuable contributions to its administration as a committee member, vice-president and ultimately its president between 1990 and 1993. It was unfortunate that his two-year term as president should have coincided with the highly contentious issue of the Club having to find new premises before its lease at 74 South Audley Street ran out. Tony, then aged 64, had retired from the army nine years earlier and was working as the sports and estate manager of the Sandhurst and Camberley Estate.

Conflicting views on the new location, in part reflecting the AC's style and future direction, engendered bitter disagreements within the membership. The full story of that saga has yet to be told but what might have precipitated a financial catastrophe for the Club had it proceeded with the absurd scheme of building 'an underground bunker' in the Royal Geographical Society's garden was only averted at the eleventh hour. Mountaineering politics were not Tony's natural metier. The heat that this tricky issue engendered gave him 'little peace' and the loss of 'quite a few nights sleep pondering on the decision that had to be taken.' In 2014, he was awarded honorary membership of the Club.

Although a skilled lecturer and a compelling raconteur with a deft literary turn of phrase, Tony never published his autobiography. *Tony Streather* attempts to redress this, but joint-authorship and the separation between Tony's military and mountaineering careers leads to a degree of duplication and tends to interrupt the flow of the narrative overall. Extracts from Tony's own writings and others (particularly Stephen Venables on K2) bring immediacy to the mountaineering expeditions that occupy the greater part of the book while the account of Tony's military career features some amusing anecdotes that well illustrate his character.

This is not a book that attempts to examine Tony's deeper motivation or his private life. Nonetheless, the authors have painted a compelling portrayal of an outstandingly courageous yet modest, generous and sensitive man who possessed the highest qualities of leadership. Tony Streather's achievements as a mountaineer will remain his principal legacy but his contributions to furthering outdoor adventure and education gave his life an extra dimension that will have benefitted many more than just the mountaineering community.

J G R Harding

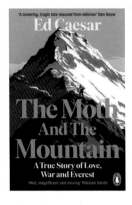

The Moth and the Mountain
A True Story of Love, War and Everest
Ed Caesar
Viking, 259pp, 2020, £18.99.

Maurice Wilson, who died making a hopeless attempt to climb Everest in 1933, has long been one of the footnotes in the mountain's history. A biography, *I'll Climb Everest Alone* by Dennis Roberts was published in 1957, but since then he has attracted only intermittent attention. The British writer Ed Caesar has returned to the subject, finding him worthy of a fresh look. Through assiduous searching he has unearthed priceless material, helping to cast Wilson in a new light. He has followed Wade Davis, author of *Into The Silence*, in framing his subject through the prism of his experiences of the First World War. Caesar has placed in him an illuminating personal and cultural context and although we may still be mystified by his apparent act of self-immolation, we have a plentiful source of information to inform our considerations.

Wilson was born in Bradford in 1898, the son of an engineer in the weaving industry who eventually ran his own company. He joined the British army in 1916 and two years later, by then a captain and winner of the Military Cross, he was seriously injured by German machine-gun fire. Although Wilson was invalided home to recover, Caesar believes he also suffered from undiagnosed shell shock, the contemporary – and controversial – name for post-traumatic stress disorder (PTSD). An older brother, Victor, suffered far worse, surviving hideous battles, incurring a near-crippling leg injury, and being effectively disabled by PTSD.

After the war Wilson's life assumed a nomadic quality, as he pursued business ventures and also a spectacular series of relationships. Having married in 1922, he immigrated alone to New Zealand in 1923, working as a travelling salesman. In 1924 he cabled to his wife to join him there. By the time she arrived, he had fallen in love with another woman and his wife sued him for divorce, spending a further 18 months in New Zealand while she saved up for her return fare home. Wilson married for a second time but that marriage ended in 1930. Wilson next headed for South Africa with a new woman by his side but they never married. In 1932 he became involved in an apparent ménage à trois with a couple named Len and Enid Evans – and it was Wilson's subsequent letters to Enid that form important new verbatim evidence in his account.

It was in 1932, during a visit to southern Germany, that Wilson was seized with the idea of climbing Everest, triggered by reading an account of the 1924 British expedition, which culminated in the disappearance of Mallory and Irvine. Caesar believes that Wilson experienced some kind of epiphany, a religious rebirth that reflected a mix of fashionable quasi-Christian theories and elements of Indian mysticism. A further contributing factor, Caesar argues, was Wilson's unresolved PTSD after the First World War.

Wilson was undeterred by the grim histories of the three 1920s Everest expeditions, with their accounts of savage weather, illness, frostbite, deprivation, the effects of high altitude, and avalanches. His aspirations achieved another level of implausibility when he resolved to travel to Everest by flying a solo Gypsy Moth from England, even though he had never piloted a plane before.

That part of his ambition he did at least fulfil, doing so wearing boots he intended for both the flight and the subsequent ascent of Everest. After a breathtaking series of adventures and mishaps, he reached Darjeeling in mid August, just a few days after the defeated British 1933 expedition passed through on its way home. He promptly engaged the services of Karma Paul, the fixer who assisted the British expeditions of the 1920s and 1930s. Running short of money, he sold his Gypsy Moth and solicited a loan from his long-suffering widowed mother; he also wrote copiously to his new love, Enid Evans.

He finally set off on the trek to Everest in March 1934, assisted by three 'Bhotia' porters. Three weeks later he arrived at the Rongbuk monastery. It is now that his great adventure appears the most preposterous, as he headed alone up the East Rongbuk glacier with a 45lb pack on his back, planning to reach the summit in five days, his 36th birthday. When that day arrived he was still floundering, without crampons, on the glacier some way short of the ascent to the North Col. Deciding to retreat, he barely survived a desperate descent to the Rongbuk glacier.

It was now that by any rational standards Wilson should have renounced his attempt. Caesar argues that what impelled him to continue was an instinctive desire to redeem the gruesome experiences of his brother Victor. Wilson left no evidence to that effect: his diary and his letters to Enid merely recounting how he set off up the glacier again some three weeks later, this time accompanied by two of his porters. He felt that the fates were with him when he found both a pair of crampons and a box of food, some of it bearing Fortnum and Mason labels, that had been abandoned by the British expedition the year before. This time he climbed halfway to the North Col before turning back once more. Three days later he made a further attempt to climb to the North Col. He died, most likely from exposure and exhaustion, a day or so later. His body was found the following year by the 1935 Everest reconnaissance expedition led by Eric Shipton.

Caesar admits that his attempt to give meaning to all he learned about Wilson was not entirely successful. He clearly relished his quest, and was rewarded for his persistence and diligence. Some of the records he used are close to home, such as Wilson's diary, which is kept in the Alpine Club Library.

His best new resource, Wilson's letters to Enid Evans, was harder to come by. They were originally in the keeping of Wilson's previous biographer, Dennis Roberts, who appears to have struck a pact with the Evanses whereby he could use information in the letters without attributing them directly, for fear of revealing their unconventional relationship. Roberts later sold the letters to a German mountaineering author, Peter Meier-Hüsing, who passed them to Caesar in return for a lunch in Berlin.

Such treasures help make a biography rich in researched and descriptive detail, adding to its authenticity. Caesar incorporates his quest into his narrative, although appearing to distance himself by using the second person – 'you' –instead of the first person, perhaps suggesting that said quest is universal in its nature. There is one curious lacuna however. Caesar adopts a radical approach to chronology in his opening chapters, which works well, apart from the fact that he nowhere provides the precise date or location of Wilson's birth (21 April 1898, according to Wikipedia), leaving us to deduce the year from inferential references. There are just four photographs of Wilson (one is used twice) and because they are incorporated within the text the two that are not portraits are difficult to read. The book has no index.

Those quibbles apart, this is a rewarding read, with a power and clarity to the writing, not quite answering all the questions it poses and leaving you to ponder them after you have closed the book – a sign of its enduring qualities.

Peter Gillman

• A shorter notice of *The Moth and the Mountain* appeared in last year's *Alpine Journal* despite having this long and more considered review to hand, an error on the part of the editor.

For a decade from the mid 1970s, British climbing enjoyed a creative renaissance as a group of young radicals with small budgets and high ambitions arrived on the scene determined to take alpinism back to a purer form. Brian Hall was at the heart of that process and his new book, published too late for review in this year's *Alpine Journal*, recalls 11 people from that seminal period of his life and the dramatic and sometimes fatal events that defined them all. They include familiar stars like Joe Tasker, Alan Rouse and Alex MacIntyre, but also cultural lodestones like Paul Nunn, the prodigiously gifted in the shape of John Syrett, whose biography is reviewed in this year's *Alpine Journal*, and Brian's childhood friend Sam Cochrane, visiting his early years in an essay that reveals much about Hall's own life's journey. After a tricky start, Hall found new direction as a mountain guide and film-industry regular, working in location safety and rigging for a host of high-profile projects, including the award-winning movie *Touching the Void*. *High Risk, Climbing to Extinction*, Brian Hall. Sandstone Press, 2022, 400pp, £24.99.

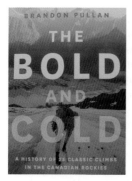

The Bold and Cold
A History of 25 Classic Climbs in the Canadian Rockies
Brandon Pullan
RMB, 2016, pp264, £30.75.

Back in the early 1990s a close group of five of us in the Edinburgh Section of the Junior Mountaineering Club of Scotland started looking for interesting objectives outside Scotland and the western Alps. Possible peaks and routes were entered into our little black books including a few pages of Canadian objectives, added when we came across two articles in *Mountain* magazine, the first by the great Canadian alpinist Dave Cheesmond, titled 'Starlight and Storm: The Great North Faces of the Rockies', and Eric Brand's 'Mount Thor: Direct West Face'. The routes featured were way above our standard but a few trips to the Graham Brown collection at the National Library of Scotland generated some mere-mortal material for our black books. Alas, our plans for the Arctic and an Alberta summer never happened and while a couple of our group later discovered Alberta's winter ice climbing, I have to confess I have never made it to Canada.

Although this book was published in 2016, winning a special jury mention that year at the Banff Mountain Book Festival, there has not been a review in the *Alpine Journal* and until this year there wasn't even a copy in the Alpine Club Library, despite several members being mentioned, quoted or featuring in the book's photography.

As the introduction states, this is not a guidebook, rather a collection of stories about 25 classic climbs brought together by the author. The idea though came from Swiss alpinist Urs Kallen. When Urs moved to Canada, he couldn't find a book that would help him find the classics. He travelled back to Switzerland in 1970 for a few years, where he came across the recently published *Im Extremen Fels* by Walter Pause. By 1979, having been back in Canada for several years, he had put together a mock-up book of his favourite routes and mountains. It was his version of Pause's book for the Canadian Rockies. Together with Dave Cheesmond, the idea of the book developed and the plan was to publish it after Cheesmond returned from the Yukon in the summer of 1987. Cheesmond's death on the Hummingbird ridge of Mount Logan led to the project being abandoned. Then, in 2005, Brandon Pullan met Urs, who told him about the idea. Urs handed over his material and said:

> Go climb these 25 routes and then you can write the book Dave and I never finished. The goal of the book is to climb as well as Dave climbed. He was one of the best alpine climbers to have ever climbed in the Rockies. You cannot change the routes or the order and you have to call it The Bold and Cold. Good Luck.

The book draws on multiple contributors who provide first-hand accounts throughout the five chapters describing the 25 climbs as you travel through the Rockies. Each chapter details five climbs of similar grade and commitment. The first five climbs are called 'The Shakedowns', then 'The Maiden Routes' and 'The Middle Earth Routes'. 'The Gladiator Routes' are climbs 16 to 20, opening with a stunning double-page image of Mount Geike. 'The Titans' opens with number 21, the north face of Alberta. There are two icefall routes: *Polar Circus* on Cirrus Mountain and *Gimme Shelter* on Mount Quadra. Some might consider pure ice routes to be secondary to alpine climbing but the inclusion of these two obvious classics ensures the list reflects the multi-faceted world of modern alpinism.

Generally, the photography is inspiring and many of the shots bring home the scale of the emptiness of this mountain range. Each of the 25 climbs is introduced by a full-page portrait image. A number of these appear to be aerial shots taken by John Scurlock, photographer and pilot, often taken in excellent light picking out the line in question. Scurlock's shot of the seventh climb, the *Beckey-Chouinard* on South Howser Tower is a good example, helped by the fact it's a granite peak rather than grey limestone. This use of light to pick out the line shows the obvious influence of *Im Extremen Fels* where Jurgen Winkler's superb photographs of each face, taken in sunlight at exactly the correct moment, illuminates so very precisely the line of the climb described in the text that follows. The shots of The Titans, the north face of Alberta, the east face of Assiniboine and the north face of North Twin capture that north-face atmosphere of brooding, sullen shade. The dour limestone of The Titans makes for a less than warm glow but underlines the sombre nature of the terrain. Some of the pictures of Mount Robson's Emperor face were a little misleading, perhaps because they had less of its grey limestone but once again the full-page portrait introducing the face communicates its vast scale. It is no wonder that *Running in the Shadows* (2,300m, VI, M6, AI5, A0) climbed on Robson during the fall of 2020, was one of the ascents honoured at the 2021 Piolets d'Or.

One frustration was the lack of maps. Even a single introductory map, like the one published on the endpapers of *Im Extremen Fels*, would have at least offered an overview of where the mountains are in relation to one another. And yet the book contained a glossary of mountaineering phrases. (I never understand why pure mountaineering books need to spell out basics such as crag, crux, ice screw, pitch and similar terms.) The omission of something so simple and effective as a locator map seemed a missed opportunity.

Regardless of the grade you climb at there is ample in this book for anyone interested in the Canadian Rockies. It's an incredibly absorbing read. Historical essays and quotations (printed in a shade of red close to that used on the Canadian flag) supplement the text, adding depth to the story of these big faces climbed between the 1960s and 1990s during what must rank as the golden age of alpinism in the Canadian Rockies.

I suppose the book is just a list, despite its interesting genesis and the rich history it contains, but it isn't a list in the same way as Gaston Rébuffat's

The Mont Blanc Massif: the 100 Finest Climbs, once described by John Barry as 'slippery with lyrical prose'. *The Bold and the Cold* is rawer than Gaston's. Then again, the mountain range itself is clearly the same: no cable cars, not many huts and some very gnarly wildlife. As I read through this highly recommended book I kept coming back to a passage from Nick Bullock's introduction:

> *I feel that some of the alpine climbing we used to think about was out there in our European backyard and even some of the Greater Ranges has been reduced to holiday destinations because of all the modern world has given in the way of reports, information, rescue possibilities and communication. I'm glad to say that alpinism in Canada appears to be way behind. I take my hat off to the gents and ladies who practice going to the hills in Canada.*

Charles Stupart

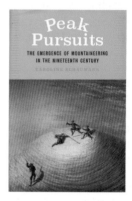

Peak Pursuits
The Emergence of Mountaineering in the Nineteenth Century
Caroline Schaumann
Yale University Press, 2020, 364pp, £30.

The emergence of mountaineering can be traced to different sources. The last *Alpine Journal* reviewed Simon Bainbridge's book *Mountaineering and British Romanticism* arguing that British mountaineering was begun in the Romantic period rather than the Victorian era. Now here is Caroline Schaumann, a German teaching in an American university, tracing the emergence of European mountaineering in the 19th century to Alexander von Humboldt in combining a delight in gaining height with scientific enquiry: the aesthetic and the empirical; exercising the body and the mind. The tension in this combination (Humboldt would forgo a summit if his instruments could not be carried there) is traced through chapters on de Saussure, Forbes and Agassiz, Albert Smith and Alfred Wills, Tyndall and Whymper, and Leslie Stephen. The last two chapters explore the American West with Clarence King and John Muir. Discussing the last chapter first reveals how the current academic writer's desire to focus, quite rightly, upon 'privileged notions of exclusivity regarding race, gender, and class' can lead to distortions in order to prove that Muir was not a modern white liberal.

Some of this is based on accusations of the sin of omission: 'Muir remained silent' on his friend's behaviour or Muir 'refused to acknowledge the rich cultural history' of Indian life in Yosemite prior to his arrival, or 'Muir remained oblivious to the Native American genocide around him.' But, more seriously, it has suddenly become fashionable to denounce Muir as a racist. In 2020 the Sierra Club apologised for Muir's 'racist remarks' against Native Americans. Actually, when Muir arrived in the Sierras, the Mariposa

Battalion had already cleared the indigenous people into the reservation at Fresno. The demoralised and isolated remnant groups of Indians Muir came across begged for tobacco and whiskey. He reported that they were dirty. But the sentence that follows this observation in *My First Summer in the Sierra* is now ignored: 'Yet it feels sad to feel such desperate revulsion from one's fellow beings, however degraded.' This is not the guilt of a racist who harbours a 'dislike of the Yosemite Miwok' as Schaumann puts it, or who therefore apparently argues for a 'depopulated wilderness'. Muir's notion of wilderness did not 'facilitate the expulsion and extermination of Native American populations' as Schaumann claims. *Travels in Alaska* is testimony to Muir's respect for the culture, skills and resilience of indigenous people, a respect that was apparently reciprocated.

'Meanwhile his gaze towards "wilderness" turned a blind eye toward social injustice, especially when it came to those not privileged to enjoy nature's remedies, such as minorities and most women.' Schaumann expects Muir in the 1890s to have solved the problem of access to mountains for minorities that remains to this day. She has to write 'most women' because there are photographs of Muir leading Sierra Club summer camps which are mostly populated by, admittedly middle-class, women. Unlike British clubs, the Sierra Club which Muir co-founded, as with most other American mountain clubs, admitted women from the start. Perhaps Muir's biggest error was his optimistic belief in the national park visitor as voter and his confidence that 'only Uncle Sam' can save trees and protect landscapes. This, however, is an issue on which Schaumann remains silent.

A revisionist contextualisation of Victorian 'muscular science' by mountaineers and their social attitudes is to be welcomed. Some readers may be excited to find 'Bigotry' and 'Prejudice' announced in the subheadings of this book, or that 'queer studies have since outed Humboldt.' But it is one thing to say that John Tyndall was 'a staunch opponent of women's suffrage and emancipation', and another to point out that he nevertheless 'admired a female climber' who had gone high on the Matterhorn, but it is quite another to write that, 'During their youthful years, both Tyndall and Whymper focussed on their professional careers and times spent with other males in the mountains, excluding women from both of these areas,' or that Whymper had 'not investigated the political causes of such living environments' when commenting on the prevalence of cretinism and goitres in the Aosta valley. Sometimes criticising Victorian male mountaineers is just too easy for Caroline Schaumann and at such moments Schaumann undermines her achievement in this book, which is to explore the tension between science and the sublime in the writings of these men. That project gets displaced by a focus on 'questions about privilege, exclusivity, and bias'. These are, of course, legitimate questions, but in this book contextualisation overwhelms its starting point and misplaced claims distract from convincing critique.

Perhaps the best chapter is the epilogue in which Schaumann not only sums up the book she thinks she has written, but relates its lessons to our Anthropocene present. 'Place attachment as a means of fostering environmental awareness' includes knowing our local uphill places in both a cognitive and an embodied way, combining close curiosity with close physical contact, recording the purple saxifrage whilst scrambling above Blea Water, for example, adding to the scientific record whilst taking in the view achieved by breathless, booted, bodily movement. It may be a long way from Humboldt's Andean researches but may redirect and enrich performance in mountaineering. For this suggestion and for this Humboldt-derived model we can be grateful for Schaumann's book.

Terry Gifford

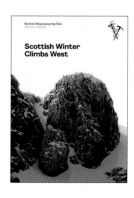

Scottish Winter Climbs West
Neil Adams
SMP, 2022, 424pp, £30.

Sumptuous quality and refreshed design are the hallmarks of the latest incarnation of the Scottish Mountaineering Press, judging by its latest offerings, including the highly collectable *The Fox of Glencoe*, reviewed elsewhere in this edition. *Scottish Winter Climbs West* arrived too late to find an appropriate reviewer for 2022 but we'll return to it next year. However, the guidebook clearly reveals a shift of gears from the narrower format of its previous and hugely popular offerings. (The deep margins in this version allow you to photograph the pages on your phone, meaning the book can stay at home.) Two more volumes, north and east, are on the way.

While including the classic winter climbing venues of Glen Coe and Ben Nevis, *Scottish Winter Climbs West* also stretches from the Southern Uplands all the way to the rugged hinterland of Knoydart and Glen Shiel, a grand tour of the best winter climbing destinations across western Scotland. With over 1,300 routes and an abundance of newer lines on familiar and lesser-known crags, its scope and range offers options for climbing across all levels and styles in almost all conditions. Crag and route information is accompanied by high-resolution photographic topos, beautifully rendered maps and detailed advice on conditions to help you be in the right place at the right time. Hugely absorbing and beautiful to look at, it will be fascinating to see how this latest offering is judged against the successes of the past.

Ed Douglas

Also Received

The dedicated Polish mountain cartographer and climber **Jerzy Wala** was born in Krakow in 1930 but he remains active into his nineties, producing two recent monographs for exploratory mountaineers with **Janusz Majer**, the latest on the **Chiantar glacier** in the eastern Hindu Kush, the largest in the range or indeed the Hindu Raj, which fills the gap between the former and the Karakoram. A German expedition was active there in 1967 but little

Massimo Faletti on the lower wall of *WaterWorld* on the north-east face of Kiris Peak in the Shimshak mountains, featured in the new monograph from Jerzy Wala and Janusz Majer. (Maurizio Giordani)

since until 2019 when Pierre Neyret led a largely French team to the glacier's head, reporting back that there are plenty of exciting objectives left to do and that the region is 'far from any Taliban'. His *American Alpine Journal* report is included in Wala's collection of maps and reports that provide a useful resource for those contemplating a visit. Wala and Majer published a similar but more extensive monograph on the **Shimshak mountains** of the Karakoram, the range south of the Mango Gusor group and east of Skardu. The region attracted a lot of attention recently thanks to an impressive bigwall first ascent on Kiris Peak (5428m) called *Waterworld* from an Italian team led by Maurizio Giordani. As Giordani himself put it of their summit day: 'On this clear day, we could see from Nanga Parbat to K2 and K6. There were hundreds of unnamed peaks with no climbing history, future projects for those, like us, who want genuine adventure among the high mountains of the Karakoram.' Wala and Majer continue to offer mountaineers new horizons.

Ditto the equally venerable **Tamotsu Nakamura**, now in his late eighties but still producing inspiring results from his decades of mountain travel. His latest offering is *Unclimbed Summits and Three Parallel Rivers*, another glossy picture book from the Tibetan marches, taking in east and south-east Tibet, south-west Qinghai, west Sichuan and north-west Yunnan. The three great rivers are, of course, the Yangtze, Yellow and Mekong. He notes in his introduction that hardening attitudes in Beijing are making travel in there regions often impossible for foreign tourists. Pressure on indigenous Tibetan nomads, with forced resettlement now government policy, is changing the human aspect of this stunning region. But, as Nakamura points out, there is plenty new to discover. 'Some are led to believe that the experience of encountering unknown mountains in great ranges is now a thing of the past, but eastern Tibet has an incredibly vast and complex topography that hides countless unclimbed summits.'

Ed Douglas

Obituaries

'Everest from Rongbuk Base Camp', Rob Fairley, watercolour,
36cm × 55cm, 1987. (Liz Duff Collection)

In Memoriam

The Alpine Club Obituary	Year of Election (including to ACG)
Rick Allen	1975
Lutz Bormann	1994
John Brailsford	1962
John Burrows	1952
Lady Ann Chorley	LAC 1966
David John Ford	Asp 1975, 1991
Edwin Hammond	1977
Stewart Hawkins	Assoc 1962
Malcolm Howells	1977
Jim Milledge	1975
Piero Nava	1973
Ted Norrish	1975
Brian Peart	1996
Kev Reynolds	1979
Neil Sawyer	1988
Richard Sykes	1971

Rick Allen
1954 - 2021

On 25 July 2021 a series of avalanches swept down the east flank of K2 taking the life of Rick Allen. In an instant, Britain lost one its finest ever mountaineers.

Rick was born in London on 6 November 1954. His father introduced him to the Scottish hills with ascents of Schiehallion and Ben Nevis. When Rick joined the University of Birmingham Mountaineering Club his rock climbing took off. Although Rick was a fledgling climber his determination instantly shone through. He quickly became proficient on rock and then developed a strong interest in winter climbing. He made ascents of *Castle Ridge* and *Tower Ridge* in 1975 with Robin Walker, and the following winter climbed *Point Five Gully* with Jim Fotheringham and Chris Duck.

Rick had a strong attraction to wild places and he became a regular visitor to the Alps completing many of the Chamonix classics. His finest early ascents were in the Bernese Oberland where he climbed the east-north-east ridge of the Lauterbrunnen Breithorn and the *Welzenbach* on the north face of the Gletscherhorn with Chris Duck in 1978, both big, demanding routes that are now rarely climbed. Further afield, Rick climbed the west ridge and *Diamond Couloir* on Mount Kenya with Roy Lindsay in 1980. Later that year he visited Nepal where made the first ascent of the west face of Tharpu Chuli (Tent Peak) in the Annapurna Sanctuary.

Wild places also set the theme for his new routeing in Scotland. This often took place in the most inaccessible and serious of locations such as A'Mhaigh-dean (Scotland's remotest Munro), Ladhar Bheinn, Beinn Lair and Beinn a'Bhuird. Rick's finest contribution was the first winter ascent of *Raven's Edge* on Buachaille Etive Mor with Brian Sprunt in 1984, a spectacular route now recognised as one of the finest mixed climbs in Glen Coe.

In 1982 Rick visited the Himalaya for a second time on an expedition organised by Roy Lindsay when he made the first ascent of Kirti Stambh (6271m) in the Gangotri region of India. Climbing with longstanding partner Ernie McGlashan, the pair backed off due to dangerous snow conditions, but after the slope avalanched, Rick went back up and continued alone to the summit. During the trip Rick met Nick Kekus and two years later they visited Nepal and climbed a new route on the 2,500m south face of Ganesh II (7111m). They reached the summit on the ninth day in a storm and spent three days descending the face. Their route was a magnificent achievement, and although it was largely ignored by the mainstream climbing press, it made a big impression on the upcoming generation of British alpinists. A benchmark had been set. If your new route was not climbed in pure alpine stye and did not take at least 12 days, then you weren't really trying hard enough.

Rick's ability to acclimatise and perform strongly at high altitude was extraordinary. This became apparent on Mal Duff's expedition to the north-east ridge of Everest in 1985 when, climbing solo, Rick reached the expedition's high point at 8,170m. The remainder of the 1980s were taken up

On the summit of Nanga Parbat after climbing the Mazeno ridge.

Back in base camp, Sandy Allan and Rick Allen celebrate their epic ascent, already one of the climbs of the century.

with another trip to the north-east ridge of Everest and Makalu. Neither were successful due to difficult snow conditions, but once again Rick reached over 8,000m on both mountains, confirming his strength at altitude.

In 1991 Rick went to the Tien Shan and made the first British ascent of Khan Tengri (7010m), and the following summer he visited Tajikistan and the Fann mountains, and made the first ascent of the difficult east ridge of Chimtarga (5489m) with Doug Scott and Russian climber Sergei Efimov. This was a significant turn of events because Sergei invited Rick to join an all-Russian expedition to Dhaulagiri (8176m) in 1993. The seven-man team were successful in forging a difficult new route up the north face. This was Rick's first 8,000m peak and an astonishing achievement on a gruelling and technical route. Rick learned to speak Russian before the trip and calmly adapted to their diet; the main sustenance on the seven-day ascent was cabbage soup.

In 2000 Rick climbed Everest with a commercial expedition. Rick's success was well deserved after his previous strong performances on the north-east ridge, but Rick soon realised that large organised expeditions were not where his heart lay. Rick moved to Tajikistan in 2006 where he climbed extensively, especially in the Fann mountains. Details of his ascents are incomplete since Rick did not leave a comprehensive chronology of his ascents but in 2006 he made the first British ascent of Pik Karl Marx (6736m) and the first ascent of the north ridge of Pik Ovalnaya (5780m) with Phil Wickens (see T Sparrow, 'Top Marx in Pamirs for AC Climbers', *AJ* 2007). In 2008 he made the first British ascent of Pik Korzhenevskaya (7105m). There isn't space here to detail this, but his long and impressive fell-running record undoubtedly helped keep him fit for the mountains. He once beat Pete Livesey in the Ben Nevis Race.

Rick's pairing with Sandy Allan was the defining climbing partnership of his life. In 1986 they made a brilliant five-day new route on the south face of Pumori (7161m), a beautiful pyramid near Everest, and worked power-fully together the following year on the north-east ridge of Everest. Two years later they climbed the north face of the Eiger. In 1995 they joined an expedition to attempt the huge and unclimbed Mazeno ridge on Nanga Parbat (8126m), the longest ridge of any of the 8000m peaks. They were unsuccessful but in 2009 returned and climbed the mountain's Diamir face. This was Rick's third 8,000m peak, and two years later, he made it four by climbing Gasherbrum I (8068m).

By 2012, Rick, now in his late 50s, and Sandy had accumulated a significant amount of high-altitude experience and decided to return to Nanga Parbat and try the Mazeno ridge one last time. The 10km route had been attempted many times since the 1970s and was one of mountaineering's last great problems. To gain the main summit you have to traverse the eight Mazeno peaks – all over 7,000m – to reach the Mazeno Gap. An alternative strategy was devised where a team of six – Rick, Sandy, the South African Cathy O'Dowd and Lhakpa Rangdu, Lhakpa Nuru and Lakpa Zarok from Nepal – planned to traverse the ridge together providing more firepower for the summit push.

In the event, it took this strong team nine days to reach the Mazeno Gap, and after a failed summit attempt, only Rick and Sandy had the physical and mental energy to try again. As Cathy and the three Sherpas made a difficult descent of the dangerous *Schell* route, Rick and Sandy set off with minimal supplies for their summit bid. Deep snow meant it took two days rather than one to reach the top but it was the descent down the *Kinshofer* route where their troubles really began. Poor conditions that year meant that all teams had given up the on the Kinshofer so there was no trail in place, and they were unable to light their stove to melt water. The epic three-day descent in extreme avalanche conditions while being exhausted and de-hydrated is one of mountaineering's great survival stories, described so memorably in Sandy's book *In Some Lost Place* (2015).

Rick and Sandy's 18-day traverse of the Mazeno ridge was widely ac-claimed as one of the finest Himalayan climbs this century and hailed as the most important British success in the high Himalaya since Stephen Venables' ascent of Everest's Kangshung face in 1988. Rick and Sandy were awarded a Piolet d'Or but Rick was a humble man: rather than putting the trophy on display, he used it to prop up the creaking bookcase in his Chamonix flat.

Rick remained focused on big mountains and was determined to continue climbing them in good style. In 2017 he attempted a futuristic new route on the north-west face of Annapurna with Felix Berg, Louis Rousseau and Adam Bielecki. They were unsuccessful but came away with an ascent of Tilicho (7134m) as consolation. Later that year Rick climbed the two highest peaks in the Rwenzori mountains of Uganda with Mike Lean: prized and rarely climbed summits. In 2018, Rick climbed Broad Peak (8047m), his fifth 8,000er, although success was overshadowed by a 'rescue' aided by a drone.

Rick Allen climbing the Chardonnet in 2017. *(Simon Richardson)*

I've written about Rick the climber and the qualities that made him so successful: drive, skill, experience and an exceptional ability to perform at altitude. This was the Rick I knew best. But there was far more to Rick than mountaineering. He was an outstanding engineer and had a glittering career with Texaco culminating as safety manager for the huge Gorgon Natural Gas Project in Australia. Rick was also extremely generous. His first marriage to Alison ended in tragedy when she died of cancer in 1999. Rick remarried Zuhra in Tajikistan in 2006 and gained a step daughter Nazira and step son Farrukh. Sadly, the marriage did not survive, but Rick took on the responsibility for Nazira and Farruk's education, funding them through their degrees. Rick was proud of their achievements and was delighted to walk Nazira down the aisle at her wedding in 2018.

But most of all it was Rick's faith that drove him. He recently attended a two-year course at the All Nations Christian College in Hertfordshire and supported Mhoira Leng' work with the Cairdeas Palliative Care Trust in Uganda. On his final expedition to K2 he was raising money for refugees and children in Myanmar.

Jerry Gore, Rick's expedition partner on K2, wrote movingly about the aftermath of the avalanche. 'Pakistani guides Arshad, Shah, Waqar, Rizwan and Ahmed were at camp two when they got the news. They all knew Rick – he was a sort of legendary grandfather in these parts – and they came rushing down the mountain to help. We found Rick late that night and buried him the next morning. We stood together in the shadow of K2 with prayers in different languages and religions filling the air. It was a moment of total unity, and a good way to say goodbye to a Scotsman who loved these mountains and the people who call them home.'

This tribute has been hard for me to write. Rick was a close friend, and we had been climbing together for nearly 40 years. A few summers ago, we climbed a new route on the Grande Fourche in the Mont Blanc range. We expected to complete the route in a day and were travelling light, but we were caught in darkness near the summit. Despite a good weather forecast it rained through the night and we shivered and cuddled our way to a long-awaited dawn. Rick had survived two open bivouacs high on Nanga Parbat, so I was determined not to be the first to complain. Needless to say,

Rick remained infuriatingly cheerful all night and did not comment once about our situation. When we were safely down in Chamonix the first thing he did was take me to buy a new bivouac sack.

Rick Allen led an extraordinary life. He was one of the world's finest mountaineers and touched the lives of many. His bold alpine-style ascents in the high Himalaya will be remembered for generations. His final resting place, with the mighty K2 as his headstone, could not be more fitting.

Simon Richardson

Sandy Allan writes: Rick was a great friend and loyal companion to me. His death on K2 in an avalanche was untimely but K2 base camp is a suitable resting place for my good, respected and tenacious mountaineering companion. We were the best of friends and on our 8,000m climbs shared the same determination and commitment. We both had a high allegiance to the ethics and the art of mountaineering. We climbed worldwide together, sharing some outstanding adventures. He was a loyal, generous and trustworthy climbing partner and is sorely missed.

Lutz Bormann
1956 - 2021

Lutz Bormann.

Bormann was elected a member of the Club in 1994. He submitted an impressive list of harder Alpine ascents, mostly on rock, mostly led by himself. He was proposed by John Temple, who said, 'he has his finger on the pulse of German mountaineering at the grass roots'. Ed Douglas, his seconder, noted that with Lutz as the editor of the German mountaineering magazine *Berge*, the Alpine Club might expect contributions in the future.

In the event, Lutz appears only once in the *Alpine Journal* index. Ken Wilson in 'Traditional Climbing Values', *AJ* 1999, pp157-60, reproduces long letters from Lutz about the use of bolting on classic routes previously climbed free. Lutz had canvassed opinion in Germany and Austria and quoted comments which left no doubt where his own opinion lay:

Bolting deteriorates the climbing standard, because lots of beginners go onto routes which are too hard for them. They rely on passive protection without having the capability of active protection. And active protection makes the climber. Self-responsibility, full awareness of all difficulties, the mastering of orientation are the peculiarities of mountaineering. The result is counter-productive of the bolting intention. ... Bolting spoils the routes and is the end of alpinism. ... I experienced climbing in Norway. Every route was like a first ascent. What a delight to climb there. Once in your life you are truly awake working your way up, thinking about the equipment very carefully, etc.

There is little information on Lutz's mountaineering activities in recent years. After his editorship of *Berge* ended in 2007, he became editor-in-chief for Gault Millau, publishers of several outdoor, fitness titles. More recently he wrote online:

> My (new) marital status made the mountains steeper, the routes shorter and the texts longer, but now the work for *ÖTZTAL MAGAZIN* and the Tyrolean Mountain Rescue Service brings me closer to my passion for the mountains.
>
> Roderick A Smith

John Brailsford
1934 - 2022

John Brailsford, with MOACs.
(Stéphane Pennequin)

I first met John in the Vallouise, the Écrins valley which he loved and adopted, and where he had lived with his French wife, Evelyne, for many years. At their home in Les Vigneaux I was plied with Yorkshire tea – with the emphasis on Yorkshire – whilst at ours he provided a little-known vintage of red wine: Chevalier Brailsford, locally bottled. The dinner conversation flowed freely; John was a great raconteur. His rich and varied life gave him much to relate, whilst his abiding enthusiasm brought all to life.

John's recent death has provoked a warm response across the mountaineering community, demonstrating just how well he is remembered. His early career as a blacksmith in Sheffield, where he had grown up as an orphan, is best covered by Mike Parsons, who describes John's role as creator of the Acorn and the MOAC ('John Brailsford Obituary', *outdoorgearcoach. co.uk*). The Acorn, first produced in 1961, by which time John was teaching engineering technology, is recognised as the first ever purpose-designed climbing nut. Its successor, the MOAC, is now a collector's item. (See S Pennequin, 'Nuts' Story: 2001, a Nut Odyssey', *www.needlesports.com*). Less well known is John's contribution to the design of the Curver ice axe.

Moving into the world of outdoor education, his influence extended far beyond the classroom, which for him was the great outdoors. I recently stumbled on a tribute from a member of the Clogwyn MC: 'Today, as a result of John Brailsford showing and guiding some of the founder members into climbing/mountaineering, a small active club exists with a hut, the 'Old Stable', in the Croesor valley.' John was instrumental in its purchase. Always proactive, he would see a need and make things happen.

That was in the early 1960s, whilst still living in Derbyshire, and before moving in 1966, after a spell at Loughborough College of Education, to Deiniolen where his young family grew up. As head of department at Bangor Normal College he introduced many to outdoor education; this too has elicited various fond memories and amusing anecdotes. His course 'changed my life forever', one ex-student wrote, reflecting the thoughts and feelings of many. He is remembered also for running the BMC's introduction to Alpine mountaineering course in the 1980s, recently described by another student as 'my true mountaineering starting point'. John was as demanding as he was committed but always enthusiastic. A few years ago a UKClimbing. com post included him in the 'top influential British climbers of his time'.

His new routes include *Scavenger* at Three Cliffs Bay in south Wales. He soloed it in 1955 but, as has recently been pointed out, the first nut placement above the crux is appropriately enough a perfect MOAC. He climbed with Joe Brown and others of that influential post-war generation, Don Roscoe and Doug Cook in particular. John was also a kayak senior instructor as well as a British Cycling Union coach. Father of Sir Dave Brailsford and himself a tough cyclist, he thought nothing of cycling from Bangor to Tremadog for a day's climbing and later of cycling out to the Alps, something he recommended to his charges. How many made it, I wonder.

The Écrins massif became a favourite venue. Here, despite the area being quite wild and inaccessible in the 1970s and 1980s, he made early ascents, often first British ascents, of many serious routes including the Gervasutti routes on the north-west wall of the Ailefroide and the south-east ridge of the Pic Gaspard, the south and south-west faces of La Meije, the south pillar of the Barre des Écrins and the west face of the Pointe de Bonne Pierre and the Couloir Chaud on the Trois Dents de Pelvoux, to name but a few. From that repertoire John developed an intimate knowledge of the area, unique among English-speaking climbers.

His guide, *Écrins Massif: Selected Climbs*, the most notable of a number of publications, was published in 1987 as the first of the Alpine Club's new series of guidebooks to the main Alpine regions. Over a 15-year period he was able to see it through two editions; it remained the best available source in English for decades. Many mountaineers of my own generation who started climbing in the 1970s will have similarly annotated copies; it is still the book I reach for if I want to remind myself of what we climbed in the Écrins back then. In *AJ* 2002 (pp187-98), Dennis Gray suggests it was the difficulties surrounding the production of English guidebooks to the Alps that brought together the AC and the ACG. Agreement on terms for their merger was reached at John's Derby home in June 1966, where he represented the ACG, of which he was a founder member, along with John Alexander and Terry Sullivan. A J Rawlinson in *AJ* 1967 (pp197-200) gives an interesting account. Here again we see John as facilitator, creating a fellowship that continues to serve generations of young climbers.

The Compagnie des Guides Ailefroide in 1984. John Brailsford is kneeling, centre.

I believe John Brailsford's career as a British guide – fully certificated in 1962 as an international mountain guide – to be unique. During the 2014 celebration of the 150th anniversary of Whymper's first ascent of the Barre des Écrins, John gave a well-received speech. I was with him in the square in Vallouise that evening following the day's commemorative ascent. He spoke in French (Yorkshire accent notwithstanding) and was clearly at his ease within that community, expressing gratitude for its acceptance of him. Back in 1975 John had played a key role in setting up the British Mountain Guides, becoming their training officer, formalising with Alan Kimber the early winter assessment procedures and making sure they were properly hard. In November 1977, with Peter Boardman and Colin Firth, he paved the way for the BMG's acceptance, despite initial resistance, at the general assembly of the UIAGM in the Val d'Aosta. Later, having worked for a while at ENSA in Chamonix, he figures in a 1984 photo of the assembled company outside the Bureau des Guides in Ailefroide. It is quite extraordinary that someone to whom successive generations of British guides – and their clients – owe such a debt should also have become part of the French guiding community: no easy feat and a tribute to John's character. A natural communicator, he certainly knew how to break down barriers.

Strong willed, knowing his own mind and not afraid to speak it, John generally achieved his self-set goals. Many have benefitted from those successes but he will above all be remembered for his generous and expansive character. I only met him on a few occasions but each was an unforgettable encounter. John Brailsford will be greatly missed by all those whose lives he touched.

John is survived by his family, Andy, Elaine and David and his wife Evelyne. I want to acknowledge the invaluable assistance of Terry Lowry in preparing this obituary.

Susan Hare

John 'Nick' Burrows
1929 - 2022

John 'Nick' Burrows in 1992.

John, known as Nick to his more recent friends, was adopted at the age of four by the Burrows family, owners of a colliery near Maccles-field. In 1943 he entered Rugby School where he became interested in long-distance running and met fellow student John Tyson (*AJ* 2015, pp440-1) with whom he developed his love of the mountains. Leaving Rugby he started work in surveying as an articled pupil, a career inter-rupted by national service for both him and Tyson. They were both posted to Malaya in 1948 during the communist insurgency and partici-pated in jungle operations in Penang, for which Tyson was awarded the MC. Returning from Malaya, John instructed at the Eskdale Outward Bound School and White Hall Outdoor Pursuits Centre before graduating in estate management from the University of London and settling into a successful career in estate management and surveying, which turned out to be much to the benefit of the UK climbing scene.

John was elected to the AC in 1952, enjoying a remarkably long member-ship of 70 years. He was proposed by E F Pilkington and seconded by Eric Shipton whom he would have met as warden at Eskdale. His application form for membership records that his third route was the traverse of the Weisshorn via the north ridge, made with Tyson and a guide. Although guided, that would have been a long and committing route in 1950 for some-one right at the very beginning of their Alpine career. His second season in the Alps records a bivouac at about 3,700m during the descent of the Zinal Rothorn in a storm, delayed by another party who were in difficulties.

John climbed and trekked extensively throughout the world but published only a very few details. In the 1960s he climbed in the Lyngen mountains in Norway and climbed Batian in Kenya. He visited the central Sahara where he climbed Djebel Telertheba (2455m), crossed the Arak gorge, and walked the Tassili plateau. In 1979 he visited Miyar Nullah in Lahaul on the unusual King's School, Ely Himalayan expedition (*AJ* 1980, pp154-7). Although a large party, only about one third of whom were adult, they minimised environmental impact by carrying lightweight equipment and using very little assistance from porters. All food was carried in from outside. Together with David Challis and schoolboys of age from 13 to 16, John made the probable first ascent of three peaks of heights between 5,425m and 5,912m.

In 1983 he was part of the Gwent Andean expedition attempting a new route on the north-east buttress of Nevado Veronica (5750m) in the Cordillera Urubamba. The report of this expedition (*AJ* 1984, pp161-4) mentions that John suffered badly from the altitude. At a similar period in his life, John participated in a physiological study of the affects of altitude, which involved the monitoring of various body functions of a group of climbers as they progressed in steps from the valley to the Margherita hut on the Signalkuppe (4554m). The study was run by an eminent physiologist who reported to me afterwards that the results were much as expected except for John's performance. 'The higher he got, the better he went.' This may come as no surprise to those who also find their performance at altitude to be variable. In 1992 he climbed Mera Peak and in 1993 trekked in Nepal, including a circuit of the Hinku valley, Hunku Drangka and back down the Lhotse valley and the Everest trail through Namche Bazar.

John was a keen member of the University of London MC (ULMC) and its senior relative, the University of London Graduate MC (ULGMC), to which he contributed enormously through his experience in surveying and estate management. When, in 1952, the Vaynol estate in Snowdonia was left to the National Trust following the death of Lord Penrhyn, John approached the NT on behalf of the club and obtained the rare and precious permission to build a new hut in the Ogwen valley. Funds were raised and, with the aid of a loan from the university, a new hut, Caseg Fraith, was built. Amongst the trustees were Sir Edwin Herbert, president of the AC, who was the London University solicitor at that time. In 1970 ULGMC decided to seek a further hut in Derbyshire. John did the crucial work in finding Fallcliffe Cottage near Hathersage, and obtaining planning permission to convert it to a climbing club hut. Thus, through the efforts of John, a club with fewer than 200 members created two very desirable huts, assets to the whole UK climbing community. In 1995 John was made an hon vice president of ULGMC in recognition.

John was a man of many parts. Not only did he climb and trek in many parts of the world but he was also a leading figure in the UK ballooning scene. He attained a balloon pilot's license, assisted in many charitable balloon events and festivals, but never achieved his ambition to fly across the Channel. His second wife, Valerie was also a well-known balloonist. Transcending all of John's accomplishments is the fact that he was the most kind and gentle of men, quiet and modest about his many achievements.

Mike Esten

Lady Ann Chorley
1931 - 2021

Lady Ann Chorley.

In her early 20s Ann Debenham was living with her mother in a Prince's Gate flat near the Royal Geographical Society. Her father, Archibald Scott Debenham, a director of Shell, had died when she was just one. She looked to her uncle, Frank Debenham, for advice on what she might do. Frank had been a member of Scott's Terra Nova expedition, 1910–13, and subsequently founded the Scott Polar Research Institute in Cambridge, becoming its first director. In 1931 he was elected the first Cambridge professor of geography and was extremely active at the RGS. It was he who asked Ann to take minutes for an RGS committee which he chaired. In this way, Ann made interesting connections with the mountaineering and exploration world.

Ann must have impressed with her work and in due course was appointed secretary to the 1953 Everest expedition. Her nephew Rupert (Gen Sir Rupert Smith) recalls:

> She would take me to the office, and I would wander around the building. I was able to inspect tents, boots, and other equipment such as oxygen sets that lay around the office; I expect they were trial samples. I tried dehydrated apple flakes and other mountaineering delicacies.

After Everest had been climbed, work at the office continued apace with the organisation of lecture tours, meetings and official receptions. The 1955 Kanchenjunga expedition was organised, and her team worked with John Hunt to pilot and expand the Duke of Edinburgh Award Scheme. Ann became close to George Lowe but their engagement was broken off. Lowe, *AJ* 2013 (pp310-11), subsequently married Susan, daughter of John Hunt. In 1964 Ann married Roger Chorley, the second Baron Chorley. Roger was a key figure in the mountaineering world (*AJ* 2016, pp370-5), whose mountaineering was curtailed after he developed polio during the expedition in 1957 to Machapuchare.

In 1966 Ann applied to join the Ladies' Alpine Club (LAC). In addition to some limited British rock-climbing experience, she had been to Arolla and climbed the Pigne D'Arolla. Her supporters for joining the LAC were Dorothy Pilley Richards and Katherine C Chorley. No doubt the visit to

Arolla stimulated sad memories of the accident in which John Hopkinson and his son and two daughters was killed on the Petite Dent de Veisivi in 1898.

Little can be found of any big mountaineering for both Ann and Roger later than a note on the LAC application of visits to Bernina and Bregalia and climbs of some minor peaks in 1969. Roger's strength and mobility were adversely affected by his polio but the couple travelled extensively to remote places, including north-west China, the Karakoram Highway, Patagonia and the Straits of Magellan in the company of George Band and John Innerdale together with their wives. Other trips were made in the company of Nick and Betsy Clinch. Norman and Enid Hardie and Bill Pachard in Australia received several visits.

Ann is remembered as a larger than life character. She loved a good party and was a generous hostess. She had time for everyone and the knack of finding something to engage with and making each meeting memorable and valued.

Roderick A Smith

David Ford
1947 - 2021

Dave Ford in a typically good mood motoring down Loch Linnhe in 2013.

Dave was born in Bristol and spent his early childhood there with his mother Ena, his father Kenneth, his twin sister Sue, and his elder sister Maureen. He remembered his childhood fondly all his life and maintained a keen interest in the lives of his siblings, nephews and nieces. Maureen remembers him as 'a dear, thoughtful but mischievous brother' who, later in life, earned her respect and admiration.

His love of the outdoors began to develop when he spent holidays at his uncle's house in Chewton Mendip. As a youth, he joined local running and climbing clubs and climbed with club pals in the Avon Gorge and elsewhere, as well as travelling to athletics competitions at venues across Britain and sailing with friends on the Norfolk Broads. Keen to try skiing, he even made a rudimentary (and not very successful) pair of skis out of wooden planks.

Martin Crocker, a close friend from this time, describes their adventures together:

Dave was a key friend of my formative years in the 1970s and we had great times together on the sea cliffs of Torbay, Lundy and Gower – as well as some memorable epics and close shaves, including in the Alps. I remember him as always positive and smiling with his endearing grin, loving the climbing and the mountains. He was a brilliant, optimistic partner, making you feel safe and inspired as together we discovered adventure in challenging places, dubiously transported in his shaky red van.

One of Martin's favourite photos is of the two of them on the summit of the Matterhorn.

We were both Alpine novices, but we grabbed that ascent one fine day between bouts of bad weather. Dave was super-keen and encouraging, yet solid and safe throughout, just the sort of partner needed to reach the top. One of his pet phrases used while climbing was 'Go, go, go but not like a yo-yo!' i.e. don't fall off!

Dave inherited excellent practical skills in joinery from his father and also learnt the difficult skill of bell ringing with his dad's team in various Somerset churches, an interest that was reignited after his retirement when he began to bell ring once more with the Tulloch bell ringing group.

After leaving school Dave trained as an agricultural engineer and later as a mechanical engineer. This was followed by work as a draughtsman for two companies in the Bristol area. However, eventually, the urge to spend more of his time outdoors became too strong and led to a complete change of career starting with a summer as an outdoor instructor, working with groups of young people at Outward Bound Eskdale in the Lake District. He began to combine summers at Outward Bound with winters working at a ski-training centre in Norway and made many lifelong friends at these locations.

Jim Dominy, one of these friends, recalls him being 'an ideal person to be with when things got "interesting" (i.e. a bit too exciting). Whether sailing, climbing or cycling, he was the best of partners and when relaxing, he was the best of company.'

Early in the 1980s, following a long cycle tour of Europe with his then partner Judith, the pair decided to settle down as smallholders in Cornwall. But neither could overcome their love of the mountains and Dave soon returned to Outward Bound, working as an instructor and later, when he found this too stressful, as storeman and bosun at Eskdale and Ullswater Outward Bound. He finally settled at Loch Eil Outward Bound in 1989 as bosun.

During this time he developed a deep love of literature, art and classical music. The sound of Radio 3 could often be heard drifting from the Outward Bound boatshed on the shore of Loch Eil. By studying hard in his spare time he gained an Open University MA in English literature and soon books by and about the great English novelists and poets were filling and then overflowing the shelves in Burnside Cottage. It was lucky he had the joinery skills to be able to construct more bookshelves that soon covered several walls in the cottage.

After Dave retired from Outward Bound he maintained his interest in outdoor activities. He also joined a local art club and helped set up a local branch of Men's Shed, an association for retired men who, like him, wanted to continue to enjoy the comradeship they had found in their workplaces. When he was disabled by a stroke two years ago, he was determined to regain his mobility and people who met him out walking were impressed by his bravery, good humour and cheerfulness.

I think Dave would have listed amongst the most joyful times of his life summer months spent with friends climbing (and occasionally cycling) in the Alps and Norway and walking in the Pyrenees, winter trips skiing almost the whole length of Norway and also sailing trips with Outward Bound students and friends on the beautiful west coast of Scotland.

Dave was blessed with a lovely open and sociable character, and with wit and humour, and had a wide-ranging interest in the world around him. The many dear friends he made due to his personality must, I think, be considered the main joy and achievement of his life.

Jenny Ford

Edwin Hammond
1938 - 2021

Ed Hammond enjoying success.

I first met Ed at a British Mountaineering Council AGM in 1963 in London, where the BMC was based in those days. He was quite involved with the running of the BMC at that time and was guides secretary for some years. Over the next few years I became a wandering outdoor instructor moving between Plas y Brenin, Outward Bound and the odd education authority centre. Ed and I would meet up now and then, do a route or two, have a drink or two and annoy Chris Briggs at the Pen y Gwryd. Ed was the fellow who got things done and it was he who found and arranged the purchase of Waenhir, which became the climbing hut for the Yeti Club, of which he was a member.

In 1966, with his Land Rover and trailer loaded, four of us set off for the Hindu Kush. Ed had organised another Ed – this one Ed Mcreery, an American living in Kabul – to act as our host and 'guide to life' in Afghanistan. We climbed in the Mir Samir area and then went over the Anjuman pass to climb our first 20,000-footer in the Pagar valley. Edwin then took to getting more done in north Wales and he and his wife Carolyn moved to live there. He bought, demolished and rebuilt the Waterloo Hotel in Betws y Coed after an amazing party in the old building, spanning three floors and the cellar.

With one expedition and one hotel chalked up Ed decided that it would be a good idea if we all did it again so in 1971 the grandly titled Anglo-Welsh expedition climbed another 20,000ft peak north of Jumla in western Nepal. He and Carolyn then moved to the Lake District and his next hotel was the iconic Wasdale Head Inn, which was in a sorry state internally. The occasional parties there gave some folk the opinion that Ed intended it to go the same way as the Waterloo. Not so, it was saved from the flames. The building is still recognisable from the old photographs but the interior is up to modern standards. Water always appears when you turn the tap on and mains electricity replaced the generator.

He was elected to Club membership in 1977, but by 2005 he realised his that his climbing days were over. He spent his later years in Switzerland, cruelly handicapped by ill health. Edwin passed away at his home in Verbier on 25 July 2021.

David Draper

Michael Baker writes: Ed Hammond and I in the 1970s were both members of the committee that advised the Sports Council on the running of Plas y Brenin, the National Mountaineering Centre. The business of the committee at that time was both interesting and controversial. The controversy centred on the mountain training dispute, which came to its height in the late 1970s. Sir Jack Longland, the chair, John Barry the director, and Ken Wilson and Dennis Gray representing the interests of the British Mountaineering Council were all heavily involved in the dispute – on different sides. Against that background, Sir Jack asked Ed to chair a team to produce a report on the role to be undertaken by the centre over the next decade. This was not to be an easy task. Positions were by then entrenched, and the characters involved had very strong views that they were determined to get across. The centre was potentially a battleground on which the controversy could be fought out. Ed, however, had a background in property development and business, which had honed his people skills, and he was intensely practical. Furthermore, his mountaineering qualifications, though not spectacular, were respected by the protagonists. In the end, the report 'Plas y Brenin in the Eighties' found favour with all concerned, which was no small tribute to Ed's skills and character. I greatly admired him as a person who gave a lot to the mountaineering world, of which his role at Plas y Brenin was only a small part.

Stewart Hawkins
1938 - 2022

Stewart Hawkins.

Stewart John Hawkins was a life force whose enthusiasm, courage and capacity for friendship inspired all who knew him. Born in London, he was afflicted by asthma as a child but won a scholarship to Charterhouse where Wilfrid Noyce taught him French, introduced him to climbing and a love of mountains and proposed him for the Climbers' Club. Stewart subsequently repaid his debt by writing a superb and detailed biography of Noyce, *Far, Far The Distant Peak* (Curbans Books, 2014), reviewed in *AJ* 2014, pp344-6. (See also 'Letters from the Fish's Tail', pp51-60.)

National service with the Nigerian Regiment extended Stewart's bent for languages as he learned Hausa. At Balliol College, Oxford, he switched from law to Farsi and Arabic putting the latter to good use in 1960 when serving a one-year attachment as a Colonial Service political officer in south Arabia. Entirely in his element, he settled one longstanding tribal territorial dispute and scotched dissident Yemeni incursions.

After Balliol, Stewart worked in Nigeria with Shell during 1963-4 and for the Steel Company of Wales between 1965 and 1967. He joined IBM in 1968 with spells in Paris and the Gulf States when his Arabic was key to successful negotiations. In 1992 he took early retirement aged 54 to settle in the Haute Provence village of Curbans where he devoted himself to the care of his beloved first wife Alison and played a prominent part in local affairs. Alison died prematurely in 1998. Stewart's marriage to Sandra in 2004 was to be a source of great joy and comfort during his own long years of illness.

I first got to know Stewart when we shared a house in the Yemeni city of Mukalla, climbing its limestone cliffs and exploring the wild wadis of its hinterland. In 1962, we did several classic routes together in the north-west Highlands and in later years Alpine treks including a circuit of Monte Viso in 1994 to track Hannibal's route across the Cottian Alps.

Stewart's house in Curbans, where he and Sandra so generously entertained their families (including sons, spouses and grandchildren) and innumerable friends, was within an hour of the Dauphiné. While regular excursions included the Pic de Bass and the Pain de Sucre (3250m), Stewart's ascent of the Barre des Écrins was aborted at 3,800m when a chunk of falling ice broke his arm and necessitated a helicopter rescue.

In tandem with his professional life, Stewart served as the international commissioner of the UK Scouting Association and was awarded the Bronze Wolf Award for outstanding services to scouting worldwide. He also undertook several missions to Central Asia for the European Union's Technical Aid to the Commonwealth of Independent States and in 1999 climbed to 3,800m in the Kyrgyz Altai.

Such visits so stirred youthful memories of Wilfrid Noyce that Stewart resolved to locate the stone cairn in Tajikistan's Garmo valley that Russian climbers had erected as a memorial to Noyce and Robin Smith who had perished descending Garmo Peak during John Hunt's 1962 Pamir's expedition. During his first attempt in 2008 he and his horse narrowly escaped drowning when fording the Zen-i-Zamin river while the swollen Kyrgyz Ob river proved impassable. In 2009 he returned with Noyce's son Jeremy, Peter Norton and Barry Cooper to add a commemorative plaque to the Russian memorial (*AJ* 2010-11, pp464-7).

Stewart was elected an associate member of the Club in 2006: his grandson Angus maintains the mountaineering tradition. In later years, he battled valiantly with a succession of serious illnesses never complaining and ever cheerful. Of an evening, when he and Sandra sat together watching the sun sink beneath the hills, Stewart's 'A good day, eh?' exemplified his unconquerable spirit. We will miss him dreadfully.

John Harding

Malcolm Howells
1942 - 2021

Malcolm Howells.

Malcolm Howells died of pneumonia on 24 November 2021 in Berkeley, California where he and his wife Mary Anne had lived for many years. He had been suffering from Alzheimer's for quite a while: a cruel disease.

Malcolm was born in Brighton on 23 September 1942. He attended Patcham Junior School and later Varndean Grammar for Boys. In 1962 he went up to Hertford College, Oxford to study physics, spending three formative years as an undergraduate and was a member of the Oxford University Mountaineering Club. After graduating he decided he wanted to teach and took a teaching diploma at Leeds University where he met Val who would later become his wife.

Malcolm Howells on the first ascent of
Phaedra in 1966. *(Ken Wilson)*

Malcolm moved to London and began teaching at a north London grammar but soon became disillusioned with the profession, deciding his true passion was for physics and so studied for a PhD at Westfield College, London. For the rest of his career, he would work in the field of high-energy physics travelling the world from one synchrotron to another: Oxford, Grenoble, Barcelona, New York and finally Berkeley.

I first met Malcolm in the 1960s in London where we shared a house together with a group of climbers, one of the leading lights being Ken Wilson. There was a close-knit social scene of climbers who would drive up to north Wales or the Lakes each weekend. We would meet on Thursday evenings at the Crown pub on Highgate Hill to have fun and arrange weekend transport. While this was a very London-centric scene, any climber finding himself in London on a Thursday night would likely find their way to the Crown.

In January 1968 Malcolm and Val were married and I was their best man. They bought a house in Crouch End, which became a late-night extension to Thursday evenings at the Crown. It was during this period that Malcolm and I began climbing regularly together, managing a number of new routes on Gogarth, including *Hustler*, *Ipso Facto*, *Phaedra* and *Rat Race*. We also made a number of early ascents and one in particular nearly ended in disaster: an attempt on the second ascent of Naddyn Ddu on Cloggy. Malcolm was on the main pitch and after dispensing with the aid peg Pete Crew had used on the first ascent, he took a rest on a nut.

'What's the nut like?' I shouted up to him. Before he could reply he was flying through the air, falling about 60ft into the retaining wall. Luckily a runner held but he still shattered his patella and gashed his head quite badly. Fortunately, Dave Yates, who had a lot of mountain rescue experience, was above us on *The Mostest* and abseiled down to lower me, with Malcolm on my back, in two 150ft rope lengths to the bottom of the crag and to the waiting official rescue team.

In around 1972 Malcolm began work at the Synchrotron Radiation Facility at Daresbury necessitating a move north where Val and Malcolm set up home in Altrincham. At the time there was a large group of climbers living

The 1978 expedition to Choktoi in the Karakoram. Left to right: Malcolm Howells, Dave 'Pod' Potts, liaison officer Harri, Barry Whybrow and Jim Curran. *(George Lowe)*

A bivy on Trango. Left to right: Malcolm Howells, Martin Boysen, Joe Brown and Mo Anthoine.

in the area: Chris Bonington, Martin Boysen, Nick Estcourt, Dave Potts, Dave Pearce, John Yates and Malcolm, to name just a few. This group became jokingly known as 'The Altrincham All-Stars'. At this time Malcolm climbed regularly with Dave Pearce making some difficult climbs on Anglesey. In the summer of 1974, they went to Yosemite in California where they climbed the north-east face of Half Dome, the Nose on El Capitan and Salathe Wall.

In August 1973 Val and Malcolm had their first daughter Lucy but sadly they separated in 1976 and soon afterwards he went to live and work in the States. I know he felt wretched about leaving Lucy and made every effort to see her whenever he could. Sometime later he met Mary Anne and they married in 1983 and not long after they had Laura, Malcolm's second daughter. Although he lived and worked in the States, he always maintained strong links with family and friends in Europe. He was a frequent visitor to Oxford and had a second home in Montpellier, France.

Malcolm was not just a very good rock climber he was also a fine mountaineer. He climbed extensively in the western Alps and we made a number of ascents in Zermatt and Chamonix together. His first Himalayan expedition came in 1974 with a trip to the Langtang Himal. In 1977 he went to Kishtwar Flat Top (6100m) and in 1978 to the Karakoram to climb Choktoi I (6166m). However, his most significant mountaineering exploit came in 1976, when he was invited to join Mo Anthoine's expedition to climb Trango Tower in the Karakoram (*AJ* 1976 pp184-5). Other members of the team included Joe Brown, Martin Boysen, Tony Riley and Jim Curran who made a film of the expedition and later wrote a book, *The Nameless Tower* (1978). Mo and Martin reached the summit first, followed a day later by Malcolm and Joe: a significant mountaineering achievement.

Malcolm was an enthusiastic skier. We made attempts on the winter Haute Route between Chamonix and Zermatt but were thwarted by bad weather.

We skied the Vallée Blanche on a number of occasions and Malcolm skied in many parts of Europe and North America until quite recently, when his illness made it no longer possible.

Malcolm was great fun to be around. What first comes to mind were his patience, generosity and unflappability. He could be quite argumentative though, usually egged on by friends; he was painfully logical with an underlying dogged determination. When skiing with a group of friends his jacket zip kept jamming, holding everyone up in cold and windy conditions. At lunchtime he was ordered to buy a new jacket. Malcolm returned wearing the same top but when challenged produced a pair of pliers: typical Malcolm.

Another anecdote that powerfully demonstrates his famous unflappability was while he was climbing *Shibboleth* on Buachaille Etive Mor in Scotland. He was leading the difficult traverse high up on the route when, to his second Dave Pearce's horror, Malcolm's rope just dropped off him. Dave had the unenviable decision, should I tell him? He decided he should and Malcolm's cool response was: 'Oh shit, I think I can make the peg.' Fortunately he did and was then thrown a rope from above by Nick Estcourt.

His wife Mary Anne and his two daughters, Lucy (on Zoom) and Laura, were with him when he died. He will be very sadly missed by his family, but also his many friends and colleagues all over the world. Farewell old pal.

Barry Whybrow

Jim Milledge
1930 - 2022

Jim Milledge. *(Simon Currin)*

Jim Milledge was, as Dr Dave Hillebrandt described him, 'the father of mountain medicine'. His research was pivotal in informing climbers coping with the rigours of high altitude but despite his considerable professional success he remained modest and wry, a shrewd observer of his colleagues but also a generous one. He appreciated his luck, too, at being involved in some of the most important research expeditions of his era.

Jim was born in Tianjin, north China, where his father was a medical missionary and came to Britain in 1936. He was first introduced to the hills at Rydal School in north Wales where, he recalled, 'I was very happy, but being dyslexic (though the term had not been invented), I was considered just dim.' While at Rydal, a local family asked the headmaster if he knew of a reliable but not academically bright lad who would like to spend time learning about their raspberry jam business, to manage production if they were away. Not appreciating Jim's enquiring and brilliant mind, masked as it was, the headmaster assigned him to this work-experience 'opportunity'. It made Jim determined never to work in such an environment again. Instead, he worked hard and 'just scraped the necessary results' to study medicine at Birmingham University. At Birmingham he caught the rock-climbing bug but was 'very average academically, until my final year when I was awarded the prize in Clinical Medicine, the only prize I ever won!' It was enough to start him on his long career of highly respected research, often on high-altitude medicine.

After graduating and house jobs, Jim had to do national service and joined the Royal Air Force as a medical officer. Posted to Hong Kong, he discovered his commanding officer was a member of the Alpine Club and they formed a mountain rescue team. Apart from local rock climbing, they made an expedition to Kinabalu (4095m) in Borneo in 1957. The following year, he and his first wife Betty made a two-week trek in Nepal, entirely self organised with just two porters and no common language. 'We fell in love with the country,' he recalled.

Demobbed from the RAF, Jim specialised in general medicine with an interest in respiratory disease, working in Southampton with William McLeod. They performed arterial blood sampling in the investigation of lung disease. In November 1959, he learned that Griff Pugh and Ed Hillary were organising an expedition to study the physiology of acclimatisation as well as attempting an 8,000m peak. The trip would last nine months, from the end of one monsoon to the start of the next. Jim wrote to Griff Pugh and when a member dropped out found himself on his way back to Nepal.

We set up the prefabricated hut on a glacier at 5,800m where we spent the winter doing the planned physiological projects there and at our base camp at 4,500m. On Makalu, we continued some physiology at 6,300m and even at 7,400m on Makalu Col, but we failed to climb the summit due to bad weather and illness. My wife Betty, an anaesthetist, worked in the Mission Hospital in Kathmandu for the 9 months we were in Solu Khumbu.

After this seminal life experience, Jim and Betty decided to return to Asia and try to find work that combined research and clinical medicine. Apart from a year's furlough in San Francisco as a research fellow with Dr John Severinghaus at the Cardiovascular Research Institute, they spent a decade at the Vellore Christian Medical College in south India, working with cardiothoracic surgeons just starting open-heart surgery and the attendant intensive care, as well as more conventional respiratory medicine.

Being based in India meant easier access to the Himalaya and during these years Jim made a number of trips to Solu Khumbu. In 1964, Dr Sukumar Lahiri, an Indian physiologist from the Silver Hut expedition, organised a small physiological wing as part of Hillary's second 'Schoolhouse' expedition. Their aim was to study physiological differences between Sherpas and themselves in a camp above Lukla where the expedition built the now busy airstrip.

Griff Pugh, Ed Hillary and Jim Milledge on the Silver Hut expedition.

The Silver Hut, landmark in mountain medicine.

Repeating studies he had done in the Silver Hut, on the changes in the chemical control of breathing with acclimatisation, Jim found to his surprise that the Sherpas had significantly lower hypoxic ventilatory responses. It was after these experiences that he published in 1967 what he regarded as his most significant paper, 'Respiratory control in lowlanders and Sherpa highlanders at altitude', coauthored with Lahiri and published in *Respiratory Physiology*.

Jim and Betty returned to Britain in 1972 and he took a job with the Medical Research Council at the new Clinical Research Centre at Northwick Park Hospital in Harrow. A year later, he shifted jobs into a split between research work and consultancy in the hospital, which he regarded as ideal and thought himself fortunate to have continued in this way until retirement in 1995, by which time he was first medical director. One junior member of staff described him as 'the best medical director he has ever come across; he was always building bridges and reconciling groups in conflict.'

During his 23 years at Northwick, Jim pursued his interest in high-altitude physiology and while research funds for work in the Himalaya were lacking in the 1970s, he did work in the UK and Switzerland on the effects of prolonged exercise and altitude on fluid and electrolyte balance and the hormones controlling them. The 1980s began much more brightly. In 1981 he made two trips to high altitude combining climbing with research. The first was to Kongur (7719m) with Chris Bonington's expedition, part of a research team led by Michael Ward. The second was to Everest with an American research expedition led by John West. Both leaders had been on the Silver Hut trip 20 years earlier. Later scientific expeditions took Jim to Kenya in 1987 and Bolivia in 1989. On these expeditions he was able to do further work on the hormones involved with fluid balance at altitude in relation to acute mountain sickness. The same year he went to Bolivia, he also published, with co-authors Ward and West, *High Altitude Medicine and Physiology*, now in its sixth edition.

Jim's work is still appreciated around the world and he represented the British Mountaineering Council on the International Climbing and Mountaineering federation's MedCom, including a period as president. Not only was Jim an accomplished researcher, he was also a very competent climber and mountaineer in his own right. This stood him in good stead during

Jim Milledge at work, studying exercise.

the Silver Hut expedition in 1960. He went on to reach 7,000m on Makalu and then had to evacuate Hillary who had become ill. He joined the Alpine Club in 1975 and was an active member, and of the Climbers' Club too.

Jim and Betty brought up their two children in the outdoors and their interest continues to this day. Betty died suddenly in 1991 and in 1993 Jim married Betty's friend Pat who cared for him during his final illness. Problems with his short-term memory caused him some frustrations but he was still able to describe potential routes in remote valleys in Nepal, holding court in the bar at Plas y Brenin on a mountain medicine course or at the Alpine Club. Being aware of his own failing intellect he took steps to make his final wishes known and arranged power of attorney. Alas, our health system failed to treat him with the dignity of a peaceful death that he had so richly earned.

Jim used to joke that his life was a perpetual mountain holiday. 'I have tried to follow my mother's aphorism, "to seize the opportunity of a lifetime, in the lifetime of opportunity"'. He remains much respected in medical circles. As Dave Hillebrandt wrote soon after Jim's death, 'one is struck by the number of young researchers, medical students, doctors and expedition mountaineers who are indebted to him for the time he gave them to encourage, guide and mentor them in their ventures.'

Ed Douglas & Roderick A Smith

Prof Sir Andrew Pollard writes: One of my favourite memories of the past 30 or so years of knowing Jim was a trip to a high-altitude conference in Japan, where we had an exhilarating international group excursion up a snowy peak, followed by recovery in a traditional Japanese hotel. The entertainment for the assembled 'rugged' medical mountaineers including communal bathing followed by dinner, wearing a (too short) Japanese style bathrobe cross-legged on the floor. Our after-dinner performance was fuelled with flowing Japanese wine and we led the international karaoke competition together singing 'On Ilkla Moor Baht 'at' in parts, followed by 'Let It Be'. Not sure if we won, but at least it sounded good to us! Thanks for all you have taught me about physiology, the mountains and enjoyment of life, without taking it too seriously.

Dr Nick Mason writes: I had *High Altitude Medicine and Physiology* out on almost permanent loan from our hospital library as a junior doctor and so it was with some trepidation that I first met Jim Milledge, author, researcher and veteran of the Silver Hut and the American Medical Research Expedition to Mt Everest (AMREE) at Plas y Brenin in April 1993. Little did I realise that within months Jim would be providing generous advice, not to mention an insightful and rigorous critique, for the projects that I was involved with on the 1994 British Mount Everest Medical Expedition. He would become a valued mentor and friend to those of us taking our first tentative steps in the world of high altitude research on that expedition.

Piero Nava
1932 - 2021

Piero Nava on Kanjut Sar in the Karakoram in 1959.

The young Piero Nava in the Dolomites.

Piero Nava passed away on 2 September 2021 in Bergamo, Italy at the age of 89. He was a longstanding member of the Alpine Club, joining in 1973, and was part of the prestigious Groupe de Haute Montagne.

His love for the mountains started as a young child when his parents would take him to spend the summer months near Courmayeur on the Italian side of Mont Blanc. This kindled a passion for the mountains, which he retained throughout his life. He started climbing in the Alps when he was a teenager and went on to climb important peaks in the Alps, sometimes as first or second ascents. On 30 July and 30 August 1961 he made a double ascent of the north face of the Matterhorn with companions Jean Bick and Piero Pression. This outstanding route had been climbed only 15 times in the previous 30 years since its first ascent.

He participated in 15 overseas expeditions often as a leader or with organisational responsibilities. Notably he was deputy leader of the 1973 Italian expedition to Everest that saw the first Italians reach the world's highest summit. This expedition was carried out on a grand scale. Two military helicopters were airlifted to Kathmandu, assembled and flown, first to base camp, and then beyond up the Khumbu Icefall. One crashed and was abandoned. Base camp was luxurious, carpeted and supplied with leather sofas: a luxury not to Ed Hillary's liking when he visited the site. Maybe this, 20 years after the first ascent, was the Rubicon of Everest madness?

Also at a very young age, Piero Nava developed a passion for mountain books and applied the same intense interest he had for climbing to his collection of rare antique books and prints, predominantly about the Alps, painstakingly putting together a library of more than 4,000 volumes throughout his life. 'I believe that his is the largest bibliography of the mountains in circulation,' Agostino Da Polenza of Orobie said, 'with books, photographs and postcards. There was no expedition I participated in that he didn't ask me to send him postcards. I believe that his library of mountain books is unparalleled.'

Piero also expressed the love for the mountains in all its aspects through the camera lens as a very competent photographer and recognised filmmaker. A respected and principled lawyer in his working life, he leaves his adored wife Giovanna and three children Donatella, Nicola and Armando. He had been a member of the Club Alpino Italiano since 1952 and was according to Paolo Valoti, president of CAI Bergamo, 'a man of great mountain culture and with truly exemplary intellectual honesty.'

Armando Nava

Ted Norrish
1935 - 2022

At Jasper after the ascent of Mount Robson in 1961. From left to right: Olaf Soot, Ted Norrish, Willi Pfisterer, Bill Roberts and Mike Keen.

Edward Wreyford Norrish, a member of the Club since 1975, died on 11 March 2022. He read classics at Brasenose College, Oxford, where he enjoyed three Alpine seasons, an expedition to Arctic Norway in 1955, and, in 1958, organised and part led the Oxford Chitral expedition. As classics master at King Henry VIII School in Coventry for nearly 30 years, from 1959 to 1987, Ted was much admired by his pupils, not only for his teaching but also as an inspirational athletics and orienteering coach.

At Brasenose in the mid 1950s Ted was a lively participant in college and university life, becoming a member of the Oxford University Mountaineering Club (OUMC), the college cross-country team, and the Oxford Bach Choir. Many years later he wrote his autobiography, *Cursus Honorum*, a lengthy and extremely detailed account of his life which he published privately. In it he wrote, 'I have had many fine times in my life, but the five years at Oxford were equal with the best.'

Norrish2: Norrish in the 1970 Karrimor Mountain Marathon.

His first expedition was the British Oksfjord (Finnmark) expedition of 1955 to Arctic Norway during which virgin peaks were climbed. He was organiser of the Oxford Chitral 1958 expedition to Saraghrar (7349m) in the Hindu Kush. Two members of the team reached a high point of about 7,000m but the climbing leader, Peter Nelson, a young mountaineer of great promise, fell on the descent (*AJ* 1956, pp104-7). Nearly 60 years later, Ted wrote an account of this expedition 'Chitral 1958', *AJ* 2016, pp254-64). One is astonished at either the retentiveness of his mind or his access to detailed notes made at the time – or both. In 1961 he climbed Mont Robson (3954m), highest peak in the Canadian Rockies, in a party of five that included Bill Roberts, who had also been on the Saraghrar expedition. Once again, Ted wrote a detailed retrospective account (*AJ* 2014, pp239-43).

A period as an instructor at Eskdale Outward Bound School followed the Chitral expedition, then six months in Austria before he took up his post in Coventry. Once in harness at King Henry VIII School, athletics and orienteering became a major focus but he continued to travel adventurously. He was in Turkey's Ala Dag in 1960 alone. In 1963 he visited Persepolis and climbed Mount Damavand (5609m) and in 1967 travelled to Egypt, Sudan and Ethiopia, reaching Lake Tana, source of the Blue Nile. There were three trips to Greece in 1964, 1978 and 1981, during which, Ted claimed, 'I climbed every mountain in Greece except Mt Kolykas.' In 1979, with a companion, he crossed the Afghan Hindu Kush by the Anjuman pass. After retiring from King Henry VIII School, he was in Tasmania, climbing Mount Anne and Mount Cradle and then he crossed Chitral again, this time alone and then spent six months in China. Latterly he spent a lot of time in the Balkans, particularly Bosnia, Croatia, Montenegro, Serbia and Albania. As a guide to friends between 1996 and 2006 he climbed in north-west Bulgaria Midjur and beautiful Kom 'about 40 times'.

Ted's was an extremely busy, active and fulfilled life, not easy to summarise. I leave conclusions about Ted, to his old climbing partner Bill Roberts, and an old pupil of his and colleague of mine, Hugh Shercliff.

Roderick A Smith

Bill Roberts writes: I first met Ted at an OUMC meet at Brackenclose in the 1950s. We then went to Arctic Norway together and climbed unclimbed peaks and glaciers together. Next was Saraghrar (7349m) in the Hindu Kush. He got to about 7,000m on this; it was climbed by an Italian expedition a few years later. We were together again on Mount Robson in 1961.

He became a popular trainer of athletes at King Henry VIII School in Coventry. Then he was ill and recovered, went to Bulgaria, married Emi and organised courses on mountains and monasteries. He was an extraordinary man, lively, full of energy, passion. We will miss him and so will Emi.

Hugh Shercliff writes: As for so many of us at King Henry VIII School in Coventry, Ted Norrish introduced me to orienteering, backpacking, bothies, and fell running (including the 18-mile night races he organised). He founded the orienteering club Octavian Droobers in the very early days of the sport: 'Octavian' for King Henry VIII School, 'Droobers' being a Midlands term for running through mud. He was known as 'Droob' at school. Apart from our camping club he ran athletics and cross-country, and was a leading light in Coventry and West Midlands running. The former 5,000m world record holder Dave Moorcroft wasn't at our school but gave a tribute citing Ted's influence on his career at Ted's memorial.

For me personally, one intervention proved significant. He gave me a copy of Munro's Tables when I was 14 and challenged me to climb 50 before I was 21, or the lot before I was 26. This I duly did and, typically, was rewarded by Ted with the promised case of champagne, 12 years after the challenge was issued. His widow Emi and I have agreed to scatter some of his ashes on a suitable Munro in the north-west Highlands, with old friends from the school camping club.

I lost touch for a while but visited him and his wife Emi after he returned to Coventry, and also gave one of the tributes at his memorial. He hated the description 'eccentric', but did things in a unique style, with a healthy disregard for both the rules and the sensitivities of his colleagues in the staffroom. However, he was very modest and the focus was always on the achievements of his charges. The recurrent theme at the memorial – be it from runners, hillwalkers, or his classics pupils – was that he enabled us to achieve more than any of us thought possible of ourselves. This may have been largely by sheer force of expectation and personality, but most look back with the greatest fondness and respect. Certainly, he was a great influence on many lives.

Brian Peart
1937 - 2022

Brian Peart.

Brian died at 85 having been accepted into the Club aged around 50 when he had achieved plenty to qualify as a full member. He much enjoyed coming to London from his native North East, for lectures and swapping tales. He was distinguished for his social as well as his altitudinal vigour: his climbing evolved from organising charitable walks for the Round Table, 41 Club and Rotary and he was keen to share his love of the mountains with friends, encouraging and enabling our progress.

After completing all of Wainwright's 214 Lakeland tops, he became enthralled with Scottish snow and ice climbing, following the established path to Clachaig Inn where he enjoyed animated talks by Chris Bonington and others. Scotland also triggered a habit of taking out friends on the rope, before getting his first taste of the Alps on a family summer holiday to Saas-Fee. During a haircut at Dora's Salon, he learned the owner's husband was the mountain guide Herman Bumen and Brian was promptly signed up for his first Alpine ascents, like the Alphubel and Nadelhorn.

Once he had learned the vital skills, Brian led his own climbs, starting with the Lagginhorn, Weissmies and Stecknadelhorn. Well-respected by the Supersaxo family who run Saas-Fee's Alphubel hotel, he made a total of seven ascents of the Allalinhorn with various companions. He was perhaps most satisfied with the various summits of Monte Rosa, especially Dufourspitze. Mont Blanc was climbed with friends when a recce took them so high it was judged not worth turning back.

The Himalaya were a natural evolution, initially with his wife Pauline, then two more serious treks. He trekked to Jomsom and hoped to climb one of the Annapurna Sanctuary peaks but his local guides were deterred by a forecast of heavy snow. On a second trip with the late George Band, they reached the southern base camp of Kangchenjunga. In between, he visited Georgia – despite war with Russia at the time – climbing Kazbek and Elbrus. In Africa, he climbed Toubkal and Kilimanjaro twice. Other adventures included a 21-mile day-walk and scramble up Mount Robson in British Columbia and the Bright Angel Trail in the Grand Canyon National Park.

Meeting Brian was transformative for me. Introduced to Lakeland in 1998 at half his age, I could barely keep up with him leaping bogs above Langdale. He nurtured my own passion for the mountains, patiently talking me out of early freezes first on Sharp Edge one balmy June evening and later my first proper alpine ridge. At 80, he saw me through Honister to the final leg of my Bob Graham Round, correctly telling me I would reach Keswick within 24 hours despite the scepticism of some others. What gave him the most pleasure was the Coast to Coast Walk with Pauline, carrying his young son Craig on his back. 'The simple things are often the very best.'

Edmond Jackson

Kev Reynolds
1943 - 2021

Kev and Min Reynolds in the Rätikon.

Kev Reynolds was well known for his walking and trekking guides. I am looking at his first book, *Walks and Climbs in the Pyrenees*, a modestly produced book from 1978, certainly in comparison with the current seventh edition, complete with colour photographs and neat maps. In a prolific career that produced over 50 books, Kev covered many varied terrains from the South Downs Way and the Cotswold Way to the Himalaya, via the Swiss Alps, the Bernese Oberland and the Valais.

An Essex boy, Ken left secondary school in 1958 to begin work in local government as a filing clerk. The hills of the Lake District, Snowdonia and Scotland provided his escape and he quickly developed into a strong, safe climber. In 1967 he married Min Dodsworth and the couple worked in a hostel in St Moritz. Back in the UK they took over the running of Crockham Hill youth hostel in Kent and Ken began writing articles for magazines. His guidebook career took off 10 years later when he began his long association with Cicerone, initially through his contact with Walt Unsworth.

Much of Kev's early output focused on Europe, but eventually he broadened his horizons to the Himalaya. A first trip to the region came in 1989, when he went on a trek to Kangchenjunga, the third-highest mountain in the world, and over the next 30 years he made nearly 20 visits to Nepal and bordering areas in India. Min, too, became a Himalayan trekker, joining Kev on many trips, and books naturally followed, guides to Annapurna, Everest, Kangchenjunga, Langtang and Manaslu, the last of which Kev regarded as 'the most beautiful walk in the world'.

Opinion on which books represent his best work will vary. As a trekking guidebook I would choose the fifth edition of his *Tour of Mont Blanc*, (2020), a real stimulus to lace up your boots and go. The second edition of *Walking in the Alps*, (2005) has been described as 'probably the most important guide to walking abroad that has been published in Britain.' Writing in the *Alpine Journal*, to which Kev was a frequent contributor, Ernst Sondheimer wrote: 'If I wanted to do everything listed in this marvellous book, I would need to live to just over 400 years and remain fit to the end.' The book is simply stunning and certainly a most worthy successor to J Hubert Walker's classic, *Walking in the Alps*, (Oliver & Boyd, 1951). But my own favourite is not a guidebook but *Abode of the Gods* (2015), tales of trekking in Nepal that amplify Kev's sympathy and love of Nepal's mountains and people.

My own queries to Kev were always rapidly and enthusiastically answered. His friendly nature came through even in a telephone call. His was a full and active life and outdoor exploration and writing were only parts of it. As a husband, father and active member of his church and community in Crockham Hill, he touched many lives. He will be sorely missed. After a lengthy battle with cancer, he died on 10 December 2021. He is survived by Min, their daughters Claudia and Ilsa, and grandchildren Charlie and Billy.

Roderick A Smith

Neil Sawyer
1961 - 2021

Aiguillette des Posettes on Neil's birthday Christmas day 2015.

Neil joined the Club in 1988, already an experienced and competent mountaineer. He had Alpine experience, having climbed Mont Blanc du Tacul, the Midi-Plan traverse, Aiguille d'Argentière and the Aiguille du Chardonnet, among others. In Britain, he had already rock and ice climbed, especially in Scotland. His winter routes included the now rarely formed Steall Falls, the north-east ridge of Aonach Beag and *Observatory Ridge*. His rock routes, mostly HVS leads, stretched from Pembrokeshire to Skye. He enjoyed soloing routes from *Classic Rock*. In his view, if he was confident he could down climb the route then he was happy to continue up it. At much the

Neil on the summit of the Aiguille du Bionassay.

same time he climbed and backpacked over many Munros. Finally, he was already an accomplished skier, having skied all the hardest runs in ski resorts like the Trois Vallées, including off-piste.

Neil grew up in Yorkshire and had an adventurous upbringing. His father was associated with the scout movement and wasn't afraid to let Neil have his fair share of outdoor activities. The family holidayed frequently in Scotland and always took a dinghy to sail off the north-west coast. His secondary education was hampered to say the least by the reorganisation of his school into a comprehensive but Neil did develop a strong interest in geology, which led him into the coal-mining industry: a job he loved. Neil was always a practical, hands-on person and his work at British Coal helped him develop into a skilled engineer. He progressed to pit deputy manager and would have risen further but for the collapse of the coal-mining industry during the Thatcher years. To continue in mining engineering, Neil would have had to travel abroad so instead he completed a MBA and took up a succession of jobs, mainly in sales.

Many people can claim Neil as one of the best friends they had. I am just one of those. It was always a memorable experience climbing with him. The mountains became our playground and we went looking for adventure. There was always a competitive edge to our excursions. Neil always wanted to get to the summit before anyone else. One such example was our ascent of Pigne d'Arolla (3787m). Normally parties climb up to the hut and next morning climb the mountain. We decided to climb from the valley straight past the hut and onto the summit. Some climbers had already set off from the hut when we passed by. Neil was determined to get past them and arrive at the top first. When I caught up with Neil on the summit and thought we might go back, he had other ideas. Why didn't we continue to the next summit over there? The way ahead was pristine untrodden snow, so off we went. That took us to La Serpentine (3789m) and still Neil wanted to carry on, to take in Mont Blanc de Cheilon (3870m). He would have but I declined, and we then dropped down into a valley that we had to climb back out of again to reach where we had camped: a great day out and typical of Neil. Through all the trips Neil and I made, I found him easy company, reliable in those trickier situations you often end up in when mountaineering, always enthusiastic and patient with those less gifted than he was.

Enthusiastic about all aspects of mountaineering, Neil was keen to test his limits and extend his abilities, whether it was snow and ice climbing, rock climbing, Alpine peaks, cycling or walking. He attended many of the Club's summer Alpine meets and also led one summer meet to Pralognan. But his biggest contribution to the Club's meet programme was undoubtedly the winter Alpine meets. For a number of years, Neil led this annual excursion to Chamonix. Activities included ice climbing, snowshoeing, on and off-piste skiing and iglooing.

By now Neil and his wife Moira, having both retired from work, had moved to Chamonix and were living their dream in the mountains at the foot of ski slopes with access to all the Chamonix ski areas, where Neil skied like a local and in the summer had plenty of peaks to go at. Neil had tried to sell the idea of the Club buying a hut in the Alps as the next logical development for the Club. He went one better by buying a home there instead.

Neil and Moira had met in Leeds through the outdoors and married in 1991. They had a shared passion for the mountains, climbing Kilimanjaro for their honeymoon. Moira joined Neil for many of his Munros, often waiting patiently while he went off to tick subsidiary tops. They also enjoyed many happy adventures with Neil's other hobbies, his rally car and Land Rovers over the years. Moira had to get used to Neil's need to be first on the summit, overtaking as many parties as possible. On one occasion climbing Alphubel (4206m) she had to lie down on the top to recover. Following this same pattern, Neil climbed his last 4,000m peak Grand Paradiso on 2 September 2021 with Moira. They overtook several parties who had left the hut before them and were second on the summit, beaten only by a party who had bivouacked higher up.

Neil died 21 days later on 23 September 2021 in a cycling accident near his home in Les Houches. It was a warm and sunny September day and he was surrounded by the mountains he loved. At the end of his life Neil had climbed 37 of the 4,000m peaks, including the Obergabelhorn, Dürrenhorn, Dent Blanche and Lyskamm, all graded AD. Of those 37, 21 were in the company of his wife Moira. He climbed in the Himalaya in the Kashmir region and the Karakoram. He completed all the Munros and associated tops, the last being Stuc a'Coire Dhuibh Bhig in February 2004. In total Neil climbed over 1,800 summits ranging from Himalayan and Alpine peaks to Marilyns.

So many of us feel, with great sadness, the loss of Neil, none more so than his wife Moira who shared his love and passion for the mountains. She continues to live their dream in Chamonix knowing 'he has only gone ahead to recce the biggest route of all and will be there to guide me when it's time.'

Paul Russell

Anthony Kinsey writes: I was hugely inspired, as well as intimidated, by Neil's incredible passion for mountaineering. When I met him, I was an over-confident mediocre skier and after a few hours on the mountain with Neil I realised just how much more there was to discover. I could tell a thousand stories of the many adventures we shared after that, but in short they were all unforgettable, educational, frightening and exhilarating. Safety always came first, but then a close second was pushing the envelope and taking on the potential dangers. All the while the banter and ridicule was constant, as well as lots of chat about our other shared passion, which, of course, was music.

Frank and Cath Procter write: Neil was a larger-than-life character with a sense of adventure that inspired us all. His skiing skills were legendary, maybe even kamikaze at times, but he always came up smiling after his mishaps. He seemed invincible. He also had a great sense of fun and is fondly remembered for his New Year antics in L'Igloo, particularly the Scottish ginger wig he donned on one occasion. He was a much-valued friend and we shall miss him dreadfully.

Paul Riley writes: Neil always needed a project; he wasn't one for sitting around. Sometimes we had to say, 'Neil just stop now and have a beer.' He had a real love of life and a need for adventure. Moira and Neil worked so well as a team, cycling together in the Dordogne and Chamonix and mountaineering throughout the Alps.

Richard Sykes
1932 - 2021

Richard Sykes.

Richard, known as 'Dick', grew up in Bristol where his father was a clergyman. The Sykes family consisted of five children including Richard who also had a twin brother. Following Bristol Grammar School, where he played on the first teams for rugby, cricket and hockey, he read classics at Cambridge. He was an active member of Cambridge University Mountaineering Club. He was a member of the 1957 Manchester expedition that attempted the first ascent of Masherbrum from which Bob Downes sadly did not return, (*AJ* 1958, pp169-84). He gained a PhD at Princeton in 1959 and further developed his keen interest in mountaineering.

For a short time he worked in the City, but that was not really for him. Instead, he trained as a social worker and worked in the Manchester area before moving back to Bristol where he founded a couple of charities, Bristol Home Plus, supporting families with children under five, then Westcare which provided support for those suffering from myalgic encephalomyelitis (ME), also called chronic fatigue syndrome. He sought to educate medical professionals who for many years dismissed the condition. He was among the first to take ME seriously and set up a national task force on the illness which reported in 1994, its conclusions feeding into the Chief Medical Officer's report.

He spent considerable time climbing and skiing in the Alps and regularly led ski tours for the Eagle Ski Club and Ski Club of Great Britain often using his British Association of Ski Instructors qualification to offer instruction. He was a member of the Climbers' Club as well as the AC and was a fine rock climber both in the Alps and throughout Britain, including climbing the Old Man of Hoy a couple of times with Mike Banks, so Mike could claim to be the oldest person to do so. He climbed regularly all over Britain as well as Spain and the Alps, latterly concentrating on Pembroke where he had a flat. Richard was also a member of the British Alpine ski traverse led by Alan Blackshaw that went from Kaprun in Austria to Gap in France requiring some six weeks of serious endurance (*AJ* 1973, pp13-22).

I remember an occasion on Skye when Richard took a day off from climbing and was asleep in the hut when the call came for help with an accident in Coire Lagan. This was in the days before formal rescue teams so anyone who was around was called on to help. Richard got up quickly and was to spend the rest of the day on the cliff helping to get an injured climber down. Several rescuers were still on the face at nightfall and Richard spent an uncomfortable night on a ledge before helping to retrieve a body the next day. So much for his rest day. At that point a couple climbers were reported missing and a fresh call went out for search parties. Richard went to bed. By then it was Sunday with no ferries running. After two days with just volunteers, the RAF mountain rescue arrived to assist.

Richard had considerable unassuming charm. He lived a simple life and became a regular attender at Quaker meetings. I last visited him in his residential home just before the pandemic as he was starting to write his memoirs, which are unfortunately unfinished and unavailable.

Robin Quine

Alpine Club Notes

'The Burning of Tyngboche [Tengpoche] Monastery', Rob Fairley, watercolour,
115cm × 180cm, 1998. (Lester and Christie Gray Collection)

Everest seen from the 20,000ft camp on the last day of the 1921 expedition.
(George Mallory)

Revisiting Everest

One of the highlights of the Alpine Club's year was the opening, albeit delayed by Covid-19 restrictions, of 'Everest: By Those Who Were There' in June. The curator of this landmark exhibition was our honorary librarian **Barbara Grigor-Taylor**, ably assisted by **Nigel Buckley** (keeper of artefacts), **Bernie Ingrams** (keeper of photographs), **Glyn Hughes** (honorary archivist), **Peter Gillman** and **Stuart Leggatt**. It commemorated the centenary of the first, reconnaissance expedition to Mount Everest in 1921 and the 1922 and 1924 climbing expeditions, exploring the experiences of expedition members as told in their own words and through their artefacts, correspondence and artworks. The exhibition drew together material from across the Alpine Club's collections, showcasing notable artefacts such as Sandy Irvine's ice axe, the last letters home written by **George Mallory** from camps V and VI, alongside archival documents relating to the planning of each expedition. The official opening of the exhibition was marked by a special lecture from our former president **Stephen Venables**: 'Everest: East Side Story'. During the questions afterwards, Chris Bonington remarked it was the best mountaineering lecture he had ever attended – praise indeed.

The exhibition was a great success, with many AC members and members of the public taking the opportunity to celebrate both the work of the Alpine Club and the Alpine Club Library in preserving and curating climbing history, and the Club's key role in the first expeditions to the world's highest mountain. Due to the high level of visitor demand, we ran a weekend opening in October, an event which also doubled up as the premiere of

The exhibition catalogue is now in its second impression after selling out.

the film of the same name produced by **John Porter**. This 35-minute film has been doing the rounds of the mountain film festivals in the UK, Europe and further afield, and has been very well received.

The comprehensive catalogue produced by Barbara Grigor-Taylor to accompany the exhibition reproduces every item from the exhibition, and is a compelling publication in its own right. It has proved to be a bestseller, with the original print run of 300 copies completely sold out. A second impression was therefore ordered and can still be purchased online via the Alpine Club Shop or by calling the office on **020 7613 0755**. Finally, many of the resources produced as part of the exhibition have been archived and can be found on the Alpine Club website: ***www.alpine-club.org.uk / news / everest-centenary***.

Women with Altitude

Our second showstopper exhibition in 2021 was 'Women with Altitude: 100 Years of Female Alpinism in the Pinnacle Club and the Alpine Club'. This was organised and run jointly with the Pinnacle Club to coincide with its centenary, and was curated by **Adele Long**, **Suzanne Strawther** and **Rosemary Scott**. The exhibition was organised as a series of panels celebrating the lives and climbing careers of 12 pioneering women climbers who were members of the

'Women with Altitude' proved a popular success.

Pinnacle Club and the Ladies' Alpine Club, including famous exponents such as **Dorothy Pilley** and **Eileen Healey**. One particularly innovative element of the exhibition was the inclusion of QR codes on each panel so that visitors could listen to each of the climbers describe their experiences of alpinism in their own words.

For those who are interested, the full transcription of Eileen Healey's climbing diaries, held in the Alpine Club Archives, can be accessed online at: *www.alpine-club.org.uk/EH_diaries/Contents.html*.

'Women with Altitude' was primarily funded by a grant from the National Heritage Lottery Fund, but special thanks must also go to ACL treasurer **Alan Henderson** for successfully securing an additional grant of £5,000 from Hackney Council's Hello Again, Hackney fund. This enabled the development of an accompanying series of resources for local schools. Archived versions of much of the exhibition material can also be found online at: *www.alpine-club.org.uk/events/past-future-exhibitions/907-women-with-altitude*.

Books

As previously reported, the ACL is an active library rather than a book museum. Hence, we aim to continually keep the collection up to date by obtaining as many new books published on climbing and mountaineering as possible. This requires considerable effort and significant funding. Luckily, we continued to see strong income from the sale of duplicate books from the regular lists produced by our honorary librarian. In particular, we were delighted to have the entire book collection of **John Peacock** donated to the Library by his wife Sheila, who was formerly the private secretary of **John Hunt**. We are very grateful to our former chair, **Hywel Lloyd**, for not only collecting the books from Devon but for also storing them until the lifting of Covid restrictions enabled him to deliver them to Charlotte Road. Thanks also to Library volunteer **Gordon Turner** who is overseeing a review of our guidebook collection with the aim of updating our holdings and making space for new acquisitions.

We're also pleased to report the successful outcome of some bookish detective work. In October, Gordon Turner spotted a rare book long missing from its usual place on the Library shelves for sale in an online auction catalogue: Douglas Freshfield's *Across Country from Thonon to Trent*, his first and rarest book, and published in 1865. Barbara commenced a detailed exchange with the auction house, providing the history of our missing copy and images of our bookplate in the front of the book but was unable to prevent it being sold to a bidder at a hammer price of £4,000. However, Barbara managed to trace the booksellers who had bought and sold the book since its disappearance from the Library, so after many more phone calls and emails, the sale was eventually cancelled. Finally, the volume was collected from the auctioneer's safe in mid November and restored to its rightful place on the reserve shelves of the Library, where it is now once more available for perusal. Well done, Barbara.

William Frederick Donkin's photograph of the Dent du Géant, on show again at the Alpine Club.

Photographs

The Photo Library received approximately 5,000 of Ian McNaught-Davis' slides, photos and films by kind donation from **Loreto Bonington**. This includes a film of the 1962 British-Soviet Pamirs expedition and slides of the first ascent of the Muztagh Tower. The collection continues to be sorted and archived by **Bernie Ingrams** and **Peter Payne**. Peter has also been digitising a collection of Edward Whymper's lanternslides, a donation from former archivist Peter Berg.

A fine collection of very large 19th and early 20th century photographs in their original Alpine Club carved oak frames, including works by **William Frederick Donkin**, **Edward Whymper** and **Fanny Bullock Workman**, has been stored in the Charlotte Road basement for many years. This has proved to be a less than ideal home; the large, heavy frames clutter up the space and some have become damaged when they have needed to be moved to enable access to other parts of the collections. The decision has therefore been taken to restore and renovate these stunning images. Once restored, they will be displayed as one of the planned 2022 exhibitions in the Lecture Hall before finding a permanent home hanging above the stairs between the ground and first floors.

Pictures

For many years, picture exhibitions at Charlotte Road have been run on a relatively ad hoc basis organised and curated by the keeper of pictures. More recently, the AC Committee established an exhibitions working group with the aim of taking a longer term and more structured approach to exhibitions. This has now been formalised as a standing sub-committee of the Club with former president **John Porter** as the current chair. So, a key project for our keeper of pictures this year has been the establishment of a detailed three-year exhibition schedule in concert with the Exhibitions Sub-Committee. (Two new glass exhibition cases have been purchased and installed in the Lecture Room, which enables us to showcase a far greater range of exhibition-related heritage material than has been the case hitherto.)

A full schedule for 2022 has been established with plans emerging for 2023 and 2024. The year 2022 will commence with an exhibition on 'Glaciers', curated by **Janet Johnson** and drawing on heritage material from the AC Collections. This will be followed during May to September by the exhibition of the large, restored photographs mentioned above: 'Large-scale Photographic Treasures of the Alpine Club'. From September to November, **Polly Townsend** will be organising an exhibition of contemporary paintings by a group of women mountain artists entitled 'A Wider Landscape'. The year will end with an exhibition of paintings of the Cuillin of Skye by **Helen Forde**.

This year has seen the first full year of our partnerships with ArtUK and The Watercolour World. Both are acting as showcases for much of the Club's artworks to both the membership and the wider public. Sales of images via ArtUK is now providing an income stream that is being utilised for conservation of the art collection.

A special thank you must be given to the AC honorary secretary Sherry Macliver, who worked tirelessly to arrange copyright permission for the Club's 2021 Christmas card: a stunning watercolour by T H Somervell, 'Everest from Pang La, 45 miles away', from the 1922 Everest expedition (Alpine Club Collection NA099P).

Alpine Club Christmas Card 2021

Artefacts

It was a relatively quiet year for artefacts. Two ice axes belonging to **Ian McNaught-Davis** and used on the first ascent of the Muztagh Tower were donated by **Chris Bonington**. These will make a fine addition to our ever-burgeoning historical ice-axe collection.

Nigel, Bernie, Barbara and Sue collaborated with The North Face to produce a shopfront display at their flagship store in Covent Garden. We loaned some of our historic mountain apparel to contrast with modern clothing in a large window display. We were mindful that the Club should not be seen to endorse their products over those of other manufacturers, but it provided some good publicity for the Club in a very high footfall environment.

Archives

After a long hiatus, due to the Covid-19 pandemic, the Archives re-opened for business in October and **Glyn Hughes** has been busy catching up on backdated enquiries. We have had a steady stream of research enquiries, including a visit from the BBC in relation to a proposed documentary on the life of **Eileen Healey**. A set of letters written by **James Surtees Phillpotts** following an ascent of the Jungfrau in 1862 was donated by his grandson, Roger Gwyn. Phillpotts, a notable headmaster of Bedford School, accompanied Whymper in the search for bodies following the Matterhorn accident. Other acquisitions included letters relating to the first ascent of Monte Rosa written by Smyth, Kennedy and Wethered, donated by Jerry Lovatt after finding them inside a book in his own collection. Adam Lloyd, son of **Peter Lloyd**, has donated his father's diary from the 1949 Nepal expedition. Adam has now also discovered transcripts of Peter's 1936 Nanda Devi and 1938 Everest diaries and has promised to supply us with copies.

Conservation work has continued, with restoration of one of the classic works of early Alpine climbing, *A Narrative of an Ascent to the Summit of Mont Blanc*, by **Charles Fellows**, published in 1827. No serious collection of books on this subject should be without a copy and, in addition to the copies held in the Library, the Archives have Fellows' own annotated proofs. Although the documents themselves are in good condition, the file in which they are kept has deteriorated badly. We have therefore commissioned our conservator, **Cyril Titus**, to make new, archive quality files to ensure the future of this important item.

Now that Cyril has completed the restoration of the three massive volumes of Alpine Club circulars (see the 2020 annual report for details), work has begun on the binding of membership applications and past committee minutes.

Monuments

Since the monuments are all in fixed locations, travel restrictions have made 2021 another frustrating year for the keeper, **Charlie Burbridge**. Luckily, access was still possible to the great Victorian cemeteries of London. Since many AC members were once London based, or at least London deceased, many a happy hour can be spent trawling through the well-organised boulevards of London's necropoli checking the state of repair of members' memorials.

The Mathews monument remains steadfastly in its location in the grounds of the Couttet Hotel. Various attempts to have it lifted over the terminal moraine into the Parc Couttet have come to nought, likely because the monument is estimated to weigh over 10 tonnes. Lifting the monument will therefore require a large crane. It is hoped that this will become available during the hotel refurbishment, but no start date for that has yet been agreed. The good news is that the Chamonix authorities have agreed its final resting place in the Parc Couttet.

The plaque to **Maurice Simond** has not been cleaned since the start of the pandemic, nor has the Hinchcliff memorial been checked over, nor the Tyndall memorial. However, a telephone conversation with the staff of the Britannia hut has confirmed that the plaque to Clinton Dent has survived another winter. High hopes exist for travel and monument checking in 2022.

Alpine Club Library

After closures and severely reduced capacity throughout 2020, Library services gradually started to open up more during 2021. Nevertheless, visitor numbers remain low by historical standards and it seems that many folk have become used to online searches and email enquiries. It remains to be seen if this tendency towards remote access continues into the future. After more than three decades of service to the Library, including many years as our honorary librarian, **Jerry Lovatt** stepped down as a trustee at the 2021 AGM. I would like to express our deepest thanks to Jerry, on behalf of the trustees, all the Library team and the whole AC membership, for his outstanding contribution over so many years. Jerry has also been a generous donor to the Library during that period and I am delighted that he will retain his association by remaining as a Library member. Also at the AGM we confirmed **Stephen Venables** as the new Club-nominated trustee, bringing us back up to our full complement of seven. The appointment and reappointment of trustees is

Jerry Lovatt, stepping down after long service as honorary librarian with old friend and honorary archivist Glyn Hughes. *(Ed Douglas)*

governed by article 45 of the ACL's articles of association. This is a cumbersome rule that has a number of unfortunate drawbacks: trustees serving for different length terms; and some trustees being required to retire while others of equal seniority are not. After considerable discussion within both the ACL and the AC, we therefore voted unanimously at the 2021 AGM to amend article 45 so that all trustees will in future serve for a fixed term of three years (renewable through re-election).

Halfway through 2021, our treasurer, **Alan Henderson**, was headhunted by the AC Committee to replace **Trevor Campbell Davis** as AC honorary treasurer at the end of his term of office. Luckily for us Alan has only been headhunted rather than poached, since he has agreed to remain as ACL treasurer and to take on both roles. I am not sure whether to congratulate him or commiserate with him. Many thanks are due to **David Lund** who arranged for an ICT upgrade in the library, updating our decades old PCs in the Archives, Photo Library and main Library with new generation Dells. The Library is also actively participating in the AC-wide review that aims to update, streamline and integrate our collective ICT systems. In the initial stage of this, we have already cleared out some obsolete hardware that has enabled the creation of some much-needed extra space in the Library reading room.

One truism apparent to anyone involved with the Library is that collections always seem to get bigger (except for the odd stolen book). This not only puts continual pressure on space, but also on the manual work that needs to be done. We are therefore always looking for volunteers to help out with the Collections. If you are at all interested in helping out or would like more information about volunteering opportunities then please contact me at: *p.meredith@ucl.ac.uk* or any of the keepers. While volunteering does involve work, it is also fun and it gives you access to a truly wondrous world of mountaineering heritage.

Public Engagement and Outreach
This year was a busy one for spreading the word about our collections and activities. In May, Beth gave a presentation about the 1921 Everest Reconnaissance expedition as part of a broader programme of Everest centenary events organised by Mountaineering Ireland. Then in September Philip and Beth prepared a history of the Alpine Club that was presented to a joint meeting of the Birmingham Medical Research Expeditionary Society (BM-RES) and the British Mountain Medicine Society (BMMS). September also saw Beth and Adam Butterworth running a live-stream tour of 'Everest: By Those Who Were There', which was followed up in December with a video tour of 'Women with Altitude'. Both of these tours can be found and viewed on the Alpine Club YouTube channel.

Acknowledgments
As always, I end this report by expressing my deep gratitude to everyone in the Library team, librarian, trustees, keepers, members and volunteers, who again gave their time so generously and ungrudgingly throughout the year. Thanks also to everyone who supplied me with the material necessary to compile this report, and especially to Beth Hodgett. Without all your efforts the ACL simply could not function. Thank you all.

Philip Meredith

Doré's Matterhorn Sketches
An exhibition of drawings from the Musée d'Orsay opened in Evian-les-Bains in July, including two by Gustave Doré, the 'Conquest of the Matterhorn' and the 'Catastrophe on the Matterhorn', done in August 1865 in pen and ink. You can view them in detail (but not download them) at the Musée d'Orsay website. In 1995 Alan Lyall wrote an article in the *Alpine Journal* (*AJ* 1995 215-221) entitled 'The Matterhorn Lithographs of 1865: Gustave Doré and his links with Edward Whymper' about the two subsequent lithographs, which are related to the drawings and how Doré must have consulted Whymper to get details so authentic. How sad then that Alan wrote: 'It is doubtful whether Doré's original drawings had very much in common with the published prints ... and if they are still in existence they may be hardly recognisable for what they are.' I'm sure he would love to have seen them if he had known they existed and he would have discussed them in his article. Yes they exist, yes they are recognised for what they are, and yes one of them bears a close resemblance to the subsequent lithograph. (Alan was the author of *The First Descent of the Matterhorn* (1997); his obituary appeared in *AJ* 2017 pp401-05.) The exhibition is entitled

Gustave Doré's drawings of the Matterhorn tragedy, now unearthed and on display. *(Mark Boxer)*

'Les Arpenteurs de rêves; Dessins du Musée d'Orsay' and was at the Palais Lumière Evian-les-Bains from 2 July to 1 November 2022. It transfers to the Musée des Beaux-Arts at Quimper on 15 December 2022 and closes on 13 March 2023.

Mark Boxer

Boardman Tasker Award 2021

After a year with fewer entries, there was a marked recovery in 2020, with more than 40 entries from around the world. The judges were David Canning, who was chair, UKClimbing editor Natalie Berry and Canadian author Marni Jackson. They chose six books for the shortlist, with a number of strong contenders missing out, evidence of the depth of quality in the field. The shortlisted titles were:

Ed Caesar for *The Moth and the Mountain* (Viking). Caesar's account of Maurice Wilson's attempt to fly to and climb Everest is an often tragic and pathetic story but never judgmental. Wilson could be the woefully unprepared climber we'd all like to despise but Caesar helps us to develop a warm attachment to him. Wilson deserved better in death and this book is a fitting tribute to his amazing journey.

Ed Douglas for *Himalaya: A Human History* (Bodley Head). An extensively researched book exploring the human histories of the Himalaya and how the mountains and their geological and imagined boundaries have shaped people and place. Douglas breaks down the romanticised Western stereotypes of Sherpas and other native peoples in the region and the exchanges, exploits and exploitations that have occurred on the 'roof of the world'.

Stephen Fabes for *Signs of Life: To the Ends of the World with a Doctor* (Pursuit). Engaging, heart-warming and often very funny, Fabes' accounts of his journeys around the world on a bicycle, and the people he meets along the way, are culturally sympathetic, mature, and poignant.

Helen Mort for *Never Leave the Dog Behind* (Vertebrate Publishing). Explores the deep bond that exists between people, their dogs and the mountains with delightful prose and poetry. The dogs featured are often the main characters in Mort's storytelling, but she also manages to expertly weave in personal elements too.

Élisabeth Revol for *To Live: Fighting for Life on the Killer Mountain* (Vertebrate Publishing). This compelling account of Revol's survival on Nanga Parbat in winter is a story of survivor's guilt and her need to tell her story as an act of healing. The writing is visceral and honest, and Revol speaks a universal truth about mountaineering that needs to be heard.

David Smart for *Emilio Comici: Angel of the Dolomites* (RMB). A very impressive biography, well written and researched, of one of Italy's foremost climbers, who put up some of the first big wall climbs and developed new climbing style and techniques.

Once again, because of Covid-19 restrictions, a live award event was deemed impossible and so once again it was done online and chaired as usual by Stephen Venables. The winner was announced as David Smart for *Emilio Comici*. Commenting on the winning book, David Canning said:

> This is an important chapter in the history of climbing, it deals sensitively and sympathetically with the contradictions in the character of Comici; rehabilitating in a way without revisionism, and it delves into the detail of the complex international politics of the time, the roots of Italian fascism and how this affected Italian climbing. It is a history that, as ever, is never as simple as we might first wish it to appear and we need to appreciate the historical context in which Comici and his contemporaries lived. The patriotic nationalism, at first an idealistic movement to achieve liberation from oppressive empires, might resonate with our current social and political contexts, but it soon took on the ugly face of extremism, and then of anti-Semitism. It remains a warning from history and Smart reminds us how sport is often appropriated for political ends, how individuals are never the heroes that folk memory would wish them to be and that, as with British climbing and its imperial and colonial ambitions, climbing has skeletons in its closet.

David Canning's full speech is available at ***www.boardmantasker.com***.

Ed Douglas

Contributors

TOM BELL is a paramedic who has been climbing and running in the mountains for most of his life, on his own and with good friends. The Alpine Club has given him the opportunity to visit areas that it would be difficult to access otherwise.

ROBIN CAMPBELL has held every office in the Scottish Mountaineering Club for which administrative competence is not required, including a long stint as editor in the 1960s and 1970s, and as archivist since 1997. Retired from a desultory career as an academic child psychologist, he now wastes his time and money in collecting and studying old drawings and watercolours, particularly those depicting mountains before they were trampled into familiarity by the boots of mountaineers.

JOHN CLEARE has been a freelance professional photographer for over 50 years but a climber for rather longer. Business and many expeditions have taken him all over the world, while he has several dozen books, several films and live TV broadcasts, more than a few new routes and several virgin summits to his credit. An ex-vice president of the AC and an ex-president of the Alpine Ski Club, he lives in remote Wiltshire.

ROB COLLISTER is a retired mountain guide who lives on the edge of the Carneddau in north Wales but still enjoys leading ski tours in the Alps.

LEO DICKINSON has BASE-jumped with peregrines, flown over Everest in a hot-air balloon and climbed hard north faces in the Alps. In 1970 he persuaded Yorkshire TV to commission a film of his ascent of the north face of the Eiger. He has made more than 50 films and won prizes at every major adventure film festival. The author of three books, his photography has appeared in *Life* and *Geo* magazines.

STUART DUNNING is a reader in physical geography at Newcastle University, a geologist by training, but now a geomorphologist specialising in landslides. He has been lucky enough to work on all seven continents but has a soft spot for Scottish landslides, midges and ticks. He also occasionally struggles up HVS.

continued …

CATH FLITCROFT spent years in the Scottish wilderness as an archaeologist before her PhD at Edinburgh University looking at blanket peat initiation. She moved to the Peak in 2000 as research manager with Moors for the Future and in 2006 joined the BMC as access and conservation officer. Her work covers a wide range of areas including policy, providing secretariat to the APPG for mountaineering and hill walking and leading on the BMC's sustainability and climate change work.

PETER FOSTER is a retired consultant physician. He has been a member of the Alpine Club since 1975.

ABBIE GARRINGTON is associate professor of modern and contemporary literature at Durham University, currently writing *High Modernism: A Literary History of Mountaineering, 1890-1945*. She has published articles on literary mountain cultures, and co-curated or co-produced several mountaineering exhibitions and conferences, including 'Savage Arena' about the life of Joe Tasker (2017).

TERRY GIFFORD was director of the annual International Festival of Mountaineering Literature for 21 years. Former chair of the Mountain Heritage Trust, he is the author of *The Joy of Climbing* (Whittles, 2004) and *Al Otro Lado del Aguilar* (Oversteps Books, 2011). Visiting professor at Bath Spa University's Centre for Writing and Environment and *profesor honorífico* at the University of Alicante, he celebrated his 70th birthday appropriately on Wreckers' Slab.

DENNIS GRAY started climbing on Yorkshire gritstone in 1947. Secretary of the ACG, first national officer, then general secretary of the BMC, Dennis has visited over 60 countries, most recently travelling widely in China. He has written two autobiographies, two books of stories, a novel and a volume of poetry, plays the banjo and sings on three CDs of climbing themed songs.

LINDSAY GRIFFIN lives in north Wales, from where he continues to report on developments in world mountaineering. An enthusiastic mind still tries to coax a less than enthusiastic body up pleasant bits of rock and ice, both at home and abroad. He remains the world's leading chronicler of mountaineering achievement.

J G R HARDING, a former Alpine Club vice president, no longer climbs but still writes about mountaineers and mountaineering. The article on Freda du Faur is one of a trilogy featuring some outstanding women climbers. John's mountaineering autobiography *Distant Snows* (Bâton Wicks) was published in 2016.

ALAN HEPPENSTALL was born in Newcastle-on-Tyne and now lives in Cumbria, after moving up from the south in 1978. Having gained a degree in Italian and French at Oxford, he worked for seven years for the British Tourist Authority, including three years in Rome. As a member of OUMC he climbed widely in the UK and enjoyed several seasons in the European Alps.

TOM LIVINGSTONE is a 31-year-old climber and writer originally from the south of England. He has a penchant for trad, winter and alpine climbing; his ascents include a winter ascent of *Rolling Stones* on the Grandes Jorasses, *The Great Game* on Koyo Zom and the *North Ridge Variation* on Latok I, for which he was a Piolet d'Or. In 2020 he founded the Young Alpinist Group.

JOHN MIDDENDORF was born in New York City and studied engineering at Stanford. During the 1980s and 1990s he was among the world's best climbers, particularly on big walls, with a formidable record in Yosemite and the Karakoram. A near-death experience with a portaledge led to him to establish the equipment company A5, and later, D4. He remains deeply interested in the evolution of climbing gear.

TIM MILLER is a climber, mountaineer, occasional skier, aspirant mountain guide and owner of Miller Mountain Guides. He is based in Scotland where he has contributed several new routes in summer and winter. He also climbs and works regularly in the Alps and further afield. He loves expeditions and climbing challenges that have an adventurous and exploratory nature.

SIMON PIERSE is senior lecturer emeritus at Aberystwyth University and was the Alpine Club's honorary keeper of pictures from 2019 to this year. He is an art historian with interests in mountain art and literature and a practising artist. He served as vice president of the Royal Watercolour Society 2009-12.

DONALD ORR is a member of the Scottish Mountaineering Club and recently retired from a career in theology and fine art, which does beg questions. He now spends his time climbing and writing, and being irresponsible with his grandsons. His writings on mountaineering and the mountain environment have contributed over the years to the *Scottish Mountaineering Club Journal*.

SIMON RICHARDSON lives in Aberdeen. Experience gained in the Alps, Andes, Patagonia, Canada, the Himalaya, Caucasus, Alaska and the Yukon is put to good use most winter weekends whilst exploring and climbing in the Scottish Highlands.

VICTOR SAUNDERS was born in Lossiemouth and grew up in Peninsular Malaysia. He began climbing in the Alps in 1978 and has since climbed in the Andes, Antarctica and across the Himalaya and Karakoram. Formerly an architect in London, he is now an IFMGA guide based in Chamonix. His first book, *Elusive Summits*, won the Boardman Tasker. In 2007 he received an honorary MA from the University of Stirling for services to Scottish mountaineering.

MARCELO SCANU is an Argentine climber who lives in Buenos Aires. He specialises in ascending virgin mountains and volcanoes in the Central Andes. His articles and photographs about alpinism, trekking, and mountain history, archaeology and ecology appear in prominent magazines in Europe and America. When not climbing, he works for a workers' union.

DAVID SEDDON is a physician in Nottingham. He was an indifferent member of both OUMC and CUMC but had more success as a ski mountaineer under the leadership of John Harding, Derek Fordham and Peter Edgerton. He remains enthusiastic about the pictures of T H Somervell.

RODERICK A SMITH began his fascination with mountains following the first ascent of Everest in 1953. He has travelled to the Himalaya, Svalbard, Greenland, Arctic Canada, Japan and the Alps but always returns to his favourites in the Lake District. A lifetime's enjoyment has not been hampered with overweening ambition, but he is proud of his first ascent of a peak in the Stauning Alps and that he can still enjoy climbing and skiing at a modest level, despite the onset of decrepitude.

ERIC VOLA is a French climber who lives in Chamonix and Marseille. He spent three years at University College, London, and climbed in the early 1960s with Chris Bonington, Nick Estcourt, Don Whillans and other Brits. In recent years he has translated British mountaineering books, including a selection of Chris Bonington's best stories and Andy Cave's *Learning to Breathe*.

IAN WALL worked at Plas-y-Brenin in the 1960s. Since then he has climbed extensively throughout the UK, the Alps and in Norway. He has led treks in Africa, Ladakh, Tibet and Nepal, where he now lives and acts as an advisor to the Kathmandu International Mountain Film Festival, Kathmandu Environmental Education Project and in developing the Nepal Mountain Leader programme working closely with the Nepal Mountaineering Association.

NOTES FOR CONTRIBUTORS

The *Alpine Journal* records all aspects of mountains and mountaineering, including expeditions, exploration, art, literature, geography, history, geology, medicine, ethics and the mountain environment.

Articles Contributions in English are invited. They should be sent to the Hon Editor *The Alpine Journal*, Alpine Club, 55 Charlotte Road, London EC2A 3QF, UK. (**edward.douglas@btinternet.com**) Articles, including images, can be sent as an email attachment, on a disk or memory stick. File-sharing services are also acceptable, by prior arrangement with the editor. With files created in Microsoft Word please confine formatting to italics and bold. A typical article is 2,500 words **and may be edited or shortened at the editor's discretion**. Longer pieces should be discussed with the editor.

The Alpine Journal is unable to offer a fee for articles published, but authors who are not AC members receive a copy of the issue of the *Journal* in which their article appears.

Maps and diagrams These should be well researched, accurate and show the most important place-names mentioned in the text. If submitted electronically, maps and route diagrams should be originated as CMYK *.eps* files in Adobe Illustrator, Freehand or similar ensuring embedded images are **300dpi** resolution and CMYK. Fonts must be embedded or converted to curves. Hard copy should be scanned as a **300dpi** *.tiff* or *.jpg* file at A4 finished size. This can be arranged through the editor if required.

Photographs Image files should have unique names or serial numbers **that correspond to the list of captions** appended to the article, as a separate document, or in an email. They should be large jpgs or tiff files. Captions must include the photographer's name. Colour transparencies should be originals. Pre-scanned images should be **300dpi** Greyscale or RGB, tiffs or maximum quality jpegs at A4 final size or larger.

Copyright It is the author's responsibility to obtain copyright clearance for text, photographs, digital images and maps, to pay any fees involved and to ensure acknowledgements are in the form required by the copyright owner.

Summaries A brief summary, listing team members, dates, objectives attempted and achieved, should be included at the end of expedition articles.

Biographies Authors are asked to provide a short autobiography of about 50 words, listing noteworthy highlights in their climbing career and anything else they wish to mention.

Deadline Copy and photographs should reach the editor by **1 February** of the year of publication.

Index

'Everest, Lhotse and Ama Dablam', Rob Fairley, watercolour,
15cm × 21cm, sketchbook No 609.

'Everest and Kusum Kanguru', Rob Fairley, watercolour,
15cm × 21cm, sketchbook No 393

Index 2022

⤬ **ALPEN**ADAPT
Adapt to any ascent

SWITCH FRONT SECTIONS
for flat glacier
or technical ice

SWITCH BINDINGS
for approach shoes
or mountaineering boots

SWITCH HEEL SECTIONS
for tough and durable
or fast and light

For more information, visit petzl.com

BMC INSURANCE

INSURANCE YOU CAN TRUST

www.thebmc.co.uk/**insurance**
0161 445 6111

When
nothing else
matters

Michelle Dvorak
Cassin Ridge, Denali
Alaska

mountain-equipment.co.uk